Threads of globalization

Manchester University Press

To buy or to find out more about the books currently available in this series, please go to: https://manchesteruniversitypress.co.uk/series/studies-in-design-and-material-culture/

general editors
SALLY-ANNE HUXTABLE, NATIONAL TRUST
ELIZABETH CURRIE, ROYAL COLLEGE OF ART/V&A
LIVIA LAZZARO REZENDE, UNIVERSITY OF NEW SOUTH WALES
WESSIE LING, LONDON METROPOLITAN UNIVERSITY

founding editor
PAUL GREENHALGH

Threads of globalization

Fashion, textiles, and gender in Asia in the long twentieth century

Edited by
Melia Belli Bose

Manchester University Press

Copyright © Manchester University Press 2024

While copyright in the volume as a whole is vested in Manchester University Press, copyright in individual chapters belongs to their respective authors, and no chapter may be reproduced wholly or in part without the express permission in writing of both author and publisher.

Published by Manchester University Press
Oxford Road, Manchester M13 9PL
www.manchesteruniversitypress.co.uk

British Library Cataloguing-in-Publication Data
A catalogue record for this book is available from the British Library

ISBN 978 1 5261 6340 0 hardback
ISBN 978 1 5261 9477 0 paperback

First published 2024
Paperback published 2026

The publisher has no responsibility for the persistence or accuracy of URLs for any external or third-party internet websites referred to in this book, and does not guarantee that any content on such websites is, or will remain, accurate or appropriate.

EU authorised representative for GPSR:
Easy Access System Europe – Mustamäe tee 50, 10621 Tallinn, Estonia
gpsr.requests@easproject.com

Typeset
by Cheshire Typesetting Ltd, Cuddington, Cheshire

Contents

List of figures   *page* vii
List of contributors   xv

Introduction: stitching together gender, textile and garment labor, and heritage in Asia – Melia Belli Bose   1

Part I: Fashioning identity: textiles, garments, and belonging

1. Wearing a gendered tree: a new style of garments from early modern to twentieth-century China – Yuhang Li   25

2. Women for cotton and men for wool: consuming gendered textiles in colonized Korea – Kyunghee Pyun   47

3. Gendered blue: women's jeans in postwar Taiwan – Ying-chen Peng   72

4. Bhutanese women and the performance of globalization – Emma Dick   92

5. Weaving and dyeing the ideal of reproduction among Shidong Miao in Guizhou province – Ho Zhao-hua   113

Part II: Gendering creative agency: women fashion designers, textile makers, and entrepreneurs

6. Soft power: Guo Pei and the fashioning of matriarchy – Kristen Loring Brennan   135

7. Investigating female entrepreneurship in silk weaving in contemporary Cambodia – Magali An Berthon   158

8 (Re)crafting distribution networks for contemporary Philippine textiles: women's advocacy and social enterprise – B. Lynne Milgram ... 180

9 Women weaving silken identities and revitalizing various Japanese textile traditions – Millie Creighton ... 207

Part III: Creative voices for change: textiles, gender, and artivism

10 Entangled histories of craft and conflict: the story of *phulkari* textiles in The Singh Twins's *Slaves of Fashion* – Cristin McKnight Sethi ... 231

11 The politics of wastefulness and 'the poetics of waste': Ruby Chishti's sartorial interventions – Saleema Waraich ... 258

12 Made in Rana Plaza: Dilara Begum Jolly's garment factory-themed art – Melia Belli Bose ... 284

Index ... 312

Figures

Figures

Every effort has been made to obtain permission to reproduce copyright material, and the publisher will be pleased to be informed of any errors and omissions for correction in future editions

1.1 Line drawing of a theatrical costume for an old lady role type, indigo-color silk stitched with gold metallic threads and peacock feathers, 117 × 223 cm, Qianlong period (1736–1795), L: 122 cm, W: 219.5 cm. Beijing Palace Museum collection. Line drawing by Chi-Lynn Lin. 30

1.2 Blue silk tapestry informal robe for a woman, 1890–1900, blue silk and metal-wrapped thread tapestry weave edged with brown silk and metal-wrapped thread tapestry weave, overall: 141 cm × 130.8 cm. Mactaggart Art Collection (2005.5.18), University of Alberta Museums. Gift of Sandy and Cécile Mactaggart. 33

1.3 Young merchants, Shanghai, 1870–1890s. Ferry Bertholet Lambert van der Aalsvoort collection. After Ferry Berholet and Lambert van der Aalsvoort, eds, *Among the Celestials: China in Early Photographs*. New Haven: Yale University Press, 2014. Mercatorfonds, p. 79. 36

1.4 Line drawing of a Chinese man's informal riding jacket (*magua*), cut and uncut silk velvet, early twentieth century, H: 61 cm, W: 158.5 cm. Minneapolis Institute of Art collection. Line drawing by Chi-Lynn Lin. 37

1.5 Yu Xunling (1874–1943), *Empress Dowager Cixi (1835–1908) in Snow Accompanied by Attendants*, 1904. Glass plate

	negative, 12.7 × 10.2 cm, Freer Gallery of Art and Arthur M. Sackler Gallery Archives, Purchase, 1966, Xunling, FSA_A.13_SC-GR-284.	39
2.1	Great Court uniform for civil officer of the Korean Empire; composed of a jacket, a waistcoat, and a pair of trousers. Jacket 110 (including sleeves) × 99 (length) × 42 (chest width) cm. National Folk Museum, South Korea. Object no. 65788.	48
2.2	Store Sign of a tailor named *Chulwoonok Yangbokjeom* [출운옥양복점 出雲屋洋服店] in Busan. National Folk Museum, South Korea. Object no. 88949.	49
2.3a	An Seok-ju's column with his illustration entitled *An Opinion of Street Scenes* (Gasangsogeyon 가상소견), part 1 on 5 February 1928, *Chosun Ilbo*. Its subtitle says "Modern Girls' Dressing-Up Movement," with the illustration of young women as bus passengers, dressed up with modernized *hanbok* and prominent wrist watches.	52
2.3b	An Seok-ju's column with his illustration entitled *An Opinion of Street Scenes* (Gasangsogeyon 가상소견), part 2 on 7 February 1928, *Chosun Ilbo*. Its subtitle says "Modern Boys' Stroll," with the illustration of modern boys in fancy clothing walking in front of shabby traditional-style houses on the street.	52
2.3c	Advertisement for Taegeukseong, a brand of cotton textile produced by Gyeongseong Bangjik, 1922.	52
2.3d	(bottom of the page) Advertisement for Taegeukseong, a brand of cotton textile produced by Gyeongseong Bangjik in *Gukminshinbo* [국민신보 國民新報] on 11 June 1939.	52
2.3e	Advertisement for Taegeukseong, a brand of cotton textile produced by Gyeongseong Bangjik: "Wooriga-manden-geok wooriga-sseuja" [우리가 만든 것 우리가 쓰자 (Let's use those made by ourselves)].	52
2.4	Kim Kichang, *Listening to Music* (Jeongcheong 정청), 1934. Color on silk, 159 × 134.5 cm. National Museum of Modern and Contemporary Art (MMCA), South Korea. Object no. KO-07851.	54
2.5	Kim Jung-hyun 김중현, *A Spring Sunlight* [Chunyang 춘양], 1936. Color on paper (four-panel screen painting), each panel 106 × 54.2 cm. National Museum of Modern and Contemporary Art (MMCA), South Korea. Object no. KO-07535.	61
2.6	Chosen Spinning and Weaving Factory in Busan, circa 1930s. *Busan • Busan Harbor 130 Years*, http://busan.grandculture.net/Contents?local=busan&dataType=01&contents_id=GC04200855.	62
3.1	Photograph of Cai Yueying published in *Union Times*, 22 May 1963.	77

3.2	Poster for *River of No Return*, 1954.	78
3.3	Illustration of the fashion column in *Taiwan Women's Journal*, no.130 (April 1967), p. 18.	79
3.4	Still of *A Different Love*, 1976.	80
3.5	Still of *A Different Love*, 1976.	81
3.6	Photograph of jeans featured in *Fashion n' Fashion*, no. 21, December 1980, p. 35.	85
3.7	O'Daniel's advertisement in *Fashion n' Fashion*, no. 23, February 1981, p. 13.	86
4.1	Women carrying baskets of manure to spread on fields at Sopsokha, Bhutan (2008). Nancy Hoyt Belcher/Alamy Stock Photo.	94
4.2	Technology and tradition co-exist side by side: young Bhutanese women taking selfies at the Thimpu Tshechu festival (2014). Danita Delimont/Alamy Stock Photo.	98
4.3	Women wearing traditional Bhutanese national dress, Haa district, Bhutan (2009). Image Professionals GmbH/Alamy Stock Photo.	103
4.4	Queen of Bhutan, Jetsun Pema arrives at Tashichho Dzong, in Thimphu, Bhutan, before meeting the Duke and Duchess of Cambridge on day five of the royal tour to India and Bhutan (2016). PA Images/Alamy Stock Photo.	104
4.5	The Prince of Wales and Duchess of Cornwall greet King Jigme Khesar Namgyel Wangchuk and Queen Jetsun Pema Wangchuck of Bhutan at Clarence House in London (2011). PA Images/Alamy Stock Photo.	105
4.6	Bhutan Airlines Uniform (2019): a contemporary, stitched garment made to emulate wrapped traditional dress, signifies Bhutan to those who travel by plane. © Sam Chui, aviation blogger and journalist.	107
4.7	A woman spinning yarn inside her house, Lobesa village, Punakha, Bhutan (2020). Sergi Reboredo/Alamy Stock Photo.	108
5.1	Preparing the warp, Jiob Hxangk village, 2 August 2002, image taken by author.	119
5.2	Soaking indigo plants, Dangx Vongx village, Shidong, 8 July 2007, image taken by author.	120
5.3	Soaking in reddish liquid, Jiob Hxangk village, 5 August 2002, image taken by author.	122
5.4	Beating fabric, Dangx Vongx village, 13 August 2008, image taken by author.	123
5.5	Cloth being steamed, Jiob Hxangk village, Shidong, 8 August 2002, image taken by author.	124
5.6	Drying dyed cloth before beating, Dangk Vongx village, 26 August 2007, image taken by author.	125

5.7	Young women dressed in silver, displaying their households' wealth, Nangl Hlinb village, 2 May2007, image taken by author.	129
6.1	Guo Pei, *Yellow Queen. One Thousand and Two Nights* collection, 2010. Silk cloak embroidered with metal thread and silk and 24-carat-gold-spun thread and adorned with silk bows and fox fur. Collection of Guo Pei. Photo in Guo Pei, *Couture and Beyond*, p. 12. Image: Asian Civilizations Museum/SCAD Savannah.	136
6.2	Hubert Vos, *Empress Dowager Cixi*, 1905. Oil on canvas, 200 × 121.6 cm. Gardens of Nurtured Harmony, Summer Palace, Beijing. Artwork in the public domain.	139
6.3	Court painters in Beijing, *Empress Dowager Cixi Playing Chinese Chess (Weiqi)*. Tongzhi or Guangxu period, 1862–1908. Hanging scroll, ink and color on silk, 231.1 × 142.6 cm. Photograph by Zhang Yuntian. Image courtesy of Palace Museum, Beijing. Gu6594.	141
6.4	Platform shoes. China, Guangxu period, 1875–1908. Embroidery, polychrome silk threads on silk satin with silk tassels; platforms: wood core covered with cotton and glass beads. Photograph by Li Fan. Image courtesy of Palace Museum, Beijing. Gu61391.	142
6.5	Flowerpot with peonies and birds. Imperial Porcelain Factory, Jingdezhen, Guangxu period, 1875 or 1876, Porcelain with enamels over colorless glaze, 23 × 27 × 21.9 cm. Photograph by Wang Jin. Image courtesy of Palace Museum, Beijing. Gu157098.	143
6.6	Guo Pei, *Palace Flowers. Legend of the Dragon* collection, 2012. Silk, jacquard, silver-spun thread, gold-spun thread, beads, Swarovski crystals, fur, silk peonies salvaged from private collections in the countryside. Collection of Guo Pei. Photo in Guo Pei, *Couture and Beyond*, p. 76. Image: Asian Civilizations Museum/SCAD.	145
6.7	Guo Pei, *Palace Flowers*, detail of shoes. *Legend of the Dragon* collection, 2012. Collection of Guo Pei. Photo in Guo Pei, *Couture and Beyond*, p. 81. Image: Asian Civilizations Museum/SCAD.	147
6.8	Guo Pei, *White Queen. One Thousand and Two Nights* collection, 2010. Silk mesh gown embroidered with silk-, 24-karat gold- and silver-spun thread, and embellished with crystals, gems, beads, sequins, and pearls; embroidered silk cape trimmed in fox fur; brass crown embellished with gems, Swarovski crystals, diamonds, and pearls. Collection of Guo Pei. Photo in Guo Pei, *Couture and Beyond*, pp. 46–47. Photo: Courtesy of SCAD.	150

7.1	Map of the main sericulture and weaving areas in Cambodia in 2016, based on data from the National Silk Strategy 2016–2020, by the author.	160
7.2	Qualities of silk yarn: from raw silk to the left to fine silk on the right before degumming, Koh Dach island. Author's photograph, December 2016.	161
7.3	Chin Koeur's certificate, dated October 1995, for training under master weaver Leav Sa Em, next to tie-dyed silk threads, Kanhjang village, Takeo, 17 March 2018. Author's photograph.	164
7.4	Silk Associations of Cambodia's business model, based on interview with Chin Koeur. Author's image.	166
7.5	Polychromic *hol* (ikat) silk scarves in a variety of patterns, Color Silk Facebook page, 7 September 2020.	170
7.6	Weaving training program with founder Ngorn Vanntha (in blue) at the Maybank Silk Weaving Training Center, Sla commune, Takeo province, n. d. Photograph Color Silk Foundation.	172
7.7	Color Silk weavers for the Fashion Revolution 2017 campaign, April 2017, Color Silk Facebook page.	173
8.1	A display of plain weave bags woven from re- and upcycled fabric in the Rags2Riches showroom, Quezon City, Manila, Philippines, 2018. Photo: B. L. Milgram.	186
8.2	A display of plain weave bags and cushions woven from re- and upcycled fabric in the Rags2Riches showroom, Quezon City, Manila, Philippines, 2018. Photo: B. L. Milgram.	187
8.3	Detail of a Rags2Riches woven panel on a simple wood frame loom, Quezon City, Manila, Philippines, 2019. Photo: Cambio & Co. Inc. and Gerald Gloton.	188
8.4	Artisans work on assembling bags and household products in the Rags2Riches workshop, Quezon City, Manila, Philippines, 2018. Photo: B. L. Milgram.	189
8.5	Two artisans weave in the workshop of the social enterprise, Save the IfugaoTerraces Movement, (Kiangan, Ifugao, Philippines, 2018. Photo: B. L. Milgram.	191
8.6	A naturally dyed ikat (resist tied and dyed) textile panel woven by artisans for the NGO, Save the Ifugao Terraces Movement/Ifugao Nation, Kiangan, Ifugao, Philippines, 2018. Photo: B. L. Milgram.	192
8.7	A naturally dyed ikat (resist tied and dyed) textile panel woven by artisans for the NGO, Save the Ifugao Terraces Movement / Ifugao Nation, Kiangan, Ifugao, Philippines, 2018. Photo: B. L. Milgram.	193

8.8	Woven textile 'wrap' using the ikat (resist tied and dyed) technique is displayed for sale on the SITMo/Ifugao Nation website. Photo: Ifugao Nation, 2022.	195
9.1	Women stay in a traditional Japanese-style building during the silk weaving workshops. Photo by Millie Creighton.	210
9.2	In addition to weaving, women learn to dye silk skeins from natural substances collected on the moutainside. Photo by Millie Creighton.	215
9.3	Newcomers together set up the loom's lengthwise threads (warp) before weaving their individual segments. Photo by Millie Creighton.	216
9.4	Women in the silk-weaving workshops continue the 'eating out' event despite the onset of rain. Photo by Millie Creighton.	217
9.5	The women show their silk creations at the end of the residential workshop. (The author is shown second from right.)	218
10.1	The Singh Twins with her *Slaves of Fashion* lightbox artworks series exhibition hosted by Norwich Castle Museum and Art Gallery in 2022/23. Photo credit Denisa Ilie.	231
10.2	*Indigo: The Colour of India* (*Slaves of Fashion* series), 2017. Copyright The Singh Twins: www.singhtwins.co.uk	233
10.3	*Coromandel: Sugar and Spice, Not so Nice* (*Slaves of Fashion* series), 2017. Copyright The Singh Twins: www.singhtwins.co.uk	234
10.4	*Palampore*, c. 1760, India (made). Painted cotton chintz. Victoria and Albert Museum, London. IS.43–1950.	236
10.5	*Cotton: Threads of Change* (*Slaves of Fashion* series), 2017. Copyright The Singh Twins: www.singhtwins.co.uk	237
10.6	The Singh Twins with two of her *Slaves of Fashion* tapestry artworks (inspired by the *Slaves of Fashion* lightbox artworks series). Photo credit Christopher Doyle.	239
10.7	*Phulkari: Craft and Conflict* (*Slaves of Fashion* series), 2017. Copyright The Singh Twins: www.singhtwins.co.uk	240
10.8	*Sainchi phulkari*, twentieth century, Undivided Punjab. Philadelphia Museum of Art. 2017-9-13.	244
10.9	*Phulkari Bagh*, twentieth century, Punjab. The Textile Museum Collection, Washington, D. C., 1985.57.45. Gift of Alice Bradley Sheldon; collected by Mary Hastings Bradley. Photography by Breton Littlehales.	245
10.10	'Manchester Bagh' and 'Jubilee Bagh' as depicted in Figures 27 and 28 in Flora Annie Steel's essay on *phulkaris* in the *Journal of Indian Art*, vol. 2, 1888.	246

Figures   xiii

11.1	*My Birth Will Take Place a Thousand Times No Matter How You Celebrate It* (2001). Recycled cloth, thread, straw, yarn. Height 45.7 cm each. Image Credit: Khalil Chishtee. Copyright Ruby Chishti. Courtesy of Ruby Chishti.	266
11.2	*Crows* (2001). Recycled cloth, thread, polyester, steel, wood. Approximately (crow-) life size. Image Credit: Sibte Hassan. Copyright Ruby Chishti. Courtesy of Ruby Chishti.	267
11.3	*Giving End* (2001). Fabric, straw, thread. H: approx. 96.5 cm. Image Credit: Harris Museum Preston. Copyright Ruby Chishti. Courtesy of Ruby Chishti.	267
11.4	*Live, Laugh, Love* (2009). Recycled clothing, thread, wood, paper, wire mesh. 83.8 cm × 55.9 cm × 30.5 cm. Private collection. Image Credit: Vipul Sangoi. Copyright Ruby Chishti. Courtesy of Ruby Chishti.	271
11.5	*Sublime Architecture* (2013). Recycled clothing, thread, wood (performance still). 193 cm × 10.1 cm × 76.2 cm. Image Credit: Khalil Chishtee. Copyright Ruby Chishti. Courtesy of Ruby Chishti.	272
11.6	(a) *The Present is a Ruin Without the People* (2016). Recycled textiles, thread, children's clothing, embellishments (lace, metal scraps), wire mesh, wood, paint, archival glue; with soundscape. 207.5 cm × 324.8 cm × 29.7 cm. Qatar Museums. Image Credit: Rossi & Rossi Gallery, Hong Kong; and (b) *The Present is a Ruin Without the People* (2016), detail. Image Credit: Jill Stuart Gallery, FSAD Cornell University.	274
11.7	*We Leave, We Never Leave, We Return Endlessly* (2017). Recycled textile, wire mesh, thread, wood archival glue. 209.5 cm × 327.6 cm × 34.3 cm. Kiran Nadar Museum of Art. Image Credit: Aicon Contemporary. Copyright Ruby Chishti. Courtesy of Ruby Chishti.	275
12.1	Rana Plaza collapsed on 24 April 2013, killing over one thousand garment workers and injuring thousands more. Photo by Taslima Akhter. Used with permission.	284
12.2	Dilara Begum Jolly, untitled painting from the *Lal Shallu* series, 1985, oil paint on cardboard, approx. 63 × 45 cm. Photo courtesy of the artist.	288
12.3	Dilara Begum Jolly, *Sculpting Time 2*, mixed media on paper, 2005, 60 × 76 cm. Photo courtesy of the artist.	289
12.4	Dilara Begum Jolly, *Tader Bola 4*, acrylic on canvas, 2008, 90 × 90 cm. Photo courtesy of the artist.	290
12.5	Dilara Begum Jolly, sari with missing persons posters (and detail), 2013, from the *Threads of Testimony* series. Photo courtesy of the artist.	294

12.6	Dilara Begum Jolly, *Amara*, 2012, Pen, ink, and yarn on paper, approx. 43 × 30 cm. Photo courtesy of the artist.	295
12.7	Dilara Begum Jolly, *Bayana 2*, pen and ink on paper, 2014, 76 × 56 cm. Photo courtesy of the artist.	297
12.8	Dilara Begum Jolly, *Bayana 6* from the *Bayana* series, 2013, pen and ink on paper, approx. 43 × 30 cm. Photo courtesy of the artist.	298
12.9(a)	Dilara Begum Jolly, *Threads of Testimony*, multi-media exhibition, 2014. View of the installation, consisting of a table and plates (molded resin encasing found objects)	299
12.9(b, c)	Begum Jolly, 'Object,' resin and found objects, 2014. Photo courtesy of the artist.	300
12.10(a, b)	Dilara Begum Jolly, hands (approx. 38 × 36 cm), cross-section of uterus (approx. 43 × 30 cm), pierced paper, 2015. *Wound* series, exhibited at Kala Kendra's *Celebrated Violence!*, 2016. Photo courtesy of the artist.	303

Contributors

Melia Belli Bose is Associate Professor of South Asian Art History at the University of Victoria, Canada. Her research focuses on issues of death, memorialization, gender, and public identity in the early modern courtly and contemporary art and architecture of north India, Pakistan, and Bangladesh. Her publications include *Royal Umbrellas of Stone: Memory, Political Propaganda, and Public Identity in Rajput Funerary Art* (Brill, 2015). She is also editor of a special edition of *Ars Orientalis* dedicated to the arts of death in Asia (2014), *Women, Gender, and Art in Asia* (ca. 1500–1900) (Routledge, 2016); and *Intersections: Art and Islamic Cosmopolitanism* (University Press of Florida, 2021).

Magali An Berthon is a textile historian focusing on the modern and contemporary history of Southeast Asian dress and textiles, with a specific interest in Cambodia. With prior experience in design, curation, and documentary, she earned a PhD in History of Design from the Royal College of Art of London with a thesis titled 'Silk and Post-Conflict Cambodia: Embodied Practices and Global and Local Dynamics of Heritage and Knowledge Transference (1991–2018)' in 2021. Since January 2022, she has been a Marie Skłodowska-Curie postdoctoral research fellow attached to the Centre for Textile Research at the University of Copenhagen, researching textile practices, production, and heritage during the Khmer Rouge regime.

Millie Creighton is an anthropologist, Japan specialist, Asianist and Associate Professor based in the Department of Anthropology at the University of British Columbia (UBC) in Vancouver, Canada. She was one of the founders of the Centre for Japanese Research at UBC and continues to work in conjunction with it and on the Executive Board of the Centre for Korean Research. She has carried out extensive research in Japan on department stores, consumerism, tourism, textiles, popular culture, gender, minorities, work, leisure, and identity, with comparisons to other parts of Asia. She received the Canon Prize for her work on Japanese department stores showing how department store marketing reflected nostalgia and the search for community, tradition, and cultural identity. She combined interests in textiles, tourism, and nostalgia by researching Japanese identity and women's involvement in live-in silk workshops to recover textile traditions, while engaging in a nostalgic tourism of remote Japanese locations.

Emma Dick is currently Head of the School of Design at Middlesex University, London and Director of Projects & Training for SPINNA Circle, a non-profit organization working to empower women in fashion and textiles globally. Her research practice aims to bring together the disciplines of textiles, business, and development and is often focused geographically in Asia (Bhutan, Turkey, Central and Southeast Asia). She is interested in how issues of the postcolonial collide with ideas of the postmodern to foreground issues of ethics and appropriation in cross-border trade and the global business of fashion.

Ho Zhao-hua is a Professor in the Textiles and Clothing Department, and also the Dean of Fashion and Textiles College at Fu Jen Catholic University, Taiwan. She completed her BA in Chinese Literature, Masters in Textiles and Clothing, both at Fu Jen Catholic University. She received her PhD from the Institute of Anthropology at National Tsing Hua University in 2011. Her thesis is titled 'Gifts to Dye For: Cloth and Person among Shidong Miao in Guizhou Province'. She also is the author of *A Study on the Aprons of Shidong Miao in Guizhou Province, China* (Guizhou University Press, 2018), and the editor of a dictionary titled *Glossary for Textile Conservation* (Bureau of Cultural Heritage, Ministry of Culture, 2022). Her scholarly interests include the anthropology of cloth, anthropology of art, Chinese fashion history, Miao ethnography, museum curatorship, and the reconstructions of Taiwanese aboriginal textiles.

Yuhang Li is Associate Professor of Chinese Art in the Department of Art History at the University of Wisconsin-Madison, USA. Her research interests cover a wide range of subjects and media of visual and material cultures in late imperial China. She is the author of *Becoming Guanyin: Artistic Devotion of Buddhist Women in Late Imperial China* (Columbia University Press, 2020), which was awarded the 2021 Religion and the Arts Book Award by the American Academy of Religion. She also co-curated and co-edited with Judith Zeitlin the exhibition and resulting catalog *Performing Images: Opera in Chinese Visual Culture* (Smart Museum and University of Chicago Press, 2014). She has published various articles on hair embroidery, Empress Dowager Cixi (1835–1908) dressing up as Guanyin, theatricality and narrative robes, paper as an efficacious medium, and artisanal reproduction of Chinese landscape painting on stones, among others.

Kristen Loring Brennan is a specialist in Chinese painting concerned with social status, gender, and visual culture in early modern China. She is currently Creative Director for Islandia Music Records and Content Editor for East Asian Art at Smarthistory, for which she has contributed several chapters to the *Reframing Art History* textbook and over thirty essays and videos. Previously Associate Professor at Pepperdine University, she holds a PhD from the University of California, Los Angeles, and an MA from Harvard University. She is the author of *Hua Yan (1682–1756) and the Making of the Artist in Early Modern China* (Brill, 2020) and co-edited with Lara C. W. Blanchard the volume, *Gender, Continuity, and the Shaping of Modernity in the Arts of East Asia, 16th–20th Centuries* (Brill, 2018). Her essays appear in *Artibus Asiae*, *Visual Resources*, and *Archives of Asian Art*, and translations in *Contemporary Chinese Art: Primary Documents* (Museum of Modern Art, 2010).

Cristin McKnight Sethi is a curator, educator, and writer who is passionate about cultural stewardship, histories of craft, and the production and circulation of textiles. She holds a PhD in Art History from the University of California, Berkeley (2015) and a Master's in Art History from the University of Texas at Austin (2008). She has taught at California College of the Arts, Colorado College, George Washington University, and Minneapolis College of Art and Design. Cristin is a Contributing Editor for South Asia for the non-profit Smarthistory.org, Chair of the Selection Committee for the International Folk Art Market, and serves on the editorial board of the *Textile Museum Journal*. Cristin has held curatorial and research positions at several arts institutions, including the Asian Art Museum San Francisco; the Los Angeles County Museum of Art; the Museum of International Folk Art in Santa Fe, New Mexico; the Philadelphia Museum of Art; and the Textile Museum in Washington, D. C. Her latest exhibition, *Handmade: Creating Textiles in South Asia*, was on view at the Textile Museum through May 2022. Cristin currently lives with her family in Minneapolis and is the Director of Education for the Textile Center of Minnesota.

B. Lynne Milgram is Professor Emerita and Adjunct Professor (Anthropology) at OCAD University, Canada. Her research on gender and development in the Philippines has analyzed the cultural politics of social change regarding women's work in microfinance, handicrafts, and the Philippine second-hand clothing trade. Milgram's current research investigates the role of digital technology in the transnational trade of Philippine crafts and issues of informality, extralegality, and social entrepreneurship with regard to street vending, public markets, and food provisioning. Milgram has published this research in referred articles and book chapters and in five co-edited volumes such as (2013) (with Hansen and Little) *Street Economies in the Urban Global South* (the School for Advanced Research). Recent publications include: 'Social Entrepreneurship and Arabica Coffee Production in the Northern Philippines,' *Human Organization* 80, no. 1 (2021): 72–82; and (with L. Mendoza) 'The Resilience of a Wholesale Vegetable Market in Benguet Northern Philippines,' in C. Panella and W. Little, eds, *Norms and Illegality* (Brill, 2021), pp. 137–160.

Ying-chen Peng specializes in late imperial and modern Chinese art history with a focus on gender issues and the globalization of material culture. Before joining the American University, Washington D. C. as Assistant Professor, she worked at the National Palace Museum and the Academia Sinica, both in Taiwan, and the Metropolitan Museum of Art as a pre-doctoral research fellow. She received her PhD from the University of California at Los Angeles in 2014. She is the author of *Artful Subversion: Empress Dowager Cixi's Image Making*, recently published by Yale University Press (2023). In addition to the East Asian history of jeans, Peng is also conducting research on the Chinese porcelain industry in the nineteenth and early twentieth centuries and the role it played in shaping the modern connoisseurship of Chinese decorative art in Europe and the United States.

Kyunghee Pyun is Associate Professor of Art History at the Fashion Institute of Technology, State University of New York. Her scholarship focuses on the history of collecting, the reception of Asian art, and the intersectionality of art and design, technology, and industrial history. She wrote *Fashion, Identity, Power in Modern Asia* (Palgrave Macmillan, 2018) discussing modernized dress in the early twentieth century. She also co-edited *Interpreting Modernism in Korean Art: Fluidity and Fragmentation* (Routledge, 2021); *American Art from Asia: Artistic Praxis and Theoretical Divergence* (Routledge, 2022); and *Expanding the Parameters of Feminist Artivism* (Palgrave Macmillan, 2022). She is writing a new book, *School Uniforms in East Asia: Fashioning Statehood and Self* (Palgrave Macmillan, 2023; forthcoming). Pyun holds her BA in Archaeology and Art History from Seoul National University and MA and PhD in History of Art from New York University.

Saleema Waraich is an Associate Professor in the Art History Department and a faculty affiliate of the Asian Studies Program at Skidmore College,

New York. Previously she held postdoctoral fellowships at Massachusetts Institute of Technology and Smith College, and served as an Assistant Curator of South Asian art at the Asian Art Museum of San Francisco. Her research spans the early modern to the contemporary eras of South Asia, focusing on Mughal material as well as its political, social, and aesthetic manifestations in post-Mughal contexts. Her courses are animated by postcolonial theory, the politics of representation, efforts to diversify and decenter a curriculum that emerges out of Euro-US hegemonic practices, and attempts to address systemic racism and promote social and environmental justice.

Introduction: stitching together gender, textile and garment labor, and heritage in Asia

Melia Belli Bose

Men plough, women weave.

Chinese idiom

To be a woman one must learn the details of women's work. Learn how to weave with hemp and ramie; don't mix fine and rough fibers. Don't run the shuttle of the loom so quickly that you make a mess. When you see the silkworms spinning their cocoons, you must attend to them day and night, picking mulberry leaves to feed them. ... Learn how to cut out shoes and make socks. Learn how to cut fabric and sew it into garments. Learn how to embroider, mend, and darn.

Song Ruozhao, Analects for Women, eighth century[1]

Of the many skills necessary to become a woman, sewing is the most important. Along with the inability to wield a writing brush, not being acquainted with the way of needlework is the source of great shame for a woman.

Onna daigaku takarabako, 'Treasure Chest of the Greater Learning for Women', eighteenth century[2]

A woman's foremost accomplishment is not to purchase a single garment for either summer or winter but to prepare them all with her own hands.

Japanese edict in Okiniwa, 1843[3]

They were considered an auspicious item of clothing, ancient in their form, and sacred in the time it took to create them. The fabric would transform – blossom – from a piece of simple raw khadi to a heavily embellished silken tapestry ... all the women of the family would gather to weave such a piece to include in the trousseau of a young bride. ... It can be considered a means of socializing, for when these women got together they would talk, share cups of chai and stitch the fabric. Special songs were sung. Phulkari became a language of the women, decorative and beautiful and every stitch appeared on that fabric as a rendition of that private dialect.

Hansla Chowdhary on an embroidered Punjabi phulkari textile[4]

Who makes our clothing? For most of us, no matter where in the world we live, or our socio-economic status, a brief inspection of our wardrobe reveals that the overwhelming majority of our garments – be they formal, business, leisure, athletic, or sleepwear – were made in Asia. They bear labels identifying their country of origin as China, Bangladesh, Vietnam, Cambodia, India, Indonesia, Sri Lanka, Myanmar, the Philippines, or Thailand. In fact, garments are typically made in stages, with materials and assembly the products of various countries functioning as nodes along a vast global manufacturing chain: buttons are produced in one country, zips in another, the fabric in another, with the final assembly in still another, before the finished product is shipped thousands of miles away to retail stores. The various steps undertaken to produce our garments are overwhelmingly performed by women. Approximately two-thirds of the estimated 75 million workers in the global garment, textile, and footwear industry today are women employed in factories throughout Asia, working predominantly for mega-retailers that sell to consumers in developed nations at low prices in a global supply chain.[5]

So-called 'fast' or 'disposable' fashion targeting consumers in wealthy countries dominates the contemporary fashion industry. These monikers refer to the rapid design, production, and marketing of clothing that emphasizes making trends quickly and cheaply available. Such briskly evolving fashion trends and the (relatively) democratic accessibility of individual garments ensure that consumers in the global north now purchase and subsequently discard clothing with unprecedented swift turnover. Fast fashion debuted in American high street retail clothing chains in the early 1990s. As the social activist Naomi Klein first brought to light through her path-breaking bestselling exposé, *No Logo: Taking Aim at the Brand Bullies*, first published in 1999, the key to the industry's roaring success is simple: the abundance of cheap labor in the global south (particularly Asia) allows companies to sell their products at lower prices.[6] The profusion of unskilled workers, favorable exchange and tax rates, and comparative lack of regulation and labor unions, made initially China, followed by a host of developing South and Southeast Asian countries, ideal to outsource cheap garment labor at a fraction of the cost in developed countries. The global north's current practice of outsourcing garment production to the global south repeats colonial patterns of labor and financial exploitation. 'What we've done,' comments 'artivist' (artist+activist) Robin Berson on the discrepancies between working conditions and wages for garment workers in different parts of the world, 'is exported tragedy.'[7]

The garment industry is fraught with paradoxes and disparities on both grassroots and global levels. It provides rare opportunities for millions of (predominantly young, poor, and uneducated) women throughout the developing world to contribute economically to their families. Moreover, as demonstrated in Bangladesh, the industry offers these women a path to education, and financial independence, and is linked to an elevated sense of self-worth, improved health, and lower instances of child marriage and infant mortality.[8] However, as demonstrated most infamously through the 2013 collapse of Rana Plaza, a garment factory in Dhaka, Bangladesh, that killed over a thousand workers and critically injured thousands more, workers frequently face hazardous working conditions for inadequate pay.

In addition to the human cost, the garment industry carries a heavy environmental price. It is one of the greatest forces of environmental degradation and global warming, utilizing pesticides, massive amounts of water, coal, and synthetic fibers, producing 1.2 billion tons of carbon dioxide annually.[9] According to a 2016 study, the average American throws away eighty-one pounds of clothing each year, leading to 9.5 million tons being sent to landfills.[10] The most immediate environmental consequences are felt in countries where the factories are located. Lower environmental regulations are another advantage developing countries offer to fashion companies, and the factories' by-products are a major contributor to the pronounced air and water pollution in many garment-producing countries throughout Asia, with China being a prime example.[11]

The fast-fashion industry also poses a threat to heritage. The time, skill, and costlier materials required to produce heritage textiles and garments make them beyond the reach of ordinary consumers. Such items are now predominantly consumed by affluent buyers with ethical concerns or, as Terza Kuldova examines in the Indian case, to announce their elite purchasing power, and cultural and/or symbolic capital.[12] With less business, hereditary artisans are squeezed out of work – often into fast-fashion factories. There are signs that the sartorial tide is shifting – albeit slowly. Voices of dissent, like Robin Berson's, against the fast-fashion industry's human, environmental, and cultural transgressions are growing louder and many consumers are beginning to make more ethically informed purchases.[13] In response, a few international *haute couture* designers are also beginning to make ethically sourced, sustainable, chic fashion, while artists, filmmakers, and others in Asia, Europe, and North America seek to educate through their work.[14]

This volume offers a holistic reassessment of the global garment industry from the vantage point of modern and contemporary Asia. It complements the sizeable corpus of (predominantly) social science literature dealing with policy and the industry's impacts on workers and the environment by taking the innovative approach of focusing on the visual.[15] Thus far, scholarship on modern and contemporary Asian textiles/fashion – their production (including working conditions of their makers), display, history, and meanings – has not adequately examined these fundamental issues, due in part to siloed disciplinary and geographic approaches. The chapters collected here employ heritage textiles and garments, and contemporary artworks from across the region, as lenses to investigate the industry's impacts on sartorial identity, local economies, the environment, lives of creators (designers, artists, entrepreneurs, small-scale cottage producers, and garment factory workers), and efforts to revive and preserve endangered heritage traditions. The disciplinary range of the volume's contributors – scholars of art history, history, fashion, and cultural anthropology, and museum curators working in different regions of Asia – enable us to arrive at a fuller understanding of the confluences of fashion, identity, and gendered labor in Asia from a number of perspectives. This volume presents a fresh and timely inquiry into these intersectional topics from the late nineteenth century to today.

'Venerable' women's work, embodied cultural capital, and industrial interventions

As the quotations at the beginning of this introduction demonstrate, in various parts of Asia, as elsewhere in the world, textile/garment production has historically been yoked to gender. In many premodern societies, women and girls were expected to produce these items, and their skill in doing so had a direct bearing on what, in a Bourdieuian sense, could be understood as their embodied cultural capital.[16] In the introduction to their 1989 volume *Cloth and Human Experience*, Annette B. Weiner and Jane Schneider concede that men play a fundamental role in numerous steps of textile production throughout the world. In many regions of Asia, the various steps of textile production were (and in many cases, remain) strictly gendered. For example, prior to the twentieth century in India and China, weavers and dyers were almost exclusively male.[17] And, as Weiner and Schneider note, men tended to have a greater presence in the production of urban and court textiles and garments. However, as they hasten to add, 'on a world scale and over several centuries, women have played a larger role than men in cloth production.'[18] In other regions of Asia, such as much of Southeast Asia, the various steps in textile production have historically been regarded as women's labor.[19]

In the first major study of women's domestic labor, *Women's Work: The First 20,000 Years*, Elizabeth Barber offers a cogent explanation for this: cloth and garment production is compatible with other feminine-gendered domestic duties, such as childcare.[20] Writing in relation to Chinese embroidery and building on Barber's assertion, Eva Kit Wah Man postulates, 'women's clothing production made them subjects of artistic and bodily expression, which in exchange gave them social identities and values.'[21]

Not only did women produce cloth and clothing for themselves and their families; but throughout premodern Asia, women also participated in the production of commercial cloth and garments which served as money, tribute, and markers of status throughout much of the world. Women textile makers contributed to the economic welfare of their families and to the wider society, and received social recognition for their skilled labor. Moreover, as Weiner and Schneider point out, in pre-capitalist societies where women produced and controlled the distribution of textiles, they tended to enjoy considerable social and even political power, contributions which were eroded with the advent of capitalism.[22]

The material most associated with feminine labor is undoubtedly silk. From its foundation in second-century BCE China, sericulture has been the prerogative of elite women and was the backbone of the Chinese imperial economy. In China, since at least the Shang Bronze Age dynasty (ca. 1200 BCE), the empress herself inaugurated the sericulture season each year by presiding over sacrificial rituals at the altar of the Silkworm Deity in the imperial palace. The tradition continued (albeit not without interruption) until the early twentieth century with the fall of the final Chinese Empire.[23] From China, sericulture spread throughout Asia, where it (largely) remained both a woman's purview and fundamental to the economy. During Japan's Edo period (1603–1868), women produced cotton and silk, which served as tax: the ability to produce was also a prerequisite for marriage. By the late nineteenth century, Japan had supplanted China as the world's leading producer of silk. The booming sericulture industry revived the flagging economy and assisted Japan in becoming industrialized (the first and only Asian country to do so in the nineteenth century): and in part, it also financed the Japanese Empire's colonial expansion in Asia. Until the end of the First World War, women performed over 80% of this labor. In fact, as the pioneering scholar of gender in Japan, Gail Lee Bernstein notes: 'During this period there were more women in the industrial labour force in Japan than in any other country for which we have comparable figures.'[24]

As in China, empresses in Korea and Japan presided over annual sacrifices to inaugurate the sericulture season. In Japan, the empress continues the tradition today. On 29 May 2020, despite the suspension of many regularly scheduled activities due to COVID-19, Empress Masako continued a tradition reputed to be over a millennium and a half old by feeding mulberry leaves to the imperial silkworms.[25]

Embroidery is another example of 'venerable' women's work throughout Asia. In premodern China, embroidery was upheld as a virtuous craft in which all women, regardless of class, were expected to participate. Marsha Weidner observes: 'Needlework was the premier feminine art, one measure of a woman's worth.'[26] For upper-class women, needlework was largely an elegant, cultured pastime, for lower-class women, it was more of an income-generating skill.[27]

Embroidery in China was regarded as a barometer of a woman's character and thus factored heavily in a potential bride's marriageability.[28] In the Philippines during Spanish colonial rule, girls in convent schools and orphanages were taught weaving and embroidery of *piña* in preparation for married life. Production of *piña* cloth from fibers of red Spanish pineapple leaves is arduous and labor intensive. During the textile's heyday in the eighteenth and nineteenth centuries, *piña* embroidery could match and often surpassed the finest examples of European lace.[29] Among the best-known South Asian embroidery traditions are the colorful mirrorwork textiles of Kutch and Saurashtra in the Indian states of Gujarat, parts of Rajasthan,[30] and Sindh, Pakistan[31] as well as the Punjabi *phulkari* work (northwest India and northeast Pakistan) that women create as part of their dowries.[32] Similar to the confluences of ideal femininity and embroidery exemplified through Weidner's discussion, in parts of South Asia the craft has long been upheld as a marker of a woman's character. According to Michele Hardy, the Mutwa community in Gujarat, whose textiles are internationally celebrated, believe 'embroidering is an important means of instilling good habits and moral qualities.'[33] Mutwa uphold the art as an exercise to cultivate the desirable feminine traits of discipline, industriousness, and concentration.[34]

Globally women have historically been encouraged to develop needlework skills as markers of industriousness and submissive femininity – sought-after qualities for potential daughters-in-law. Another boon for the patriarchy in having women excel in such a skill is that this labor requires immense discipline and focus. Patriarchal cultures tend to cast women as flighty, unruly, and prone to stray, which reflects poorly on their families.[35] An appropriately skilled and disciplined woman is less apt to wander (she is too busy!) and excellence in the textile arts suggests her likelihood to remain at home and out of trouble. It is therefore unsurprising that women who excelled in these arts were among the most eligible on the marriage market and heralded as virtuous and venerable by their societies. Heteronormatively masculine textile work, such as dyeing, requires a very different skillset and is typically conducted in public, as opposed to the indoor and often domestic arts of embroidery and sericulture.[36]

In this volume, Cristin McKnight Sethi, Kristen Loring Brennan, Ho Zhao-hua, Yuhang Li, and Magali An Berthon contextualize the gendered work of sericulture and embroidery in different regions of Asia throughout the long twentieth century, demonstrating that these arts remain robust expressions of women's creative and economic agency. Sericulture and embroidery also enable designers and artisans to both revive and reinterpret their heritage, and materially reassert their imagined communities.[37]

While less well known beyond their regions of production, household textiles, which are ubiquitous throughout their respective domestic landscapes across Asia, are potent signifiers of home, family, belonging, women's skills, and homo-sociability. Women's domestic textiles addressed in this volume include embroidered Punjabi *phulkaris* and *nakshi kantha* quilts of Bengal. Like Korean patchwork *jogakbo* (or *bojagi*) and Japanese *furoshiki*, *kanthas* arose from practices of frugality; women stitch these textiles from fabric swatches or single panels of repurposed material.[38]

Their making is typically a communal activity, with several women either working on their own pieces or contributing to a single textile as they socialize. Mothers include such textiles in their daughters' trousseaux – thereby reassuring their new in-laws that the new wife will be busy. In their owners' marital homes, the textiles are sites of memory, reminding new brides of their natal families. In recent decades domestic textiles such as *phulkaris*, *kanthas*, *jogakbo*, and *furoshiki* have been reinterpreted as 'high art' and exhibited in art museums or sold in high-end boutiques; appropriations of them have even graced fashion show runways. A number of Korean contemporary artists, such as Kimsooja and Chunghie Lee, employ *jogakbo* stitching or the cloth itself as a synecdoche of home and family.[39] In this volume Cristin McKnight Sethi and Melia Belli Bose present examples of how women's domestic textiles are appropriated and reinterpreted in new contexts while still retaining nostalgic accretions from their original domestic environments.

Considering the high value most world cultures place on textiles – particularly prior to the twentieth century – and women's long-standing, central roles in textile and garment production, how did it come to be that we pay those who make clothing less than a living wage in a world where the comparatively wealthy throw away clothes? We may chart the roots of our present sartorial condition to the nineteenth century, when a combination of colonialism, industrialization, and capitalist culture and production began to profoundly impact the value of women's textile labor. As Weiner and Schneider aptly comment: 'market pressures to reduce labor costs made women vulnerable to loss of recognition for their contribution to textile wealth.'[40]

Scholars of global history, material, and fashion, Beverly Lemire[41] and Giorgio Riello,[42] and economic historian Sven Beckert,[43] note that historically textile production was at the forefront of industrialization and capitalization. As historian of economics and business John Singleton notes, from the late nineteenth century to now, in the shift from handlooms to power looms 'Textile based industrialization has had its greatest success in Asia.'[44] Industrialized cloth production was initiated by the colonial state in many parts of Asia. Industrial capitalist colonialism under the British was the most devastating to local traditions and economies in the Indian Subcontinent. The trade-focused East India Company began exporting Indian textiles to Europe in the early seventeenth century. By the mid-nineteenth century, the British Empire was purchasing vast supplies of raw cotton at wholesale prices from its Indian colony and manufacturing it into yarn and cloth in industrialized mills in British cities, such as Manchester (where the majority of workers were similarly women). The products were then shipped back to India, and sold for far cheaper than Indian cloth, thereby undercutting, and ultimately crippling, the local market. By the end of the century, this practice galvanized the *swadeshi* Indian independence movement, finally leading to independence in 1947.⁴⁵ In this volume, McKnight Sethi examines recent art by the British-Indian Singh Twins which highlights the deleterious impacts of British-sponsored industrialization and trade on the *phulkari* women's heritage embroidery and other textile traditions in India. In her chapter, Kyunghee Pyun examines a similar situation in Korea under Japanese colonization (1910–1945). In occupied Korea, Koreans were prohibited from producing wool, and thus compelled to purchase material from Japan, bolstering Japan's economy.

Today, throughout Asia, women not only produce the bulk of heritage textiles and garments but they also wear them, and thus sartorially perform their ethnic, national, religious, or communal identities significantly more than men. Colonization, industrialization, globalization, and the implementation of new political systems during the long twentieth century more profoundly impacted men's fashion, making them more likely to wear European-style clothing.⁴⁶ Women throughout the region also gradually adopted European and/or Arabic-style dress (including the body-enveloping *burka*, floor-length *abaya*, headscarf, and *niqab* face covering to become what anthropologist Emma Tarlo terms 'visibly Muslim' in many parts of Asia).⁴⁷ Women also commonly traverse sartorial zones, for example wearing European-style clothing for work, school, or leisure, and heritage garments such as a *sari, shalwar kameez, choli lengha* in South Asia; *dai* in Vietnam; kimono in Japan; *hanbok* in Korea, and a variety of distinct regional garments among Chinese ethnic minorities, for formal occasions, such as weddings. Bhutan is a fashion outlier. According to the *Driglam Namzha* (the kingdom's official code of discipline or conduct, which outlines gendered dress), all citizens are required to observe the official dress code during daylight hours: men wear a *gho*, women, a *kira*.⁴⁸ However, as Emma Dick examines in this volume, despite these strict sartorial regulations, the design, cut, and material of these garments are far from homogeneous, static, or untouched by fashion and technological developments beyond the kingdom.

Women are also at the forefront of many protectionist and revival efforts throughout Asia, documenting and establishing non-governmental organizations (NGOs) and commercial enterprises to support and train heritage textile and garment producers, the majority of whom are also women. Examples include India-based American-born Sally Holkar, co-founder of Rehwa Society and WomenWeave. These initiatives, which promote heritage Maheshwari handloom textiles, subvert the normatively masculine-gendered activity of weaving by training local women in the craft, and assisting them in selling their work. Vancouver-based entrepreneur and fiber artist, Charlotte Kwon, founded Maiwa, which combines a foundation, school of textiles, and boutique. Collaborating with artisans in India, Maiwa is dedicated to promoting Indian heritage textiles and natural dyes to create 'slow clothing' (as opposed to 'fast fashion') and works with 'hand spinners, hand weavers, natural dyers, block printers, embroiderers ... all the artisans who are left behind in the rush to mass produce clothing.'[49] Judy Frater, an American who has lived and worked among nomadic Rabari women embroiderers in India for over twenty-five years, is Founding Director of Somaiya Kala Vidya, an education institute for textile artists, and the Kala Raksha Trust and Textile Museum, which promotes and preserves their work. Frater has received numerous awards for this work from both American and Indian institutions.[50]

It is beyond the scope of this volume, but it certainly bears noting that, although the women listed above (and many others) have played a major role in stimulating moribund textile traditions and changing countless people's lives for the better, they wield unequal power over the local women actors. The women spearheading the protectionist/revivalist initiatives are overwhelmingly from the global north. They are educated, urban, and have access to international capital. Equally problematic (and paradoxical) is that the primary market for the heritage textiles produced in their initiatives is wealthy urbanites in the global north and urban Asia. 'Traditional' labor and media garners hefty prices, thereby positioning the textiles beyond reach for their original communities. Meanwhile, for their new consumers, the textiles may assuage nostalgic longings for a (fictive) romanticized village idyll. For consumers purchasing heritage textiles from their own country, they may take pride in their cultural stewardship, nurturing 'their own' traditions (even if they are from an entirely different region). In purchasing 'slow clothing' whose production empowers poor village women, consumers, particularly in the global north, may congratulate themselves on their 'ethical consumerism.'[51]

Heritage textile/garment revivals are also making a splash on high-fashion catwalks in Beijing, Tokyo, Mumbai, Paris, and New York. A number of women and men *haute couture* designers, particularly from China, are outsourcing textile production to rural women artisans to produce bespoke garments that combine regional styles of needlework with local and Western designs.[52] Among the best known internationally are Lan Yu (b. 1986), who incorporates embroidery from her native Suzhou,[53] and Aniu Aga (b. 1983), who includes embroidery from her own Yi ethnic group.[54] In her chapter in this volume, Brennan explores the hybrid and intersectional designs of China's premier high-fashion designer, Guo Pei (b. 1967). Pei shot to international fame in 2015, when the Barbadian-American celebrity Rihanna wore her fifty-five pound yellow silk, fox fur-trimmed, real gold-threaded, Swarovski crystal-encrusted ball gown to the Met Ball. The event earned the designer a coveted spot on *Time* Magazine's World's 100 Most Influential People the following year. Rather than drawing exclusively from her own regional heritage, Pei's designs are more inclusive and cosmopolitan, uniting heritage embroidery techniques, regional and imperial motifs, and garment styles from across the People's Republic of China, including Occupied Tibet and Inner Mongolia, with European elements.[55]

It is vital to recognize that currents of fashion production, consumption, and stylistic appreciation/appropriation are not unidirectional. In addition to being the global center of garment production, Asia is both a nexus of fashion consumption and an international sartorial trendsetter. Fast fashion and luxury brands rely on consumption within Asia and many non-Asian designers create lines for sale exclusively in Asia. Europe's import of luxury Asian textiles, such as silk and muslin, has an ancient history. Asia also boasts a long history of setting fashion trends outside the continent. For example, late nineteenth-century *avant garde* European women, such as Madame Monet, donned kimono to announce their cosmopolitanism and refined taste, as documented in *La Japonaise*, her portrait painted by her husband, Claude Monet in 1878. In the 1990s, teenage girls in Tokyo pioneered genres of outrageous street fashion such as schoolgirl chic, Harajuku, Lolita Kawaii, and cosplay, which influence young women's counterculture fashion in various Asian metropolises and far beyond.[56]

Dialogues in cloth and gender: plan of the volume

This volume offers a uniquely interdisciplinary, truly pan-Asian investigation of modern and contemporary women's textile/garment labor, use, and shifting meanings. Its purpose is to create a platform for new scholarship on distinct regional traditions of textiles, fashion, and art that have been overlooked and warrants reassessment. Equally meaningful, when read together the chapters highlight concerns valid in other disciplines concerned with gender, labor, and visual culture. Paramount among these are considerations of the creative malleability of heritage objects, motifs, and materials; how technology and industrial labor help, hinder, and offer workers pathways towards agency; and (hopefully) reflections on the fashion industry's grassroots and global impacts.

The first section, 'Fashioning Identity: Textiles, Garments, and Belonging,' explores how garments, materials, and motifs convey identity (communal, religious, gendered, national) and how these changed throughout the long twentieth century. The prolific artistic patronage of China's last dowager empress, Cixi (r. 1861–1908) has garnered considerable scholarly attention this century.[57] Yuhang Li examines how the matriarch manipulated her imperial image through art to promote her uncommon position of authority. In 'Wearing a Gendered Tree: A New Style of Chinese Garments at the Turn of the Twentieth Century,' Li turns to a hitherto neglected topic: design developments in men's and women's imperial robes during Cixi's tenure. Li explores how this final manifestation of Chinese court attire presents reinterpretations of centuries-old gendered plant iconography, nature, and the gendered body in a rapidly changing China.

In 'Women for Cotton and Men for Wool: Consuming Gendered Textiles in Colonized Korea,' Kyunghee Pyun continues the topic of gendered expressions of fashion. Using advertisements in Korean popular magazines published during Japanese occupation in the early twentieth century, this chapter investigates gendered consumption of textiles. The advertisements present the ideal Korean woman as a patriotic consumer of Korean-made cotton. Elite men, on the other hand, are depicted wearing garments of wool, a material that the colonial government exported to Korea and prohibited Koreans from producing. Beyond expanding our knowledge of modern Korean fashion and constructions of gender, this chapter contributes to the sizeable corpus of scholarship on colonial fashion, currently dominated by studies of India.

Ying-chen Peng's chapter, 'Gendered Blue: Women's Jeans in Postwar Taiwan,' similarly engages with popular visual culture that promotes gendered ideals. The chapter analyzes women's consumption of blue jeans in post-Second World War Taiwan and asks: what does it mean when a woman from a culture guided by Confucian ideals (which promotes feminine morality, obedience to patriarchy, and modesty) dons a pair of jeans, an international signifier of rebelliousness, sexiness, and modernity?

Bhutan is the most understudied region of Asia, largely due to its self-imposed isolation. The Kingdom enjoys a thriving commercial and domestic textile industry: today, over 80% of women weave, thereby making significant contributions to their household income. In 'Bhutanese Women and the Performance of Globalization,' Emma Dick builds on Diana K. Myers and Susan S. Bean's 1994 pioneering volume, *From the Land of the Thunder Dragon: Textile Arts of Bhutan*, and offers an updated study of textiles, fashion, and gender in the kingdom.[58] Focusing on the dress of both the Queen, Jetsun Pema Wangchuck, and that of ordinary female citizens, Dick explores what changes the Royal Government, globalization, NGOs, and technology have initiated in Bhutanese women's fashion this century. Beyond Bhutan, Dick's study contributes to wider debates surrounding the politics of identity, dress, and globalization tethered to the creation, consumption, appropriation, and display of heritage textiles and garments.

Ho Zhao-hua takes up several of Dick's points in 'Weaving and Dyeing the Ideal of Reproduction among Shidong Miao in Guizhou Province,' an ethnographic study of the heritage cloth making and clothing of Shidong Miao ethnic minority communities in Guizhou, China. Ho explores how Miao consider cloth making – weaving, dyeing, and finishing – to cosmologically invest the cloth. As the various steps of cloth making are women's work, the Miao accord the skill and its performers special regard. Ho also offers a gendered and iconographic reading of common Miao needlework motifs on their distinct jackets, considering their stylistic evolution during the long twentieth century.

The second section, 'Gendering Creative Agency: Women Fashion Designers, Textile Makers, and Entrepreneurs,' turns to the diverse spheres of palace, runway, home, and getaway to consider women's textile labor, creative agency, and innovative ways their work bridges local heritage, the global market, and museum. In 'Soft Power: Guo Pei and the Fashioning of Matriarchy,' Kristen Loring Brennan considers the myriad cosmopolitan influences of Asia's most successful international high-fashion designer, Guo Pei. Shirking the Spartan and gender-obscuring Chinese communist uniforms that were *de rigour* in her youth during the 1970s, Pei's designs appropriate from such seemingly discordant muses as the Qing dynasty Dowager Empress Cixi and contemporary American model, Carmen Dell'Orefice (b. 1931). Brennan examines how the designer's *haute couture* gowns and the 'brand' that is Guo Pei create a truly global identity for her elite buyers, presenting them not as sexualized, or cunning consumers, but as empowered women of means – matriarchs who define history.

The two essays 'Investigating Female Entrepreneurship in Silk Weaving in Contemporary Cambodia' by Magali An Berthon and '(Re) crafting Distribution Networks for Contemporary Philippine Textiles: Women's Advocacy and Social Enterprise' by Lynne Milgram turn our attention to women as cloth makers and entrepreneurs in Southeast Asia today. Berthon charts the history of sericulture in Cambodia, from its thirteenth-century foundation, to its demise under the Khmer Rouge in the 1970s, to its reinvigoration under foreign and domestic NGOs in the late twentieth century. Using the anthropological methodologies of Actor Network Theory and ethnography, Berthon assesses the aims and successes of two women-owned Cambodian NGOs, paying particular attention to issues of ownership, female leadership and empowerment, and their ramifying effects on the nation's silk industry. Milgram considers relationships between women social entrepreneurs and women cotton ikat weavers in Ifugao province, northern Luzon, Philippines. The collaboration produces innovative designs on indigenous-inspired textiles that respond to the global market for ethically sourced artisanal goods. In dialogue with chapters in the volume's first section, Milgram also considers the roles of heritage and 'authenticity' as weavers and embroiderers adapt their indigenous designs.

In 'Women Weaving Silken Identities and Revitalizing Various Japanese Textile Traditions,' Millie Creighton similarly examines intersections of gender, heritage textile production, identity, and cultural stewardship, in this case in contemporary Japan. Unlike the women in Berthon's and Milgram's essays, whose textile labor is a vital source of revenue generation for their families, Creighton's subjects are upper-middle-class urbanites who participate in sericulture and silk-weaving workshops in rural Japan as personally edifying leisure. Their sanitized and curated experiences with sericulture are thus also markedly different from those of earlier generations of Japanese women and girls, who particularly during the Meiji (1868–1912) and Taisho (1912–1928) eras, when Japan was the world's largest producer of silk, endured tedious and dangerous working conditions. Creighton also examines women's wool-crafting and indigo-dyeing workshops, and how urban Japanese women of means similarly fit into constructions of regional and national identities.

The three chapters in the final section, 'Creative Voices for Change: Textiles, Gender, and Artivism,' present works of visual art from South Asia (or its diaspora) referencing textiles or actual fibers as synecdoches of the global textile/fashion industry and its devastating impacts on local economies, the working conditions of its producers, the environment, and systemic racism. '"Artivism" is a hybrid neologism that signifies work created by individuals who see an organic relationship between art and activism', notes scholar of Chicana Studies, Chelsea Sandoval, and historian of Latinx and Latin American art, Guisela Latorre, in their analysis of Judy Baca's collaborative digital art. Artivism can 'Create new angles of vision to challenge oppressive modes of thinking … artivism is a form of political activism that seeks egalitarian alliances and connections across difference. It requires a mode of consciousness that replicates the digital potentialities and egalitarianism.'[59] Chapters in this section read works of art as a means to inform and galvanize viewers in hopes of correcting various inequalities. Textile-related artivism comes to the fore in South Asian contexts more so than elsewhere in Asia where art (or at least literature on it) focuses more on dissidence or other media of protest. This is not surprising, considering that textiles were such charged loci of local disaffection in the region during the colonial era. Bengal's monopoly on muslin, coveted by elites throughout Asia, Europe, and the Middle East for over two thousand years, remains a source of great cultural pride, while the decimation of the industry under the British East India and later Raj is still widely resented.[60] Gandhi's directive to Indians to spin *khādī* established the fabric as the synecdoche *par excellence* of non-violent resistance and demands for *swaraj* (self-rule).

In 'Entangled Histories of Craft and Conflict: The Story of *Phulkari* Textiles in The Singh Twins's *Slaves of Fashion*,' Cristin McKnight Sethi analyzes the long-standing connection between textile labor, particularly hand embroidery, and constructions of gender in South Asia through a detailed study of Punjabi *phulkari* embroidery from India and Pakistan. The essay offers a counterpoint to Berthon's and Milgram's as it explores craft revival initiatives as income generation projects geared towards female textile makers. The region's most popular textile, *phulkari*, is a synecdoche of Punjabi identity within South Asia and the diaspora, as well as the homeland, which the British partitioned in 1947. McKnight Sethi explores the UK-based artist The Singh Twins's incorporation of *phulkari* motifs in her paintings to critique the deleterious impacts of colonization on Indian textile traditions, histories of exploitative garment labor, luxury consumerism, and their enduring, global legacies.

Saleema Waraich continues the theme of linking the colonial appetite for Indian textiles (particularly raw cotton) and its devastation of local industries to detrimental contemporary circumstances. In 'The Politics of Wastefulness and "the Poetics of Waste": Ruby Chishti's Sartorial Interventions,' Waraich highlights the trajectory from colonial material exploitation to the global north's current mass consumption of fast fashion. Waraich examines this relationship through Pakistani-American artivist Ruby Chishti's sculptures fashioned from discarded garments, which critique the fast-fashion industry's impacts on the environment and self-identity.

Melia Belli Bose turns from the environmental to the human cost of fast fashion in 'Made in Rana Plaza: Dilara Begum Jolly's Garment Factory-Themed Art.' Contemporary Bangladeshi multi-media feminist artivist Dilara Begum Jolly created a series of visceral, affective artworks that present the victims of two recent deadly garment factory disasters in her country as relatable individuals. Jolly herself opines that if viewers of her work connect empathetically with her victim subjects, it may inspire them to buy more ethically and demand grassroots changes, thus transforming her artivism into a small but powerful act of resistance to a global system of structural violence. Much like The Singh Twins's incorporation of *phulkari* motifs that McKnight Sethi describes, in her garment factory-themed art, Jolly incorporates references to Bengali *nakshi kantha* domestic textiles to highlight Bangladesh's enduring traditions of women's textile production.

Knitting together myriad topics from across Asia (and beyond) that represent nearly a century and a half of women's engagement with textiles, the proceeding chapters illuminate broader imbrications of gender, labor, industrialization, heritage, globalization, consumption, agency, and sartorial performances of identity. This volume also presents examples of cultural stewards who work to reinvigorate moribund textile traditions and provide pathways towards workers' economic empowerment, and artivists who reference textiles to expose abuses and injustices. Fast-fashion production is not confined to Asia; numerous countries throughout the global south participate in the international supply chain that caters to the global north's voracious appetite for up-to-the-minute cheap apparel. Ethiopia, Honduras, Guatemala, El Salvador, Nicaragua, and Turkey are also major fast-fashion exporters, again, with women performing the bulk of the labor. Each of these countries similarly boasts august heritage textile traditions and the authors in this volume hope that our efforts initiate similar inquiries into these countries' textile traditions and the lives of those who produce them.

Acknowledgments

I am grateful to Saleema Waraich, Kyunghee Pyun, Allan Antliff, and the anonymous readers for their insightful comments on earlier drafts of this chapter.

Notes

1. Wm. Theodore de Bary and Irene Bloom, comp., *Sources of Chinese Tradition*, 2nd ed., vol. 1 (New York: Columbia University Press, 1999), pp. 827–831.
2. Marcia Yonemoto, *The Problem of Women in Early Modern Japan* (Berkeley: University of California Press, 2016), p. 67.
3. Louise Allison Court, 'The Changing Fortunes of Three Japanese Archaic Textiles,' in Annette B. Weiner and Jane Schneider, eds, *Cloth and Human Experience* (Washington, D. C.: Smithsonian Institution Press, 1989), p. 405.
4. Aanchal Malhotra, *Remnants of Partition: 21 Objects from a Continent Divided* (New Delhi: Oxford University Press, 2019), pp. 106–107.
5. Facts obtained from 'The Clean Clothes Campaign,' https://cleanclothes.org/ (accessed 23 June 2020). Founded in 1989 to improve the working conditions of garment workers, the Clean Clothes Campaign is the largest alliance of non-governmental organizations (NGOs) and labor unions in the global garment industry.
6. Naomi Klein, *No Logo: Taking Aim at the Brand Bullies* (Toronto: Random House, 1999). More recent studies include Kate Fletcher, *Sustainable Fashion and Textiles: Design Journeys* (New York: Routledge, 2014) and Dana Thomas, *Fashionopolis: The Price of Fast Fashion and the Future of Clothes* (New York: Penguin, 2019).
7. Ariful Islam, 'Triangle to Tazreen and Rana Plaza: Memories of Artist Robin Berson,' in Tasleema Akhtar, ed., *Chobbishe April: Hazar Praner Chitkar'* [24th April: Outcries of a Thousand Souls] (Dhaka: Bangladesh Garment Sromik Samhoti, 2014), p. 37.
8. Rachel Heath and Mushfiq Mobarak, 'Manufacturing Growth and the Lives of Bangladeshi Women,' *Journal of Development Economics*, 115 (2015): 1–15.
9. 'How Your Love of Fashion could be Harming the Environment,' BBC, 23 April 2019, www.bbc.co.uk/newsround/45756754 (accessed 15 June 2020).
10. Eleanor Goldberg, 'You're Probably Going to Throw Away 81 Pounds of Clothing This Year,' *Huff Post*, 6 September 2016, www.huffingtonpost.ca/entry/youre-likely-going-to-throw-away-81-pounds-of-clothing-this-year_n_57572bc8e4b08f74f6c069d3?ri18n=true (accessed 24 June 2020).
11. Elizabeth C. Economy, 'The Great Leap Backward? The Costs of China's Environmental Crisis,' *Foreign Affairs* 86, no. 5 (September–October 2007): 38–59.
12. In *Luxury Indian Fashion: A Social Critique* (London: Bloomsbury, 2017), Kuldova explains how luxury artisanal garments have become a significant force defining contemporary elite Indian society.
13. Elizabeth Cline, *Overdressed: The Shockingly High Cost of Cheap Fashion* (New York: Penguin, 2012), p. 41; Harry Moser and Sandy Montalbano, 'Why Made-in-USA Fashion Is Turning Heads,' *Industry Week*, 18 January 2018, www.industryweek.com/economy/why-made-usa-fashion-turning-heads (accessed 2 August 2020).
14. In 2019 the contemporary art exhibition *Fast Fashion/Slow Art* was held at Bowdoin College and the George Washington University. Installations, performances, and

films interrogated the global garment industry, workers' rights, and the industry's environmental impact (Bibiana Obler and Phyllis Rosenzweig, eds, *Fast Fashion/Slow Art* (London: Scala Art Publishers, 2019)).

15 Recent scholarship on labor and policy in the Asian garment industry includes: Sanchita Banerjee Saxena, *Made in Bangladesh, Cambodia, and Sri Lanka: The Labor Behind the Global Garments and Textiles Industries* (Amherst: Cambria Press, 2014); Sanchita Banerjee Saxena, ed., *Labor, Global Supply Chains, and the Garment Industry in South Asia: Bangladesh after Rana Plaza* (New York and London: Routledge, 2019); Vicki Crinis and Adrian Vickers, eds, *Labour in the Clothing Industry in the Asia Pacific* (New York and London: Routledge, 2016); Dev Nathan, Silliman Bhattacharjee, Rahul S. Shikha, Purushottam Kumar, Immanuel Dahagani, Sukhpal Singh, and Padmini Swaminathan, *Reverse Subsidies in Global Monopsony Capitalism: Gender, Labour, and Environmental Injustice in Garment Value Chains* (Cambridge: Cambridge University Press, 2022).

16 In 'The Forms of Capital,' sociologist Pierre Bourdieu describes embodied cultural capital as knowledge (both passively acquired and consciously cultivated) acquired over time that impacts a person's social status (in ed., J. G. Richardson, *Handbook of Theory and Research for the Sociology of Education* (New York: Greenwood, 1986), pp. 241–259).

17 Numerous NGOs, commercial enterprises, and the state of Uttar Pradesh are reinvigorating the hand-weaving industry in Varanasi, one of India's most celebrated weaving centers. As in much of the country, Varanasi's weavers have historically been Muslim men (in south India, the majority are Hindu men). Women typically perform ancillary jobs of spinning, loading, and stretching the yarn. This gendered division of textile labor continues today. For more on Varanasi's weaving industry (particularly its famed Banarsi *saris*, and its revival, see Shivani Vora, 'For Indian Weavers in Varanasi, Help for an Endangered Craft,' *New York Times*, 17July 2015, www.nytimes.com/2015/07/19/travel/for-indian-weavers-in-varanasi-help-for-an-endangered-craft.html (accessed 27 July 2020);

Helen Regan and Omar Khan, 'Fine Silk Over Fast Fashion: The Last Handweavers of India's Holiest City,' CNN, 9 November 2019, www.cnn.com/style/article/silk-weavers-varanasi-banarasi-sari-intl-hnk/index.html (accessed 27 July 2020).

18 Weiner and Schneider, *Cloth and Human Experience*, p. 21.

19 Jennifer Harris, ed., *5000 Years of Textiles* (Washington, D. C.: Smithsonian Books, 2010), p. 13.

20 Elizabeth Barber, *Women's Work: The First 20,000 Years* (New York: W. W. Norton & Company, 1995), pp. 29–32.

21 Eva Kit Wah Man, *Bodies in China: Philosophy, Aesthetics, Gender, and Politics* (Albany: State University of New York Press, 2019), p. 61.

22 Weiner and Schneider, *Cloth and Human Experience*, pp. 23–24.

23 For more on women's roles in sericulture in China (particularly during the Ming dynasty), see Yi Jo-lan, 'Gender and Sericulture Ritual Practice in Sixteenth-Century China,' *Journal of Asian History*, 48, no. 2 (2014): 281–302.

24 Gail Lee Bernstein, 'Women in the Silk-Reeling Industry in Nineteenth-Century Japan,' in Gail Lee Bernstein and H. Fukui, eds, *Japan and the World* (London: Palgrave Macmillan, 1988), pp. 54–55. Bernstein details the vital role of women's sericulture labor on Japan's path to industrialization: silk thread was Japan's major export, generating funds for the Japanese Empire to acquire machines and raw materials to initiate other industries (ibid.).

25 Tatsuro Sugiura, 'Masako Carries on Tradition of Sericulture at Imperial Palace,' *Asahi Shimbun*, 3 June 2020, www.asahi.com/ajw/articles/13426699?fbclid=IwAR2CrPz1PFgFi7kHyPX2llLpbocT7tVsT1cfuxbOpKaq7wepZaP_W99aQkc (accessed 29 June 2020).

26 Marsha Weidner, 'Women in the History of Chinese Painting,' in Marsha Weidner, Ellen Johnston Lang, Irving Yucheng Lo, Christina Chu, and James Robinson, eds, *Views from the Jade Terrace: Chinese Women Artists 1300–1912* (Indianapolis: Indianapolis Museum of Art, and New York: Rizzoli, 1988), p. 21; Wah, *Bodies in China*, p. 67.

27 Rachel Silberstein's recent publications (*A Fashionable Century: Textile Artistry and Commerce in the Late Qing* (Seattle: University of Washington Press, 2020); 'Cloud Collars and Sleeve Bands: Commercial Embroidery and the Fashionable Accessory in Mid-to-Late Qing China,' *Fashion Theory*, 21 (2017): 245–277; 'Eight Scenes of Suzhou: Landscape Embroidery, Urban Courtesans, and Nineteenth-Century Chinese Women's Fashions,' *Late Imperial China* 36, no. 1 (June 2015): 1–52) offer greater analysis of confluences of women's clothing and accessories, and women's work (particularly needlework) in late Qing dynasty China. Silberstein also explores women's participation in the commercialization of textile handicrafts and the flourishing of urban popular culture during this period.

28 See Wah, *Bodies in China*, pp. 61–72.

29 A recent exhibition on *piña* textiles at the San Francisco International Airport, *Pineapple to Piña*, emphasized links between a woman's skill producing and embroidering the textile and her perceived virtue in the colonial Philippines.

30 Judy Frater, *Threads of Identity: Embroidery and Adornment of the Nomadic Rabaris* (Ahmedabad: Mapin, 1997) remains the definitive work on Rabari textiles from the Kutch region of Gujarat.

31 See Nasreen Askari and Rosemary Crill, *Colours of the Indus: Costumes and Textiles of Pakistan* (London: Victoria and Albert Museum, 1997).

32 Recent scholarship on *phulkari*s includes Darielle Mason, ed., *The Embroidered Textiles of Punjab from the Jill and Sheldon Bonovitz Collection* (New Haven: Yale University Press, 2017); and Cristin McKnight Sethi, 'Producing, Collecting, and Displaying Phulkari Embroidery from Punjab, c.1850 to Present,' PhD dissertation (University of California, Berkeley, 2015).

33 Michele Hardy, 'Embodying Embroidery: Researching Women's Folk Art in Western India,' *Textile Society of America Symposium Proceedings*, (2000): 158–166, at 161.

34 Ibid.

35 In *Renaissance Clothing and the Materials of Memory* (Cambridge: Cambridge University Press, 2000), Ann Rosalind Jones and Peter Stallybrass discuss spinning and weaving and fairy tale literature in the early modern European context in relation to discipline. Rebecca M. Brown also addresses Gandhian rhetoric around discipline and textile production in late colonial India (*Gandhi's Spinning Wheel and the Making of India* (London: Routledge, 2010)).

36 See for example Yi, 'Gender and Sericulture Ritual Practice.'

37 Writing on nationalism, political scientist and historian Benedict Anderson coined the term 'imagined communities.' He describes the nation as a socially constructed community that is imagined by its citizens who perceive themselves as part of that group (*Imagined Communities: Reflections on the Origin and Spread of Nationalism* (London and New York: Verso, 1991)). Scholars have since used the term to refer to other communities too large for all members to know each other.

38 For more on *furoshiki*, see Hideyuki Oka, *How to Wrap Five Eggs* (New York: John Weatherhill, 1976); Kazua Takaoka, *Furoshiki* (Tokyo: PIE Books, 2012).

39 For a discussion of the history of these cloths and their meanings in Kimsooja's multi-media art, see Joo-eun Lee, 'Sooja Kim's Wrapping Cloth: The Aesthetics of Paradox,' *Woman's Art Journal*, 36, no. 1 (Spring/Summer 2015): 19–26.

40 Weiner and Schneider, *Cloth and Human Experience*, p. 24.

41 Beverly Lemire, *Global Trade and the Transformation of Consumer Cultures: The Material World Remade, c.1500–1820* (Cambridge: Cambridge University Press, 2018).
42 Giorgio Riello, *Cotton: The Fabric that Made the Modern World* (Cambridge: Cambridge University Press, 2013).
43 Sven Beckert, *Empire of Cotton: A Global History* (New York: Vintage Books, 2015).
44 John Singleton, *The World Textile Industry* (New York and London: Routledge, 1997), p. 27.
45 See Riello, *Cotton*, pp. 269–270; Rosemary Crill, *The Fabric of India* (London: Victoria and Albert Museum, 2015); Susan S. Bean, 'Gandhi and *Khadi*, the Fabric of Indian Independence,' in Weiner and Schneider, eds, *Cloth and Human Experience*, pp. 355–365; Susan S. Bean, 'Freedom Homespun,' *Asian Art and Culture*, 9, no. 2 (1996): 53–67.
46 For a discussion on gendered practices of adopting Western-style clothing in colonial and postcolonial India, see Emma Tarlo, *Clothing Matters: Dress and Identity in India* (Chicago: University of Chicago Press, 1996).
47 Emma Tarlo, *Visibly Muslim: Fashion, Politics, Faith* (London: Bloomsbury, 2008).
48 Manmath Padhy, 'A Study of Socio-cultural History of Bhutan,' *Proceedings of the Indian History Congress*, 74 (2013): 1052–1053.
49 https://maiwa.com/pages/our-story (accessed 13 July 2020).
50 https://www.ashoka.org/en-ca/fellow/judy-frater (accessed 28 June 2020).
51 For a greater discussion of these three perceived boons, see Chloe J. Tibert, who addresses these issues in relation to Punjabi *phulkari* and Bengali *nakshi kantha* in'Collective Repositories: The Social Lives of *Phulkari* and *Nakshi Kantha* Embroideries, MA (University of Victoria, 2023).
52 For recent work on this in India, see Tara Mayer, 'From Craft to Couture: Contemporary Indian Fashion in Historical Perspective,' *South Asian Popular Culture*, 16, no. 2–3 (2018): 183–198.
53 Ellen Sheng, 'Chinese Fashion Designer Lan Yu On Why "Made In China" Will Succeed In Going Global,' *Forbes*, 26 October 2016, www.forbes.com/sites/ellensheng/2016/10/26/chinese-fashion-designer-lan-yu-on-why-made-in-china-will-succeed-in-going-global/#1120980c2482 (accessed 13 July 2020).
54 Liu Zhongyin, 'Chinese Fashion Designer Keeps the Culture of China's Yi Ethnic Group Alive through Innovative Clothing Design,' *Global Times*, 15 April 2019, www.globaltimes.cn/content/1145960.shtml (accessed 13 July).
55 For more on Guo Pei's designs, see Paula Wallace, ed., *Guo Pei: Couture Beyond* (New York: Rizzoli Electa, 2018).
56 See Philomena Keet, *Tokyo Fashion City: A Detailed Guide to Tokyo's Trendiest Fashion Districts* (London: Tuttle, 2019). Arguably the best-known appropriator (who some critique as cultural appropriator) of Japanese teenage girl street fashion is the American singer, Gwen Stefani, who sings about and dresses Japanese and Japanese-American backup dancers as 'Harajuku Girls.' For a discussion of the ongoing controversy of Stefani's practice, see Christopher Luu, 'Gwen Stefani Says Her Harajuku Girls Phase Wasn't Cultural Appropriation,' *In Style*, updated 19 November 2019, www.instyle.com/news/gwen-stefani-harajuku-girls-wasnt-cultural-appropriation (accessed 12 January 2022).
57 Carlos Rojas, *The Naked Gaze: Reflections on Chinese Modernity* (Cambridge: Harvard University Asia Center, 2009); Yuhang Li and Harriet T. Zurndorfer, 'Rethinking Empress Dowager Cixi through the Production of Art,' *Nan Nü*, 14 (2012): 1–20; Yuhang Li, 'Oneself as a Female Deity: Representations of Empress Dowager Cixi as Guanyin,' *Nan Nü*, 14 (2012): 75–118; Yuhang Li, 'Painting Empress Dowager Cixi as Guanyin for Missionaries' Eyes,' *Orientations*, 49 no. 6 (November/December 2018): 50–61; Yuhang Li, *Becoming Guanyin: Artistic Devotion of Buddhist Women in*

Late Imperial China (New York: Columbia University Press, 2020); Ying-Chen Peng, 'Lingering Between Tradition and Innovation: Photographic Portraits of Empress Dowager Cixi,' *Ars Orientalis*, 43 (January 2013): 157–174; Ying-Chen Peng, 'Staging Sovereignty: Empress Dowager Cixi (1835–1908) and Late Qing Court Art Production,' PhD dissertation (University of California, Los Angeles, 2014).

58 Diana K. Myers and Susan S. Bean, *From the Land of the Thunder Dragon: Textile Arts of Bhutan* (Chicago: Serinida Publications, 1994).

59 Chelsea Sandoval and Guisela Latorre, 'Chicana/o Artivism: Judy Baca's Digital Work with Youth of Color,' in Anna Everett, ed., *Learning Race and Ethnicity: Youth and Digital Media* (Cambridge and London: MIT Press, 2007), pp. 82, 83.

60 Veronica Murphy, 'Textiles,' in R. Skelton and Mark Francis, eds, *Arts of Bengal: The Heritage of Bangladesh and Eastern India* (London: Whitechapel Gallery, 1980), pp. 63–70.

Bibliography

Anderson, Benedict. *Imagined Communities: Reflections on the Origin and Spread of Nationalism*. London and New York: Verso, 1991.

Askari, Nasreen and Rosemary Crill. *Colours of the Indus: Costumes and Textiles of Pakistan*. London: Victoria and Albert Museum, 1997.

Barber, Elizabeth. *Women's Work: The First 20,000 Years*. New York: W. W. Norton & Company, 1995.

Bean, Susan S. 'Freedom Homespun.' *Asian Art and Culture* 9, no. 2 (1996): 53–67.

Bean, Susan S. 'Gandhi and *Khadi*, the Fabric of Indian Independence.' In *Cloth and Human Experience*. Edited by Annette B. Weiner and Jane Schneider. Washington, D. C.: Smithsonian Institution Press, 1989.

Beckert, Sven. *Empire of Cotton: A Global History*. New York: Vintage Books, 2015.

Bernstein, Gail Lee. 'Women in the Silk-Reeling Industry in Nineteenth-Century Japan.' In *Japan and the World*. Edited by Gail Lee Bernstein and H. Fukui. London: Palgrave Macmillan, 1988.

Bourdieu, Pierre. 'The Forms of Capital.' In *Handbook of Theory and Research for the Sociology of Education*. Eited by J. G. Richardson. New York: Greenwood, 1986.

Brown, Rebecca M. *Gandhi's Spinning Wheel and the Making of India*. London: Routledge, 2010.

Cline, Elizabeth. *Overdressed: The Shockingly High Cost of Cheap Fashion*. New York: Penguin, 2012.

Court, Louise Allison. 'The Changing Fortunes of Three Japanese Archaic Textiles.' In *Cloth and Human Experience*. Edited by Annette B. Weiner and Jane Schneider. Washington, D. C.: Smithsonian Institution Press, 1989.

Crill, Rosemary. *The Fabric of India*. London: Victoria and Albert Museum, 2015.

Crinis, Vicki and Adrian Vickers, eds. *Labour in the Clothing Industry in the Asia Pacific*. New York and London: Routledge, 2016.

de Bary, Wm. Theodore and Irene Bloom, comp. *Sources of Chinese Tradition*. 2nd ed., volume 1. New York: Columbia University Press, 1999.

Economy, Elizabeth C. 'The Great Leap Backward? The Costs of China's Environmental Crisis.' *Foreign Affairs* 86, no. 5 (September–October 2007): 38–59.

Fletcher, Kate. *Sustainable Fashion and Textiles: Design Journeys*. New York: Routledge, 2014.

Frater, Judy. *Threads of Identity: Embroidery and Adornment of the Nomadic Rabaris*. Ahmedabad: Mapin, 1997.

Goldberg, Eleanor. 'You're Probably Going to Throw Away 81 Pounds of Clothing This Year.' *Huff Post*, 6 September 2016. www.huffingtonpost.ca/entry/youre-likely-going-to-throw-away-81-pounds-of-clothing-this-year_n_57572bc8e4b08f74f6c069d3?ri18n=true (accessed 24 June 2020).

Hardy, Michele. 'Embodying Embroidery: Researching Women's Folk Art in Western India.' *Textile Society of America Symposium Proceedings* (2000): 158–166.

Harris, Jennifer, ed. *5000 Years of Textiles*. Washington, D. C.: Smithsonian Books, 2010.

Heath, Rachel and Mushfiq Mobarak. 'Manufacturing Growth and the Lives of Bangladeshi Women.' *Journal of Development Economics* 115 (2015): 1–15.

'How Your Love of Fashion could be Harming the Environment.' BBC, 23 April 2019. www.bbc.co.uk/newsround/45756754 (accessed 15 June 2020).

Islam, Ariful. 'Triangle to Tazreen and Rana Plaza: Memories of Artist Robin Berson.' In *Chobbishe April: Hazar Praner Chitkar*' [24th April: Outcries of a Thousand Souls]. Edited by Tasleema Akhtar. Dhaka: Bangladesh Garment Sromik Samhoti, 2014.

Jo-lan Yi. 'Gender and Sericulture Ritual Practice in Sixteenth-Century China.' *Journal of Asian History* 48, no. 2 (2014): 281–302.

Jones, Ann Rosalind and Peter Stallybrass. *Renaissance Clothing and the Materials of Memory*. Cambridge: Cambridge University Press, 2000.

Keet, Philomena. *Tokyo Fashion City: A Detailed Guide to Tokyo's Trendiest Fashion Districts*. London: Tuttle, 2019.

Klein, Naomi. *No Logo: Taking Aim at the Brand Bullies*. Toronto: Random House, 1999.

Kuldova, Terza. *Luxury Indian Fashion: A Social Critique*. London: Bloomsbury, 2017.

Lee, Joo-eun. 'Sooja Kim's Wrapping Cloth: The Aesthetics of Paradox.' *Woman's Art Journal* 36, no. 1 (Spring/Summer 2015): 19–26.

Lemire, Beverly. *Global Trade and the Transformation of Consumer Cultures: The Material World Remade, c.1500–1820*. Cambridge: Cambridge University Press, 2018.

Liu Zhongyin. 'Chinese Fashion Designer Keeps the Culture of China's Yi Ethnic Group Alive through Innovative Clothing Design,' *Global Times*, 15 April 2019. www.globaltimes.cn/content/1145960.shtml (accessed 13 July).

Luu, Christopher. 'Gwen Stefani Says Her Harajuku Girls Phase Wasn't Cultural Appropriation.' *In Style*, updated 19 November 2019. www.instyle.com/news/gwen-stefani-harajuku-girls-wasnt-cultural-appropriation (accessed 12 January 2022).

Malhotra, Aanchal. *Remnants of Partition: 21 Objects from a Continent Divided*. New Delhi: Oxford University Press, 2019.

Man, Eva Kit Wah. *Bodies in China: Philosophy, Aesthetics, Gender, and Politics*. Albany: State University of New York Press, 2019.

Mason, Darielle, ed. *The Embroidered Textiles of Punjab from the Jill and Sheldon Bonovitz Collection*. New Haven: Yale University Press, 2017.

Mayer, Tara. 'From Craft to Couture: Contemporary Indian Fashion in Historical Perspective.' *South Asian Popular Culture* 16, no. 2–3 (2018): 183–198.

McKnight Sethi, Cristin. 'Producing, Collecting, and Displaying Phulkari Embroidery from Punjab, c.1850 to Present.' PhD dissertation, University of California, Berkeley, 2015.

Moser, Harry and Sandy Montalbano. 'Why Made-in-USA Fashion Is Turning Heads.' *Industry Week*, 18 January 2018. www.industryweek.com/economy/why-made-usa-fashion-turning-heads (accessed 2 August 2020).

Murphy, Veronica. 'Textiles.' In *Arts of Bengal: The Heritage of Bangladesh and Eastern India*. Edited by R. Skelton and Mark Francis. London: Whitechapel Gallery, 1980.

Myers, Diana K. and Susan S. Bean. *From the Land of the Thunder Dragon: Textile Arts of Bhutan*. Chicago: Serinida Publications, 1994.

Nathan, Dev, Silliman Bhattacharjee, Rahul S. Shikha, Purushottam Kumar, Immanuel Dahagani, Sukhpal Singh, and Padmini Swaminathan. *Reverse Subsidies in Global Monopsony Capitalism: Gender, Labour, and Environmental Injustice in Garment Value Chains*. Cambridge: Cambridge University Press, 2022.

Obler, Bibiana and Phyllis Rosenzweig, eds. *Fast Fashion/Slow Art*. London: Scala Art Publishers, 2019.

Oka, Hideyuki. *How to Wrap Five Eggs*. New York: John Weatherhill, 1976.

Padhy, Manmath. 'A Study of Socio-cultural History of Bhutan.' *Proceedings of the Indian History Congress* 74 (2013): 1052–1053.

Regan, Helen and Omar Khan. 'Fine Silk Over Fast Fashion: The Last Hand-weavers of India's Holiest City.' CNN, 9 November 2019. www.cnn.com/style/article/silk-weavers-varanasi-banarasi-sari-intl-hnk/index.html (accessed 27 July 2020).

Riello, Giorgio. *Cotton: The Fabric that Made the Modern World*. Cambridge: Cambridge University Press, 2013.

Rojas, Carlos. *The Naked Gaze: Reflections on Chinese Modernity*. Cambridge: Harvard University Asia Center, 2009.

Sandoval, Chelsea and Guisela Latorre. 'Chicana/o Artivism: Judy Baca's Digital Work with Youth of Color.' In *Learning Race and Ethnicity: Youth and Digital Media*. Edited by Anna Everett. Cambridge and London: MIT Press, 2007.

Saxena, Sanchita Banerjee, ed. *Labor, Global Supply Chains, and the Garment Industry in South Asia: Bangladesh after Rana Plaza*. New York and London: Routledge, 2019.

Saxena, Sanchita Banerjee. *Made in Bangladesh, Cambodia, and Sri Lanka: The Labor Behind the Global Garments and Textiles Industries*. Amherst: Cambria Press, 2014).

Silberstein, Rachel. *A Fashionable Century: Textile Artistry and Commerce in the Late Qing*. Seattle: University of Washington Press, 2020.

Silberstein, Rachel. 'Cloud Collars and Sleeve Bands: Commercial Embroidery and the Fashionable Accessory in Mid-to-Late Qing China.' *Fashion Theory* 21 (2017): 245–277.

Silberstein, Rachel. 'Eight Scenes of Suzhou: Landscape Embroidery, Urban Courtesans, and Nineteenth-Century Chinese Women's Fashions.' *Late Imperial China* 36, no. 1 (June 2015): 1–52.

Singleton, John. *The World Textile Industry*. New York and London: Routledge, 1997.

Takaoka, Kazua. *Furoshiki*. Tokyo: PIE Books, 2012.

Sugiura, Tatsuro. 'Masako Carries on Tradition of Sericulture at Imperial Palace.' *Asahi Shimbun*, 3 June 2020. www.asahi.com/ajw/articles/13426699?fbclid=IwAR2CrPz1PFgFi7kHyPX2llLpbocT7tVsT1cfuxbOpKaq7wepZaP_W99aQkc (accessed 29 June 2020).

Tarlo, Emma. *Clothing Matters: Dress and Identity in India*. Chicago: University of Chicago Press, 1996.

Tarlo, Emma. *Visibly Muslim: Fashion, Politics, Faith*. London: Bloomsbury, 2008.

'The Clean Clothes Campaign.' https://cleanclothes.org/ (accessed 23 June 2020).

Thomas, Dana. *Fashionopolis: The Price of Fast Fashion and the Future of* Clothes. New York: Penguin, 2019.

Tibert, Chloe J. 'Collective Repositories: The Social Lives of *Phulkari* and *Nakshi Kantha* Embroideries. MA, University of Victoria, 2023.

Vora, Shivani. 'For Indian Weavers in Varanasi, Help for an Endangered Craft.' *New York Times*, 17 July 2015, www.nytimes.com/2015/07/19/travel/for-indian-weavers-in-varanasi-help-for-an-endangered-craft.html (accessed 27 July 2020).

Wallace, Paula, ed., *Guo Pei: Couture Beyond*. New York: Rizzoli Electa, 2018.

Weidner, Marsha. 'Women in the History of Chinese Painting.' In *Views from the Jade Terrace: Chinese Women Artists 1300–1912*. Edited by Marsha Weidner, Ellen Johnston Lang, Irving Yucheng Lo, Christina Chu, and James Robinson. Indianapolis: Indianapolis Museum of Art, and New York: Rizzoli, 1988.

Ying-Chen Peng. 'Lingering Between Tradition and Innovation: Photographic Portraits of Empress Dowager Cixi.' *Ars Orientalis* 43 (January 2013): 157–174.

Ying-Chen Peng. 'Staging Sovereignty: Empress Dowager Cixi (1835–1908) and Late Qing Court Art Production.' PhD dissertation, University of California, Los Angeles, 2014.

Yonemoto, Marcia. *The Problem of Women in Early Modern Japan*. Berkeley: University of California Press, 2016.

Yuhang Li. *Becoming Guanyin: Artistic Devotion of Buddhist Women in Late Imperial China*. New York: Columbia University Press, 2020.

Yuhang Li. 'Oneself as a Female Deity: Representations of Empress Dowager Cixi as Guanyin.' *Nan Nü* 14 (2012): 75–118.

Yuhang Li. 'Painting Empress Dowager Cixi as Guanyin for Missionaries' Eyes.' *Orientations* 49 no. 6 (November/December 2018): 50–61.

Yuhang Li and Harriet T. Zurndorfer. 'Rethinking Empress Dowager Cixi through the Production of Art.' *Nan Nü* 14 (2012): 1–20.

PART I

Fashioning identity: textiles, garments, and belonging

1

Wearing a gendered tree: a new style of garments from early modern to twentieth-century China

Yuhang Li

Introduction

From the eighteenth century on, the novel design known as *yishu mei*, or 'single tree with plum blossoms,' which was associated with theatrical costume, appeared now and again in both textual and visual references in China.[1] From the mid-nineteenth century to the first half of the twentieth century, tree designs expanded to a wide range of vegetation. These became increasingly popular and appeared on assorted garments, from theatrical robes for a wide range of characters, to men and women's attire. These plant images break conventional associations with masculine or feminine attributes and blur gender boundaries. Unlike the use of flowers and plants as a repetitive modular pattern or as a symmetrically programmed composition, with this style the shape of the garment serves as a framing device for the imagery. A complete single tree or a cluster of assorted plants are arranged on both sides of a full-length garment. The vegetation is explicitly depicted as growing from the earth, and the anatomical body of the wearer beneath the attire and the vegetation on the clothing coincide. This new design was widely reproduced in woven silk and cotton, embroidered silk, and cut velvet. Scholars have addressed the long-established tradition of anthropomorphizing plants in Chinese painting and decorative arts from social, political, and cultural perspectives.[2] However, the allegorical meanings of painting-like vegetation on garments have not been studied.

Surviving visual and textual sources suggest that certain whole-tree designs might be closely related to some commemorative purpose, such as a birthday. Birthday celebrations are perhaps the most common social, cultural, ritual, and religious practice in China and they were one of the driving forces behind artistic production in early modern China. Thus far, birthdays have not been singled out to explore the complicated issues around fashion design, and by making birthdays an explicit focus of discussion this chapter uncovers early modern notions of time, theatricality, the body, and subjectivity. I will first trace the historical development of this aesthetic and then discuss how the new design engaged different notions of the body. In particular, I will show how these textiles were employed to express a new relationship between body and nature over the span of a person's lifetime.

In a recent groundbreaking book on fashion history and market economy in nineteenth-century China, Rachel Silberstein points out that to break from the Western-dominated discourse around fashion history, we need to provide a different logic to fashion theory; we must unlink fashion from the exclusive focus on Europe and capitalism. Following Jennifer Craik, Silberstein explains, 'To define fashion as necessarily cast from capitalist economies is to imply a misleading homogeneity to fashion as a social and cultural force.'[3] She thus poses the question of how to think about fashion in non-capitalist societies. The problem of Chinese fashion in this period is parallel to the problem of thinking about late imperial China as early modern China. We need to affirm that this period is modern, but in a way that is not derivative from the West. Consequently, modernity must be defined at a higher level of abstraction, which can encompass both the West and China without prioritizing one region. We must proceed similarly with the concept of fashion and define fashion at a higher level of abstraction so that it can supervene over both Chinese and European social realities. From Silberstein's description, we get a sense of the conceptual conditions of this new concept of fashion and how they connect to early modernity. Agreeing with the cultural historian of Chinese fashion BuYun Chen, she writes, 'As innovations in the textile industry stimulated new forms of consumption, women in and outside the court used luxury silks to "fabricate" self.'[4] Although the whole-tree design discussed here differed from the module structured design and patterned trimmings on the everyday dresses discussed in Silberstein's book, the fact that both of these means to construct the self emerged in new spatial conditions is still crucial. I will discuss those spatial conditions in the context of theatricality; namely, how spectacles on a theatrical costume and a picturized design impacted on garments used by people offstage for a celebrative and commemorative purpose, if not exclusively, at least as one of the major reasons behind such productions. Hence fashion was linked to new forms of consumption that were part of the fabrication or construction of the self.

Pictorial technique and theatrical costumes

When a garment carries a whole-tree design, its contour line is perceived as a frame that encloses the image, with the moveable 'picture' doubled.

The crux of the issue of pictorial images on clothing is the conceptual shift it gives rise to, from the body enclosed in clothing to a body that has dual statuses, at once enclosed *and* supporting a painting-like image.[5] This radical change is implied by the surviving dress objects and custom-made fabrics, yet not explicitly explained in textual sources. The exact moment when the whole-tree design was invented for garments is unclear, but it is connected to the development of theatrical costumes on which the subject first appeared late in the Ming period (1368–1644). Two elements may help us trace the pictorialization of this new textile motif. First is the connection between pictorial technique and theatrical costume, namely 'painting' as a method that was used to design performance costumes. Second, the pictorial image on theatrical costume functioned as a form of spectacle that not only provided allegorical information on a character but also added festivity to performance by the omnipresence of its auspicious signs. In other words, the body became the very agent that presented the vital message carried by the whole-tree design.

In the official history of the Ming dynasty, *hua* (to paint) is codified as a technique that distinguishes the principal pattern on a performance costume from a pattern on other garments such as court robes and regular official robes. For instance, during the fifth year of the Hongwu reign (1372), the court promulgated a dress code for performances conducted by ceremonial apprentices, male musicians, and dancers for both civil and military dances. A sunflower with entangled floral branches in a square shape is painted on both the front and back of a red silk robe with wide or narrow sleeves.[6] The positioning of the central pattern echoes a long-established Chinese tradition of having a square-shaped insignia sewn onto the chest area of a surcoat as a way to indicate the wearer's civil service status.[7] The difference is that the pattern is directly depicted on the performance outfits and no clear decorative borders are arranged along the central image. The painted pattern is clearly distinguished from embroidered and woven patterns. Embroidered and woven insignias, which are produced by expensive material, time, and labor, are graded with higher social status. BuYun Chen argues that 'the [Ming] court's sumptuary order constituted one among multiple systems of value that invested meaning in dress. The Ming dress code, as envisioned by the emperor and his bureaucrats and codified in texts, expressed a pointed interest in maintaining distinctions both within the official bureaucracy and between the official and non-official realms.'[8] The privilege of consuming embroidered and woven patterns was reserved for the imperial and aristocratic classes and ranked officials. Painting was an efficient and economical way to replicate identical designs for group performances at the court.[9] As a result, the notion of 'painted patterns' is associated with theatricality throughout the Ming period.

That distinction is further complicated from the perspective of gender. In the early Ming period, female musicians' outfits were regulated to allow *yunjian*, or a collar with painted cloud patterns. Not until 1530, when the court conducted rituals to venerate the Goddess of the Silkworm in the Jiajing period (1521–1567), was the sunflower pattern assimilated to the female musicians' performing uniform of wide-sleeved robes made of black gauze. The pattern, golden in color, was stamped onto the garment.[10]

When the Manchu conquered Ming China in 1644, the new regime established a different design for state ritual dance and musical costumes. The large central pattern was no longer stressed; instead, a small floral pattern in gold was stamped repetitively onto the red robes, the material being similar to that used during the Ming period.[11] Painted patterns, the established convention for performance garments, combined with embroidery and woven materials, continued to be used to decorate borders on opera costumes during the Qing period (1644–1911). That is to say, painted patterns, sometimes even used to describe pleats, became part of an accepted collection of treatments.[12] As the use of pictorial techniques on theatrical garments fell away, fabrics with woven pattern and embroidered silks became the dominant materials for operatic costume. Although the painting technique was marginalized in Qing theatrical costume production, the compositional structure of a painting was manifested in woven silk and embroidered images on costumes. The appearance of pictorial images on costumes, including the whole tree, coincides with its use in pictorial tapestry, curtains, and other objects.

The whole-tree design as a pictorial image on garments

As part of creating an air of festivity and spectacle, indexing imperial prosperity with the omnipresence of auspicious signs, theatrical costume underwent major transformations during the eighteenth century and was further distinguished from everyday garments with respect to style and materials.[13] We can see this in the comments of the well-known playwright Li Yu (1611–1680), who detested the trend in extravagant theatrical costume and dance outfits.[14] But by the Qianlong reign (1735–1796), when another playwright and poet, Li Dou (1749–1817) published his *Record of Painted Boats of Yangzhou* (*Yangzhou huafang lu*, 1795) to celebrate material life in Yangzhou, one of the most prosperous cities in the lower Yangze River delta, a wide range of theatrical costumes are described. Among them is a type called 'a bright red Daoist robe with golden branches of a tree of plum flowers.'[15] A Daoist robe, also referred to as *Xuezi*, is a long robe with side openings that can be worn by characters from a wide range of social strata and by both men and women.[16] The theory and the pictorial techniques on drawing the plum flower compiled in the *Plum Painting Manual* (*Meipu*) in the second edition, *The Mustard Seed Garden Manual of*

Painting (Jieziyuan huapu) in 1701 demonstrate that a plum tree does not simply stand for a man nor for a woman. The different parts of a plum tree are associated with the characteristic of *yang* or *yin* or both, such as buds or two roots and trunks pairing husband and wife.[17] In the situation of one tree, a trunk as wood stands for the *yin* force that connects to the earth. Plum blossoms, in contrast, possess *yang* and reach to heaven. When depicting the form of a trunk, the visual references could be a dragon or a whirling phoenix.[18] The flexibility of masculinity and femininity in the discourse of plum tree and the visual reference for creating a plum tree coincide with the fact that a plum tree was shared by both male and female theatrical robes during the Qianlong period.

The earliest visual evidence of a robe with a plum tree can be observed in a painting entitled *Prince Hongli Practicing Calligraphy on a Banana Leaf*, which was created by an anonymous court artist in 1730. Within a full-moon-shaped frame, Prince Hongli, the future Qianlong Emperor (1711–1799), is portrayed as a young Han Chinese scholar holding a brush in his right hand, his other hand pressing on a large banana leaf.[19] The iconography of 'writing on a banana leaf' carries a Buddhist connotation of emptiness. It suggests the contradiction between the extreme desire to possess the interior of the body and the negation of that desire – by realizing that the interior and exterior are both empty.

Prince Hongli's intricately figured robe indicates that he might be masquerading as a fictional character in the male role type of a young Confucian scholar. On his brown robe, a flourishing plum flower tree seems to start from his back, its asymmetrical branches crossing both of his shoulders to the front. Two pairs of phoenixes face inward in the midst of the blossoms and are arranged on his sleeves. The combination of plum flowers and phoenixes is unusual and deciphering its precise meaning will require further investigation. More importantly, the details of a tree growing from the ground are not specified on Prince Hongli's garment. The blossoms spread to the bottom of his robe and green shoots are clearly portrayed as the ending of the pattern. The naturalistic representation of the garment suggests that the depiction might have been based on actual patterns on a robe. A rosy theatrical jacket made in the Qianlong period from the Beijing Palace Museum collection supports such speculation.[20] This damask jacket, embroidered with a curling plum tree, just like a curling dragon, was designed for a young female character who was likely from a wealthy family.[21] On the right chest part of the jacket, three root strands are stitched and embraced by a twig of bamboos. The bare root often suggests that the root is removed from its natural surroundings; however, such treatment may hinge on the idea that the plant is a whole tree. In the *Plum Painting Manual*, the roots are specified as the beginning of a vital plum tree.[22] Since the historical context of this theatrical garment has been lost, it is difficult to speculate about the exact symbolic meaning of the plant that might have been associated with the original character. But there are at least two types of whole-tree designs in the Qianlong period: unrooted from the ground and rooted in the ground. The former completely disappeared from the nineteenth century onwards.

After Qianlong ascended the throne, such flamboyant styles of theatrical robes were often incorporated into a sign system of festivity represented on paintings at the Qing court. For instance, at Qianlong's request, the court painter Ding Guanpeng (active 1737–1768) created a handscroll entitled *Picture of a Peaceful Spring Market* (*Pingan chunshi tu*) in the seventh year of his reign (1742). This painting represents a wide range of street performances during the Lunar New Year Festival. A male performer with his back facing viewers, wears a tangerine-color robe decorated with tree branches and white plum blossoms that echo the female theatrical jacket.[23] Plum flowers bloom in winter. When they bloom, it means that the spring will arrive. The pictorialized design of whole-tree blossoms and the bold color stage the signs of upcoming spring and enhance the festivity.

A long indigo *pi* jacket for the role type of an old lady held in the Beijing Palace Museum collection provides a clearer example of the second design model (Figure 1.1). Both the front and back of the garment are embroidered with a design of pine tree and cranes. The branches from both sides are jointed at the shoulders to create the illusion that they extend back and forward on the garment. Stitched in gold metallic threads, a gnarled trunk is positioned on the right-front. Its branches reach onto the right sleeve and circle back from the neck, extending to the left sleeve. The density of needle-clusters is gradually reduced from right to left. Two novel factors can be observed: first, this asymmetrical composition breaks with a long-established principle that patterns have a central focus and are arranged symmetrically on a garment.[24] Second, its single

1.1 Line drawing of a theatrical costume for an old lady role type, indigo-color silk stitched with gold metallic threads and peacock feathers, 117 × 223 cm, Qianlong period (1736–1795), L: 122 cm, W: 219.5 cm. Beijing Palace Museum collection. Line drawing by Chi-Lynn Lin.

tree is planted in the ground. There is no decorative border on the bottom of the robe, which is instead defined by a foreground of shallow mounds. The sameness of front and back is part of the structuring principle of Chinese garments. Nonetheless, as a theatrical costume, the asymmetrical composition suggests movement on the part of the wearer and allows the audience to consistently see the same pattern as the character moves onstage.

This raises some simple questions: What does it mean to use the shape of a garment as a frame? And, how are we to understand the phenomenon of using the body to support a picture? What are the differences between a vase decorated with a representation of a whole-tree design and a robe stitched with the same design? In his study of the relationship between painting and Japanese *kosode* design in early modern Japan, Robert Singer alerts us to the fact that in Edo Japan, the division of artists versus artisans was not explicit. Hence, using the shape of a garment as a frame for painting reflects the fluidity of boundaries around different artistic media and objects in the early modern period.[25] Singer's insights can help us rethink the puzzle of whole-tree designs on garments and other objects from the perspective of practices across media.[26] Still, the human body, even as a vehicle of display, cannot be so easily reduced to an object. Human bodies, like other objects, exist taking up space in the world. However, unlike other objects, human bodies reflect our wills and subjectivities immediately. A whole tree design on a garment becomes efficacious only through the mediation of the body, only by being worn and becoming an expression of subjectivity.

During the nineteenth and the beginning of the twentieth century, particularly during the Guangxu reign (1875–1908) when Empress Dowager Cixi (1835–1908) was the *de facto* ruler of Qing China, the whole-tree design was not only produced for theatrical costumes, but was also incorporated on Manchu men and women's jackets and women's informal long gowns and vests. We see a tendency that the garments worn on stage and off stage share similar aesthetics. In the surviving imperial textile collections at the Beijing Palace Museum, there are nearly three hundred bolts of fabric and garments labeled *zhengzhi*, or whole branch, another term for the whole-tree pattern in the Museum's inventory system.[27] During the Tongzhi reign (1862–1875) when Emperor Dowager Cixi co-reigned with her young son, such design for an everyday robe was considered a new pattern. A tag attached to a bolt of custom-made fabric helps us to understand how this pattern was named. Two crucial phrases, *yizhi*, or one branch, and *tongshen*, or full-length body, are inserted in between the terms used for color, fabric, and pattern. The text on the tag can be roughly translated as 'one violet blue Nanjing twill damask robe with a new pattern of three abundances [consisting of] one branch of peach and [one branch of] pomegranate [that run through the] whole body.'[28] The term 'one branch' emphasizes oneness rather than completeness. In other words, one branch that crosses the full-length body is the design focus. On the fabric, three complete trees of peach, pomegranate, and citron symbolize three abundances, namely longevity, offspring, and happiness.

The types of vegetation expand from plum and pine trees to bamboo, peach, pomegranate, citron, peony shrub, magnolia, begonia, wisteria vines, orchid clusters, lotus, palm, pine, and grape. Some of them are grouped together or pair with an animal to formulate an auspicious symbol. From the limited selection of plum and pine trees on theatrical costume in the eighteenth century to a wide range of plants on everyday garments between the middle of the nineteenth and early twentieth centuries, the whole-tree design underwent a drastic change with respect to its meaning and its function to decorate garments. The initial association of the plum tree with a particular character and emotion or its symbolic meaning correlating to the universe was changed to assorted plants that can generate various good meanings. There is a long-established tradition to using auspicious symbols to decorate a garment in China. As Wu Hung explains the logic behind image making of auspicious omens from the Western Han period (202 BC–8 AD), 'the people of that time believed that the portrayal of *xiangrui* (auspicious omen) images on clothes and objects of daily use would invoke the appearance of real *xiangrui*.'[29] This practice is called 'invoking omens' (*farui*).[30] By the time of the Qing dynasty, invoking omens deeply rooted in image making of auspicious signs crossed various mediums. Sometimes, the very expensive material itself would serve such purpose. For instance, on the aforementioned theatrical robe (Figure 1.1), the peacock feathers and gold metallic threads were used to create images of rocks, pine trees, and cranes to generate the efficacy of longevity. Furthermore, compared with repetitive patterns of one branch of a flower on fabric, a picture like a whole-tree graph bears a closer resemblance to its subject. As Jessica Rawson reminds us, the mimetic likeness of an image 'gave the image the powers of the thing or person depicted.'[31] Hence, a pictorialized whole-tree design can be more effective with respect to invoking the good meaning embedded in the auspicious flowers.

When a whole-tree design was represented on a theatrical costume, the contour lines of the gown served as a frame for the picture, and the 'picture' was completely preserved. Particular pictures were associated with particular characters in a narrative on stage. The subjectivity of the wearer was subordinate to the character. However, when a whole-tree design was transferred to an everyday garment, it had to fit into a structured secular garment that conformed to certain social protocols. In nineteenth-century Manchu women's informal dress, borders and trim were crucial components of garments. On the issue of morality and proper dress in nineteenth-century China, Silberstein emphasizes how the obsession with elaborate borders on the sleeve bands and openings of both Han and Manchu women's garments in late Qing China expressed a new aesthetic that decentralized the ground fabric of a garment. The consumption of fripperies such as luxurious fabrics was critically attacked by orthodox scholars, who considered them *fuyao* (outrageous dress), an old category in a long-lived discourse that referred to any peculiar trend beyond the regular dress code as improperly flaunting marginal decorations and flourishes.[32] The garment with a whole-tree pattern made with twill damask fits Silberstein's observation perfectly, since the subtle image created through twill-weaving techniques is not as eye catching as the vibrant borders. The use of a whole-tree design created with other materials such as embroidered silk, *kesi* woven silk, and cut velvet, then, demonstrates a counter-practice that reclaimed the background material.

In both situations, the whole-tree image had to be suitably enclosed within a decorative trim and cuff bands, as well as along the neck band and on the front overflap closing to the right side. The picture on the robe is fragmented into several sections. The underflap of this gown (Figure 1.2, right), which I will discuss in more detail in the following section, carrying partially duplicated images from the overflap, shows that during construction, by stitching the fragmented picture back into a complete one, some part of the whole-tree design is multiplied. In addition, the gown could be used as the underlayer of a set of garments. Although we cannot know the original context as to when this garment would have been worn, in theory an exterior gown with a similar design could be worn over this one.

More importantly, a whole-tree design on a theatrical garment and on an everyday secular garment suggests two different spaces when a garment would be used. In theatrical use, the totality of the design was connected to a plot, a character, and an actor. The actor is blended into the character

1.2 Blue silk tapestry informal robe for a woman, 1890–1900, blue silk and metal-wrapped thread tapestry weave edged with brown silk and metal-wrapped thread tapestry weave, overall: 141 cm × 130.8 cm. Mactaggart Art Collection (2005.5.18), University of Alberta Museums. Gift of Sandy and Cécile Mactaggart

and has agency within the scripted plot. The garment and the totality of the image reflect this specific type of agency. During the early twentieth century, the whole-tree design on theatrical costume became more ostentatious with the addition of birds and animals to energize the characters.[33] However, when the image is employed on an everyday robe, it undergoes multiple mediations and instead of being one structure, it becomes a conjuncture of structures. The image ceases to be a totality because it is interrupted by the borders and other structural conditions of clothing. One could wear multiple layers of garments with a whole-tree design, which would create the effect of multiple partial totalities. The material conditions of secular clothing thus fracture the totality of the theatrical image. That fractured totality and the conjuncture of structures open a space for secular agency. This situation enables one to instrumentalize the theatrical image, which can function as metonym or synecdoche, where a part symbolizes the whole. But one can become conscious of that whole and its symbolic meaning in different ways. The plot is no longer a given but gets created in dialogue with concrete political contexts.

Wearing a tree and embodying longevity

Each of the woody and floral trees is loaded symbolically and may indicate a specific meaning when paired with different plants, birds and flowers, and even Chinese characters. For instance, the established composition of bamboo (*zhu*) and the Taihu rock or rock of longevity (*shoushi*) involve a pun on the phrase 'celebrating longevity' (*zhushou*). Bamboo trunks were one of the most popular designs on Manchu women's garments. From the surviving dress objects and bolts of custom-made textiles produced for the Qing court, we see that this unique pattern was manufactured in a wide range of silk and cotton materials that were used for exterior and interior gowns. The interior gown (*chenyi*) could be worn under the exterior gown (*changyi*) and vest or as an independent garment. A blue *kesi* woven silk *chenyi* gown (Figure 1.2, left: front; middle: back) from the University of Alberta Museums collection reveals a style from the last decade of the nineteenth century. On an indigo blue silk background, a thick bamboo trunk, woven in metal-wrapped threads, is arranged across the body from the garment's bottom left corner to the right armpit. Several smaller bamboo stalks are positioned in front of and behind the main trunk, which suggests depth of space. Following the whole-tree convention, the foreground is represented as a gently sloping open field decorated with clusters of flowers and grasses.[34]

The whole-tree design is surely part of a long tradition that draws analogical meaning between plants and human beings in the Chinese cultural context. The most cliché combinations are the scholarly *si junzi* (four gentlemen), which include the orchid, plum, bamboo, and chrysanthemum, and the *suihan sanyou* (three friends in the winter), comprising pine, bamboo, and plum. Depicted together, these plants signal the four characteristics of the Confucian nobleman: honesty, uprightness, frugality, and purity.[35] However, those meanings could shift when the plant images were used individually or in a different context, and the correspondence between a natural sign and a human being could vary.[36] The conventional male gendering of these plants could also be altered. For instance, pine and bamboo have been standard symbols for longevity and can be associated with both genders.

In a late sixteenth-century *chuanqi* opera entitled *Yuhuan ji*, or *Story of the Jade Bracelet*, an episode celebrating the birthday of a regional military governor, Zhang, he reveals how his wife, daughter, and a female servant together presented him embroideries made by their own hands. These embroideries include a pine tree, bamboo, plum flowers, and a pair of cranes and a turtle. The connotation of the images is explicitly explained in each gift giver's own voice: The pine tree (embroidered by his wife) stands for longevity like that of pine and cypress trees; several bamboos (stitched by his daughter) signify incorruptibility and uprightness; the branch of plum flowers (made by the female servant) wishes general fulfillment in managing state affairs. A pair of thousand-year-old cranes and a ten-thousand-year-old turtle (unclear who the maker is) symbolizes the general's life lasting for a thousand years.[37] Although only the pine tree, crane, and turtle are directly related to the idea of long life, the juxtaposition of symbols for uprightness and service to the state along with longevity suggest that birthday celebrations in premodern China were not solely about someone's age, but part of a larger visual program asserting goodness and decency.

This raises the question of the relation between goodness or righteousness and longevity. Normally, longevity is associated with a number. People live for a certain number of years. However, the quantity also has a qualitative dimension. People who are ethical live long lives, so moral quality is associated with longevity. The pine tree, bamboo, and plum flower express human qualities. They are the externalization of human values, which are also connected to a long life. Birthday celebrations brought uprightness and longevity together in specific objects, often themselves representations of things in nature.

On a photograph likely taken between 1870 and 1890, two young merchants sit in a professional studio in Shanghai (Figure 1.3).[38] The man on the left has a waist-length jacket that displays a plum tree design. This type of garment is often called a *magua* (riding jacket) and was an informal style developed from a type of military garment used in the early Qing dynasty.[39] By the late nineteenth and early twentieth centuries, it was commonly worn by the gentry. Unlike the Manchu women's dress with layered trimmings, the man's jackets are not decorated with

36   Fashioning identity

1.3 Young merchants, Shanghai, 1870–1890s. Ferry Bertholet Lambert van der Aalsvoort collection. After Ferry Bertholet and Lambert van der Aalsvoort, eds, *Among the Celestials: China in Early Photographs*. New Haven: Yale University Press, 2014. Mercatorfonds, p. 79

borders. The character *shou* (longevity) appears on the long gown worn under his jacket. The right sitter's short-waisted jacket, likely made of cut velvet, reveals a much clearer pattern combining a bat and the character *shou*, which signal the expression *fushou* (happiness and longevity). Since both young men wear clothing bearing symbols of longevity, it is reasonable to suppose that this photograph was taken as part of a birthday celebration.

A surviving man's waist-length jacket, now in the Minneapolis Institute of Art (Figure 1.4), was another garment used for birthday celebrations. This jacket is sewn with the front overflap closing to the right, fastened with five knot-and-loop toggle buttons. Unlike earlier examples, the front and back of this jacket have slightly different designs, though the overall structure of the massive pine trees is identical, with a standing crane on the front amid auspicious *lingzhi* mushrooms, and a spotted deer on the back. The combination of crane, deer, and pine tree also carries the meaning of longevity. The massive pine branches cross the shoulders and neck to the front. This design suggests the wearer's body, more precisely a male body beneath the attire, that coincides with the thick tree trunk. Although a pine tree design can appear on a female character's outfit on stage, women often chose other plants such as bamboo, plum flowers, peach trees, and peony shrubs.

At the Qing court, the whole-tree model became a field for experiments in new design. Under Cixi's rule, through an established convention

1.4 Line drawing of a Chinese man's informal riding jacket (*magua*), cut and uncut silk velvet, early twentieth century, H: 61 cm, W: 158.5 cm. Minneapolis Institute of Art collection. Line drawing by Chi-Lynn Lin.

of a homophonous relationship, new flowers and birds for prosperity, continuity, and life cycle, such as peach and bat, peony, magnolia, and plum, were added to the group of images for celebration of longevity. A bolt of light purplish-grey velvet material carries a combination of peony and plum flower trees, even more directly coveying the meaning of longevity through creating two big characters of *shou* or longevity, similar to Cixi's handwriting, on the blank background.[40] Some of these designs were produced only for birthday celebrations while some were not associated with a particular event but invoked omens of longevity in everyday life.

These garments and custom-made fabrics reveal the complexity of a whole-tree design. The externalization of human values in the natural world is then re-internalized when the wearer in effect embodies the tree. The externalized value is not simply represented by the symbolic object but is situated directly on the body. From this perspective, the value does not simply function as an outer layer but becomes almost identical with one's body. In her discussion of the practice of foot binding, Dorothy Ko insightfully reminds us how in imperial China, the body itself was attire.[41] When one wears a garment with a whole pine tree, one's body becomes such a tree. And yet, there is a kind of space between the person and the garment s/he wears. The tree is embroidered or woven onto a textile, which suggests material complexity or hybridity. The material object creates a situation in which one is both identical to the tree and not identical to it. This allows for a sense of becoming eternal in this life.

Staging the plant on the garment

During the thirtieth day of the lunar year in February 1904, six designs for Manchu vests by an unknown court painter from the Qing imperial painting academy (*Ruyi guan*, or Hall of Fulfillment of Wishes) were submitted to the Imperial Household Department (*Neiwufu*).[42] The attached yellow tags show that this set of designs was made for celebrations of the seventieth birthday of Empress Dowager Cixi. All six designs carry the subject of bamboo: three of them depicting grouped bamboo with rock and the other three only branches of bamboo leaves. Eight months later, a few days before her seventieth birthday, which was on 10 October in the lunar calendar, Empress Dowager Cixi had two groups of photographs taken at the Summer Palace: the first group is relatively formal, showing Cixi and a crowd of imperial women lined up before the Gate of Dispelling Clouds (*Paiyunmen*).[43] This architectural compound had been renovated and was used by Cixi as her birthday celebration venue from the late nineteenth century.[44] The second set of photographs was taken in a snowy garden. Cixi either poses by herself or with her eunuchs, the Fourth Princess (1881–?), and her ladies in waiting, Der Ling (1885–1944) and Rongling (1882–1973) and their mother. This session is briefly described in Der Ling's memoir *Two Years in the Forbidden City*. According to Der Ling, Cixi was inspired by the heavy snow and wanted to be photographed on the hillside in the Summer Palace. She ordered Der Ling's brother, Yu Xunling (1874–1943), an amateur photographer who had learned the technique in France, to take the photograph.[45] In both sets of photographs, Cixi wears a vest with bamboo and rocks that echoes some of the designs painted by the court artist. In most of these photos, Cixi holds open her outer cape and tries to display the vest (Figure 1.5).

Two surviving vests from the Beijing Palace Museum and Metropolitan Museum collection are very similar to the one worn by Cixi in the photos.[46] Compared to the court artists' design and final product, it seems that Cixi favored a style that carries less depth and even less color than the painted design and the fabric vest. I will use this vest and the related photographs to discuss how Cixi could have been involved in designing the vest and how she pointedly 'displays' her longevity in front of the camera's eye.

The Beijing Palace Museum vest with wide armholes and a stand-up collar is a typical Manchu waistcoat. Instead of a center or side opening, it has a totally removable front, and a back section that folds over at shoulder level to fasten horizontally with round jade buttons across the

1.5 Yu Xunling (1874–1943), *Empress Dowager Cixi (1835–1908) in Snow Accompanied by Attendants*, 1904. Glass plate negative, 12.7 × 10.2 cm, Freer Gallery of Art and Arthur M. Sackler Gallery Archives, Purchase, 1966, Xunling, FSA_A.13_SC-GR-284

top chest. Three more buttons down each side secure the lower part. The front piece is a *kesi* woven image representing a Taihu rock erected on a hilly ground painted in light green. The rock is woven in gold-wrapped threads. Two small bamboos with spread leaves are arranged symmetrically behind the rock. The bamboo is woven with different tones of purple or perhaps originally blue colors to indicate layers of bamboo leaves. Small pinkish lotus flowers are scattered evenly on the ground. Each flower is surrounded by elongated leaves. The back of the vest is a similar *kesi* woven tapestry.

These vests might have been produced by Cixi's personal textile manufactory in the Pavilion of Elegant Flowers (*Qihuaguan*) in the West Imperial Garden (*Xiyuan*) next to the Forbidden City, which was built on 4 September 1890. Indeed, one bolt of blue gauze fabric woven with complete bamboo trunks bears the manufactory marker of Pavilion of Elegant Flowers.[47] A textual source for Cixi's order to correct these particular designs has not been discovered, but Cixi had a habit of making corrections directly on design drafts.[48] And without Cixi's final consent, no design would be sent to the imperial workshop.

Comparing Cixi's vest with the six drawings by the court painter, the most distinctive difference is that she enhanced the visual effect of the whole-tree convention. All the bamboos are rearranged behind the rock and the color palette has been reduced to two or three colors. The naturalistic style and three-dimensionality of the rock and bamboo on the court painters' design draft are reduced to flat figures with a more decorative quality. The rock and bamboo become more prominent in this rendering to more directly express the message of celebrating longevity. Such treatment was gradually developed during the Guangxu period and became a prototype of whole-tree design on woven silk under Cixi's rule. By returning to a pictorial convention of bamboo and rock on a garment likely established by her, she reconfirmed her own way of invoking efficacious signs. More importantly, the central position of rock and bamboo echoes the design on a theatrical garment worn by the character of Boddhisattva Guanyin. On Guanyin's costume, the bamboo and rock represent Guanyin's dwelling within the bamboo forest, and an auspicious symbol of long life simultaneously. As an important character in operas performed during imperial birthday celebrations, Guanyin becomes a messenger celebrating longevity. Cixi used the incarnating power of portraiture to harness the spiritual authority of the goddess Guanyin by making her costumed portrayal of the goddess coincident with her own person.[49] Hence the centrality of the rock and bamboo on her birthday vest is further enhanced through such mimetic practice.

In the photographs taken on the snowy hillside, Cixi seems to incorporate the bamboo on her vest into the natural surroundings, bringing to mind pine trees and plum blossoms, both also associated with winter.

These symbols together lead viewers to think of the visual convention, 'Three Friends of Winter,' originally associated with literati culture, but which became a popular motif in the late imperial period. In one shot Cixi stands alone next to a rock and under a pine tree with a straight trunk, she extends one hand to grip the rock beside her, and her right hand holds a pine branch, a sign that could be interpreted as both uprightness and longevity. Her eyes and the front view of her vest presented to the camera show great confidence.

Two other group pictures reveal Cixi's idea of exhibiting her vest in an authoritative manner. In both photographs, she is surrounded by her eunuchs. Her central position with arms extended reveals her absolute superiority. She completely opens her cape and rests her arms on the two eunuchs' hands. While other people are looking at the camera, she sets her gaze to either front left or right as a way to distinguish herself from the rest of her entourage. Xunling uses a lower-angle shot to enhance Cixi's power. The central image on her birthday vest is fully displayed, and, instead of her eyes, the bamboo and rock standing for her longevity face us directly and send the clear message of her immortality, which is embedded in the auspicious snow.

In the modern period, time is often described as empty and homogeneous, and this vision of time affects the commemoration of birth. Late Qing China is an interesting case because, on the one hand, there were enormous changes taking place in the realm of calculating time, but simultaneously the Qing court continued to organize events and rituals according to dynastic time and traditional cosmological principles. Through a birthday vest that was profoundly influenced by the whole-tree design mode, and her exhibiting this garment in front of the camera lens, Cixi managed to blur the conventional gendered visual field. More importantly, she turned time into space where her self-inscription in a symbolic and ritual world secured her legitimacy as *de facto* ruler. From this perspective, we could say that Cixi's birthday celebration is really about the ideology of the ruling class. However, by the early twentieth century, the dynastic time Cixi invoked could no longer be thought of as hegemonic. In that context, Cixi, as a female ruler of a dynasty in decline, could be read as embodying another phenomenology of time and eternity. Her effort to commemorate her birthday through symbolism implies a time that is neither linear nor empty; it represents the possibilities of enchantment in an increasingly disenchanted world.

Conclusion

In this chapter, we have seen how the whole-tree image underwent numerous transformations from its early modern expression to the eve of the modern period, with Empress Dowager Cixi. In all these cases, fashion was mediated with politics, but this mediation became more intense in Cixi's case. In the earlier period, transposition of the motif from theatrical to secular settings created a fractured totality that left room for secular agency and the instrumentalization of the images. In Cixi's case, this agency reaches its apex in the intersection of dynastic and national space-time. This ideological formation anticipates what we see in later years.

Notes

1. 'One bolt of damask with one tree plum flowers from Nanjing' is listed as one of the gifts presented to the grandmother of a county-level official responsible for arrests and prisons during the Ming period. Xizhousheng [pseudo], *Xingshi yinyuan zhuan*, volume 1 (Hong Kong: Zhonghua shuju, 1959), p. 145.
2. Richard M. Barnhart, *Peach Blossom Spring: Gardens and Flowers in Chinese Painting* (New York: Metropolitan Museum of Art, 1983), pp. 25–56.
3. Rachel Silberstein, *A Fashionable Century: Textile Artistry and Commerce in the Late Qing* (Seattle: University of Washington Press, 2020), p. 4.
4. Ibid., p. 5.
5. Ming Wilson with the Palace Museum, Beijing, eds, *Imperial Chinese Robes from the Forbidden City* (London: V & A Publishing, Victoria and Albert Museum, 2010), p. 81.
6. Zhang Tingyu, comp., *Mingshi* (Beijing: Zhonghua shuju, 1974), vol. 6, juan 67, p. 1653.
7. Chung Young Yang, *Silken Threads: Embroidered Court Costume, and Rank Insignia of China, Japan Korea, and Vietnam* (New York: Harry N. Abrams, 2005).
8. BuYun Chen, 'Wearing the Hat of Loyalty: Imperial Power and Dress Reform in Ming Dynasty China,' in Giorgio Riello and Ulinka Rublack, eds, *The Right to Dress: Sumptuary Laws in a Global Perspective, c.1200–1800* (Cambridge and New York Cambridge University Press, 2020), pp. 418–419.
9. According to *Mingshilu* (Veritable Records of the Ming dynasty), at a martial arts dance performed before an imperial banquet, there were some thirty-two dancers wearing identical outfits. Zhongguo zhexueshu dianzi jihua, *Mingshilu, Taizu shi lu*, juan 55, 82.
10. Zhang, comp., *Mingshi*, p. 1653.
11. *Daqing Huidian* (Collected Statutes of the Great Qing), juan 33, in *Siku quanshu* electronic database (University of Wisconsin-Madison library).
12. For examples, please see the 'theatrical robe with flowers and butterflies' in Daisy Yiyou Wang and Jan Stuart, eds, *Empresses of China's Forbidden City, 1644–1912* (Salem and Washington, D. C.: Peabody Essex Museum and Freer Sackler, Smithsonian Institution, 2018), p. 160.
13. Zhang Rui, 'Beijing gugong bowuyuan cang qinggong xiyi yanjiu,' *Zhongguo xiqu xueyuan xuebao*, issue 38.4 (November 2017): 129–133, at 129.
14. To Li, the only acceptable dance outfit was embroidered with phoenix and birds at the top and rosy clouds on the lower part of the garment, which he considered an established archaic form. Li Yu, *Xianqing ouji*, annotated by Juang Jurong and Lu Shourong (Shanghai: Shanghai guji chubanshe, 2000), p. 125.
15. See the term in Chinese, '*Dahong jingeng yishumei daopao*,' in Li Dou, *Yangzhou huafang lu*, annotated by Zhou Chundong (Jinan: Shandong youyi chubanshe, 2002), p. 158.
16. Liu Yuemei, *Zhongguo jingju yixiang* (Shanghai: Shanghai cishu chubanshe, 2002), pp. 114–122.
17. Mai Mai Tze, trans., *The Mustard Seed Garden Manual of Painting: A Facsimile of the 1887–1888 Shanghai Edition* (Princeton: Princeton University Press, 2015), p. 404.

18 Ibid., p. 402.
19 Gerald Holzwarth, entry of cat. 187, in Evelyn S. Rawski and Jessica Rawson, eds, *China: The Three Emperors, 1662–1795* (London: Royal Academy of Arts, 2005), p. 435.
20 From Beijing Palace Museum collection, gu 00215711. I examined this garment at the Beijing Palace Museum in the autumn of 2022.
21 I thank Zhang Rui for pointing out the similarity of a dragon on a dragon robe and the plum tree on this garment.
22 Tze, trans., *The Mustard Seed Garden Manual of Painting*, p. 404.
23 This handscroll is in the National Palace Museum, Taipei collection. The size of the painting is 30.3 × 233.5 cm.
24 I thank Dorothy Ko for alerting me to the fact that this is the central issue of changes in design.
25 Robert T. Singer, 'A Wearable Art: The Relationship of Painting to Kosode Design,' in Dale Carolyn Gluckman and Sharon Sadako Takeda, eds, *When Art Became Fashion: Kosode in Edo-Period Japan* (Los Angeles: Los Angeles County Museum of Art, 1992), pp. 181–209.
26 Since the pictorialization on Japanese *kosode* emerged earlier than the Chinese whole-tree design, scholars have suggested there might be the influence of Japanese design at the Qing court. However, further research needs to be conducted. Mary M. Flowers Dusenbury, *Dragons and Pine Trees: Asian Textiles in the Spencer Museum of Art* (New York and Manchester: Hudson Hills Press, 2004), p. 156. For discussion of how the Japanese company Takashimaya deliberately created a hybrid mandarin robe with pictorialized bamboo designs in the early twentieth century, see Mei Mei Rado, 'The Hybrid Orient: Japonisme and Nationalism of the Takashimaya Mandarin Robes,' *Fashion Theory*, 19, no. 5 (2015): 583–616.
27 In the Beijing Palace Museum inventory system, *zhengzhi* refers to both the whole-tree design and a module design of a branch of a flower. Since not every object has been photographed, it is difficult to determine the exact number of garments and amount of unused fabric with the whole-tree design at the present stage. For examples of the repetitive pattern of a branch of a flower, see a blue theatrical costume with a design of peach and crane patterns, Beijing Palace Museum collection gu00218511. For a brief discussion of this robe used in different periods, see Zhang, 'Beijing gugong bowuyuan cang xiyi yanjiu,' p. 129.
28 See the object with catalog number gu 00013147 in the Beijing Palace Museum database.
29 Wu Hung, 'A Sanpan Shan Chariot Ornament and the Xiangrui Design in Western Han Art,' *Archives of Asian Art*, vol. 37 (1984): 38–59, at 45.
30 Ibid.
31 Jessica Rawson, 'The Power of Images: The Model Universe of the First Emperor and Its Legacy,' *Historical Research*, 75, no. 188 (May 2002): 123–154, at 126.
32 For a discussion on this issue, please see Silberstein, *A Fashionable Century*, pp. 57–58.
33 For instance, see 'Embroidered Blue Silk Actor's Robe' from the University of Alberta Museums collection. The robe was made around the 1930s. The accession number is 2005.5.403.1. https://search.museums.ualberta.ca/21-20974 (accessed 18 April 2022).
34 The bottom of bamboo trunks is sometimes removed. See another *kesi* woven woman's robe entitled 'Purple Silk Tapestry Weave Robe for a Woman' from the University of Alberta Museums collection. The accession number is 2005.5.322. https://search.museums.ualberta.ca/21-20974 (accessed 18 April 2022).
35 There are different accounts of the development of the subjects of *si junzi*. Some scholars think that during the Yuan dynasty (1279–1368), Wu Zhen (1280–1354) was the first to add the orchid to the combination of plum, bamboo, and chrysanthemum,

and formulate this combination as *siyou* or 'four friends.' During the Wanli period (1573–1619), Huang Fengchi edited the *Plum, Bamboo, Orchid, and Chrysanthemum in Four Manuals* (*Meizhulanju sipu*) (Beijing: Wenwu chubanshe, 1982). Chen Jiru (1558–1639) started referring to this compositional arrangement as *sijun*, the four gentlemen or four noble qualities. See Chen's preface in Huang's book.

36 The painted patterns on performance costumes during the Ming period often draw the equivalence of an animal to a male performer's specialization. For instance, the male singers' wide-sleeved red gauze robes for the grand state ceremony are painted with parrots and yellow orioles, and the male dancers' green robes for the 'dance to pacify the world under heaven' are decorated with dancing cranes. See Zhang, comp., *Mingshi*, p. 1653. The metaphoric meaning of these singing birds could vary from the early Ming to the late Ming period and from the court to outside the court. For a discussion of the late Ming gendered metaphorical meanings of the oriole and crane, please see Peng Xu, 'Courtesan vs. Literatus: Gendered Soundscapes and Aesthetics in Late-Ming Singing Culture,' *T'oung Pao*, 100, fasc.4/5 (2014): 404–459.

37 Yang Ruosheng, *Yuhuan ji*, Act 3, 6a–6b, in Mao Jin, comp., *Liushi zhong qu*, vol. 8, Maoshi jigu ge mingmo keben. *Diaolong zhongri guji quanwen ziliaoku*, digital database at the University of Wisconsin-Madison library.

38 I would like to express my gratitude to Tingting Xu, who shared her expertise on the date of this photograph and her knowledge of the history of early Chinese photography. Ferdinand M. Bertholet, *Among the Celestials: China in Early Photographs* (New Haven: Yale University Press, 2014), p. 79.

39 Antonia Finnane, *Changing Clothes in China: Fashion, History, Nation* (New York: Columbia University Press, 2008), Fig. 1.1 caption.

40 Please see the object with the catalog number gu00023184 in the Beijing Palace Museum collection.

41 Dorothy Ko, 'The Body as Attire: The Shifting Meanings of Footbinding in Seventeenth-Century China,' *Journal of Women's History*, 8, no. 4 (Winter 1997): 8–27.

42 See 'Xiaoqin hou yiyang,' in *Gugong zhoukan*, vol. 4, issues 301–400. No. 1, No. 2, and attached slip, in issue 376: p. 984. No. 3 and 4 in issue 378, p. 992. No. 5 and 6, in issue 379, p. 996.

43 For a general understanding of Cixi's portraiture in photographs, see Ying-chen Peng, 'Lingering between Tradition and Innovation: Photographic Portraits of Empress Dowager Cixi (1835–1908),' *Ars Orientalis*, 43 (2013): 157–175.

44 For a fruitful discussion of Cixi's involvement in the architectural renovation of the Summer Palace, see Ying-chen Peng, 'Reconfiguring Patriarchal Space: Empress Dowager Cixi (1835–1908) and the Reconstruction of the Gardens of Nurtured Harmony,' in L. C. W. Blanchard and K. Chiem, eds, *Gender, Continuity, and the Shaping of Modernity in the Arts of East Asia, 16th–20th Centuries* (Boston: Brill, 2017), pp. 191–223.

45 Princess Der Ling, *Two Years in the Forbidden City* (New York: Moffat, Yard and Company, 1912), p. 378.

46 Wilson, *Imperial Chinese Robes*, p. 81. There is a third vest with same design but woven with an indigo background. University of Alberta Museums collection, accession number 2005.5.6, https://search.museums.ualberta.ca/21-19228 (accessed 15 May 2022).

47 See object with the catalog number gu00021860 in the Beijing Palace Museum collection.

48 See entry 'Xiaoqin hou shan shuhua,' in Xu Ke, *Qingbai leichao*, vol. 8, *yishu lei* (Taibei: Taiwan shang wu yin shu guan, 1966), p. 11.

49 For a more detailed discussion, see Yuhang Li, 'Oneself as a Female Deity: Representations of Cixi Posing as Guanyin,' *Nan Nü: Men, Women, and Gender in China*, 14, no. 1 (2012): 75–118.

Bibliography

Barnhart, Richard M. *Peach Blossom Spring: Gardens and Flowers in Chinese Painting*. New York: Metropolitan Museum of Art, 1983.

Bertholet, Ferdinand M. *Among the Celestials: China in Early Photographs*. New Haven: Yale University Press, 2014.

Chen, BuYun. 'Wearing the Hat of Loyalty: Imperial Power and Dress Reform in Ming Dynasty China.' In *The Right to Dress: Sumptuary Laws in a Global Perspective c.1200–1800*. Edited by Giorgio Riello and Ulinka Rublack. Cambridge and New York: Cambridge University Press, 2020.

Finnane, Antonia. *Changing Clothes in China: Fashion, History, Nation*. New York: Columbia University Press, 2008.

Flowers, Mary M. Dusenbury. *Dragons and Pine Trees: Asian Textiles in the Spencer Museum of Art*. New York and Manchester: Hudson Hills Press, 2004.

Holzwarth, Gerald. Entry of cat. 187. In *China: The Three Emperors, 1662–1795*. Edited by Evelyn S. Rawski and Jessica Rawson. London: Royal Academy of Arts, 2005.

Huang Fengchi. *Plum, Bamboo, Orchid, and Chrysanthemum in Four Manuals (Meizhulanju sipu)*. Beijing: Wenwu chubanshe, 1982.

Ko, Dorothy. 'The Body as Attire: The Shifting Meanings of Footbinding in Seventeenth-Century China.' *Journal of Women's History* 8, no. 4 (Winter 1997): 8–27.

Li Yu. *Xianqing ouji*. Annotated by Juang Jurong and Lu Shourong. Shanghai: Shanghai guji chubanshe, 2000.

Liu Yuemei. *Zhongguo jingju yixiang*. Shanghai: Shanghai cishu chubanshe, 2002.

Li, Yuhang. 'Oneself as a Female Deity: Representations of Cixi Posing as Guanyin.' *Nan Nü: Men, Women, and Gender in China*, 14, no. 1 (2012): 75–118.

Peng Xu. 'Courtesan vs. Literatus: Gendered Soundscapes and Aesthetics in Late-Ming Singing Culture.' *T'oung Pao* 100, fasc.4/5 (2014): 404–459.

Peng, Ying-chen. 'Lingering between Tradition and Innovation: Photographic Portraits of Empress Dowager Cixi (1835–1908).' *Ars Orientalis* 43 (2013): 157–175.

Peng, Ying-chen. 'Reconfiguring Patriarchal Space: Empress Dowager Cixi (1835–1908) and the Reconstruction of the Gardens of Nurtured Harmony.' In *Gender, Continuity, and the Shaping of Modernity in the Arts of East Asia, 16th–20th Centuries*. Edited by L. C. W. Blanchard and K. Chiem. Boston: Brill, 2017.

Princess Der Ling. *Two Years in the Forbidden City*. New York: Moffat, Yard and Company, 1912.

Rado, Mei Mei. 'The Hybrid Orient: Japonisme and Nationalism of the Takashimaya Mandarin Robes.' *Fashion Theory* 19, no. 5 (2015): 583–616.

Rawson, Jessica. 'The Power of Images: The Model Universe of the First Emperor and Its Legacy.' *Historical Research* 75, no. 188 (May 2002): 123–154.

Silberstein, Rachel. *A Fashionable Century: Textile Artistry and Commerce in the Late Qing*. Seattle: University of Washington Press, 2020.

Singer, Robert T. 'A Wearable Art: The Relationship of Painting to Kosode Design.' In *When Art Became Fashion: Kosode in Edo-Period Japan*. Edite by Dale Carolyn Gluckman and Sharon Sadako Takeda. Los Angeles: Los Angeles County Museum of Art, 1992.

Tze, Mai Mai, trans. *The Mustard Seed Garden Manual of Painting: A Facsimile of the 1887–1888 Shanghai Edition*. Princeton: Princeton University Press, 2015.

Wang, Daisy Yiyou and Jan Stuart, eds. *Empresses of China's Forbidden City, 1644–1912*. Salem and Washington, D. C.: Peabody Essex Museum and Freer Sackler, Smithsonian Institution, 2018).

Wilson, Ming with the Palace Museum, Beijing, eds. *Imperial Chinese Robes from the Forbidden City*. London: V & A Publishing, Victoria and Albert Museum, 2010.

Wu Hung. 'A Sanpan Shan Chariot Ornament and the Xiangrui Design in Western Han Art.' *Archives of Asian Art* vol. 37 (1984): 38–59.

Xizhousheng [pseudo]. *Xingshi yinyuan zhuan*. Volume 1. Hong Kong: Zhonghua shuju, 1959.

Xu Ke. *Qingbai leichao*. Volume 8. *Yishu lei*. Taibei: Taiwan shang wu yin shu guan, 1966.

Yang, Chung Young. *Silken Threads: Embroidered Court Costume, and Rank Insignia of China, Japan Korea, and Vietnam*. New York: Harry N. Abrams, 2005.

Zhang Rui. 'Beijing gugong bowuyuan cang qinggong xiyi yanjiu.' *Zhongguo xiqu xueyuan xuebao*, issue 38.4 (November 2017): 129–133.

Zhang Tingyu, comp. *Mingshi*. Beijing: Zhonghua shuju, 1974.

2

Women for cotton and men for wool: consuming gendered textiles in colonized Korea

Kyunghee Pyun

Introduction

East Asians started to recognize a new style of dress in the late nineteenth century. As merchants, missionaries, diplomats, and military officers from Europe or North America arrived in ports such as Jemulpo (now Incheon), Kore ans became interested in *yangbok* and *yangjang*, Western-style men's attire and women's attire. American politician Percival Lawrence Lowell (1855–1916) stayed in Seoul as Counselor to the Korean Embassy in 1883 and left many photos dated to 1884 and now kept at the Museum of Fine Arts, Boston. In these images, most Koreans sport well-pressed, clean *hanbok* in accordance with their social statuses and professions.[1] As dress historian Kyungmee Lee and others have pointed out, progressive thinkers and politicians in the late Joseon dynasty were aware of the need for new clothing for conducting official business with their counterparts from Europe and North America.[2] Kim Ok-gyun (1851–1894), Seo Jae-pil (1864–1951; known as Philip Jaisohn), Park Young-hyo (1861–1939), and Yun Chi-ho (1864–1945), for example, surprised people by abandoning *hanbok* and choosing Western-style suits and short hair after their visit to Japan to explore new world affairs in 1881–1882. Thus, Jemulpo and Seoul saw the increasing emergence of general goods stores selling Western-style clothes and accessories for gentlemen.[3]

The Korean Empire began in 1897 and following the Gabo Reform in 1894–1896 assigned Western-style garments for high-ranking officials for public affairs and modernized military uniforms (Figure 2.1). An official high-ceremonial ensemble called *daeryebok* included a pair of trousers, a waistcoat, and an embroidered jacket carefully designed with rose of Sharon patterns to symbolize the Empire. This ensemble has buttons inscribed 'SUPERFINE PARIS' on the trousers. Made of fine woollen

2.1 Great Court uniform for civil officer of the Korean Empire; composed of a jacket, a waistcoat, and a pair of trousers. Jacket 110 (including sleeves) × 99 (length) × 42 (chest width) cm. National Folk Museum, South Korea. Object no. 65788

textiles, the ensemble represented the dignity and the authority of a civil officer in both domestic and diplomatic official affairs.

The wave of new fashion was irreversible in other sectors including ordinary citizens on the streets. Most male adults had one or two garments or accessories in Western style such as leather shoes, hats, walking canes, or watches, as shown on the sign of a tailor's shop in Busan called *Chulwoonok Yangbokjeom* (Figure 2.2).[4] However, it was still rare to encounter a man fully dressed in Western clothes in 1910: only upper-class citizens and imperial family members, mostly male, had access to them. When Emperor Sunjong and his consort were shown in modernized dress in official photographs around 1910, viewers noted Empress Sunjeonghyo's traditional court attire called *wonsam* embellished with a European-style sash and a medal.[5] The emperor's high-ceremonial ensemble was made of woollen textiles and the *wonsam* of silk. This is the dichotomy of gendered textile consumption in early twentieth-century Korea.

A full set of menswear was still beyond the means of most citizens. After the Korean Empire was annexed to Japan in 1910 and citizens gathered for Emperor Gojong's funeral in January 1919, most male citizens dressed in hybrid fashion: traditional *hanbok* ensembles with short hair, European hats, and leather shoes for those who could afford them. Ordinary women, shown in photos during the March First Movement in 1919, retained *hanbok* as their primary garment. In the 1920s, the Japanese Government-General brought economic and cultural policies to suppress resistance among Korean citizens. And this had ramifications for how people dressed.

Using advertising campaigns in popular magazines from the early twentieth century, this chapter analyzes gendered consumption of textiles in colonized Korea. The dichotomy between cotton woven textiles and woollen woven textiles is also visible in public space and resulted from economic disparity between rural and urban communities.[6] This study

2.2 Store sign of a tailor named *Chulwoonok Yangbokjeom* [출운옥양복점 出雲屋洋服店] in Busan. National Folk Museum, South Korea. Object no. 88949

will conclude that the dichotomy between men's labor and women's labor in textile production was perpetuated even after the Independence of Korea. Men worked as supervisors and managers while women worked as low-skilled laborers on the factory floor. Gendered consumption of luxury versus ordinary textiles is a mirroring image of gendered production systems in textile mills and factories.

Korean women's consumption of cotton and silk in the 1920s

During the late Joseon dynasty, women were aware of new types of cotton textiles. *Okyangmok*, 'jade-color Western cotton,' refers to imported textiles known as calico: plain-woven cotton fabric originally from Calicut (Kozhikode), a coastal city in southern India. In the late nineteenth century, British bleached white cotton textiles were considered as bright and white as 'jade' among Korean consumers.[7] This imported textile was commonly used in lining traditional garments (especially *jeogori* jackets for *hanbok* ensembles) among upper-class people. *Okyangmok* was also used for special purposes, as shown in the Heung-guk-sa temple's colossal 1902 Buddhist painting of Amitabha and six attendants. Measuring 628 cm long and 381 cm wide, the hanging banner was made of *okyangmok* from Manchester. It was commissioned by Emperor Gojong's consort, Eom.

Domestic cotton had grown since the fourteenth century during the Mongol Invasion in the Goryeo dynasty and along with hemp was the most common textile for ordinary people. Mun Ik-jeom (1329–1398) brought cotton seeds in the 1360s and planted them successfully in his hometown in Gyeongsang province. Cotton prefers a mild climate, and southern regions such as Gyeongsang and Jeolla were ideal. Ramie is also an ancient fiber in Korea, but was produced in smaller amounts than cotton. Before cotton fabrics were disseminated, ramie and hemp were main sources of textiles in addition to silk. Among the extant garments from the late nineteenth century are *hanbok* ensembles comprising a short jacket (*jeogori*) and a long skirt (*chima*) made of silk, homespun natural fibers of cotton, ramie, or hemp, and veils for women called *ssegaechima* made of *okyangmok* cotton.[8]

Okyangmok imported from the British Empire or via intermediaries such as Japanese merchants from 1876 was a novelty, and its pure white surface attracted consumers. A newspaper article in 1898 noted that imported cotton textiles were cheaper and convenient so that weavers in rural villages could not make a living.[9] Dress historian Eun-soo Choi noted that the linings of silk jackets for women (*jeogori*) from 1890 to 1910 were made of *okyangmok*.[10]

Patterned and solid-color cotton textiles were also popular. Female school uniforms were modernized *hanbok*-style ensembles of cotton with a white jacket and a black skirt. American missionary Mary Scranton founded Ewha School for Girls in 1886 and introduced a uniform consisting of a red *hanbok* ensemble of Russian cotton;[11] the students were called *hong-deung-yi*, red-robed children. In 1911, A. J. Walter and O. F. Pye, American missionaries and teachers at Ewha, designed a cotton vest attached to a *hanbok* skirt to facilitate physical education classes. In the 1920s, many women's magazines carried sewing patterns for this type of modernized *hanbok* and other school uniforms.[12] However, Japanese-style sailor suits became more prevalent in the 1930s. Ewha briefly adopted the black sailor suit in the 1930s. Girls' school uniforms in the design of a sailor suit jacket and a pleated skirt were ubiquitous in the 1930s in colonized Korea following the Japanese custom.[13] Except in winter, cotton was the main fabric, either in modernized *hanbok* or in Western-style skirt ensembles.

While women were producing a small amount of ramie, hemp, or silk textiles in addition to cotton, industrially manufactured cotton textiles inundated the market, leading to the cessation of domestic production and consumption: it was much more efficient and convenient to buy machine-produced cotton textiles. Korea, Japan, and China were the main exporters of raw silk from 1850 to 1930.[14] Japan was a dominant exporter of raw silk as well as woven silk textiles throughout the 1930s.[15] Sewing was taught to women in educational institutions.[16] Women's magazines also carried sewing patterns for children's clothes or new styles of basic garments. People sewed *beoseon* (traditional socks), underwear, and shirts. Knitted cotton socks, underwear, or garments were also introduced in the early twentieth century.[17]

Bridal registries from the early twentieth century list garments made predominantly in various types of silk and occasionally *okyangmok* or *gwangmok* (광목, which literally means broad cotton textile). Eun-soo Choi's analysis of women's jackets from the 1920s notes that pink *okyangmok* or white *seoyangmok* (서양목, which literally means Western or foreign cotton textiles) were used for the outer shells while linings were made of *gwangmok*.[18] For example, a 1934 bridal registry at the National Folk Museum includes a Western-style modernized tailored dress of *seoyangbok* for a bride, but all the other items are *hanbok* ensembles for different seasons, distinguished by patterns, colors, and types of weaving, mainly cotton and various silks.[19]

Studies of 'modern girls' and 'new women' in colonized Korea based on newspaper illustrations, opinion columns, or articles in women's magazines have emphasized that women expressed their modernistic experiences in sartorial consumption.[20] *The Arrival of New Women*, an exhibition held at the National Museum of Modern and Contemporary Art (MMCA) in 2018, documented the lives and voices of new women through visual and musical art.[21] Women faced steadfast legacies of Confucianism, imperialism and colonialism, and emerging mercantile capitalism while they sought escape from the morals and demands of the Confucian patriarchal family structure. As demonstrated in An Seok-ju's illustrations of a modern boy and a modern girl in 1928, new women who were educated, more visible in public space, and perhaps ambitious for careers and material success were viewed with worry (Figure 2.3a–b). Women standing in trams and buses are shown with conspicuous gold watches, fine rings, and purses. They are new women (*shinyeoseong*), represented by their hybrid fashion of modernized *hanbok* ensembles, short hair styles, knee-length skirts which reveal the legs, patterned jackets made of imported textiles, and custom-made leather shoes (Figure 2.3a). Modern boys strolled like

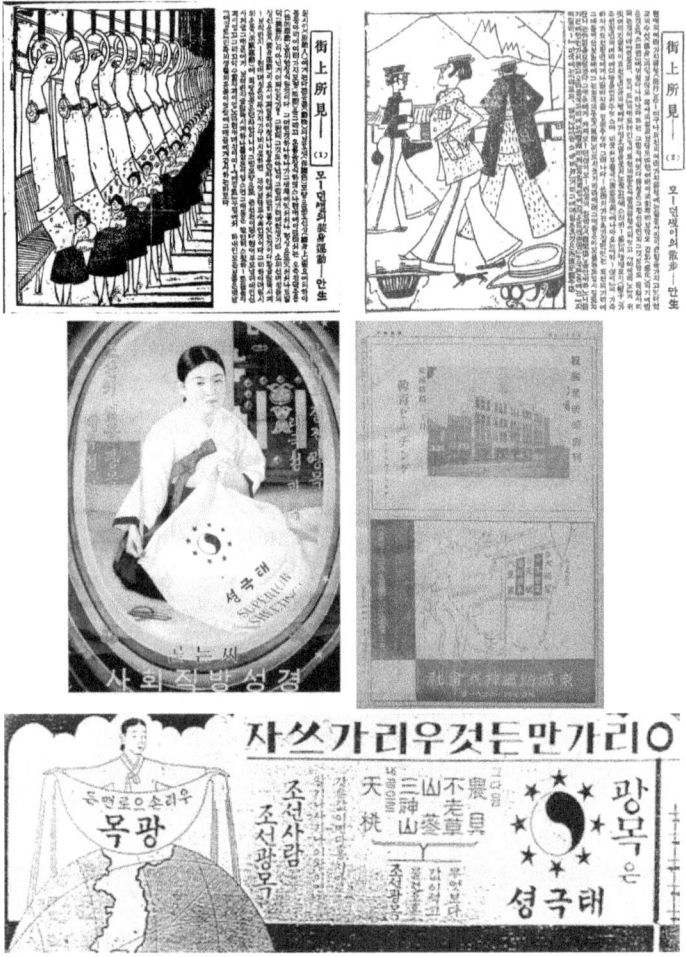

2.3 Advertisement for Taegeukseong Cotton by Kyungseong Bangjik, 1930s
  a An Seok-ju's column with his illustration entitled *An Opinion of Street Scenes* (Gasangsogeyon 가상소견), part 1 on 5 February 1928, *Chosun Ilbo*. Its subtitle says "Modern Girls' Dressing-Up Movement," with the illustration of young women as bus passengers, dressed up with modernized *hanbok* and prominent wrist watches
  b An Seok-ju's column with his illustration entitled *An Opinion of Street Scenes* (Gasangsogeyon 가상소견), part 2 on 7 February 1928, *Chosun Ilbo*. Its subtitle says "Modern Boys' Stroll," with the illustration of modern boys in fancy clothing walking in front of shabby traditional-style houses on the street
  c Advertisement for Taegeukseong, a brand of cotton textile produced by Gyeongseong Bangjik, 1922
  d (bottom of the page) Advertisement for Taegeukseong, a brand of cotton textile produced by Gyeongseong Bangjik in *Gukminshinbo* [국민신보 國民新報] on 11 June 1939
  e Advertisement for Taegeukseong, a brand of cotton textile produced by Gyeongseong Bangjik: "Wooriga-manden-geok wooriga-sseuja" [우리가 만든 것 우리가 쓰자 (Let's use those made by ourselves)]

fashionable *flâneurs* in Paris or any cosmopolitan city, with glasses, hats, musical instruments, and other luxury accessories (Figure 2.3b). These illustrations were published in *Chosen Ilbo*, a popular Korean-language newspaper founded in 1920. It is important to note that Korea was undergoing rapid transformation from an agrarian, rural country to an industrial, urban society – at least in several cosmopolitan cities. In a satirical criticism of women's predilection for gold watches and fine jewelry, both women's economic activities and their fashion items are scrutinized for censure.[22]

Simultaneously, queerness in sartorial choices, such as men looking like women or women dressed as men, often raised attention among the public or in the media. As in the traditional Confucian society, gender norms were imposed on both men and women, with men in a more privileged position and with women condemned vociferously for any wrongdoing. The gender aspect, in a heteronormative mode, was still enforced, and those celebrities deviating from the norm were much censured. For example, Hyun Hui-un was a pioneer in establishing the first beauty salon in Gyeongseong (Seoul) and publishing a beauty and style magazine called *Hyangheun*, equivalent to *Cosmopolitan*. An Seok-joo and Hyun Hui-un were collaborators on other magazines.[23] Hyun was noted as an eccentric, wearing makeup and grooming himself to an excessive degree. Modern boys were criticized in a similar tone that they spent resources and time cultivating their fashionable looks while overlooking other manly duties. There are cases of women dressed as men. Equivalent to *flâneurs* in Paris, these fashionable women were *giseang*, public entertainers and escorts to business tycoons. Bae Jungja (1870–1952), for example, was famous for dressing herself as a man in impeccable business attire and collecting confidential information for Japanese espionage.[24] In a sartorial criticism by conservative columnists, one can see that the ways in which people might counter that heteronormative mode are in social scandals or in entertainment news. In Hyun's case, he was a founding member of the new theater movement after he came back from study abroad in Japan; his circle of writers, actors, and designers seemed to be rather tolerant of Hyun's eccentric mode of fashion.[25] However, women violating heteronormative modes were often criticized in the context of anti-patriotism, overt consumerism, or easy virtue.

Patterned textiles are symbols of fashion in a 1934 painting by Kim Ki-chang (1914–2001) of his younger sister Kim Ki-ok and a young woman named Soje. A young beauty, Soje is dressed in a modernized *hanbok* (Figure 2.4). The jacket is of blue fabric with small patterns, and the skirt of plaid cotton. The midi skirt would reveal her calves but was not as short as those in An Seok-ju's illustration (see Figure 2.3a). Both women wear modern shoes. The room, with a phonograph and Western-style furniture, unusual in the 1930s, was in a doctor's house in Kim's neighborhood.

2.4 Kim Kichang, *Listening to Music* (Jeongcheong 정청), 1934. Color on silk, 159 × 134.5 cm. National Museum of Modern and Contemporary Art (MMCA), South Korea. Object no. KO-07851

A cream-color lace-trimmed tablecloth and matching cushion cover provide a calm balance against the pattern-rich fabrics of an upholstered rattan sofa and the two women's clothes. Awarded recognition at the Joseon Art Exhibition in 1934, the painting gives a glimpse of moderate styling in patterned textiles for modernized *hanbok* ensembles.

Korean men's consumption of woollen textiles and the tailoring business

During the Three Kingdoms period from the fourth to the seventh centuries CE, animals were raised for felt. Baekje, for example, sent sheep to Japan.[26] During the Goryeo dynasty, a record shows that two thousand sheep were imported into Korea.[27] Camels were also known to Korean people from the Three Kingdoms period. Camel and sheep wool was available in felt. However, to make tailored garments new types of woollen textiles were needed. Serge, worsted flannel, gabardine, crepe, and jacquard were introduced to consumers. In the last two decades of the nineteenth century, a handful of reformist politicians and thinkers wore Western-style suits with accessories and underwear purchased at foreign goods stores in In-cheon and Busan called *yanghaeng*.[28] During the Korean Empire, civil officers' Western-style Great Court attire called *daeryebok* and *soryebok* were made of woollen textiles (Figure 2.1).

Historian Rachel Silberstein notes that the British and Dutch East Asia Companies spent years encouraging sales of British textiles among the fashionable urban elite in China. Eventually, courtesans, gentlemen, and wealthy ladies in Suzhou, Yangzhou, and Shanghai became fond of light woollen textiles for their garments.[29] Chinese overcoats in the late Qing dynasty – *changyi* gowns, *magua* jackets, and *doufeng* cloaks – Silberstein demonstrated, had bright colors or linings made of British wool. After the Opium War and subsequent foreign occupations in coastal cities, men, both Chinese and non-Chinese, dressed in Western-style suits. The art of tailoring in Shanghai and Hong Kong quickly gained recognition among international businessmen. Korean resistance leaders based in Shanghai in the 1920s were often shown in well-tailored suits in newspaper or anniversary photographs. Just like wealthy Chinese consumers, male Korean elites were fond of well-tailored, light-weight woollen suits.[30]

While school uniforms were mostly made of cotton in the early twentieth century, overcoats or cloaks for winter uniforms could be made of wool. After the fall of the Korean Empire, the social elite employed by banking, governmental offices, or commerce consumed woollen textiles for tailor-made suits. Public spaces were modernized with tables and chairs, but private residences were still equipped with traditional furniture for sitting on the floor. It was thus customary that the elite men had two sets of sartorial languages: Western-style suits in the office and modernized *hanbok* ensembles for wearing at home – just as they spoke Japanese in public and Korean at home. Men not in public office also consumed woollen textiles to make modernized *hanbok* overcoats called *durumagi*. It was common for those who could afford those modern luxuries to wear a *hanbok* ensemble (jacket and trousers) in silk with a woollen *durumagi*, a woollen felt hat, and leather shoes.

A man dressed in a full ensemble of Western-style jacket, trousers, waistcoat, and a hat created an aura of economic power and political influence. Park Young-hyo (1861–1935), for example, was a pro-Japanese politician who served as Interior Minister under King Gojong in 1895. As son-in-law of King Cheljong, he lived a luxurious and privileged life and studied at the University of Edinburgh. After the 1910 annexation of Korea into the Japanese Empire, he was awarded the title of Marquess in the Japanese peerage and held a seat in the House of Peers in the Diet of Japan. He served as President of the *Dong-A Ilbo* newspaper in 1910, Director of the Bank of Chosen in 1918, and President of Gyeongbang Corporation (originally Gyeongseong Bangjik 경성방직) in 1921. Another fashionable man was Kim Seong-su (1891–1955). His family founded both *Dong-Ah Ilbo* and Gyeongbang Corporation.

People like Kim Seong-su and Park Young-hyo were prominently featured in photographs in newspapers. Their impeccable suits and ties were symbols of progress and enlightenment, symbols of modernity.[31] Their clothes could have been tailored in Japan. For most people, Western clothing and suits were initially regarded as pro-Japanese and anti-patriotic, but gradually came to be objects of envy. Western-style outfits as a fashion trend flowed from men to women and from the upper to the middle classes: from upper-class men to their female counterparts in high society, then to middle-class men and later middle-class women, and later to the lower classes. The transition from traditional to modernized dress originated in uniform culture in the military or in the educational institutions.[32]

Fashionable neighborhoods in Seoul were filled with people dressed in various degrees of hybridity. Western-style garments and accessories, often mixed with traditional ones, denoted a person's worldview as much as their economic status. Woollen textiles were much more expensive than cotton. Manufactured cotton shirts were also more expensive than home-made versions. Tailors flourished in commercial centers in Seoul, Busan, Daegu, Pyeongyang, and Hamheung: Jongro Tailors, subject of a research project undertaken by the National Folk Museum, was established in 1916.[33] Tailoring schools also became popular among young people. According to a study of products sold at tailors' shops, both ready-to-wear and custom-tailored suits were sold for men, while women's clothes were made at dressmakers' shops in the 1930s.[34] From 1938 to 1945, the wartime emergency economic system impacted tailors. Main workers at tailoring boutiques are the owner, chief, clerks, salespersons, workers, and apprentices. Owners could be tailors or non-tailors. Chiefs were assumed to be the most senior tailors. Clerks were shop employees. Salespeople were dispatched to make orders and receive payments, and workers were in charge of the production of clothes. Among the workers were apprentices who were training in tailoring and sewing.

Tailors were regular advertisers in newspapers. *Dong-A Ilbo* or *Chosun Ilbo* carried seasonal advertisements for trendy coats or new suits for men and women, although women were still rare among customers until 1945. Rarity of woollen clothes for women was common in other countries. The introduction of woollens in women's clothing was relatively recent in Britain as well as in East Asia. Dress historian Lou Taylor analyzed the use of wool and reception of tailored woollen clothing among British women in the late nineteenth century.[35] As light-weight woollen textiles were advertised for women, outdoor coats for walking or jackets for horse riding had become common for wealthy ladies by the 1880s. Although women's dresses were made of silk or cotton, by the 1920s gradually fashionable women also began to own coats, jackets, or capes of woven woollen textiles in addition to felt hats and leather gloves.[36]

In East Asia, woollen coats were being advertised to elite women by the early 1930s, according to newspaper advertisements. Fur-lined coats were status symbols for wealthy housewives.[37] However, women were still restricted to the private domain, with limited access to public space. A few women were able to wear Western-style, tailored suits.[38] However, most women, whether working or staying at home, wore modernized *hanbok* in public and in private. Women's *jeogori* in the 1930s were made of rayon or woollen textiles in addition to the prevalent textiles of silk and cotton.[39] Ordinary brides and housewives made their *jeogori* in cotton textiles in solid colors throughout the period, while well-to-do women used wool muslin or serge to make modernized *hanbok* ensembles. Serge was imported to make military uniforms, coats and trench coats. As it was used to make durable outer garments, dark colors of navy blue, grey, brown, and black were popular. In the 1930s 'new women' were often shown in modernized *hanbok* ensembles in woollen textiles with jackets (*jeogori*) and skirts (*chima*) of the same color.[40] Silk georgette fabric was common for Western-style women's ensembles (*yangjang*) and was occasionally used to make *hanbok* among upper-class ladies.[41]

Most tailors were young men who had attended tailoring academies. There were a few pioneering women tailors, like Choi Kyung-ja, who studied Western-style dressmaking at Ochanomizu College of Fashion and opened *Eunjwaok* (은좌옥; pronounced *Ginjaya* in Japanese) in Hamheung, a port city in the northern part of Korea in 1937. Choi opened a dressmaking school called *Hamheung Yangjae Hakwon* and educated women dressmakers from 1938.[42] This was, though, an exceptional case. Most women worked as assistants, seamstresses, needle workers or shop keepers in tailoring houses. Until Choi returned and opened her own boutique for women, women also visited tailors to have Western-style clothes made, just like their fathers and husbands.

After the division of Korea, Choi moved her dressmaking school to Seoul in 1949 and called it Kookje Fashion Academy (*Kookje Yangjang*

Jeonmun Hakwon). When the Korean War broke out, Choi took refuge in Daegu and operated it there. After the war, she relocated her academy and boutique back to Seoul and opened *Kookje Yangjang-sa* in Myung-dong in 1954. Other tailors in Gwang-gyo and Jong-ro also relocated their shops to Myung-dong, which became the fashion center of Korea until the 1980s. At Choi's Kookje Academy, both men and women were trained to become fashion designers in womenswear.[43]

Although women like Choi created a platform for other women to become dressmakers, tailoring remained a male-dominated business among both owners and customers. As men occupied most white-collar office positions until the late twentieth century, tailors and consumers of woollen textiles were primarily men while their assistants or garment caretakers were women.

Colonial capitalism and textile manufacturing in Japanese-occupied Korea

Historian Carter Eckart and other historians have studied colonial capitalism under the Japanese occupation.[44] Eckart analyzed the business history of textile manufacturer Gyeongbang, owned by the Gochang Kim clan and operated by Korean people in Seoul as a representative of ethnic capital enterprise imbued with patriotic support for their home country. Eckart named the 'patriotic capitalism,' or construction of national capital, *minjok jabon* 민족자본 in Korean.[45] Like any imperialist government, Japan saw Korea as a convenient market for the growth of its economy. Scholars of Korean department stores have shown a hierarchy of merchandise, giving privilege and brand power to products made in Japan. And when Japanese visitors needed souvenirs reminiscent of the 'folk' nature of the colony, they bought crafts or ceramics made by Korean artisans in a Japanese-owned studio.[46]

Economic historian Mitsuhiko Kimura argues that Japan did not maintain a monopoly in cotton textiles exported to Korea. Japanese textile companies were keen on competition among themselves and also with Korean companies, which did not generate significant profits.[47] However, it is important to recognize the Japanese monopoly of cotton textiles before 1910. The Korean market for Japanese cotton textiles from 1890 to 1910 is significant, as the Korean market was as large as the Chinese.[48] This is because Korea's machine-operated cotton-weaving industry was small. After the March First Movement in 1919, the Japanese Government-General allowed Koreans to manufacture cotton or cotton-mix synthetic textiles for domestic consumption while they monopolized supplies of woven woollen textiles and raw synthetic fibers.

In advertisements for Gyeongbang, women were often portrayed as major consumers and patrons of cotton textiles (Figure 2.3c).[49] Woollen textiles were not allowed for manufacturing within Korea until 1945. Japanese companies or Japanese-owned wholesalers monopolized the supply and advertised woollen clothes as a luxury for the elite – affluent men and dandies ('modern boys') (Figure 2.3b). Colonial capitalism fit well with the view of gendered textile production and consumption. Gyeongseong Bangjik, for example, created a brand called *Taegeukseong* (Taegeuk Star) and featured a woman in white *hanbok* holding a piece of cotton cloth (Figure 2.3c–d). In its advertising campaign, Gyeongbang was careful to promote the patriotic consumption of '*gwangmok*' (Korean-grown, Korean-made cotton) as opposed to '*okyangmok*,' imported textiles.[50] This patriotic stance mirrors examples in other colonial societies. Historian Nancy Reynolds, for example, argued that Egyptian textile companies used tropes of 'foreign silks,' 'durable Egyptian cottons,' or 'artificial silks.' These terms were used to urge Egyptian consumers from the 1930s to the 1950s to buy Egyptian cotton products.[51] Historian Lisa Trivedi followed the development of Indian cotton textiles and other national products in India during British colonial rule,[52] where the patriotic consumption of Indian cotton textiles was emphasized. China also had a similar movement to patronize domestic products.[53]

The advertisements of Gyeongbang used the tagline 'We [Koreans] should use what we make' (*Joseon saram Joseon gwangmok*, literally Korean People; Korean Cotton) in Korean-language newspapers such as *Dong-Ah Ilbo*.[54] Gyeongbang was founded in 1919 in the aftermath of the March First Movement of Independence to empower Korean people's economic potential and founded with principles of national capital (*minjok jabon*) and economic independence (*gyeongje jaju*).

Women were viewed as instrumental in household consumption of domestic products. The advertisement with a middle-aged housewife holding *gwangmok* cloth like a flag was effective in reaching potential consumers: ordinary Korean people. According to Cha's statistics, there were three kinds of cotton textiles around 1909: bleached cotton (*sarashi-momen*) was the cheapest while white cotton (*shiromomen*) and striped cotton (*shimamomen*) were more expensive. White cotton was 27% more expensive and striped cotton 46% more than bleached cotton.[55] As shown in An Seok-ju's illustration of 1928, fancy jackets were made of either striped or patterned textiles (Figure 2.3a, b). Around 1923, the consumer price for cotton textiles in Korea was the second most expensive among major cities in East Asia.[56]

In this view of national capital, consumers of imported and expensive foreign products were often criticized in Korean-language magazines and newspapers. Women in particular were admonished for extravagant purchases in novels, films, popular stories, and opinion columns.[57] Historian Theodore Jun Yoo focused on the inner dynamics of the department store and its promotion of fashion and consumption.[58] Both sectors of fashion and consumption were viewed as largely gendered, as they belonged to the exclusive domains of women. Women's extravagant consumption was a concern among social commentators who called for social control and the rationalization of spending. Yoo's research stems from his earlier work on female workers in colonized Korea.[59]

Cotton textiles, available from domestic manufacturers, were widely available by the 1930s, whereas woollen textiles were not allowed for manufacturing within Korea until 1945, as mentioned above. Historically, ordinary people wore cotton clothing in layers for the cold season while the social elite could use silk, felt, or fur to keep them warm. Woollen woven textiles are relatively new, as Western-style suits emerged at the turn of the twentieth century. The dichotomy between cotton woven textiles and woollen woven textiles is visible in public space and resulted from economic disparity between rural and urban communities. At the beginning of the colonial period, the Japanese government used the pretext of public hygiene and sumptuous consumption to eradicate community-based funerary customs while promoting domestic production of ramie or hemp linen by women for funerary clothing in rural areas. By 1943, production of raw cotton in Korea had increased to 320 million pounds, which provided more than enough materials for textile factories.[60] It is evident that cotton production was not in shortage, and that Koreans had been forced to give up their traditions.

As the Second Sino-Manchurian War loomed in the mid-1930s, the war effort swept the country. The type of peaceful, sunny afternoon depicted in Kim Jung-hyun's 1936 painting *A Spring Sunlight* would soon disappear (Figure 2.5). Unlike Kim Ki-chang's well-appointed, modern urban living room, families in rural villages lived in traditional houses without modern kitchens, as shown in Kim Jung-hyun's painting (compare Figure 2.4 and Figure 2.5). Women sat on a raised wooden floor attached outside a main room, overlooking the yard. This is what the Japanese expected to see as an 'exoticized' image of their colonial citizens in Korea called *hyangtosaek*, meaning 'return to the land.'[61] While women and children prepared meals at home, men would probably be working outside, and thus invisible. Far from being stylish, with patterned textiles of cotton or rayon shown in Kim Ki-chang's painting, this family are dressed in traditional *hanbok* of solid colors and in traditional rubber shoes (compare modern girls in Figure 2.3a with women in Figure 2.5).[62]

The nostalgic view of a happy family preparing a meal disguised the reality of supply shortages. Ordinary women were introduced to a work uniform called *momppae*, resembling bloomers with tight ankles. When the National Mobilization Law (국가총동원법 国家総動員法) was issued in 1938, women made work trousers out of rugged cloth and endured manual labor. For durability and easy of washing, cotton or synthetic textiles were preferred. Wartime propaganda by the Japanese regime

2.5 Kim Jung-hyun 김중현, *A Spring Sunlight* [Chunyang 춘양], 1936. Color on paper (four-panel screen painting), each panel 106 × 54.2 cm. National Museum of Modern and Contemporary Art (MMCA), South Korea. Object no. KO-07535

encouraged married women to replace male labor during their husbands' absence on the battlefields. Oro-Japanese organizations like the Women's Labour Volunteer Corps also urged younger, unmarried women to work in factories to show their loyalty to the Japanese emperor.[63]

The condemnation of modern girls and new women of the 1920s diminished in the 1930s with a slowly increasing number of female social elite in art, music, and education.[64] More and more female workers were also active in retail, service, and manufacturing industries. However, textile factory workers, who were overwhelmingly women, were almost invisible in public space and neglected in the nationalist newspapers (Figure 2.6).

Women's role in production and consumption of cotton and synthetic textiles, whether in traditional, pre-industrial households or in colonial capitalism, was vital in expanding the quantity and the geopolitical influence of Korean textiles. A survey in 1948, after Korean Independence, reported that production had declined 70% from 1940.[65] Table 2.1, of production volume by textile type, created in 1948, shows an overwhelming amount of cotton textiles (71.5%) as opposed to silk (25.6%), wool (1.1%), and linen (1.8%). The paucity of wool production is another sign of colonial capitalism: lucrative, innovative skills were not transferred to the colonized. Korean citizens were forced to be dependent on the Japanese supply of woollen textiles or on imported products.

2.6 Chosen Spinning and Weaving Factory in Busan, circa 1930s. *Busan · Busan Harbor 130 Years*, http://busan.grandculture.net/Contents?local=busan&dataType=01&contents_id=GC04200855

Table 2.1 Production volume by textile type (*Economic Statistics Yearbook* 1948 by Chosen Bank).

Textile type	Production volume (km)	Ratio (%)
Silk textiles	10,862	25.6
Cotton textiles	30,413	71.5
Woollen textiles	472	1.1
Linen textiles	768	1.8

Source: Data from the *Korean Economic Yearbook* [Hanguk geongje yeongam 한국경제연감 韓國經濟年鑑] (Seoul: Joseon Bank, 1948). Quoted in Kwon Byeongtaek 권병택, 'Bangjik 방직 紡織,' *Encyclopedia of Korean Culture* [Hanguk minjok munhwa daebaekgwa sajeon 한국민족문화대백과사전] (Seongnam: Academy of Korean Studies, 1995).

Conclusion: gendered labor

As scholars of colonialism have argued, colonized people were essential consumers of cheap goods. The British Empire inundated the Indian market with coarse cotton textiles manufactured in Birmingham and Manchester. A popular belief of a hemp ensemble for the deceased was an 'invented tradition' in the colonized era by the Japanese intervention. As discussed by historians of Korean dress, in the Joseon dynasty the dead and dying were dressed in their best outfits, as confirmed by the discovery of surviving garments in the tombs of privileged families of the period. Due to the shortage of goods caused by the Japanese military campaign in Manchuria, Japan enforced thrift and frugality across its colonies. Thus, in 1934, the Japanese Governor-General promulgated regulations on rituals (*Euiryejunchik* 의례준

칙 儀禮準則); folk customs were reformed in the name of improved public hygiene and discouraging sumptuous consumption. The rules stated that expensive silk should not be used for funerals, and robes were to be made of homespun hemp cloth or ramie, eradicating community-based funerary customs of several hundred years. As a result, there was a sudden increase in hemp cloth prices. In Kim Jung-hyun's painting (Figure 2.5), the women preparing the meal would have had difficulty finding proper hemp garments if there had been a death in the family.

In this account of gendered textiles, women were targeted with advertising campaigns by national capitalists such as Gyeongbang, and were simultaneously producers of homespun textiles. Expensive materials such as woven woollen textiles or felt hats were not in the domain of women's household labor. They were for professional tailors – usually men – and the urban elite. Women were the main workforce in modern factories producing cotton, synthetic, and silk textiles. At home and at work, the care of garments was often placed on women's shoulders. The gendered labor and gendered consumption of luxury textiles continued after 1945 as the hierarchical system of men in public space and women in private space changed little until the late 1960s.[66]

Notes

1. For example, see *His Majesty – The Prime Minister of Korea* (NRICP Relic No.: 2911), 1884, albumen print at the Museum of Fine Arts, Boston Photograph Library (acc. no. 2003.728). There are about sixty photos in Lowell's collection, starting with 2003 in the accession numbers.
2. Kyungmee Lee, 'Dress Policy and Western-Style Court Attire in Modern Korea,' in Kyunghee Pyun and Aida Yuen Wong, eds, *Fashion, Identity, and Power in Modern Asia* (New York: Palgrave Macmillan, 2018), pp. 49–54.
3. Kyunghee Pyun, 'Hybrid Dandyism: European Woollen Fabric in East Asia,' in Pyun and Wong, eds, *Fashion, Identity, and Power*, p. 288.
4. See ibid., pp. 290–293 for tailors emerging in the 1920s.
5. Kyeongmi Joo, 'Gendered Differences in Modern Korea toward Western Luxuries,' in Pyun and Wong, eds, *Fashion, Identity, and Power*, p. 146; figure 7.1.
6. Mary Beth Mills, 'Gender and Inequality in the Global Labour Force,' *Annual Review of Anthropology*, 32 (2003): 41–62, www.jstor.org/stable/25064820 (accessed 4 February 2021).
7. Gary R. Saxonhouse and Gavin Wright, 'National Leadership and Competing Technological Paradigms: The Globalization of Cotton Spinning, 1878–1933,' *Journal of Economic History*, 70, no. 3 (2010): 535–566, www.jstor.org/stable/40836579 (accessed 4 February 2021).
8. The National Folk Museum has several examples of women's ordinary clothes, including skirts and jackets, made of *okyangmok*: minsok 067426; minsok 090571; over 250 items in all. See the entry for 'okyangmok' in the *Encyclopedia of Korean Folk Culture* (Seoul: National Folk Museum, 2001), https://folkency.nfm.go.kr/kr/topic/detail/7120 (accessed 4 February 2021). *Okyangmok* was a translation of 'calico' in registries and inventories in the early twentieth century.
9. *Maeil Sinmun*, 3 June 1898: 'Everybody would buy a cheap, convenient product. Thus, country folks who used to weave cotton textiles in rural villages before

seoyangmok was imported cannot maintain a living these days.' Kwon Byeongtaek 권병택, 'Bangjik' 방직 紡織, *Encyclopedia of Korean Culture* [Hanguk minjok munhwa daebaekgwa sajeon 한국민족문화대백과사전] (Seongnam: Academy of Korean Studies, 1995), http://encykorea.aks.ac.kr/Contents/Item/E0021794 (accessed 4 February 2021).
10　Eun-soo Choi 최은수, '1890nyeon–1960nyeondae yeoja jeogori gamjeong' 1890 년–1960년대 여자 저고리 감정 [Appraisal of female Jeogori from 1890 to 1960], *Bokshik*, 복식 服飾 [*International Journal of Costume and Fashion*] 58, no. 5 (2008): 178–180, at 180.
11　Kyunghee Pyun, 'Transformation of Monastic Habits: Student Uniforms for Christian Schools in East Asia,' *Journal of Religion and the Arts*, 24, no. 4 [Special Issue: Faith/Fashion/Forward: Dress and the Sacred] (2020): 622–625, at 624.
12　See magazines such as *Bu-in* or *Shinyeoseong*. Read Yuri Seo, 'Magazine Covers and Colonial Modernity: Politics of the Korean Face,' in Kyunghee Pyun and Jung-Ah Woo, eds, *Interpreting Modernism in Korean Art: Fluidity and Fragmentation* (New York: Routledge, 2021), pp. 108–110.
13　For Korean school uniforms in the early twentieth century, see Pyun, 'Transformation of Monastic Habits,' 604–640.
14　Debin Ma, 'The Modern Silk Road: The Global Raw-Silk Market, 1850–1930,' *Journal of Economic History*, 56, no. 2 (1996): 330–355, www.jstor.org/stable/2123969 (accessed 7 February 2021). See especially p.331: 'Between 1927 and 1930, the trade volume of raw silk reached 65 percent of the value of wool and 35 percent of cotton. Before World War I, share of raw silk was 40 percent of total export value in Japan; 30 percent of the total in China.' Ma's research does not mention Korea as a separate nation. From p. 339, note 25, the export of raw silk from Japan to the United States reached 50% of the raw silk supply in the US between 1909 and 1920; about 70% after 1912; and more than 70% after 1916. From 1925 to 1937, Japan provided 70–90% of raw silk in the worldwide trade to the US and Europe; and its silk-reeling engineering facilities were the most advanced at the time. See p. 342ff. Korea's raw silk production was beneficial for Japan to focus on export of its silk products to North America and Europe.
15　Lawrence B. Clickman, '"Make Lisle the Style": The Politics of Fashion in the Japanese Silk Boycott, 1937–1940,' *Journal of Social History*, 38, no. 3 (2005): 573–608, www.jstor.org/stable/3790646 (accessed 7 February 2021). It is interesting that Japanese silk products in the US prompted consumer activism in 1937 as women boycotted Japanese fashion goods because the profits funded Japanese militants in the Second Sino-Japanese War.
16　Maeng Mun-jae 맹문재, '1930nyeondae yeoja godeunghaksaengdeul-eui hakgyo saenghwal gochal' 1930 년대 여자고등학생들의 학교생활 고찰 [A study of school life of female high school students in the 1930s] *Hangukhak-yeongu* 한국학연구 [*Journal of Korean Studies*] 29 (2008): 31–56. This article studies school life in the 1930s based on the school magazine *Baewha*, published by Baewha Girl's High School students and graduates in Seoul from 1929 to 1943. It confirms that female students learned physical education, fine arts, music, English literature, geography, chemistry, botany, sewing, embroidery, and home economics.
17　Korean modern knitted cotton socks, silk stockings, women's nylon hosiery, and other garments need more research. Pyun's essay includes the development of women's hosiery and knitted cotton socks in the mid and late twentieth century: Kyunghee Pyun, 'Body Autonomy and Miniskirt Controversy in South Korea,' *Berg Encyclopedia of World Dress and Fashion*, Berg Fashion Library edited by Joanna Eicher (digital database) (Oxford: Berg Publishers/Bloomsbury, 2021). doi: 10.5040/9781847888556.EDch062019.
18　Choi, '1890nyeon–1960nyeondae yeoja jeogori gamjeong,' 182.

19 Called *Honsumulmok* (혼수물목 婚需物目) at the National Folk Museum, min070775 (acc. no.). The list on pink paper is 22.5 cm long × 37.4 cm wide.
20 Kim Eun-jung 김은정, 'Geundaejeok pyusang-euroseo-eui yeoseong fashion yeongu: modeon geol (gaehwagi–1945nyeon)eul jungshim-euro' 근대적 표상으로서의 여성패션 연구: 모던 걸(개화기–1945년)을 중심으로 [A study of women's fashion as a symbol of modernity: focusing on the modern girl from the enlightenment period to 1945], *Ashia-yeoseong-yeongu* 아시아여성연구 [*Journal of Asian Women*] 43, no. 2 (2004): 331–359.
21 *The Arrival of New Women* was held at the MMCA from December 2017 to April 2018. See Theodore Jun Yoo, *The Politics of Gender in Colonial Korea: Education, Labour and Health, 1910–1945* (Berkeley: University of California Press, 2008); especially ch. 2: 'The "New Woman" and the Politics of Love, Marriage, and Divorce in Colonial Korea.'
22 For rising concerns around consumerism, see Kate E. Taylor-Jones, 'Shopping, Sex, and Lies: *Mimong/Sweet Dreams* (1936) and the Disruptive Process of Colonial Girlhood,' *Journal of Japanese and Korean Cinema*, 10, no. 2 (2018): 98–114. The article discusses the perils of modern womanhood including consumerist pleasure.
23 Yongkeun Chun, 'Displayed Modernity: Advertising and Commercial Art in Colonial Korea, 1920–1940,' PhD diss. (Royal College of Art, 2020). See Shin Hyeon-gyu 신현규, 'Choecho ui miyong japji hyangheun gwa buin e yeonjaedoen miyong ganghwa e daehayeo' 최초의 미용잡지 '향혼'과 '부인'에 연재된 미용강화에 대하여 [On the beauty enhancement in Korea's first beauty magazines *Hyang-heun* and *Buin*], 근대서지 [*Modern Bibliography Review*], no. 4 (2011): 351–370; Ryu Suyun 류수연, 'Hyeon Huiun ui hwajang damnon' 현희운의 화장 담론 [Hyeon Hui-un's discourse of makeup], *Eomun yeongu* 어문 연구 [*Society for Korean Language and Literary Research*] 43, no. 1 (2015): 201–223. See Seo Yuri's chapter in this volume (note 5) for *Hyang-heun* and *Buin*.
24 Bae was the adopted daughter of Itō Hirobumi, http://encykorea.aks.ac.kr/Contents/Item/E0021921 (accessed 15 July 2021).
25 For Hyeon Hui-un, see Moon Kyoung-Yeon 문경연, '1920 nyeondae choban Hyeon Cheol ui yeongeungnon gwa geundaejeok gihoek' 1920 년대 초반 현철의 연극론과 근대적 기획 [Hyeon Chul's drama theory and modern project in the early 1920s], *Han'guk yeongeukak* 한국연극학 [*Journal of the Korean Theatre Studies Association*], no. 25 (2005): 5–38.
26 The seventh year of Empress Suiko corresponds to the early seventh century. Min Gil-ja 민길자, 'Mojik' 모직 毛織, *Encyclopedia of Korean Culture* [Hanguk minjok munhwa daebaekgwa sajeon 한국민족문화대백과사전] (Seongnam: Academy of Korean Studies, 1995), http://encykorea.aks.ac.kr/Contents/Item/E0018563 (accessed 4 February 2021).
27 During the reign of Uijong of Goryeo (1146–1170). Min, ibid.
28 Pyun, 'Hybrid Dandyism,' p. 288.
29 Rachel Silberstein, 'Fashioning the Foreign: Using British Woolens in Nineteenth-Century China,' in Pyun and Wong, eds, *Fashion, Identity, and Power*, p. 243.
30 Pyun, 'Hybrid Dandyism,' p. 289.
31 Gong Je-wook 공제욱, 'Hanmal, iljeshigi Euibok-eui byeonhwa-wa saenghwal yangshik: Yangbok-eui doyibeul jungshimeuro 한말, 일제시기 의복의 변화와 생활양식: 양복의 도입을 중심으로 [Changes in clothing trends in the last period of the Chosôn dynasty and Japanese colonial period: the Westernization of Korean clothing culture], *Saheowa yeoksa* 사회와 역사 [*Society and History*] 122 (2019): 117–158; Lee Yu-kyung 이유경 and Kim Jin-gu 김진구, 'Woorinara yangbok suyong gwajeong-eui bokshik byeoncheon-ei daehan yeongu: Munhwajeonpa yiron-eul jungshimeuro' 우리나라 양복수용 과정의 복식변천에 대한 연구: 문화전파 이론을 중심으로 [A study of changing fashion styles during the introduction of Western-style attire: focusing on

the diffusion theory of culture], *Bokshik* 복식 服飾 [*Journal of the Korean Society of Costume*] 26 (1995): 123–143.

32 For the standardization of Western-style school uniforms in East Asia, see Pyun, 'Transformation of Monastic Habits,' 604–611.

33 A field research project on *Jongro Tailor of 100 Years* was published by the National Folk Museum: *A Centennial Anniversary of Tailor History-Chongro Tailor's* [Baengnyeon-eui taeileo: Jongro yangbokjeom] (Seoul: National Folk Museum, 2014). Another exhibition was created based on this research. It was called *Tailors of 100 Years and Daegu* [Baengnyeon-eui taeileo geurigo Daegu] and held at Daegu Textile Museum in 2016.

34 Kim Soon-Young 김순영, 'Hanguk geundae yangbokjeom-eui panmae mulpum-gwa saengsan-mit panmae juche' 한국 근대 양복점의 판매 물품과 생산 및 판매 주체 [Production, sales, and salespeople of merchandise at Korean modern tailors], *Bokshik* 복식 服飾 [*Journal of the Korean Society of Costume*] 67, no. 5 (2017): 89–107.

35 Lou Taylor, 'Wool Cloth and Gender: The Use of Woollen Clothing in Women's Dress in Britain, 1865–85,' in A. de la Haye and E. Wilson, eds, *Defining Dress: Dress as Object, Meaning and Identity* (Manchester: Manchester University Press, 1999), p. 35; Susan North, 'John Redfern and Sons, 1847 to 1892,' *Costume*, 42 (2008): 145–168.

36 Ann Smart Martin, 'Makers, Buyers and Users – Consumerism as a Material Culture Framework,' *Winterthur Portfolio*, 28, no. 2/3 (1993): 141–157.

37 For example, see the 1936 film *Sweet Dream* (*Mimong* 미몽). It depicts a department store displaying various types of fancy clothes where the main character shops for a dress for her daughter.

38 Kwon Hye-young 권혜영 and Yi Gyeong-ja 이경자, 'Hanguk yeoseong yangbok-eui byeoncheon-ei gwanhan yeongu: 1900nyeon–1945nyen-eul jungshimeuro' 한국 여성 양복의 변천에 관한 연구: 1900 년–1945 년을 중심으로 [A study of transformation of Korean women's Western-style suits: from 1900 to 1945], *Bokshik* 복식 服飾 [*Journal of the Korean Society of Costume*] 7 (1983): 21–37. Lee Kyungmee 이경미, 'Daehanjeguk-gi Gojong hwangje, Sunjong hwangje, Sunheonhwang-gwibi sajin-eui yangbok' 대한제국기 고종황제, 순종황제, 순헌황귀비 사진의 양복 [Western-style attire in photographs of Emperor Gojong, Emperor Sunjong, and Imperial Consort Sunheon during the Korean Empire], *Hanguk euiryuhakoe haksuldaehoenonmun-jip* 한국의류학회 학술대회논문집 [*Proceedings of the Korean Society of Clothing and Textiles*] (2009): 57–59, at 59.

39 Choi, '1890nyeon–1960nyeondae yeoja jeogori gamjeong,' 184.

40 Ibid., 184.

41 See ibid., 186 for examples dating from the 1940s.

42 For tailoring academies in Korea, see Pyun, 'Hybrid Dandyism,' p. 31 n. 27.

43 Among the well-known male graduates of *Kookje Bokjang Hakwon*, established in 1961, are Andre Kim and Lie Sang-bong; female graduates include Lee Kwang Hee, Kim Chang-sook, Jin Taeok, and Lee Cinoo.

44 Carter J. Eckart, *Offspring of Empire: The Koch'ang Kims and the Colonial Origins of Korean Capitalism, 1876–1945* (Seattle: University of Washington Press, 2017).

45 Patriotic capitalism or national capitalism could be comparable to the post-war theory of 'moral economies.' Reinhild Kreis, 'Make or Buy? Modes of Provision and the Moral Economy of Households in Postwar Germany,' *Geschichte Und Gesellschaft. Sonderheft* 26 (2019): 187–212, www.jstor.org/stable/26632298 (accessed 4 February 2021). Renegotiation of household production and consumption is still under the competing agencies of governmental institutions, regulatory bodies, advertisers and marketers, and activist movements.

46 See Younjung Oh, 'Shopping for Art: The New Middle Class' Art Consumption in Modern Japanese Department Stores,' *Journal of Design History*, 27, no. 4 (2014): 351–369.
47 Mitsuhiko Kimura, 'The Economics of Japanese Imperialism in Korea, 1910–1939,' *Economic History Review*, New Series 48, no. 3 (1995): 555–574. See especially pp. 556–557.
48 Ibid., 'p. 557, nn. 11–13: the Tōyō Spinning and Weaving Company and Kanegafuchi Spinning and Weaving Company were major providers of cotton textiles to Korea. Kimura also notes that British cotton textiles fell to 6.5% in Korea after 1924 as Japanese companies took a predominant position.
49 The advertisement campaigns are also evidence of 'family capitalism.' Dennis McNamara, 'The Keishō and the Korean Business Elite,' *Journal of Asian Studies*, 48, no. 2 (1989): 310–323. See especially pp. 311–312. Park Jong-min 박종민 and Kwak Eun-kyung 곽은경, 'Shinmun gwanggo-nae yeoseong-eui teukjing-gwa yeokwal: 1920nyeonbuteo 2005nyeon ggaji Chosun Ilbo, Dong-A Ilbo gwang-go bunseok' 신문광고 내 여성의 특징과 역할: 1920 년부터 2005 년까지 조선일보, 동아일보 광고 분석 [Characteristics and function of women in newspaper advertisements: an analysis of Chosun Ilbo and Dong-A Ilbo advertisements from 1920 to 2005], *Gwanggo yeongu* 광고연구 [*Advertising Research*] 77 (2007): 59–93.
50 See a comparable process of effeminizing textile labor by indigenous people in eighteenth-century Britain. Emily M. West, 'Labour and the Literary Technologies of Mechanization in the British Cotton Industry,' *Journal for Early Modern Cultural Studies* 17, no. 4 (2017): 49–74. Race and gender were crucial factors in inventing a fictional image of Britain's technological and industrial mastery against indigenous Indian laborers in the cotton trade.
51 Nancy Y. Reynolds, 'National Socks and the "Nylon Woman": Materiality, Gender, and Nationalism in Textile Marketing in Semicolonial Egypt, 1930–56,' *International Journal of Middle East Studies*, 43, no. 1 (2011): 49–74, www.jstor.org/stable/23017342 (accessed 7 February 2021).
52 Lisa Trivedi, *Clothing Gandhi's Nation: Homespun and Modern India* (Bloomington: Indiana University Press, 2007).
53 Karl Gerth, *Consumer Culture and the Creation of the Nation* (Cambridge: Harvard University Press, 2003); Michael Zakim, 'Sartorial Ideologies: From Homespun to Ready-Made,' *American Historical Review*, 106, no. 5 (2001): 1553–1586. See also Zakim's book, *Ready-Made Democracy: A History of Men's Dress in the American Republic, 1760–1860* (Chicago and London: University of Chicago Press, 2003).
54 One can easily compare this with an Egyptian advertisement of 1933: 'Only buy what you need from an Egyptian – in that way the wealth of your country will grow. Visit the Egyptian Products Sales Company: its employees are Egyptian, its wares are Egyptian, its raw materials are Egyptian, and [its products were] made by the hands of Egyptian workers.' Reynolds, 'National Socks,' 53.
55 Myung Soo Cha, 'Unskilled Wage Gaps within the Japanese Empire,' *Economic History Review*, 68, no. 1 (2015): 23–47, www.jstor.org/stable/43910009 (accessed 4 February 2021). See especially 33 n. 37.
56 See Table 4 in ibid., 34. According to Cha's prices, calculated in grams of pure silver in 1923, cotton textile in Seoul was equivalent to 27 grams of silver while it was 17 in Tokyo, 18 in Dalian, 10 in Taipei, and 33 in Beijing.
57 See the character Ae-sook in the 1936 film, *Mimong*, as discussed by Taylor-Jones, 'Shopping, Sex, and Lies.'
58 Theodore Jun Yoo, 'Fashioning Identities: The Emergence of the Department Store and Consumer Culture in Colonial Korea,' *Yinmungwahak* 인문과학 人文科學 [*Journal of the Humanities*] 118 (2020): 263–296.

59 Yoo, *The Politics of Gender*; see esp. ch. 3: 'The Female Worker: From Home to the Factory' and chapter 4: 'Discoursing in Numbers: The Female Worker and the Politics of Gender.'
60 Timothy C. Lim, 'The Origins of Societal Power in South Korea: Understanding the Physical and Human Legacies of Japanese Colonialism,' *Modern Asian Studies*, 33, no. 3 (1999): 603–633; esp. 613, www.jstor.org/stable/313078 (accessed 4 February 2021).
61 See Yeon Shim Chung, '"Vernacular Modernism" in Modern Korea: Lee Quede's Hyangtosaek,' in in Pyun and Woo, eds, *Interpreting Modernism*, pp. 79–84.
62 One can compare Kim's painting with the department store scene in the aforementioned 1936 Korean film, *Sweet Dream*. The main character and the department store salesperson wear modernized *hanbok* while ready-to-wear children's, women's, and men's clothes in all colors and patterns are on display.
63 Janice C. H. Kim, 'The Pacific War and Working Women,' *Signs*, 33, no. 1 (2007): 81–103; esp. 90.
64 For this aspect, see essays by Youngna Kim, In-hye Kim, and Younjung Oh, in, Pyun and Woo, eds, *Interpreting Modernism*.
65 Byeongtaek 권병택, 'Bangjik' 방직 紡織, *Encyclopedia of Korean Culture*.
66 Another paper, on gendered textile consumption and gendered labor practices in textile manufacturing facilities after 1945 in Korea, was 'Gendered Labour in Korean Textile Industry: Transition of Knowledge from Colonial Capitalism to Industrial Conglomerate.' It was presented at the panel entitled *Transforming Knowledge and Human Resources into Wealth and Power: Comparative Perspectives on Engineers, Merchants and Labour in East Asia, 1850–1945* at the 19th World Economic History Congress (WEHC), Campus Condorset, Paris, 25–29 July 2022 (organizers: Hailian Chen and Naofumi Nakamura; chair: Weipin Tsai). It is being edited for the *Journal of the Royal Asiatic Society*'s special volume for 2025 or so.

Bibliography

Byeongtaek, Kwon 권병택. 'Bangjik' 방직 紡織. *Encyclopedia of Korean Culture* [Hanguk minjok munhwa daebaekgwa sajeon 한국민족문화대백과사전]. Seongnam: Academy of Korean Studies, 1995). http://encykorea.aks.ac.kr/Contents/Item/E0021794 (accessed 4 February 2021).

Cha, Myung Soo. 'Unskilled Wage Gaps within the Japanese Empire.' *Economic History Review* 68, no. 1 (2015): 23–47. www.jstor.org/stable/43910009 (accessed 4 February 2021).

Choi, Eun-soo 최은수. '1890nyeon–1960nyeondae yeoja jeogori gamjeong' 1890년–1960년대 여자 저고리 감정 [Appraisal of female Jeogori from 1890 to 1960]. *Bokshik*, 복식 服飾 [International Journal of Costume and Fashion] 58, no. 5 (2008): 178–180.

Chun, Yongkeun. 'Displayed Modernity: Advertising and Commercial Art in Colonial Korea, 1920–1940.' PhD dissertation, Royal College of Art, 2020.

Chung, Yeon Shim. '"Vernacular Modernism" in Modern Korea: Lee Quede's Hyangtosaek.' In *Interpreting Modernism in Korean Art: Fluidity and Fragmentation*. Edited by Kyunghee Pyun and Jung-Ah Woo. New York: Routledge, 2021.

Clickman, Lawrence B. '"Make Lisle the Style": The Politics of Fashion in the Japanese Silk Boycott, 1937–1940.' *Journal of Social History* 38, no. 3 (2005): 573–608. www.jstor.org/stable/3790646 (accessed 7 February 2021).

Eckart, Carter J. *Offspring of Empire: The Koch'ang Kims and the Colonial Origins of Korean Capitalism, 1876–1945*. Seattle: University of Washington Press, 2017.

Encyclopedia of Korean Folk Culture. Seoul: National Folk Museum, 2001. https://folkency.nfm.go.kr/kr/topic/detail/7120 (accessed 4 February 2021).

Eun-jung, Kim 김은정. 'Geundaejeok pyusang-euroseo-eui yeoseong fashion yeongu: modeon geol (gaehwagi–1945nyeon)eul jungshim-euro' 근대적 표상으로서의 여성패션 연구: 모던 걸(개화기–1945 년)을 중심으로 [A study of women's fashion as a symbol of modernity: focusing on the modern girl from the enlightenment period to 1945]. *Ashia-yeoseong-yeongu* 아시아여성연구 [*Journal of Asian Women*] 43, no. 2 (2004): 331–359.

Gerth, Karl. *Consumer Culture and the Creation of the Nation*. Cambridge: Harvard University Press, 2003.

Gil-ja, Min 민길자. 'Mojik' 모직 毛織. *Encyclopedia of Korean Culture* [Hanguk minjok munhwa daebaekgwa sajeon 한국민족문화대백과사전]. Seongnam: Academy of Korean Studies, 1995. http://encykorea.aks.ac.kr/Contents/Item/E0018563 (accessed 4 February 2021).

Hyeon-gyu, Shin 신현규. 'Choecho ui miyong japji hyangheun gwa buin e yeonjaedoen miyong ganghwa e daehayeo' 최초의 미용잡지 '향혼'과 '부인'에 연재된 미용 강화에 대하여 [On the beauty enhancement in Korea's first beauty magazines *Hyang-heun* and *Buin*]. 근대서지 [*Modern Bibliography Review*], no. 4 (2011): 351–370.

Hye-young, Kwon 권혜영 and Yi Gyeong-ja 이경자. 'Hanguk yeoseong yangbok-eui byeoncheon-ei gwanhan yeongu: 1900nyeon–1945nyen-eul jungshimeuro' 한국여성 양복의 변천에 관한 연구: 1900 년–1945 년을 중심으로 [A study of transformation of Korean women's Western-style suits: from 1900 to 1945]. *Bokshik* 복식 服飾 [*Journal of the Korean Society of Costume*] 7 (1983): 21–37.

Je-wook, Gong 공제욱. 'Hanmal, iljeshigi Euibok-eui byeonhwa-wa saenghwal yangshik: Yangbok-eui doyibeul jungshimeuro 한말, 일제시기 의복의 변화와 생활 양식: 양복의 도입을 중심으로 [Changes in clothing trends in the last period of the Chosôn dynasty and Japanese colonial period: the Westernization of Korean clothing culture]. *Saheowa yeoksa* 사회와 역사 [*Society and History*] 122 (2019): 117–158.

Jong-min, Park 박종민 and Kwak Eun-kyung 곽은경. 'Shinmun gwanggo-nae yeoseong-eui teukjing-gwa yeokwal: 1920nyeonbuteo 2005nyeon ggaji Chosun Ilbo, Dong-A Ilbo gwang-go bunseok' 신문광고 내 여성의 특징과 역할: 1920년부터 2005 년까지 조선일보, 동아일보 광고 분석 [Characteristics and function of women in newspaper advertisements: an analysis of Chosun Ilbo and Dong-A Ilbo advertisements from 1920 to 2005]. *Gwanggo yeongu* 광고연구 [*Advertising Research*] 77 (2007): 59–93.

Joo, Kyeongmi. 'Gendered Differences in Modern Korea toward Western Luxuries.' In *Fashion, Identity, and Power in Modern Asia*. Edited by Kyunghee Pyun and Aida Yuen Wong. New York: Palgrave Macmillan, 2018.

Jun Yoo, Theodore. 'Fashioning Identities: The Emergence of the Department Store and Consumer Culture in Colonial Korea.' *Yinmungwahak* 인문과학 人文科學 [*Journal of the Humanities*] 118 (2020): 263–296.

Kim, Janice C. H. 'The Pacific War and Working Women.' *Signs* 33, no. 1 (2007): 81–103.

Kimura, Mitsuhiko. 'The Economics of Japanese Imperialism in Korea, 1910–1939.' *Economic History Review* New Series 48, no. 3 (1995): 555–574.

Kreis, Reinhild. 'Make or Buy? Modes of Provision and the Moral Economy of Households in Postwar Germany.' *Geschichte Und Gesellschaft. Sonderheft* 26 (2019): 187–212. www.jstor.org/stable/26632298 (accessed 4 February 2021).

Kyoung-Yeon, Moon 문경연. '1920 nyeondae choban Hyeon Cheol ui yeongeungnon gwa geundaejeok gihoek' 1920 년대 초반 현철의 연극론과 근대적 기획 [Hyeon Chul's drama theory and modern project in the early 1920s]. *Han'guk yeongeukak* 한국연극학 [*Journal of the Korean Theatre Studies Association*] no. 25 (2005): 5–38.

Kyungmee, Lee 이경미. 'Daehanjeguk-gi Gojong hwangje, Sunjong hwangje, Sunheonhwang-gwibi sajin-eui yangbok' 대한제국기 고종황제, 순종황제, 순헌황귀비 사진의 양복 [Western-style attire in photographs of Emperor Gojong, Emperor Sunjong, and Imperial Consort Sunheon during the Korean Empire]. *Hanguk euiryuhakoe haksuldaehoenonmunjip* 한국의류학회 학술대회논문집 [*Proceedings of the Korean Society of Clothing and Textiles*] (2009): 57–59.

Lee, Kyungmee. 'Dress Policy and Western-Style Court Attire in Modern Korea.' In *Fashion, Identity, and Power in Modern Asia*. Edited by Kyunghee Pyun and Aida Yuen Wong. New York: Palgrave Macmillan, 2018.

Lim, Timothy C. 'The Origins of Societal Power in South Korea: Understanding the Physical and Human Legacies of Japanese Colonialism.' *Modern Asian Studies* 33, no. 3 (1999): 603–633. www.jstor.org/stable/313078 (accessed 4 February 2021).

Ma, Debin. 'The Modern Silk Road: The Global Raw-Silk Market, 1850–1930.' *Journal of Economic History* 56, no. 2 (1996): 330–355. www.jstor.org/stable/2123969 (accessed 7 February 2021).

Martin, Ann Smart. 'Makers, Buyers and Users – Consumerism as a Material Culture Framework.' *Winterthur Portfolio* 28, no. 2/3 (1993): 141–157.

McNamara, Dennis. 'The Keishō and the Korean Business Elite.' *Journal of Asian Studies* 48, no. 2 (1989): 310–323.

Mills, Mary Beth. 'Gender and Inequality in the Global Labour Force.' *Annual Review of Anthropology* 32 (2003): 41–62. www.jstor.org/stable/25064820 (accessed 4 February 2021).

Mun-jae, Maeng 맹문재. '1930nyeondae yeoja godeunghaksaengdeul-eui hakgyo saenghwal gochal' 1930 년대 여자고등학생들의 학교생활 고찰 [A study of school life of female high school students in the 1930s]. *Hangukhak-yeongu* 한국학연구 [*Journal of Korean Studies*] 29 (2008): 31–56.

National Folk Museum. *A Centennial Anniversary of Tailor History-Chongro Tailor's* [Baengnyeon-eui taeileo: Jongro yangbokjeom]. Seoul: National Folk Museum, 2014.

North, Susan. 'John Redfern and Sons, 1847 to 1892.' *Costume* 42 (2008): 145–168.

Oh, Younjung. 'Shopping for Art: The New Middle Class' Art Consumption in Modern Japanese Department Stores.' *Journal of Design History* 27, no. 4 (2014): 351–369.

Pyun, Kyunghee. 'Body Autonomy and Miniskirt Controversy in South Korea.' *Berg Encyclopedia of World Dress and Fashion*. Berg Fashion Library edited by Joanna Eicher (digital database). Oxford: Berg Publishers/Bloomsbury, 2021.

Pyun, Kyunghee. 'Hybrid Dandyism: European Woollen Fabric in East Asia.' In *Fashion, Identity, and Power in Modern Asia*. Edited by Kyunghee Pyun and Aida Yuen Wong. New York: Palgrave Macmillan, 2018.

Pyun, Kyunghee. 'Transformation of Monastic Habits: Student Uniforms for Christian Schools in East Asia.' *Journal of Religion and the Arts* 24, no. 4 [Special Issue: Faith/Fashion/Forward: Dress and the Sacred] (2020): 622–625.

Reynolds, Nancy Y. 'National Socks and the "Nylon Woman": Materiality, Gender, and Nationalism in Textile Marketing in Semicolonial Egypt, 1930–56.' *International Journal of Middle East Studies* 43, no. 1 (2011): 49–74. www.jstor.org/stable/23017342 (accessed 7 February 2021).

Saxonhouse, Gary R. and Gavin Wright. 'National Leadership and Competing Technological Paradigms: The Globalization of Cotton Spinning, 1878–1933.' *Journal of Economic History* 70, no. 3 (2010): 535–566. www.jstor.org/stable/40836579 (accessed 4 February 2021).

Seo, Yuri. 'Magazine Covers and Colonial Modernity: Politics of the Korean Face.' In *Interpreting Modernism in Korean Art: Fluidity and Fragmentation*. Edited by Kyunghee Pyun and Jung-Ah Woo. New York: Routledge, 2021.

Silberstein, Rachel. 'Fashioning the Foreign: Using British Woolens in Nineteenth-Century China.' In *Fashion, Identity, and Power in Modern Asia*. Edited by Kyunghee Pyun and Aida Yuen Wong. New York: Palgrave Macmillan, 2018.

Soon-Young, Kim 김순영. 'Hanguk geundae yangbokjeom-eui panmae mulpum-gwa saengsan-mit panmae juche' 한국 근대 양복점의 판매 물품과 생산 및 판매 주체 [Production, sales, and salespeople of merchandise at Korean modern tailors]. *Bokshik* 복식 服飾 [*Journal of the Korean Society of Costume*] 67, no. 5 (2017): 89–107.

Suyun, Ryu 류수연. 'Hyeon Huiun ui hwajang damnon' 현희운의 화장 담론 [Hyeon Hui-un's discourse of makeup]. *Eomun yeongu* 어문 연구 [*Society for Korean Language and Literary Research*] 43, no. 1 (2015): 201–223.

Taylor, Lou. 'Wool Cloth and Gender: The Use of Woollen Clothing in Women's Dress in Britain, 1865–85.' In *Defining Dress: Dress as Object, Meaning and Identity*. Edited by A. de la Haye and E. Wilson. Manchester: Manchester University Press, 1999.

Taylor-Jones, Kate E. 'Shopping, Sex, and Lies: *Mimong/Sweet Dreams* (1936) and the Disruptive Process of Colonial Girlhood.' *Journal of Japanese and Korean Cinema* 10, no. 2 (2018): 98–114.

Trivedi, Lisa. *Clothing Gandhi's Nation: Homespun and Modern India*. Bloomington: Indiana University Press, 2007.

West, Emily M. 'Labour and the Literary Technologies of Mechanization in the British Cotton Industry.' *Journal for Early Modern Cultural Studies* 17, no. 4 (2017): 49–74.

Yoo, Theodore Jun. *The Politics of Gender in Colonial Korea: Education, Labour and Health, 1910–1945*. Berkeley: University of California Press, 2008.

Yu-kyung, Lee 이유경 and Kim Jin-gu 김진구. 'Woorinara yangbok suyong gwa-jeong-eui bokshik byeoncheon-ei daehan yeongu: Munhwajeonpa yiron-eul jungshimeuro' 우리나라 양복수용 과정의 복식변천에 대한 연구: 문화전파 이론을 중심으로 [A study of changing fashion styles during the introduction of Western-style attire: focusing on the diffusion theory of culture]. *Bokshik* 복식 服飾 [*Journal of the Korean Society of Costume*] 26 (1995): 123–143.

Zakim, Michael. *Ready-Made Democracy: A History of Men's Dress in the American Republic, 1760–1860*. Chicago and London: University of Chicago Press, 2003.

Zakim, Michael. 'Sartorial Ideologies: From Homespun to Ready-Made.' *American Historical Review* 106, no. 5 (2001): 1553–1586.

3

Gendered blue: women's jeans in postwar Taiwan

Ying-chen Peng

The herstory of jeans

Jeans, the five-pocket trousers made from durable denim fabric, are a staple in wardrobes around the globe. After being patented by Levi Strauss & Company in 1873, this item of clothing swiftly made its name as the best companion for gold diggers and rangers in the American West. Although dismissed for decades as a blue-collar garment unsuitable for middle-class men and women, jeans were welcomed by American society during the Second World War for their practicality.[1] In the postwar era, blue jeans went through several identity transformations and began their global expansion as one facet of American cultural and military hegemony. Hollywood stars, particularly James Dean (1931–1955) and Marlon Brando (1924–2004), played an essential role. Their portrayals of rebellious, angry young men in blue jeans reflected and further cemented a seminal part of the iconography of angry young men disappointed with the world they lived in – a world busy with regional conflicts but lacking in opportunities.[2] Such association between jeans and discontent sparked the popularity of jeans in the counterculture in the following decade, but the hippies developed more sophisticated ways to make a statement with their jeans. Wearing personalized second-hand jeans was considered the most visible critique of consumerism and the mechanical repetition of middle-class life.[3] At this point, jeans acquired a new symbolism as a critique of middle-class hypocrisy and rage against the machine. After the 1980s, the dominance of jeans was challenged by other fashion trends, and expensive designer jeans eroded the garment's rebellious cachet. Even though jeans are no longer in the fashion spotlight, a T-shirt, a denim jacket, and a pair of jeans have become firmly imprinted in the popular perception as the uniform of young men discontented with society.[4] As such, masculinity has been woven into this garment, and with its widening popularity a pair of blue jeans is now the icon of 'American masculinity' in the global context.

As for the development of women's jeans, however, the story is more complex. On the one hand, female agency in the herstory of jeans is often overshadowed by the masculine nature of denim fabric. In her seminal historical analysis of denim in fashion, Emma McClendon astutely points out that the conventional characterization of this fabric (and, by extension, of blue jeans) as 'menswear' ignores the contributions by women to the design as well as the production of jeans.[5] On the other hand, the herstory of jeans largely mirrors the patriarchal control of women's familial and social roles and the constant objectification of the female body. Indeed, images of the patriotic, independent Rosie the Riveter wearing jeans or denim jumpsuits were popularized by mass media when the US government mobilized women to fill the labor market during the Second World War, but this icon soon gave way to model housewives when most women were discharged from their professional positions to make room for the returning veterans.

Meanwhile, women's jeans were incorporated into the accoutrement of sexy, passive female companions to male stars that Hollywood had created to promote the fixed gendered stereotypes. Although hippies, student activists, and feminists produced a contemporary female equivalent to men's jeans that advocated for the liberation of women's bodies and minds in the 1960s and 1970s, their efforts were strategically offset by advertisements proffering a different message. Brook Shields's infamous and oft-cited line in a 1980 television commercial – 'You wanna know what comes between me and my Calvins? Nothing' – exemplifies the trend of tying tightly fitted jeans to sex.[6] While it reflected the enlightened awareness of women's subjectivity in their body and desire, this notion was reduced to a body fetish by consumerism.

When jeans fever rode the tide of US economic and cultural expansion across the Pacific Ocean, these pre-set stereotypes of masculinity and femininity were packaged together. In recent years, scholars have moved beyond the conventional interpretation of the global success of jeans that equates jeans with the American dream, exemplified in the anthology *Global Denim* (2010). As its editors state, 'jeans are a quintessential example of material culture [and] transcend any simple opposition of subjects and objects.'[7] New scholarship has excavated unique local histories of this garment that negate universalism and provide further meaning and depth to the parochial encounter and vice versa.[8] Nonetheless, most attention has been paid to the geographical regions that have a long association with the Anglo-American world. Moreover, the gendered dimension of jeans under the umbrella of 'global denim' remains a topic awaiting further investigation.[9] Do blue jeans wield the same currency for women as an icon of modernity, independence, and freedom when they enter the daily life of East Asian societies, where the dominant Confucian patriarchy defines female virtue as a domestic attachment to men? How do local designs of women's jeans reflect the adaptation, appropriation, and even rejection of the Western feminist discourse in local societies?

The herstory of women's jeans in postwar Taiwan stands out as a compelling story about how this garment is emblematic of local societal change. While the political identity of the island has shifted multiple times (from a province of Qing China to a Japanese colony in 1895, and then to a province and the main territory of the Republic of China in 1945 and 1949, respectively), Neo-Confucianism – the Chinese philosophy that evolved into various local versions across East Asia beginning in the eleventh century – remains the backbone of Taiwanese society. In its early years, the ruling Nationalist government enjoyed an intertwined relationship with the US that was vividly reflected in the political, economic, and cultural milieus. But, after its defeat in the civil war against the communists and its retreat from the mainland to Taiwan, the alliance with the US gradually eroded. The US began phasing out its economic support of Taiwan in the 1960s, but it was the normalization of diplomatic relations with the People's Republic of China in 1979 that eventually led to the termination of formal ties with the Republic of China in Taiwan. On the cultural front, American popular culture and modernist literature, art, and philosophy continued to be introduced through Hollywood movies and activities hosted by the local office of the United States Information Service, offering a breath of fresh air to a society that was largely restricted by government surveillance and censorship. In the 1970s, after the relationship between the two countries had broken down, Taiwanese intellectuals relinquished their formerly receptive stance and began to recognize and even promote the importance of local, that is, Taiwanese, identity.

Because blue jeans are a commodity that originated in the US, they serve as an ideal case study of the *glocal* – the internalization that comes after globalization. But the popularity and ordinariness of jeans make them unlikely subjects for scholarly inquiry. Experts in fashion history are keener to trace the history of designer fashions and the textile industry than that of ordinary ready-to-wear garments. For example, Ye Li-cheng's *History of Costume in Taiwan* (2014), the most comprehensive research on this subject, provides a detailed chronology of costume and fashion evolution, but jeans are never explicitly discussed.[10] Although they did not spark the interest of fashion scholars, jeans caught the attention of those studying gender issues because of their association with queers and lesbians in early postwar Taiwanese cities.[11] Discussions about jeans also appear in personal memories. The novelist Chang Bei-hai's essay 'The Great Jeans, the Amazing Levi's' is by far the most detailed description outlining the early history of jeans in Taiwan.[12] Taking the existing scholarship as a starting point of this chapter, I utilize primary sources, including newspaper reports, magazine articles, and films, to articulate the herstory of jeans in Taiwan from the 1950s to the early 1980s. The changing designs and production of jeans and the public discourse on women's jeans are scrutinized to contextualize how this imported garment was woven into the fabric of gender and identity in Taiwanese society. As I will show, jeans empowered Taiwanese women to pursue subjectivity and active participation in the public sphere, but these ends were achieved not through wholesale stylistic adoption but rather through nuanced adaptation.

Dangerous trousers

Jeans made their first appearance in Taiwan along with the US marines in the early 1950s. The social atmosphere at the time was tense; anything foreign was viewed with suspicion, an outcome of the conflict between local Taiwanese and the army from the mainland, which resulted in the tragic incident of 28 February 1947, when nearly thirty thousand people were killed.[13] Before the ripples had quieted down an even more devastating event occurred: the Nationalists lost the civil war to the communists and retreated to Taiwan in 1949. Anxious to assert its superiority over local elites and to solidify its authority on the island, the government took strict control over the circulation of information, capital, and commodities. Off-duty American marines and sailors who wore blue jeans aroused the curiosity of young people in Dadaocheng, the most prosperous neighborhood near the harbor in Taipei. Since only those with resources could get a taste of imports, blue jeans soon became a symbol of affluence and class distinction. These young men and women were also notorious troublemakers who were frequently caught by the police but quickly released thanks to their well-connected families. Among them, young women in jeans especially caused a social spectacle because they violated martial law and the moral expectations for women in Taiwanese society.

It had long been considered inappropriate and boundary transgressing for a woman to wear trousers in public. Although Han Chinese women had traditionally worn trousers under a long robe, a standard set before the Japanese colonization in 1895, these garments were gradually replaced by the *qipao*, a close-fitting, high-collared one-piece dress that took inspiration from traditional Han Chinese and Manchu costumes and flourished in urban Taiwan after the 1920s. Towards the end of the Second World War, when the Japanese occupation government forged the Japanization (*kōminka*) policy, which required all colonial subjects to adopt the Japanese language and dress, *kimono* became the proper wear for women.

Rapid urbanization and industrialization during the colonial period enabled women to pursue new vocations, such as office assistant and shopkeeper, and to gain financial independence. Yet these jobs were not labor intensive enough to allow women employees to wear trousers.

After the Nationalist government took power, women who wore trousers in public were often interrogated by the police for their 'improper' clothes.[14] The queer appearance of women gang members, with their short hair, printed shirts, and trousers, became such a spectacle that a photograph of one of them was published in a newspaper. Smoking before the camera, her casual demeanor poses an exciting contrast to the headline, which claimed the woman 'acknowledged her improper behavior' (Figure 3.1).[15] Within such a social atmosphere, blue jeans were doubly suspicious in the eyes of conservatives: they were not just trousers, they were *foreign* trousers. Wanting a pair of jeans could evolve into a crisis for a young woman and her family: a twenty-one-year-old woman committed suicide after her mother accused her of acting like a gang member and punished her for buying a pair of jeans.[16] But the mother's accusation was not completely unfounded, as the members of the most infamous girl gang, 'Thirteen Gals,' were indeed the earliest street models of jeans.[17]

If young gang members triggered the connection between jeans and fallen morality in the public imagination, Hollywood movies introduced the link between jeans and rebellion to the conservative Taiwanese society as a whole. American movies were exempt from government restrictions thanks to the treaty signed between the two countries in 1946 that granted US merchants business advantages. Hollywood's dominance was overwhelming: of the 444 foreign movies permitted to be shown in 1954, 349 were from the US. Moreover, unlike other foreign imports, which were forced to wait two to three years to clear customs, these movies passed quickly enough to allow for local release less than a year after their US premieres.[18] James Dean's *Rebel Without a Cause* set a milestone for the popularity of jeans in 1955, and within a year young Taiwanese people got to see the movie in theaters. The newspaper advertisement makes a specific connection to the infamous 'Thirteen Young Gangsters,' the male equivalent to the aforementioned 'Thirteen Gals,' to localize the plot, and the film indeed became a decisive factor in the linking of jeans with rebellious youths.[19] The movie was so popular that it was released for a second time later that year.

At the same time, Marilyn Monroe's role as the dance hall singer Kay in *River of No Return* (1954) instilled blue jeans with sweetness and vulnerability (Figure 3.2). Wearing this garment on a dangerous journey in the Wild West, the heroine embodies qualities opposite to her male companions. She was motherly, passive, and sexually attractive. The commercial success of these Hollywood movies contributed to the jeans frenzy in Taiwan and possibly encouraged a changed public perception of women's jeans, as reflected in reportages to be discussed shortly. Young men and women, whose main sources of fashion were films, movie magazines from Hong Kong, and limited Japanese- and English-language magazines, were quickly drawn to buying jeans, most of which were imported. According to

Women's jeans in postwar Taiwan   77

3.1 Photograph of Cai Yueying published in *Union Times*, 22 May 1963

one 1958 newspaper report, there were roughly fifty thousand young people in Taiwan who wore jeans. The report was also the first to outline the origin of jeans and to call for a distinction between 'cowboy clothes' and jeans. It acknowledged that jeans were a fashionable item for girls in the US and even ended by quoting a certain American fashion expert, Mme Mary: 'Maybe one day [men and women] will wear jeans at their weddings.'[20]

Public condemnation of women's trousers, jeans included, gradually disappeared over the next decade for several reasons. The Nationalist government's strategy of developing the textile industry proved to be an economic boon: international fashion trends were embraced and local infrastructure was put in place to mass market ready-to-wear clothing such as jeans. The thriving industry offered further opportunities for women to participate in the labor market and acquire financial independence. These social and economic changes did much to remove the gender-transgressing stigma of women wearing trousers.

Interestingly, although the feminine quality of the jeans introduced by Monroe was in line with patriarchal expectations of women, the casualness and inklings of sexual desire that a woman in jeans might arouse in men, particularly amplified in the poster design in Figure 3.2, still conflicted with Taiwan's social conservatism. Women from 'decent' families were always encouraged to wear a dress. In the leading women's journal

3.2 Poster for *River of No Return*, 1954

Taiwan Women's Monthly (*Taiwan funü yuekan*), the fashion column would introduce occasions suitable for wearing trousers. For example, in one 1967 entry the editor recommends wearing a striped sleeveless top and light-colored nylon trousers for spring outings (Figure 3.3).[21] Like other journals in postwar Taiwan, this one was available only by subscription and thus had a limited readership, mainly middle-class housewives and mothers who had spare time and money to buy and read magazines. Because the fashion column often provided tailoring instructions to help readers make proper clothes for themselves and their children, jeans, which existed primarily as imported, ready-to-wear items, were beyond the range of discussion. Indeed, jeans were first mentioned in *Taiwan Women's Monthly* in the January 1977 issue, at a time when the local ready-to-wear market had reached maturity; the focus of the article was not the style of jeans but how to identify quality.[22] The contrast between the widespread popularity of jeans among young people and their absence in the women's journal certainly testifies to the class distinction that blue jeans embodied. They remained dangerous and improper for middle-class women throughout the 1960s and early 1970s.

3.3 Illustration of the fashion column in *Taiwan Women's Journal*, no. 130 (April 1967), p. 18

Domesticated fashion

The blue wave of jeans wearing showed no sign of ebbing in the next decade. Jeans' popularity widened from gang members and young fashionistas to college students seeking to demonstrate their distrust of the establishment and quest for intellectual freedom – stances similar to those of their Western counterparts. The expanded circle of wearers gave rise to two types of women's jeans in Taiwan. At one end of the spectrum were jeans embroidered with floral patterns or traditional Chinese motifs that effectively domesticated the subversive or sexual undertones. At the other end, the unadorned, washed-out wide-leg versions preserved the spirit of resistance.

The ongoing restrictions on print media in Taiwan made locally published fashion magazines a latecomer to the game. It was not until 1975 and 1978, respectively, that the first of these – *Fashion Magazine* (*Liuxing zazhi*) and *Fashion 'n Fashions* (*Wang Rongsheng shizhuang*) – published their inaugural issues. What filled the void until their appearance was a new type of romance film, particularly those adapted from the works of novelist Chiung Yao. Unlike earlier movies, which essentially served as government propaganda, these works always centered around the love affairs of middle-class young people. The romantic stories, catchy melodies, and beautiful screen idols constituted the formula for box office success. The stars of these films also became the most persuasive models for the audience to find inspiration for the latest fashions.

The prolific use of denim in *A Different Love* (1976), one of the popular Chiung Yao movies, offers direct visual evidence of the gendered codification of this fabric in Taiwanese fashion. The story portrays a classic love triangle: a young, attractive pink-collar employee, Song Xiaoyu (played by Brigitte Lin), is pursued by her banker boss, but she has fallen in love with the gardener (played by Charlie Chin), whom the banker's father has hired to experiment with a new breed of rose. In his role, Chin almost always dons a navy-blue Levi's jacket adorned with a signature red flag and a pair of blue jeans to emphasize his image as a young, idealistic college graduate working outdoors and to contrast with his rival. (The young banker is never shown in jeans.) Brigitte Lin, on the other hand, models at least four different after-work outfits that include denim: a pair of dark blue jeans, a pair of wide-leg patchwork trousers in different shades of denim (Figure 3.4), a similarly collaged vest plus indigo-dye patchwork, and another vest with colorful floral embroidery (Figure 3.5). Although such

3.4   Still of *A Different Love*, 1976

3.5 Still of *A Different Love*, 1976

fashion trends followed styles that had been created earlier by American hippies, they signified very different local meanings to the Taiwanese.

Patchwork and embroidery were common techniques that hippies had used to personalize their second-hand jeans in order to manifest their opposition to materialistic middle-class values. The famous light wash was a feature of second-hand jeans. Yet in Taiwan these techniques took on a gendered aspect. In place of large, bold embroideries, small floral motifs were preferred and these were limited to women's wear exclusively. A report on street fashion best defines this new look: the combination of 'jeans from the West and soft, elegant embroidery from the East is … a cultural integration.'[23]

The emphasis on traditional elements was a local aesthetic choice in response to the changing political climate in Taiwan. The domino effect of losing the legitimacy of sovereignty in the international community prompted patriotic calls to boycott imported goods and launched the Domestic Movement in literature and art, which emphasized local identity rather than the latest foreign theories and trends. Experiments with traditional textile patterns and decoration, for example embroidery and indigo wax dye, were also undertaken and developed by the domestic ready-to-wear market. The Taiwanese textile industry, which had been export based, was hampered by the global economic decline following the two oil crises in the 1970s. Factories that had previously taken foreign orders now turned to the domestic market and modified the fit and design of their products to satisfy the needs and preferences of local customers.[24] All these factors together created the jeans styles featured in *A Different Love*.

More critically, Brigitte Lin's jeans reflected the ongoing debate about the morality of women's jeans. Although trousers were no longer considered antithetical to traditional social values, the blue-collar origin of jeans and their rebellious undertones always bothered conservatives. An insignificant incident in Japan that was widely covered by Taiwanese newspapers exemplifies such anxiety. In its 27 May 1977 issue, the *Union Times* reported on a dispute between a fifty-six-year-old American professor of English literature at the University of Osaka and a twenty-one-year-old female student. The professor had dismissed the woman from his class for wearing jeans. A subsequent meeting between the American and a group of students only yielded sharply differing views on the symbolism of women's jeans. The students asserted that jeans were 'an outfit that liberates women from domestic roles rather than a blue-collar uniform'; the professor admonished that women in college 'should work hard to make themselves the best of women rather than dressing like a second-class man.'[25] The incident ended with the professor's departure from the university, indicating the students' victory over the outdated, conservative stance.[26] A woman columnist for the *China Times* responded to this report in an essentialist piece claiming that women should move men with their sweet smiles and tenderness – in other words, the femininity within them. She opined that women's jeans could be appropriate, as long as they appeared 'feminine,' such as those decorated with floral embroidery.[27] The report cited above on street fashion also mentions how stylish young female consumers welcomed elegant light blue jeans for similar reasons.[28] This preference is another indicator of how women's jeans were shedding the original, masculine characteristics of denim: a fabric and identity that is strong and enduring.

Such discourse on the necessity of 'reforming' women's jeans to fit them back into the framework of traditional expectations of women also echoed the unique nature of the rising feminist movement in Taiwan.

Hsiu-lien Anette Lü, the originator of the campaign, was the first to publish a statement advocating for women's equal rights in education and the workplace. Distancing herself from the Western feminist discourse that criticized women's subjugation to family responsibilities, Lü initially watered down her rhetoric. The slogan 'wielding the spatula in your left hand and writing with the pen in your right hand' acted as a compromise and cushion to ensure the general acceptance of her movement to improve women's social standing.[29] Yet, as the historian Doris Chang has pointed out, Lü's assertion that traditional feminine qualities were strengths that could play a critical role in emancipation essentially implied that women's liberation had to rely on men's approval.[30] It is worth noticing how precisely the new design of women's denim fits into Lü's discourse. Indeed, Brigitte Lin's character in *A Different Love* is a vernacular manifestation of Lü's theory. Xiaoyu is a hardworking young woman who pursues love for its own sake rather than for financial security. She is also a filial daughter who supports her father's business and even risks her love by asking for a loan from her boyfriend's rival. In other words, Xiaoyu, and the embroidered denim she wears, is the manifestation of urban women's nuanced social standing between total liberation and conservative Confucianism.

Coda: from sweetness to sassiness

In the twenty years after their first appearance in Taiwan, the annual sales of jeans nearly tripled, to 140,000 units.[31] Although the fervent interest in jeans in Taiwan's domestic market gradually quieted in the early 1980s, women's jeans saw another critical transition that echoed their wearers' changing identity in the public sphere. As noted above, fashion information before the 1980s did not have a dedicated channel for circulation. While movies offered a convenient platform to showcase the latest trends, they left little room for a deeper discussion about fashion and its impact on daily life. In this regard, magazines created a dynamic space to serve such a purpose. My analysis of *Taiwan Women's Monthly* above demonstrated how fashion was discussed in the context of the social expectations of women, and its new competitors in the late 1970s and early 1980s followed in those same footsteps. However, the publications now embraced a more diverse population of women. In these new magazines, we find women's jeans that are both sexy and professional, and these are the new faces of women in urban Taiwan as well.

Launched in May 1978, *Fashion 'n Fashions* was one of the earliest fashion magazines entirely produced and published domestically. Its founder, Eliza Wang, was the first Taiwanese model who made her name in the New York fashion scene in early 1970s.[32] Wang defined her magazine not only as a window into the latest international fashion trends, but more importantly as a platform for career women to explore various aspects of their professional lives – an area previously overlooked in the mass media. In other words, the editorial board followed the format of prominent international fashion magazines such as *Cosmopolitan* and *Elle* and became a sensation in the publishing industry. At its height, the magazine even collaborated with textile tycoons and designers to host fashion shows. Though it lasted for only seven years, *Fashion 'n Fashions* paved the way for the local editions of famous-name international magazines.[33]

Jeans did not feature frequently in *Fashion 'n Fashions*'s content or advertising as the magazine mainly centered on designer apparel. But whenever jeans made an appearance, they were more provocative than those the columnists and movie stars of the 1970s had advocated. For instance, in a three-page presentation of jeans in different colors that introduced the garments as the 'symbol of youth,' the models displayed a new kind of youthfulness: a mixture of lightheartedness and sex appeal (Figure 3.6). Their relatively stiff body postures impliy the women's unfamiliarity with this new way of posing. Nevertheless, they proudly show off their curves and the labels on their back pockets for the camera while making suggestive facial expressions.[34] In a more explicit representation of the link between sexiness and jeans, a local fashion brand, O'Daniel, put out an advertisement featuring a half-naked female model looking provocatively into the camera while embracing a man in jeans.[35] Not surprisingly, the model is a white, blond woman whose sheer 'foreignness' reinforces the company's self-branding as a 'pseudo' foreign designer label in order to stand out from its domestic competitors. The choice of model also served to avoid censorship.

The distinct new identity of women's jeans can be found in O'Daniel's other advertisements. In one a woman in blue jeans, high heels, and a suit jacket stands confidently (Figure 3.7). She is the new career woman – no longer a mere pink-collar employee but a professional in charge. The acceptance of jeans as professional workwear was indeed on the rise. In a serial article introducing appropriate work apparel for career women, jeans are singled out as a standard for journalists, editors, and professionals in creative fields such as the entertainment industry.[36] The strong variety of professions mentioned here also signifies women's strengthening prospects in more advanced career fields. If the previous decades had witnessed women's gradually increasing presence in low-end vocations, the new era saw a surge in women college degree holders eligible to compete in more highly paid and competitive professions, and they confidently replaced the sweet characteristics of women's jeans with sassiness.

The dominance of jeans in the ready-to-wear industry ended when jeans gradually changed from blue to a rainbow of colors in early 1980s Taiwan. The era's economic prosperity created a diverse market that offered consumers a greater variety of clothes to choose from. Denim was challenged by corduroy, and young people were not as attached to

3.6 Photograph of jeans featured in *Fashion n' Fashion*, no. 21, December 1980, p. 35

3.7 O'Daniel's advertisement in *Fashion n' Fashion*, no. 23, February 1981, p. 13

jeans as in the previous decades.[37] Despite losing their earlier symbolism to become a staple in everyone's wardrobe, jeans manifested the critical transition of women's roles in the public sphere in postwar Taiwan. This chapter has articulated the local herstory of jeans, which belies the general assumption that jeans became popular in the world because of the American spirit they embodied. In reality, this one garment type could be tweaked or adapted to suit local needs. In other words, jeans may be gendered blue, but each local history is a unique wash.

Notes

1 Sandra Curtis Comstock has shown that blue jeans gained popularity among middle-class consumers during the Great Depression due to the shared sense of suffering that they felt while wearing them. Sandra Curtis Comstock, 'The Making of an American Icon: The Transformation of Blue Jeans during the Great Depression,' in Daniel Miller and Sophie Woodward, eds, *Global Denim* (Oxford and New York: Berg, 2011), pp. 35–36.
2 James Sullivan, *Jeans: A Cultural History of an American Icon* (New York: Gotham Books, 2006), pp. 92–93.
3 Ironically, their anti-materialism stance would eventually be co-opted by the fashion industry. In their advertisements, jeans makers would often use photographs showing myriads of jeans wearers at the Woodstock Art and Music Fair in 1969. Emma McClendon, *Denim: Fashion's Frontier* (New York: Fashion Institute of Technology, 2016), p. 24.
4 Levi Strauss & Company's Vintage Clothing campaigns have emphasized this spirit in recent years: they have showcased 1957, when the space race began (www.levi.com/US/en_US/blog/article/levis-vintage-clothing-spring-summer-19/); 1960s Greenwich Village (www.tmrwmagazine.com/features/style/levis-vintage-clothing-folk-city); and 1975, the year the San Francisco Museum of Art was founded (www.levi.com/US/en_US/blog/article/soapbox-derby-of-75/).
5 McClendon, *Denim*, pp. 15–16.
6 Although the ad was quickly banned by ABC and CBS in New York soon after its release, it made the New York-based designer Calvin Klein's first high-fashion denim line a huge success and remains a classic in the history of jeans.
7 Daniel Miller and Sophie Woodward, eds, *Global Denim* (Oxford and New York: Berg, 2011), p. 19.
8 Ibid., p. 12. Note that the editors subsequently published another book that incorporated the fruit of *Global Denim* into a theoretical monograph on the ordinary characteristics of jeans. See Daniel Miller and Sophie Woodward, *Blue Jeans: The Art of the Ordinary* (Berkeley: University of California Press, 2012). Another example of this kind of approach, focusing on local production that has transformed the meaning of jeans, is Leila Zaki Chakravarti, 'Material Worlds: Denim on the Globalized Shop Floor,' *Textile: The Journal of Cloth and Culture*, 9, no. 1 (2011): 62–74.
9 Sophie Woodward's chapter on jeans is one example of scholarship that looks at this garment from a gendered perspective. Sophie Woodward, 'Dressing Up and Dressing Down: Can You Wear Jeans?' in *Why Women Wear What They Wear* (Oxford and New York: Berg, 2007), pp. 135–151.
10 Ye Li-cheng, *Taiwan fuzhuang shi diancang erban* [History of costume in Taiwan, collectible second edition] (Taipei: Shangding, 2014).
11 Jeans are mentioned as a type of trouser in this scholarship. See Huang Meng-wen, 'Xizhuang yu xianghua: Zhanhou chuqi Taiwan "chuanku de" nüxing de shenying' [Suits and corsages: Taiwanese women in trousers during the early postwar

period],Master's thesis (Taipei National University of the Arts, 2018), pp. 30–32; and Eno Pei Jean Chen, '"Kuer" shengcun moshi: *Sheizai zhao mafan* he *Richang duihua* Zhong de kuer Shijian yu xiufu zhuanxiang' [Mrs. Trouser's modes of life: queer temporalities and reparative turns in *Troublers* and *Small Talk*], *Route: A Journal of Cultural Studies*, no. 31 (Fall 2020): 7–42, at 36.

12 Chang Bei-hai, 'Weida de niuzaiku, liaobuqi de Levi's' [The great jeans, the amazing Levi's], in *Meiguo: Bage gushi* [America: eight stories] (Shanghai: Shanghai renmin chubanshe, 2007), pp. 1–42.

13 According to the official report the number of dead ranges between eighteen thousand and twenty-eight thousand people. See Yu Yihui, *Taiwan yishi de duomianxiang: Bainian liang'an de minzu zhuyi* [The multifaceted Taiwanese identity: nationalism on both sides of the Taiwan Strait in the past century] (Taipei: Liming wenhua, 2001), p. 118.

14 In 1962 police detained and interrogated a handicapped woman for appearing in public with short hair, a red shirt, and black trousers. See 'Zhiti shangcan, bunan bunü: qizhuang zhaoyao guoshi, jingju miaoyu jieyi' [Handicapped, neither man nor woman: (a woman wore) a strange outfit in public and offered a funny explanation at the police station], *Union Times*, 5 June 1962.

15 'Banzuo naner yang, zucheng taimeibang, Cai Yueying shexian youdang, yi tancheng xingwei budang [Adopting a man's appearance and organizing a woman's gang: Cai Yueying is accused of loitering in public and acknowledges her misdeeds],' *Union Times*, 22 May 1963.

16 'Yao chuan niuzaiku, nülang ziyi wang' [Young woman commits suicide for desiring to wear jeans], *Union Times*, 12 January 1956.

17 Although news reports on these gang members do not indicate what kind of trousers they wore, the writer Zhang Beihai, who witnessed the rise of these gangs, specifies jeans in his personal history of jeans. See Chang, 'Weida de niuzaiku, pp. 2–4. It should be noted that jeans also played a role in coining the lesbian identity in modern Taiwanese society. While female companionship that bears lesbian undertones has a long history in China and Taiwan, the growing popularity of jeans coincided with the rise of gay bars and American-style restaurants during the 1960s Vietnam War and contributed to the conceptual and visual construction of tomboys. Their defeminized appearance included a pair of trousers or jeans, as exemplified in Figure 3.1. For the discussion of the construction of the 'T-*po*' lesbian community in Taiwan, see Antonia Chao, 'Global Metaphors and Local Strategies in the Construction of Taiwan's Lesbian Identities,' *Culture, Health and Sexuality*, 2, no.4 (October–December 2020): 397–399.

18 Liu Xiancheng, 'Meiguo jiqi dianyingye jieru Taiwan dianying shichang de lishi fenxi' [A historical analysis of the US film industry's intervention in the film market in Taiwan], *Film Appreciation Journal*, no. 130 (January–March 2007): 41–42.

19 The movie was initially banned but then released in June. For the advertisement that includes the phrase 'Thirteen Young Gangsters,' see *China Times*, 24 June 1956.

20 Jintang, 'Qingliang jijie hua "niuzaiku",' [Talk about jeans in this cool season], *Union Times*, 19 October 1958.

21 Shuyuan, 'Zhongchun ri de nilong xianzhi fushi' [Nylon knitwear for spring], *Taiwan funü yuekan*, April 1967, p. 18.

22 Cheng Liangxia, 'Xuangou chengyi you xuewen' [There is much to learn about choosing ready-to-wear clothes], *Taiwan funü yuekan*, January 1977, p. 16.

23 Zhang Baole, 'Chuanshang niuzaiku, yangyi huoli yu qing chun, bufen nan yu nü, jietou manshi niuzaiku' [Wearing jeans to show off your youth and energy: the street is filled with men and women in jeans], *China Times*, 28 September 1975.

24 Li-cheng, *Taiwan fuzhuang shi diancang erban*, pp. 172–180.

25 'Riben shaonü xin zuofeng: meiji jiaoshou laogudong, chuan niuzaiku shangke bei zhuchu, shesheng jian huitan buhuan ersan' [The new demeanor of Japanese girls

versus the old-fashioned] American professor: [A female student] wears jeans to school and is expelled; unpleasant meeting afterwards ends without resolution], *Union Times*, 27 May 1977.
26 'Rehuo de niuzaiku: xiaoyuan nei qi fengbo Meiji jiaoshou fener tingjiang' [The jeans are to blame: campus incident results in American professor's enraged cancellation of lectures], *Union News*, 22 June 1977.
27 Lai Liqiong, 'Niuzaiku fengbo' [The jeans incident], *China Times*, 25 June 1977.
28 Zhang, 'Chuanshang niuzaiku, yangyi huoli yu qing chun.'
29 The next phase of her discourse – abandoning the traditional dichotomy of male/public sphere versus female/domestic sphere and the negative stereotyping of the power struggle between the two sexes – was cut short in 1979 when Lü was charged with violent sedition and jailed for five years for her involvement in the Kaohsiung Incident, the Nationalist government's repression of pro-independence activists on the island.
30 Doris Chang, *Women's Movements in Twentieth-Century Taiwan* (Urbana: University of Illinois Press, 2009), pp. 91–93.
31 Song Naiyi, 'Niuzaiku pinpai baiyu zhong' [There are more than one hundred brands of jeans (on the market)], *China Times*, 9 December 1981.
32 Chang Wang, 'Strategic Analysis for Eliza Fashion School of Art,' Master's thesis (Simon Fraser University, 2009), pp. 4–5.
33 The first local edition of an international magazine was *Cosmopolitan*, which appeared in 1989. Before that there were other translated fashion magazines such as *Non-No* (a pirate of the Japanese *No-no*, which was geared towards teenage fashion), first issued in 1984. Fang-chih Irene Yang, 'International Women's Magazines in Taiwan,' in Catherine Farris, Anru Lee, and Murray Rubinstein, eds, *Women in the New Taiwan: Gender Roles and Gender Consciousness in a Changing Society* (Armonk: M. E. Sharp, 2004), pp. 127–128.
34 'Xiangzheng qingchun zhaoqi de niuzaiku zuhe' [Jeans combinations: the symbol of youth], *Fashion 'n Fashions*, December 1980, pp. 35–37.
35 See *Fashion 'n Fashions*, July 1981, p. 17.
36 'Yun xiang yishang hua xiang rong, di si zhang: wei zhiye er chuan' [Making clothes like beautiful clouds and makeup as refined as flowers, chapter 4: dress for your job], *Fashion 'n Fashions*, May/June 1982, p. 90.
37 'Niuzaire qie tuichao, dengxinrong ku dengchang' [Jeans lose shine as corduroy becomes popular], *China Times*, 30 January 1983.

Bibliography

'Banzuo naner yang, zucheng taimeibang, Cai yueying shexian youdang, yi tancheng xingwei budang [Adopting man's appearance and organizing a woman's gang: Cai Yueying is accused of wandering in public and acknowledged her wrong doings].' *Union Times*, 22 May 1963.

'Niuzaire qie tuichao, dengxinrong ku dengchang [Jeans lose shine while corduroy becomes popular].' *China Times*, 30 January 1983.

'Rehuo de niuzaiku: xiaoyuan nei qi fengbo: Meiji jiaoshou fener tingjiang [The jeans to blame: incident on campus resulted in the American professor's enraged cancellation of lectures].' *Union News*, 22 June 1977.

'Riben shaonü xin zuofeng: Meiji jiaoshou laogudong, chuan niuzaiku shangke bei zhuchu, shesheng jian huitan buhuan ersan [The new demeanor of Japanese girls versus the old antique American professor: [woman student] wearing jeans to school and is expelled; unpleasant meeting afterwards ends without resolution].' *Union Times*, 27 May 1977.

'Xiangzheng qingchun zhaoqi de niuzaiku zuhe [Jeans combinations – the symbol of youth].' *Fashion n' Fashion*, no. 21, December 1980.

'Yao chuan niuzaiku, nülang ziyi wang [A young woman committed suicide for desiring to wear jeans].' *Union Times*, 12 January 1956.

'Yun xiang yishang hua xiang rong, di si zhang: wei zhiye er chuan [Making clothes like beautiful clouds and makeup as refined as flowers – chapter four: dress for your job].' *Fashion n' Fashion*, no. 38, May/June 1982.

'Zhiti shangcan, bunan bunü: qizhuang zhaoyao guoshi, jingju miaoyu jieyi [Handicapped, neither man nor woman: [a woman wore] strange outfit in public and offered funny explanation in the police station].' *Union Times*, 5 June 1962.

Chakravarti, Leila Zaki. 'Material Worlds: Denim on the Globalized Shop Floor.' *Textile: The Journal of Cloth and Culture* 9, no.1 (2011): 62–74.

Chang, Bei-hai. 'Weida de jiuzaiku, liaobuqi de Levi's [The great jeans, the amazing Levi's].' *Meiguo: Bage gushi* [America: eight stories]. Shanghai: Shanghai renmein chubanshe, 2007.

Chang, Doris. *Women's Movements in Twentieth-Century Taiwan*. Urbana: University of Illinois Press, 2009.

Chao, Antonio. 'Global Metaphors and Local Strategies in the Construction of Taiwan's Lesbian Identities.' *Culture, Health & Sexuality* 2, no. 4 (October–December 2020): 377–390.

Chen, Eno Pei Jean. '"Kuer" shengcun moshi: Sheizai zhao mafan he Richang duihua Zhong de kuer Shijian yu xiufu zhuanxiang [Mrs. Pants' modes of life: queer temporalities and reparative turn in *Troublers* and *Small Talk*].' *Route: A Journal of Cultural Studies* no. 31 (Fall 2020): 7–42.

Cheng, Liangxia. 'Xuangou chengyi you xuewen [There is much to learn about choosing ready-to-wear clothes].' *Taiwan funü yuekan* no. 271 (January 1977): 15–48.

Huang, Meng-wen. 'Xizhuang yu xianghua: zhanhou chuqi Taiwan "chuanku de" nüxing de shenying [Suits and corsages: Taiwanese women in pants during the early post-war period].' MA thesis, Taipei National University of the Arts, 2018.

Jintang. 'Qingliang jijie hua "niuzaiku."' *Union Times*, 19 October 1958.

Lai Liqiong. 'Niuzaiku fengbo [The jeans incident].' *China Times*, 25 June 1977.

Levi. 'Campaigns.' *Off the Cuff*. www.levi.com/US/en_US/blog/category/campaigns (accessed 26 January 2022).

Liu, Xiancheng. 'Meiguo jiqi dianyingye jieru Taiwan dianying shichang de lishi fenxi [A historical analysis of the US film industry's intervention in the film market in Taiwan].' *Film Appreciation Journal* no. 130 (January–March 2007): 40–46.

McClendon, Emma. *Denim: Fashion's Frontier*. New York: Fashion Institute of Technology, 2016.

Miller, Daniel and Sophie Woodward, eds. *Global Denim*. Oxford and New York: Berg, 2011.

Shuyuan. 'Zhongchun ri de nilong xianzhi fushi [Nylon knitwears for the spring time].' *Taiwan funü yuekan* no. 130 (April 1967): 17–18.

Song, Naiyi. 'Niuzaiku pinpai baiyu zhong [There are more than one hundred brands of jeans (on the market)].' *China Times*, 9 December 1981.

Sullivan, James. *Jeans: A Cultural History of An American Icon*. New York: Gotham Books, 2006.

Woodward, Sophie. 'Dressing Up and Dressing Down: Can You Wear Jeans?' In *Why Women Wear What They Wear*. Oxford and New York: Berg, 2007.

Yang, Fang-chih Irene. 'International Women's Magazines in Taiwan.' In *Women in the New Taiwan: Gender Roles and Gender Consciousness in a Changing Society*. Edited by Catherine Farris, Anru Lee, and Murray Rubinstein. Armonk: M. E. Sharp, 2004.

Ye, Li-cheng. *Taiwan fuzhuang shi diancang erban* [History of costume in Taiwan, collectible second edition]. Taipei: Shangding, 2014.

Yu, Yihui. *Taiwan yishi de duomianxiang: bainian liang'an de minzu zhuyi* [The multifaceted Taiwanese identity: nationalism on both sides of the Taiwan Strait in the past century]. Taipei: Liming wenhua, 2001.

Zhang, Baole. 'Chuanshang niuzaiku, yangyi huoli yu qing chun, bufen nan yu nü, jietou manshi niuzaiku [Wearing jeans to show off your youth and energy: the street is filled with men and women in jeans].' *China Times*, 28 September 1975.

4

Bhutanese women and the performance of globalization

Emma Dick

Introduction

> Bhutanese women ... 'have a hard lot of it – Besides all this [agricultural work]. The Economy of the Family falls to their Share. They have to dress the victuals and feed the Swine ... not unfrequently one sees them with a Child at the Breast, staggering up a Hill with a heavy Load, or knocking Corn, a Labour scarcely less arduous.'[1]

Thus wrote George Bogle, a Glaswegian envoy from the East India Company. Bogle was sent by Warren Hastings, the first Governor-General of Bengal, to Tibet in 1774–1775 to try to establish favorable trading relations with the Qing dynasty in China. Bogle traveled through Bhutan to befriend the Panchen Lama, as a possible advocate to support British East India Company trading interests with Peking. Kate Teltscher has written a history of this journey, reconstructed through George Bogle's letters, journals, and documents. Teltscher reminds us that,

> Bogle's interest in the conditions of women was typical of eighteenth-century travel accounts; the way in which women were treated was considered a measure of society's level of civilisation. Bhutanese women appeared to Bogle to lead lives of unremitting toil, unsweetened by amusement or adornment; they engaged in hard labour and drank strong liquor, they mixed freely and washed infrequently. This lack of feminine refinement was, for Bogle, related to the Bhutanese neglect of rank: finer feelings grew out of a sense of superiority that was derived from class status. Although he enjoyed the formality of Bhutanese society, Bogle saw the unconstrained behaviour of the women as one of its flaws.[2]

Bogle's journey from Bengal through Bhutan to Tibet is a fascinating insight into the early centuries of globalization, how relationships developed between different political, economic, and geographic states and systems, and how the British East India Company, originally founded in the Elizabethan era, became one of the first proto-multinational trading companies, establishing colonial domination of the East by the West and consecrating the foundations of the capitalist political economy of the modern world, a system which is still being played out today in different ways. Bogle's account, as with all travelers' tales, provides us with an insight into inter-cultural semiology – how to read another culture through one's own cultural and temporal norms.

However, it is not meaningful to impose such a value system emerging from the eighteenth-century European Enlightenment onto Bhutan – a country which has never been colonized and has a culture that has independently evolved its own entirely different logic of enlightenment. In Buddhist terms, to be 'enlightened' means to have woken up and to understand the world, so that the mind and the body are not separated but are in perfect harmony with one another. Bhutan's experience of globalization has been driven by a different rate of development, of 'modernity', from Western Europe. Characters like George Bogle are so interesting as they allow us to appreciate the touch points at which these two world orders have met and interacted.

In this chapter I explore the gendered myths of globalization currently in circulation by examining the roles which Bhutanese women occupy in signifying and organizing meanings around modernity and how Bhutanese women have experienced modernity. This has been shaped in the twenty-first century by the competing and complementary forces of the Royal Government of Bhutan, contact with international development agencies, and the growth of digital technology in the kingdom as it is developing economically. I discuss the impact of national policies such as *driglam namzha*, a sumptuary dress code for conduct and etiquette, and Gross National Happiness (GNH), Bhutan's holistic measurement of development, on women's dress and identity, alongside discussion and analysis of Her Majesty the Gyaltsuen Queen Jetsun Pema Wangchuck and how her royal sartorial identity is crafted both within Bhutan and globally. Bhutan provides an interesting paradox to consider in discussing globalization because the country is used to signify both 'poverty' and 'luxury' at the same time, depending on how it is contextualized.

Myth acts economically: the paradox of Shangri La against everyday life in Bhutan

Recent shifts in fashion studies scholarship[3] have begun to move beyond simple binary construction of West vs non-West, and ways of understanding global and inclusive narratives of dress, textiles, and national/ethnic identity emerge. This is a very welcome part of a greater global shift to decolonize the humanities. There has never been a more urgent time to address the systemic vestiges of colonialism and acknowledge global power structures that have acted as inherent biases in the foundations of knowledge, by acknowledging our collective human experience in various modes of online and offline existence.

Despite our highly advanced potential for technological connectivity and growing critical consumer awareness of the dangers of what Shoshana Zuboff has termed 'surveillance capitalism', images of the 'exotic Other' are still very much everywhere.[4] Stereotyped images of the smiling pre-industrial woman are present in popular narratives in fashion magazines, marketing, and advertising, as well as tourism campaigns based on cultural heritage and sometimes even also in well-meaning activism campaigns designed to break the cycle of commodity fetishism and reveal the people behind opaque global supply chains who make our clothes. The same kind of images may be used as marketing tools by charities who want us to donate money to 'empower' the 'deserving' poor in the 'least developed' corners of the world (Figure 4.1). Similar images represent success stories for intergovernmental development agencies furthering agendas for economic growth in locations either already previously ransacked by colonial enterprises or neglected and overlooked as unproductive regions of the world where resources could not easily benefit the commodification of the natural world for the mass manufacture of consumer products.

Bhutan's relative lack of industrial development is sometimes mythologized to connote an excess of natural beauty, depending on the context.

4.1 Women carrying baskets of manure to spread on fields at Sopsokha, Bhutan (2008)

Roland Barthes wrote about the fundamental power of myth in naturalizing belief as follows:

> In passing from history to nature, myth acts economically: it abolishes the complexity of human acts, it gives them the simplicity of essences, it does away with all dialectics, with any going back beyond what is immediately visible, it organizes a world which is without contradictions because it is without depth, a world wide open and wallowing in the evident, it establishes a blissful clarity; things appear to mean something by themselves.[5]

First, consider the 'productive' realm in which images of Bhutan operate. From the perspective of the World Bank, Bhutan is ranked as a lower-middle-income country with a GDP of 3,316 USD per capita, based on 2019 figures. Using GDP per capita data gives only a blunt measure for understanding the relative poverty or wealth of a country, as it does not indicate the income distribution of individual people, and it also disguises the purchasing power of that country by presenting all data as unified in USD equivalent, which can fluctuate enormously according to exchange rates and access to banking infrastructure and financial mechanisms. The relative proportions of different employment activities within Bhutan highlights some of the inequalities and differences which make up the economic wealth or poverty of Bhutan. For example, Agriculture contributes only 10% to Bhutan's GDP but accounts for 54% of employment. Bhutan is a vastly pre-industrial society. The growth of the economy continues to be led by hydropower, which Bhutan exports to India, and Bhutan's economy is closely linked to India's. Overall unemployment is low, but high youth unemployment represents Bhutan's challenge to create more employment and better jobs for future generations as it nudges towards internationally agreed indicators of a 'well-developed' nation.[6]

In tasteless contrast to this backdrop of an economically precarious nation, images of Bhutan circulate globally in a mythical context entirely motivated by consumer culture. In July 2019 Bulgari launched its *Cinemagia* high jewellery collection in Bhutan. Editor-in-chief of *Thailand Tatler*, Naphalai Areerson, flew to Bhutan for the launch and wrote about it in her Diary of society events for the week.

> (Bhutan) The name conjures images that are magical and mystical. And the country itself is like a place stuck in time. Bhutan is high on the bucket list of many tourists, but with its 'high value, low impact' policy, it doesn't really welcome all visitors with open arms. Which is why Bulgari, in trying to give its clients and media an unparalleled experience, chose this tiny Himalayan kingdom for the regional launch of its Cinemagia high jewellery collection.[7]

Sarah Cheang has written about high fashion's long history of exploiting 'the Other'– either using distant impoverished lands as an exotic background to editorial photoshoots of predominantly white models, or its ethnic clothing providing a dress-up wardrobe of 'costumes' for models and stylists to use to 'go native':

> Fashion is shown to be a globetrotting overlay in endless juxtapositions of designer-clad models, who are citizens of the world, with indigenous people, who belong root and branch to one particular place. The products of the Vogue fashion world, although centred on the capitals of Paris, London, Milan and New York, are projected as a free-floating, universal phenomenon in opposition to an explicitly geographically grounded ethnicity.[8]

This phenomenon is very clearly present in fashion industry usage of Bhutan as a 'geographically grounded' utopia, what Foucault would term a 'heterotopia', for the staging of luxury. Bhutan acts as a rooted backdrop for the 'globetrotting overlay' of the performance of luxury, eco-consciousness, sustainability, and ethereal virtues associated with 'fairy tales' and other patronizing stereotypes not grounded in the lived realities of ordinary Bhutanese people. 'Bhutan' is used and abused as the signifier of luxury, rarity, purity – to be commodified by the wealthy Western consumer or brand. This system negates Bhutan's possibility for self-determination to fashion its own identity within the dominant visual culture of globalization whose authors are predominantly 'Western', or 'Western owned'. A strong association with the myth of Shangri La is present in almost all fashion narratives about Bhutan. Bhutanese companies and organizations themselves have begun to use this myth as an effective shorthand for communicating the notion of a timeless refuge from the problems of modernity that is such an attractive quality to consume for tourists and image makers, exhausted, alienated, and worn down by the opposing but equally pervasive myth of economic growth at all costs.

Shangri La is the name of the pristine utopia described in James Hilton's 1933 novel *Lost Horizon*. McMillin suggests that George Bogle's letters established the possibility of the idea once they were first published by Clements Markham in 1876 and gained wide popularity through his lens. George Bogle may in fact provide the archetype for the myth of epiphany that is experienced in the Himalayas, evidenced nowadays through everything from mountaineering to yoga practice. The myth of Shangri La is naturalized as truth and continues to haunt the Western imagination on page and screen, used as the driving force for development projects and tourism campaigns up to the present day.[9] *Lost Horizon* was made into a film by Frank Capra in 1937 and established Columbia Pictures as a successful film production company. In 1939 *Lost Horizon* was chosen as Pocket Book #1 by Simon & Schuster, and it became the first paperback book to have mass market production and distribution techniques applied to its promotion. Pocket Books were published in small format with glued bindings, rather than stitched, and they were sold at a cheap price for mass market distribution and readership. Michael Dirda explains the mass and enduring popularity of the Shangri La myth established by *Lost Horizon* in the 1930s as a reaction to the repulsion towards the twentieth century's noisy industrialism after one world war and 'the cultural apprehension widely felt in the early 1930s' throughout Europe and the West.[10]

I have written elsewhere about the enduring Condé Nast discourse on Bhutan,[11] whereby only the very wealthy and privileged can afford to travel there, including fashion industry leaders such as Derek Lam, Sir David Tang, Christina Ong, Diane von Furstenberg, and Christian Louboutin, among many others. Diane von Furstenberg's Diary from 2012 speaks of meeting the Bhutanese Royal Family and is a perfect example of the extremely patronizing language that continues to mythologize Bhutan as a one-dimensional utopia which exists for the benefit of only the global super-elite: 'It's like being in a fairy tale. They look and behave like a fairy tale King and Queen. They are so incredibly nice, simple and caring about their lovely Kingdom.'[12]

Royal patronage, *driglam namzha*, and nation building through textiles and dress

Rooted firmly on the ground, the Royal Family of Bhutan have historically played a fundamental role in shaping the identity of Bhutan in their own image through textiles and dress, and continue to do so in the twenty-first century. Susan S. Bean, Diana K. Myers, and Rinzin O. Dorji, who are three of the foremost scholars on Bhutanese textiles, write with fascinating detail about the importance of the royal women as patrons of textile heritage in Bhutan.[13] In the 1950s, the Royal Family, which originated in Bhutan's most textile-rich region, Lhuentse in eastern Bhutan, introduced a renewed interest in the aesthetic and social significance of cloth to western Bhutan, an area not previously known for its weaving. The Dowager Queen, Gyalyum Ashi Phuntsok Choden was a committed patron of textiles and employed weavers in central and eastern Bhutan and also in a palace weaving workshop near her residence in Thimphu. The Dowager Queen Gyalyum employed weavers near Dechencholing Palace to make royal commissions. In 1967 she set up a training institute for traditional arts, especially Buddhist painting and sculpture, in Trashigang. This institute has now evolved into the National Institute of Zorig Chusum (the 'thirteen traditional arts') with branches in Thimphu and Trashi Yangtse, which continues to flourish, and combines traditional master–apprenticeship training with an art school-style curriculum.

The third king, Jigme Dorji Wangchuck, supported the women of the family in these cultural nation-building undertakings and reinforced their importance. He chose to wear handwoven Bhutanese garments in all his official portraits, never the Chinese brocades that the first and second kings sometimes wore. His wife, Queen Ashi Kesang Choden, appears in the July 1967 issue of *Vogue USA*, photographed in London when the children were on holiday from their English schools. While the *Vogue* article evidences patronizing language, describing the rulers as 'a charming family from a small, imperilled kingdom in the Himalayas … an aerial Shangri La suspended … so isolated, so locked in the past that it had, until recently, no wheeled vehicles', it also draws attention to the role of the Queen in encouraging traditional crafts such as silver working and weaving, noting the 'costumes' (note the word 'costume' is used, not 'clothes') she and her children wear in the photos.

> The costumes she and her children wear on these pages – some of silk, some of yak wool – were woven in Bhutan and dyed with indigenous dyes: wools in strong rich colours – dark red, blues, purples – silks in pale-gold, pink, or bright turquoise. On the facing page, the Queen's robe is of green-and-gold silk brocade woven with designs of the sacred chrysanthemum, over a pale-pink silk blouse: her hair is braided with black silk and wool cords. The magnificent necklace and earrings are of pure turquoise and seed pearls, set in heavy gold.[14]

The National Museum was established by the Royal Family at Paro in 1968, as another example of fostering appreciation for traditional crafts and textiles. Bhutan adopted the Indian model of state-supported handicraft emporia, establishing the National Handicraft Emporium in 1971 with

4.2 Technology and tradition co-exist side by side: young Bhutanese women taking selfies at the Thimpu Tshechu festival (2014)

Princess Ashi Sonam Choden as official patron. Together, the museum and the emporium were intended to promote textile heritage and textile innovation among Bhutanese and also tourists, who were at that time mainly Indian.[15]

The mutual benefit between tourism industries and culture industries is well attested in innumerable case studies globally as a support framework to preserve traditional craft skills and provide livelihoods for artisans. Calls for sustainable development and a growing interest in supporting more ethical approaches towards the production of clothing and textiles form part of the same ecosystem. In Bhutan there exists an official code of etiquette, behavior, and dress, *driglam namzha*, based on seventeenth-century social norms, which continues to encourage and promote the use of traditional textiles and dress in twenty-first-century life and has been used to guide the cultural identity of Bhutan as the country experiences globalization.

Driglam namzha is based on a Buddhist monastic code of conduct and dress, which formed part of Bhutan's cultural heritage and was enacted inconsistently in various ways at different times according to the historical context. It became enshrined in law in 1989 as part of a conscious agenda of nation building by the fourth king, providing an 'authentic' blueprint for Bhutanese to follow in challenging times as the country began to connect with various aspects of global modernity. Based on antiquated modes of dress and rank, *driglam namzha* continues to regulate official public dress and etiquette, although it does not apply to Hindu priests or foreigners, an exception which promotes potentially problematic ideas about national and ethnic identity within an otherwise relatively non-hierarchical society.[16]

The official dress code for men and women is based on the traditional dress of the Ngalop ethnic group, the dominant social and religious group within Bhutan, said to descend from the earliest bearers of Tibetan Buddhism who entered the country in the ninth century CE. Shortly after the institution of the strict 'national' dress code in 1989, an estimated eighty thousand Lhotsampa people of Nepali origin from the south of Bhutan fled as refugees to Nepal, reflecting the challenges of establishing a nation state built for 'One Nation, One People' to represent and include both dominant and minority ethno-linguistic groups harmoniously. Bhutanese refugees have remained in limbo in refugee camps in Nepal or been resettled to the USA and other countries.[17]

For women, the traditional national dress consists of a *kira*, a rectangle of handwoven textile, usually about three meters in length, which is wrapped around the body, folded into a wide pleat in the front, fastened at the shoulders with brooches (called *tinkhup*, or *koma*) and secured with a tight narrow cloth belt (*kera*) wrapped around the waist. The *kira* is worn on top of a loose long-sleeved Tibetan-style blouse (*wangu*) and the look is completed with a short wide-sleeved jacket (*tego*) often fastened with a brooch. The jacket sleeves are aligned with the blouse sleeves, which are then folded back over the jacket to form long cuffs worn a little above the wrist. A shoulder cloth (*rachu*) is worn draped across the left shoulder.[18] For men the national dress is the *gho*, the same garment worn by most Tibetan males, but hitched up to the knees to give greater freedom of movement. A discourse of nostalgia for the loss of authentic national dress practices has emerged as older styles of traditional garments have become superseded by modern hybrid garments with stitched elements to emulate the appearance of wrapped and folded cloth, and modern closures and fastenings adopted instead of the brooches for reasons of practical wearability. For example, a writer for the Bhutan Broadcasting Service wrote in a blog in 2007 (now archived): 'Today, it is very rare to see Bhutanese women wearing the complete National Dress. With the hook, *half-kira* and the *jacket-tego*, *kera* and *wangu* may soon also be heading for the museum like the *thinkhab*.'[19]

In private, Bhutanese people often wear Western-style clothing in a variety of styles, imported from Bangladesh, Thailand, and surrounding countries which mass manufacture clothing, but all public life should officially abide by the rules of *driglam namzha*. The two contexts of 'official' and 'off-duty' dress have allowed the Bhutanese to hold both sets of values in their minds simultaneously, to exhibit a dual-consciousness of dress, what Keats would have referred to as 'negative capability.' Fines enforced for breaking the *driglam namzha* amount to approximately three days' wages for the average Bhutanese, so the incentive to dress within the law is quite strong. However, if you look on the pages of the Facebook group Bhutan Street Fashion[20] you will see how diverse the ways of wearing *gho* and *kira* have become and the enlarged vocabulary of dress practices on the streets of Bhutan. *Driglam namzha* has also encouraged patriotism in consumption, with more and more women commissioning local artisans to weave the best they can afford, and favoring heritage styles from their grandmothers, rather than opting for cheaper imports from India.

However, in 2018 it was reported that 90 % of the handicrafts on sale at some of the most popular tourist destinations are 'imported from neighbouring countries'[21] and often bear no resemblance to local traditions and techniques, other than a printed label claiming these are 'Made in Bhutan.' While this may seem that tourists are undiscerning and will buy anything apparently 'rooted' in the location of their travels, regardless of the actual provenance of the product, this practice is unfortunately widespread in many tourist industries worldwide and not unique to Bhutan. Furthermore, it is also deeply embedded in the ambiguities of labeling regulations regarding country of origin for textiles and clothing – the factual denotation of provenance and the connection between production and consumption are so very often shrouded in mystery. Hence – commodity fetishism.

Browning mentions one incident where the Royal Government of Bhutan in 2010 emphasized the need to tone down 'the brightness of our textiles' with the more 'sober colours that the affluent Western markets prefer,' thus arguing that in some instances national identity and culture need to be molded and packaged with the preferences and tastes of outsiders in mind.[22] I think here it is important to remember that products developed specifically for a target market of foreign tourists are often not at all the same as products responding to the needs and tastes of local customers. These are two different things, and they are not mutually exclusive. One need not infect the other.

Richard Whitecross examines the impact that regulation has had on the acceptance and performance of 'correct' *driglam namzha* in Bhutan, and argues that all claims to 'tradition' require some form of legitimacy, whether regulatory or derived from some other authority. Tradition can be based on a temporal framework that lacks a clear beginning and marks off the historical period from 'modernity.' Used in this way, Whitecross argues, 'tradition aggregates and homogenises pre-modern culture and posits a historical past, against which the modern can be measured.'[23]

Alternatively, tradition can be thought of as 'strongly normative, the intention and the effect is to reproduce patterns of culture … it is this normative transmission which links the generations of the dead with the generations of the living.'[24] So, tradition is not left behind in the transition to modernity; instead tradition is what modernity requires to prevent society falling apart. It is this second approach to tradition which seems to be implied in the reaffirmations and training sessions of *driglam namzha* in ministry departments continuing in 2020, to provide unity in a time of crisis. Whitecross demonstrates how an individual or a group's subjective experiences of 'tradition' and law become synthesized into beliefs that demonstrate the highly relational nature of political, cultural, and legal legitimacy. Whitecross believes that the fact that *driglam namzha* is so very often contested reveals 'the complex and dynamic relationship between ordinary Bhutanese and law in contemporary Bhutan.'[25]

The Royal Family continue to be almost universally admired within Bhutan as equitable, forward-thinking bearers of modernity as well as the living embodiment of Bhutanese tradition and culture. The sartorial choices of the current Queen, Her Majesty the Gyaltsuen Jetsun Pema Wangchuck, are immaculately crafted to present her as the embodiment of *driglam namzha*. For her wedding in 2011 Queen Jetsun Pema wore a supplementary-warp patterned *kira*, full of rich supplementary-weft motif patterning, echoing the style of the queens of the second and third kings. She wore this with an imported silk brocade jacket. Her beautifully embroidered silk *rachu* had a yellow rather than a red ground, echoing the color of the ceremonial shoulder cloth worn by the King. The style of embroidery was based on the embroidered silk *rachu* introduced by the four queens of King Jigme Singye[26] decorated with dragons, phoenixes, and the eight auspicious symbols of Buddhism. In April 2016, the Home Ministry issued a notice to all local officials to let local women know that a 'patterned' (i.e. embroidered) *rachu* was only for royalty. As one official said, 'today many women can afford different patterned *rachu*, cheaper versions are available from India … but [women] are not aware of the type they are entitled [to wear].'[27]

Queen Jetsun Pema is often photographed wearing an embroidered *rachu*, as seen in Figure 4.4 in 2016 on her way to meet the Duke and Duchess of Cambridge on their royal visit to Bhutan. Only her feet betray her as a paid-up member of the global fashion system – she wears burgundy-colored platform stiletto sandals and bright red nail varnish on her toes. When she travels abroad Queen Jetsun Pema is more flexible with her clothing choices, dressing to fit in with the appropriate contexts of the countries she visits. So stark is the contrast between Queen Jetsun Pema *in* Bhutan and Queen Jetsun Pema *not in* Bhutan, that Sarah Cheang's observations on the rootedness of indigenous people to one particular place take on a different inflection.[28] The anonymous people who perform 'geographically grounded ethnicity' (after Cheang, 2013) in the background of the *Vogue* fashion shoot (represented in Figure 4.3) are vastly different from the royal subject of the monarch, whose agency and claim to reflexivity in dress practices allow her to perform dual-consciousness of dress on the global stage seamlessly.

Globetrotting: Bhutanese women mediating modernity and tradition

Flying into Bhutan is one of the most memorable travel experiences I have ever had. You can see the summit of Mount Everest and several of the other highest mountains in the world poking through the clouds, towards the heavens. It is easy to understand why the Shangri La myth is so effective and enduring. 'It organizes a world which is without contradictions because it is without depth, a world wide open and wallowing in the evident, it establishes a blissful clarity; things appear to mean something by themselves.'[29] There is something completely otherworldly about how to physically reach Bhutan and how inaccessible it is. As you prepare to land at Paro International Airport, the pilot has to turn off all flight navigation systems because the planes have to fly so close to the mountains that the systems won't work accurately, and this is very dangerous. Only the most experienced of flight captains are permitted to land and take off from Paro Airport. The landing strip is literally hidden behind a mountain, and you do not see it until you are only five hundred feet above the ground. It is both a terrifying and an exhilarating experience.

The majority of ordinary Bhutanese will never experience that journey.[30] Those who make this journey on a regular basis, the pilots and the

4.3 Women wearing traditional Bhutanese national dress, Haa district, Bhutan (2009)

4.4 Queen of Bhutan, Jetsun Pema arrives at Tashichho Dzong, in Thimphu, Bhutan, before meeting the Duke and Duchess of Cambridge on day five of the royal tour to India and Bhutan (2016)

4.5 The Prince of Wales and Duchess of Cornwall greet King Jigme Khesar Namgyel Wangchuk and Queen Jetsun Pema Wangchuck of Bhutan at Clarence House in London (2011)

cabin crew who work for the two airline companies operating, Drukair and Bhutan Airlines, are important globetrotting bearers of both modernity and tradition. To the outside world the cabin crew uniforms embody Shangri La and *driglam namzha*. To the Bhutanese audience rooted on the ground, the uniforms present certain practical and technical problems of garment production and manufacture.

A skills gap in tailoring was identified through a series of events during the process of nation building made evident through *driglam namzha*. It was not possible to make predictably sized garments of consistent quality as uniforms for civil servants, airline staff, the military or police, and this production was generally outsourced to India or Bangladesh. The growing demand for quality items of national dress to clothe the civil service contributed to the formulation of a development project to request capacity-building training in garment design and manufacture through the United Nations Development Programme (UNDP) in Bhutan. A national design competition was organized by UNDP Bhutan[31] to design and manufacture uniforms for the Drukair female cabin crew, and this highlighted the difficulties of manufacturing standardized garments in Bhutan. Singapore International Foundation won the bid for proposals to provide a Training of Trainers to tailors in Bhutan and identified Lasalle College of the Arts in Singapore as the appropriate academic partner to provide expertise in curriculum development and technical skills training in tailoring. I was working as Head of Fashion in Lasalle College of the Arts at this time and contributed to the design, development, and delivery of the training in 2008–2009.[32]

It is very interesting to note how the Drukair uniform has evolved from the late 1980s to the present day and how this resonates with evolving ideas of dress code and Bhutanese national identity as it connects with modernity and literally connects Bhutan to the rest of the world through aviation. The Drukair uniform and the Bhutan Air uniform encapsulate both the problems of manufacturing modernity and the free-floating signifiers of consuming tradition.

Gross National Happiness? Or lives of unremitting toil, unsweetened by amusement or adornment[33]

In addition to the policy of *driglam namzha*, the Royal Government of Bhutan developed its own metric to measure development: Gross National Happiness. The concept was developed by the fourth king, King Jigme Singye Wangchuck, in 1972 when he declared, 'Gross National Happiness is more important than Gross Domestic Product.' The measurement of GNH is based on four pillars (good governance; sustainable socio-economic development; cultural preservation; and environmental conservation), nine domains (psychological well-being; health; education; time use; cultural diversity and resilience; good governance; community vitality; ecological diversity and resilience; living standards), and thirty-three individual indicators (of which one is *driglam namzha*), aligned across these domains. GNH categorizes respondents into four groups of people – unhappy, narrowly happy, extensively happy, and deeply happy. The analysis explores the happiness people enjoy already, then focuses on how policies can increase happiness and sufficiency among the unhappy and narrowly happy people.[34]

The results broken down by gender are quite striking. Happiness is not equally distributed across the population. According to a report of detailed analysis of the 2010 GNH census in Bhutan, 11.1% of men are deeply happy and 37.4% of men are extensively happy, compared with only 5.4% of women who are deeply happy and 27.7% who are extensively happy. Among women, 52.5% are narrowly happy, and fully 14.3% are unhappy; in comparison, 45% of men are narrowly happy and only 6.5% are unhappy. In the past few decades, Bhutan has seen major socio-economic transformation and a rapidly growing per capita income. Yet, despite progress in achieving gender equality in education and participation in the labor force, the 2010 GNH survey findings have shown that the gender differences are greatest in negative emotions, work, leisure time, schooling, literacy, political participation, safety from human harm, and wildlife damage, all to the disadvantage of Bhutanese women.

Bhutanese women and the performance of globalization 107

4.6 Bhutan Airlines uniform (2019): a contemporary, stitched garment made to emulate wrapped traditional dress, signifies Bhutan to those who travel by plane

Matrilineal inheritance, as practiced in Bhutan, means that some 60% of rural women and about 45% of urban women have land and properties registered in their name. However, land cannot be used to access finance, but ties women to the land, which may not produce any income from agriculture, and thus makes it difficult for women to migrate for better

4.7 A woman spinning yarn inside her house, Lobesa village, Punakha, Bhutan (2020)

opportunities for work and to acquire skills. Research by the World Bank acknowledges that more input and representation from women in how to manage land is needed, in addition to further access to secondary and higher education and changing social norms to encourage more men to share housework and raise children.[35] The average working hours for females is higher than for males. On average, rural women work the longest, followed by urban women.[36] George Bogle's observations on ordinary Bhutanese women who 'lead lives of unremitting toil, unsweetened by amusement or adornment' have not materially advanced much since 1775.

Comparing these findings with a comparable global survey of happiness, the happiness experienced by women in Bhutan is *less* than the global average, as women globally report *higher* levels of happiness than men, by an amount that is highest at about the age of thirty. Across all age categories, females average 0.09 points higher on the 0 to 10 life evaluation scale, or 1.5% of the global average life evaluation.[37]

Conclusion

Images of Bhutanese women bear witness to the contradictory narratives of the Bhutanese experience of globalization, their image celebrated in so many global development and luxury contexts, yet without the majority of ordinary Bhutanese women themselves experiencing many of the benefits of that increased global connectivity, visibility, and happiness.

Notes

1. MSS Eur E226/14, APAC, BL. George Bogle's letters cited in Kate Teltscher, *The High Road To China: George Bogle, the Panchen Lama and the First British Expedition to Tibet* (London: Bloomsbury, 2006), pp. 90–91.
2. Teltscher, *The High Road to China*, p. 91.
3. For example Research Collective for Decolonizing Fashion (https://rcdfashion.wordpress.com/about/) and the Fashion and Race Database (https://fashionandrace.org/), along with International Journal of Fashion Studies (www.intellectbooks.com/international-journal-of-fashion-studies) are a few significant resources.
4. Shoshana Zuboff, *Surveillance Capitalism* (London: Profile Books, 2019).
5. Roland Barthes, *Mythologies* (London: Vintage, Random House, 2000), p. 143.
6. www.worldbank.org/en/country/bhutan/overview#2 (accessed 14 February 2019).
7. www.thailandtatler.com/society/naphalais-diary-july-22–28 (accessed 14 February 2019). See also www.linkedin.com/pulse/never-been-done-before-luxury-event-bhutan-2019-chabri%C3%A8res (accessed 24 August 2023).
8. Sarah Cheang, '"To the Ends of the Earth": Fashion and Ethnicity in the Vogue Fashion Shoot,' in D. Bartlett, S. Cole, and A. Rocamora, eds, *Fashion Media Past and Present*. 1st edn. (London: Bloomsbury, 2013), p. 37.
9. Teltscher, *The High Road to China*, p. 257.
10. Michael Dirda, 'Hiding From Our Troubles in Shangri-La; James Hilton's "Lost Horizon" Captures the Cultural Apprehension Widely Felt in the Early 1930s,' *Wall Street* Journal, Eastern edition, 2017.
11. Emma Dick, 'Constructing Fashionable Dress and Identity in Bhutan,' in M. Angela Jansen and Jennifer Craik, eds, *Modern Fashion Traditions: Negotiating Tradition and Modernity through Fashion* (London: Bloomsbury, 2018), pp. 185–206.
12. Von Furstenberg (2012) cited in Dick, 'Constructing Fashionable Dress', p. 187.
13. Susan S. Bean, Diana K. Myers, and Rinzin O. Dorji, 'Modeling a Future for Handmade Textiles: Bhutan in the Twenty-First Century,' *Textile Museum Journal*, 46 (2019): 53–73.
14. 'Fashion: H.M. the Queen of Bhutan, and Her Children,' *Vogue*, 150, no. 1 (1967): 84–87.
15. Bean, Myers, and Dorji, 'Modeling a Future for Handmade Textiles,' 53–73.
16. Francoise Pommaret, 'Textiles in Bhutan I: Way of Life and Identity Symbols', in Michael Aris and Michael Hutt, eds, *Bhutan: Aspects of Culture and Development* (Gartmore: Kiscadale Ltd, 1994), p. 173.
17. Dhurba Rizal, 'The Unknown Refugee Crisis: Expulsion of the Ethnic Lhotsampa from Bhutan', *Asian Ethnicity*, 5, no. 2 (2004), 151–177, doi: 10.1080/1463136042000221861.
18. Diana K. Myers and Susan S. Bean, eds, *From the Land of the Thunder Dragon: Textile Arts of Bhutan, London and Salem* (Chicago: Serindia Press, 1994).
19. *Thinkhab* is an alternative spelling of *tinkhup*. Original reference was BBS (2007), www.bbs.com.bt/There%20it%20goes,%20to%20the%20museums.html (accessed 14 July 2012).
20. www.facebook.com/BhutanStreetFashion/ (accessed 24 August 2023).
21. https://thebhutanese.bt/90-percent-of-local-handicraft-products-imported-from-the-neighboring-countries-apic-ceo/ (accessed 24 August 2023).
22. Christopher S. Browning, 'Nation Branding and Development: Poverty Panacea or Business As Usual?' *Journal of International Relations and Development*, 19, no. 1 (2016): 50–75, at 63.
23. R. W. Whitecross, 'Law, "Tradition" and Legitimacy: Contesting Driglam Namzha', in J. D. Schmidt, ed., *Development Challenges in Bhutan: Perspectives on Inequality and Gross National Happiness*. Edinburgh

Napier University Repository, https://napier-repository.worktribe.com/output/169905/law-tradition-and-legitimacy-contesting-driglam-namzha, p. 17 (accessed 24 August 2023).
24. Edward Shils, cited in Whitecross, 'Law, "Tradition" and Legitimacy,' p. 17.
25. Whitecross, 'Law, "Tradition' and Legitimacy,"' p. 2.
26. Polygyny and polyandry are both legal in Bhutan and though considered to be becoming rarer are still practiced in rural areas, especially where land ownership is economically challenging and inheritance would mean dividing small plots of land into even smaller plots as sons and daughters establish their own families. In Bhutan land can pass down matrilineal or patrilineal ownership, hence fraternal polyandry (where a woman is married to multiple brothers) or sororal polygyny (where a man is married to multiple sisters) both exist to preserve land ownership and share domestic and agricultural duties.
27. https://kuenselonline.com/only-ada-rachu-for-women/ (accessed 24 August 2023).
28. Cheang, '"To the Ends of the Earth",' p. 37.
29. Barthes, *Mythologies*, p. 143.
30. According to the Department of Air Transport, the number of passengers flying through Paro Airport increased to 397,599 in 2018. According to Bhutan Tourism Monitor in 2018, a total of 274,097 foreign individuals visited Bhutan in 2018. International leisure arrivals grew by 1.76% to 63,367 over 2017 while arrivals from the regional market grew by 10.37%. Without more nuanced analysis it is difficult to know how many of the remaining 123,502 passengers were international consultants working on development projects or business ventures and how many were Bhutanese citizens traveling overseas for work or leisure. The percentage of ordinary Bhutanese people who fly regularly or have ever left Bhutan is very small. A Bhutanese passport ranks nintieth on the Henley Passport Index worldwide, meaning a visa is required for Bhutanese to travel to 173 destinations.
31. UNDP, *UNDP Bhutan Annual Report 2006–7* (Thimpu: UNDP, 2007), p. 16.
32. Dick, 'Constructing Fashionable Dress.'
33. Teltscher, *The High Road to China*, p. 91.
34. https://ophi.org.uk/gnh-and-gnh-index/ (accessed 24 August 2023).
35. Aphichoke Kotikula, 'Bhutan gender policy note' (English) (Washington, D. C., World Bank Group, 2013). http://documents.worldbank.org/curated/en/960591468017989867/Bhutan-gender-policy-note, pp. v–vi (accessed 24 August 2023).
36. K. Ura, S. Alkire, T. Zangmo, and K. Wangdi, *An Extensive Analysis of The Gross National Happiness Index, 2012*. Centre of Bhutan Studies, https://ophi.org.uk/wp-content/uploads/Ura_et_al_Extensive_analysis_of_GNH_index_2012.pdf, p. 155 (accessed 24 August 2023).
37. Nicole Fortin, John F. Helliwell, and Shun Wang, 'How Does Subjective Well-Being Vary Around The World By Gender And Age?' in John Helliwell, Richard Layard, and Jeffrey Sachs, eds, *World Happiness Report 2015* (New York: Sustainable Development Solutions Network, 2015), p. 43, https://worldhappiness.report/ed/2015/ (accessed 24 August 2023).

Bibliography

Bean, Susan S., Diana K. Myers, and Rinzin O. Dorji. 'Modeling a Future for Handmade Textiles: Bhutan in the Twenty-first Century.' *Textile Museum Journal* 46 (2019): 53–73.

Brooks, Andrew. *The End of Development: A Global History of Poverty and Prosperity*. London: Zed Books, 2017.

Browning, Christopher S. 'Nation Branding and Development: Poverty Panacea or Business as Usual?' *Journal of International Relations and Development* 19, no. 1 (2016): 50–75.

Capra, F. *Lost Horizon*. Film. Columbia Pictures, 1937.

Cheang, S. '"To the Ends of the Earth": Fashion and Ethnicity in the Vogue Fashion Shoot.' In *Fashion Media Past and Present*. Edited by D. Bartlett, S. Cole, and A. Rocamora. 1st edn. London: Bloomsbury Publishing Plc, 2013.

Choden, Karma. 'Imprints of Happiness.' *Kuensel*, 9 April 2007. https://web.archive.org/web/20120305053530/http:/www.kuenselonline.com/modules.php?name=News&file=article&sid=8308 (accessed 24 August 2023).

Dick, Emma. 'Constructing Fashionable Dress and Identity in Bhutan.' In *Modern Fashion Traditions: Negotiating Tradition and Modernity through Fashion*. Edited by M. Angela Jansen and Jennifer Craik. London: Bloomsbury Academic, 2018.

Graham, M. 'Warped Geographies of Development: The Internet and Theories of Economic Development.' *Geography Compass* 2, no. 3 (2008): 771–789.

Hilton, J. *Lost Horizon*. London: Vintage Classics, [1933] 2015.

Jackson, Tim. *Prosperity Without Growth: Foundations for the Economy of Tomorrow*. 2nd edn. London: Routledge, 2017.

Kumar, Deepa. 'Framing Islam: The Resurgence of Orientalism During the Bush II Era.' *Journal of Communication Inquiry* 34, no. 3 (July 2010): 254–77. https://doi.org/10.1177/0196859910363174.

Lo, Joseph, Lisa Macintyre, and Britta Kalkreuter. 'Investigating Markers of Authenticity: The Weavers' Perspective: Insights from a Study on Bhutanese Hand-woven Kira Textiles.' *Textile* 14, no. 3 (2016): 306–325. doi: 10.1080/14759756.2015.1119576.

Lowenthal, David. *The Heritage Crusade and the Spoils of History*. Cambridge: Cambridge University Press, 2004.

Myers, D. K. 'Bhutanese Fashion and Textiles in the 21st Century.' *Marg* 66, no. 4 (2015): 40–51.

Myers, Diana K. and Susan S. Bean, eds. *From the Land of the Thunder Dragon: Textile Arts of Bhutan*. London and Salem: Peabody Essex Museum and Serindia Press, 1994.

Norbu, Khyentse. *Travellers and Magicians*. Film. Prayer Flag Pictures, 2003.

Palden, Tshering. 'Druk Air's New Look.' *Kuensel*, 13 March 2008. https://web.archive.org/web/20120305053525/http:/www.kuenselonline.com/modules.php?name=News&file=article&sid=10006 (archived from the original 5 March 2012. Retrieved 20 February 2021).

'Promoting Bhutanese culture through the national airline Drukair' (PDF) (Press release). United Nations Development Programme Bhutan. 21 March 2007. Archived from the original (PDF) on 11 June 2007 (accessed 20 February 2021).

Rebellato, D. *Theatre and Globalization*. Basingstoke: Palgrave Macmillan, 2009.

Rizal, Dhurba. 'The Unknown Refugee Crisis: Expulsion of the Ethnic Lhotsampa from Bhutan.' *Asian Ethnicity* 5, no. 2 (2004): 151–177. doi: 10.1080/1463136042000221861.

Royal Government of Bhutan. *Economic Development Policy of the Kingdom of Bhutan*. https://events.development.asia/system/files/materials/2023/05/2023 05-bhu-economic-development-policy-kingdom-bhutan-2010.pdf (accessed 19 August 2023).

Schroeder, R. and K. Schroeder. *Happy Environments: Bhutan, Interdependence and the West. Sustainability* 6, no. 6 (2014): 3521–3533.

Stokes, F. 'Applied Theatre and Political Change in Bhutan.' *Postcolonial Studies* 18, no. 2 (2015): 174–188. doi: 10.1080/13688790.2015.1044487.

Teltscher, Kate. *The High Road to China: George Bogle, the Panchen Lama and the First British Expedition to Tibet.* London: Bloomsbury, 2006.

Verma, R. 'Business as Unusual: The Potential for Gender Transformative Change in Development and Mountain Contexts.' *Mountain Research and Development* 34, no. 3 (2014): 188–196.

Whitecross, R. W. 'Law, "Tradition" and Legitimacy: Contesting Driglam Namzha.' In *Development Challenges in Bhutan: Perspectives on Inequality and Gross National Happiness*. Edited by J. D. Schmidt. Cham: Springer, 2017. doi.org/10.1007/978-3-319-47925-5_7.

Zuboff, Shoshana. *Surveillance Capitalism*. London: Profile Books, 2019.

5

Weaving and dyeing the ideal of reproduction among Shidong Miao in Guizhou province

Ho Zhao-hua

Introduction

To Shidong Miao, cloth is not a mere object. The goal of making cloth is to create a textile that is cultivated and invested with personhood. Likewise, for a Shidong Miao woman, making clothes is an essential way to show her identity and personhood. People always say that 'a woman who cannot make clothes, is not a Shidong Miao woman; a woman who cannot make Shidong Miao clothes, does not belong to the place of Shidong.' In this way, weaving, dyeing, embroidering, and making clothes present the core values of Shidong Miao women.

This chapter examines the significance of cloth in the traditional Shidong Miao cultural and social fabric. Through ethnographic research,[1] it clarifies the key concepts through which Shidong Miao construct their ideal of reproduction and how this is expressed in textile production. I argue that the process of reproduction has two steps: the first is creation, the second cultivation. The first step, creation, comes about through the process of *yenbyangx* fusion; however, birth for humans and weaving for textiles is only the first step. In both cases what is created is still in a raw and immature condition. Both require a second step, cultivation, to be transformed into a cooked, mature, and civilized form which is invested with Shidong Miao personhood.

Shidong Miao

The Miao are one of the ethnic minorities officially recognized by the People's Republic of China (PRC), and their population is spread over Guizhou, Guangxi, Yunnan, Hunan, and Sichuan provinces. The term 'Miao' may mislead one to regard these approximately eight million people as a single group, but it should be noted that the diverse population of 'Miao' are considered a single group as the result of the Ethnic Identification Campaign (Ch. *minzu shibie* 民族識別) that the PRC government has pursued since the 1950s.[2] People designated 'Miao' are also found in a number of Southeast Asian countries, and there is a small diaspora of Miao known as 'Hmong.' The Hmong have emigrated from China to Thailand, Laos, Vietnam, and Burma over the past hundred years.[3] There are three Miao languages and thirty to forty highly mutually intelligible dialects, which form the Miao branch of the Hmong-Mien (Miao-Yao) language group in the Sino-Tibetan language family. As Zhengwen Yang and Inez De Beauclair have noted, this complexity of ethnicity is in need of further examination.[4]

In the middle reaches of the Qingshui River in Guizhou province lies the small river port town of Shidong.[5] Politically and culturally speaking, Shidong was in one of the 'shatter zones,'[6] one of the 'barbarian,' 'raw' Miao areas outside the reach of imperial China. Over time, these 'shatter zones' have become smaller and smaller, due to imperial Chinese military force and increased colonial bureaucratic control.[7]

The attitudes and actions of the state towards this area changed dramatically through different historical regimes. The Native Chieftain (Ch. *tusi* 土司) system was first established in 1277, during the Yuan dynasty. As in other areas of southwest China, this system created a tutelary relationship with the state which left governance to local leaders. In the early Ming dynasty, the soldier-settler system (Ch. *tuntian* 屯田) was established, but the general attitude of avoidance of this outlying population remained, and, to that end, the Miao Boundary Wall was built during the Wanli Era (1572–1620) to quarantine the 'raw' Miao and keep them outside of China.

The coming of the Qing marked a dramatic change in state policy towards this area and towards the Miao people. Where the Ming had sought to avoid and isolate, the Qing sought to incorporate this area into the state through direct control and violence. The war of conquest started in 1727. Ertai, Governor of Guizhou, sent General Zhang Kwang-si to pacify the area,[8] which had become a hotbed of conflicts between locals and the rising population of soldier-settlers. Zhang Kwang-si slaughtered eighteen thousand Miao and burned numerous hamlets. This was the first time that 'raw' Miao living in the middle stream of the Qingshui River suffered in what can now be seen as a long, continuous brutal war that had begun as a revolt against new taxation. However, it is the rebellion of Zhang Xiu-mei that lives strongest in social memory.

As the Taiping rebellion (1851–1864) shook China, in order to fund its campaign against the Taiping rebels, the state taxed the southwest, causing great hardship. In 1853–1873, Zhang Xiu-mei led an uprising that lasted eighteen years; his army established a Miao territory along the Qingshui River, covering the eastern parts of Guizhou. In the end, food shortages and traitors caused the members of this rebellion to defect. For the Shidong people, this was the most significant event that changed 'raw' Miao to 'cooked' Miao as Miao people chose either to revolt or to obey.[9]

Through these experiences, indigenous people learned how to negotiate with different kinds of outsiders. By adopting Confucian educational symbolic capital and official bureaucratic skills, Shidong Miao found a way to play a dual policy. On the one hand, they were pretending to be Han to negotiate with Han Chinese. On the other hand, they were controlling the flow of women to keep China out of Shidong.[10] Economically, life in Shidong today remains dependent on agriculture and trade. In terms of Shidong's cloth production, Guizhou's history of using and trading cotton fabric dates back to at least the Ming dynasty. After 1850, Miao people learned how to make cotton fabric and started cultivating cotton, but they have never achieved the quality of Han Chinese fine blue cotton cloth. The climate also precludes growing enough cotton, so cotton yarn has been available in the local market for a long time. Trade in yarn was also greatly promoted by the government store in the 1960s, and since then people have seldom spun their own yarn. Most cotton yarn comes from Hunan province, along with silk thread and other fabrics.

Yenb, yangx, gender, host, and guest

The Shidong Miao concepts of *yenb* and *yangx* are similar to the Han concepts of 'yin' and 'yang.' Shidong Miao view life as a series of stages between transition points: birth and death are examples – newborn babies having the afterbirth removed and putting on clothes signifies a transition from the *yenb* spirit-world to the *yangx* earth. Cutting the ties off the clothes worn in life and putting on 'ghost clothes' (the clothes people are buried in) to live another life is another transition of returning from the *yangx* earth to the *yenb* spirit-world. Metaphors involving transformation are often used to describe transitions and change. For example, if an old woman dies, locals say *jangx life* (she 'turned into a butterfly') and that she returned to the soil in the (*yenb*) south. If a male dies, locals say *jangx vongx* (he 'turned into a dragon') and that he returned to the hills in the (*yangx*) west. Of things that turn out unexpectedly, they say *jangx ghangd jangx dlix* ('it turned into a frog and became a tadpole'); if things turn out as expected, they say *jangx vongx jangx hob* ('it has become a dragon; it has become thunder').[11]

In *yenb* and *yangx*, the concepts of 'cold and hot' and 'male and female' are extended to the practice of 'fusing *yenb* and *yangx*' through festivals. Rituals and their practice construct a time of social ideals that can lead to an exchange of heaven and earth which concludes in marriage. The timing of different stages of the entire sequence of setting up and finally holding a marriage is related to the natural cycling of *yenb* and *yangx*.

The Sisterhood Festival and Chimao Festival occur at the times of year when *yenb* becomes *yangx*, and *yangx* becomes *yenb* respectively. The Sisterhood Festival is female centered: it is a time to attract men; Chimao is centered around men who want to court a young woman and eventually take a wife. Both festivals enable men and women to engage with each other. Looking-for-clothes events, which deal with inner relationships, maintain reproduction inside the defined group – the Miao cannot marry non-Miao. And their characteristic sharing of food enhances the intimacy between the opposite sexes. The boundaries of the in-group are reinforced through these social practices.

Shidong Miao society is an oral one. Their rich culture is passed on to the next generation by storytelling, singing, and through their ritual life, and is reflected in various aspects of traditional clothing. Their myths and metaphors reflect how Shidong Miao understand and explain the universe and their place in it, and also constitute and underpin their cultural imagination.

Cloth, clothing, and dressing up play a uniquely important role in the culture of Shidong Miao people. The women are renowned for their clothing, particularly their intricately embroidered jackets, which exhibit an extensive range of variety and visual styles.[12] Needlework and embroidery is not only a skill but also a representation of a woman's cleverness, artistry, and gentle demeanor. At festivals, clad in their handsewn jackets, girls show off their ingenuity and try to attract a young man for marriage. In terms of social admiration or admonition, the goal of showing off their handmade clothing at festivals is to establish the boundaries between "home" and "guest" that organize Shidong Miao sociality.

Shidong Miao people use 'flowers' as a metaphor to describe the daughters in the family, and 'trees' to describe the sons. Although they are children of the same parents, the family is inherited by the son 'tree.' Although the daughter's 'flowers' are beautiful, they cannot stay at home. They must be married out. There will be a new daughter-in-law at home. Women leave their original 'tree' and go to their husband's family so that every family will have blossoms and fruit. A man's family welcomes the new bride, but the house still belongs collectively to the men. Therefore, they establish the concepts of 'host' (*ghaib*) and 'guest' (*khat*) under the framework of a gender binary of mutually constructive ideals.

Echoing the above, local people consider the relationships between male and female as follows: women are like water, men are like soil; women are classified as guests and men are the immobile hosts. It is a man's job to cultivate land, and he is responsible for his family's continuity and productivity. In contrast, women are flowing guests and women who have not married out or who have married into the family are in charge of everything to do with cloth.[13] This duality establishes Shidong Miao society.

A Shidong Miao household is an integrated complex of the two genders. The patrilineage controls the land, money, and food. Everything related to production and reproduction is the domain of males. The human body is similarly a combination of male and female domains. The trunk and limbs of the body, the skeleton, blood, head, hands, liver, intestines, and mouth, activity and motion, and eating, for example, are contributed by the father. The body's flesh, skin, breasts, belly, buttocks, heart, and eyes all come from the mother, the matrilineal side, along with emotion, feeding, and breast feeding. This is how a Shidong Miao child is seen as being formed from different parts contributed by each parent.

The basic Shidong Miao understanding of the construction of a life is that the life energy is provided by the father; the mother's body is simply a container which can become pregnant, providing feeding and breeding for the child. The father provides the food to nourish the household, and the mother makes clothes to grow the flesh and skin for the child and husband. Similarly, the whole process of making fabric is the same as making the body of a person with flesh and blood, skin, and personhood.

Marriage demonstrates that it is important to have a constant exchange of women between *ghaib* (host) and *khat* (guest), the wife takers and wife givers. The woman marrying in from the *khat* side will become a container for the *ghaib* side. This allows the patrilineal side to maintain the fertility of the household and avoid incest and other prohibitions. The kinship structure constructs relationships of descent and marriage, affinal and consanguineal, and defines social roles and identity and thereby affects social interaction.[14]

Shidong Miao measure a woman's diligence by how much cloth she produces. They believe the value of good fabric lies in its beauty but it is hard to put a price on the aesthetic quality; that requires good fortune and blessings from the Thunder God.[15] Beautiful fabric does, however, have economic ramifications: along with beautiful embroidery it contributes to a household's reputation, a cultural asset which helps a young woman, and her family with her, marry successfully.

Each article she produces and wears is imbued with symbolic meaning. For example, headcloth colors directly indicate a Shidong woman's age, sexual maturity, and status. Shidong Miao girls (*ad*), brides (*niangb*), mothers (*mais*), grandmothers both paternal and maternal (young *wud* and old *wud*), and great-grandmothers (*wud tais*) wear distinctly different color combinations. Starting from bright red and white in their youth, the colors gradually shift to darker shades of red and blue, with white becoming a decorative element.

As well as age, colors indicate marital and fertility status. Red represents fertility. When a young girl develops sexually and begins to menstruate, her headcloth becomes red, orange, and white. With increasing maturity, white disappears, and green and blue colors appear. The very reddest color is for marriageable or newly married women: it represents a teenage girl's growing glory and energy. People associate this red color with chili peppers which symbolize and promote good health. A menopausal woman wears a blue headcloth. The red totally disappears from a woman's headcloth when it is no longer necessary for her to have sex in order to have children. An older woman's headcloth is mainly black and dark blue, a reminder that she is approaching her death.

Create cloth, cultivate cloth

As mentioned in the introduction, to Shidong Miao cloth is not a mere object. Weaving and dyeing cloth present the Shidong Miao concept of personhood and the social ideal of reproduction. The goal of making cloth is to create cloth that is invested with personhood. The process of imbuing raw materials with personhood has several distinct stages. The warp constructs the skeleton and the weft determines the gender of the cloth. The skillful manipulation of warp and weft grows the cloth and gives birth to patterns. During the indigo-dyeing process, oxidization, fermentation, and stabilization transform the raw materials into a living and lively object. Adding a reddish hue with bramble roots and holly leaves gives the fabric blood; finishing with a glossy layer of cowhide glue completes its skin. Finally, the addition of the physical labor of pounding and steaming the cloth transforms the 'raw cloth' into a 'cooked cloth' and completes the 'cultivation' process. The pounding process makes the cloth tender and soft, to reveal the jade-like texture. The steaming process stabilizes color fastness and cowhide glue permeability. When these two steps are complete, the personhood presents and reproduction is fulfilled.

Step 1: creating cloth

Setting up the warp is very labor intensive. It requires the cooperation of at least four to six people, including one person who is skilled in the process. Members of the husband's patrilineal family, such as her husband's mother, her husband's father's brother's wife, and her husband's brother's wife, teach the daughters-in-law by helping set up the warp for each household together (Figure 5.1). The different households congregate to help a particular household in turn. They share the traditional knowledge and skillset as well as the labor required to make it possible to produce the skeleton of the fabric.

After setting up the warp and inserting a warp beam, the women prepare the weft threads. This stage is where the gender of the cloth is determined. This usually involves separating ground and pattern weft threads: single undyed threads for the ground and either one or two blue threads

5.1 Preparing the warp, Jiob Hxangk village, 2 August 2002

for the pattern weft.[16] When asked why Shidong Miao did this and the difference between using one or two threads for the pattern, one woman said dismissively, 'Threads are divided into male and female: male is heaven, female is earth. When you set up the warp and weft correctly, the road will appear naturally. The children will only come when the threads interlace male and female.' She explained that 'children' is a metaphor for 'patterns.' The weaving of the warp and weft threads creates the physical cloth and is a process of *yenb–yangx* fusion.

Weaving itself is a very labor-intensive activity. It may take one and a half months to weave a 1.5 meter-length cloth. Shidong Miao women weave four different types of cloth. *Dob* is a plain weave cloth. The warp and weft both use single threads, so *dob* is classified as male cloth. This is mainly used for jacket sleeves, skirts, and children's wear. Second, *linx pat* is a small diamond pattern cloth or twill.[17] People say the pattern represents a bird's eye; some that it represents a seed. The warp and weft both use a single thread, so *linx pat* cloth is considered male. Male fabrics like *dob* and *linx pat* are used to make things like belts and clothes. *Linx pat* cloth is used to make the front pieces of clothes. Third, *linx dix*, the most complicated pattern to make, is a middle-size diamond pattern cloth. It uses eight pattern rods to separate and organize the warp threads and create a special farmland pattern. *Linx dix* cloth is considered parent cloth: the weft uses single thread (i.e. male) as ground and two threads (i.e. female) for the float pattern: *linx dix* is therefore a *yenb–yangx* fusion cloth. This type of cloth is used on the back of women's jackets and on aprons, and cannot be used for men's clothing. Finally, *linx qub bongk* is a large diamond pattern cloth. *Linx qub bongk* is a cloth used only for baby carriers, woven on the same type of loom as that used for *linx dix*. It is woven using nine pattern rods to construct the pattern, a two-thread weft making the pattern larger. It represents the mother's family's land. *Linx qub bongk* cloth is given as a gift from the maternal grandmother to a newborn grandchild. This is a female cloth.

Indigo dye making is a complex, tedious process. The various steps in the process of traditional indigo dyeing are expressions of *yangx* and *yenb* forces, and *yenb–yangx* fusion. The dye is extracted from the fresh plant and prepared in an exacting and elaborate process taking about a month. At this first stage, the soaking indigo plant (Figure 5.2) and water are both considered female and domestic, that is, non-wild. When the water goes green in color, the plant material is scooped out of the water, and a small cup of lime is stirred into the indigo water. The lime is considered wild and male and able to give life to the sludge. At this next fermentation step, boiling water is poured over ash (considered wild) and the mixture is filtered to produce alkaline water. The ash and the resulting alkaline liquid are considered male. Twenty-eight *jin*[18] of indigo sludge and twenty-eight *jin* of wine are mixed together, then added to the alkaline water. The indigo

5.2 Soaking indigo plants, Dangx Vongx village, Shidong, 8 July 2007

sludge is food, and the wine is yeast to keep the alkaline indigo-water alive and produce the 'flesh' of the fabrics. This alkaline liquid forms the foundation for the dyeing.

The cloth is put into the vat for perhaps twenty minutes, then hung on a rack to drip dry, the fluid dripping from it collected to be reused for the next fabric-dyeing process. The cloth is then dried in the *yangx* sunlight to speed up the oxidization. Once dry, the cloth is continually beaten with a wooden mallet until it is shiny and smooth. To get dark blue cloth takes a minimum of six days, putting the cloth into the vat once each day, but cloth normally undergoes this dyeing and daily beating for twelve days to give a much darker color which is preferred.

Shidong Miao people like the fabric to have a rosy or reddish color. If a cloth is dark blue, they say it is 'not activated' whereas cloth that is dark black and shiny with a reddish sheen is considered energetic. Dyeing the cloth reddish gives the cloth 'flesh' enough 'blood' to live and to make it mature. Bramble roots and holly leaves, both wild and male, are mixed to produce the blood-color dye liquor (Figure 5.3).

Shidong people say of the most beautiful cloth that its skin is in 'good taste.' To give the skin the desired aesthetic quality, cowhide (considered wild and male) is boiled to make into glue and smeared on the surface of the fabric. The cloth is then laid in the sun to bring out the final glossy effect.

Step 2: cultivating cloth

As outlined above, the warp provides the basic 'skeleton' structure which is woven with the weft. The weaving 'gives birth' to a figure, but without indigo dyeing it remains a raw person: such pale and bloodless 'flesh' is considered an immature woman. When observing the Miao people dyeing cloth, I often hear women say that undyed cloth represents a girl who has not yet matured enough to have reached her first menstrual period. A further series of steps are taken to make the cloth appear mature, rosy, submissive, and glossy. The crucial processes involve pounding and steaming to transform the cloth into a cultivated object. Most importantly, Wud Ying said, 'you must make flesh which is in good taste, otherwise, nobody will notice the beauty of the girl.' Their efforts are designed to achieve 'skin' with the desired aesthetic quality. This is a significant part of preparation for the marriage exchange.

Pounding the surface and adding the glue creates a jade-like cloth with highly prized glossy skin. The entire transformation requires spending a month and a half pounding with a heavy mallet (Figure 5.4). Every woman describes the process as extremely difficult and exhausting; nevertheless, 'no pounding, no cultivated cloth.' Shidong Miao women say they like 'a calm and tender cloth, as sophisticated as jade.'

5.3 Soaking in reddish liquid, Jiob Hxangk village, 5 August 2002

5.4   Beating fabric, Dangx Vongx village, 13 August 2008

Wud Ying commented, 'Pounding the cloth educates it to become a beautiful girl, just as we teach our daughters. They must learn how to behave like a girl. Cloth that hasn't been pounded is like a vulgar and tasteless girl; this is a guiding principle for both: making cloth and making a girl.'

The final step is to steam the cloth in a steamer to stabilize color fastness and cowhide glue cohesively (Figure 5.5). The steaming process makes 'raw cloth' into 'cooked cloth.' The method of steaming a cloth is the same as steaming rice. Shidong Miao women use a wooden steaming bucket on the large stove in the kitchen. There are holes in the bottom of the bucket to allow hot air to enter. Before placing the cloth inside, the bottom will be covered with straw. Several rolls of cloth are placed inside in a vertical direction, then the steamer is covered with the lid and steamed for about thirty minutes. When the time is up, these cloth rolls are put on the ground and opened one by one. The cloth is then taken to the Qingshui River, lightly patted wet and dried in the sun (Figure 5.6). It is now mature; rosy, submissive, and glossy. It has both flesh and blood.

Weaving, dyeing, and personhood

For Shidong Miao people, making a cloth is similar to giving birth. The contribution needs to come from both patrilineal and matrilineal family.

5.5 Cloth being steamed, Jiob Hxangk village, Shidong, 8 August 2002

5.6 Drying dyed cloth before beating, Dangk Vongx village, 26 August 2007

The first step of making cloth in Shidong is building the skeleton. The warp forms the bones of the cloth being made as the weft is woven, growing the body. A Shidong woman always sets up her warp with her patrilineal family. The young daughter-in-law does not learn weaving in her natal home. Setting up the warp in the matrilineal home is actually forbidden.

In Shidong, dyeing is also considered the mother's responsibility. However, in contrast to weaving, a Shidong woman always does indigo dyeing with members of her matrilineal family, such as her mother and sisters. The matrilineal side is the 'container of life,' and indigo dyeing uses the matrilineal 'container.' The dyeing is considered the same as pregnancy and the dyeing vat is a container that symbolizes a woman's womb. A married daughter goes back to her mother's home to share the indigo container and labor, and they do the indigo dyeing together.

Unmarried women and girls are forbidden from touching the dyeing vat, and newly married or pregnant women are not allowed to touch or even go anywhere near the indigo dyeing vat. If they did, the dyeing liquid would decay and die. Shidong Miao believe that a spiritual being lives in the vat. The spiritual being would be frightened by the unborn baby of a gestating woman.

On one occasion I saw a woman's fabric which had taken the dye unevenly, leaving some areas uncolored. I began to ask her why but another woman, Zhang Zhiyin, quickly stopped me, and later explained some local beliefs and ritual aspects. The woman doing indigo dyeing was afraid that someone's inappropriate words in front of the vat would interfere with the dyeing outcome, which was why Zhang Zhiyin stopped me from saying anything. She also did not want any public discussion of her failure. It is equally inappropriate to say 'Oh what beautiful cloth!' because malevolent spirits might hear this and be jealous, and then come and interfere with the vat.

Unsuccessful dyeing, understood as a Shidong Miao woman being unable to bring the indigo water to life, is put down to a number of possible causes. One possible cause is interference from ghosts who have frightened the spiritual being who lives in the indigo vat. The best remedy for this situation is to ask a ritual specialist to do a purification ritual. If a woman constantly has trouble with indigo dyeing and has sought the help of a ritual specialist without effect, people would consider the problem as perhaps coming from her previous life. She might have picked up the wrong item in the Thunder God's garden: 'this is related to destiny.'

There is no special ritual practice normally undertaken for beginning the dyeing if it has gone successfully in previous years, although a woman needs blessings from the Thunder God to successfully make beautiful fabrics. As mentioned above, Shidong Miao believe that a spiritual being lives in the vat. If a woman did not produce well-dyed fabric the previous year, then the best remedy is to ask a ritual specialist to do a purification ritual this year. This kind of ritual is classified as *ait dliang* (done with ghosts). These are not normal rituals and it is not good to hold them publicly; they are done secretly. Giant knotweed rhizome is boiled in water to later put into the indigo dyeing water to bring it to life. The ritual specialist kills a chicken which is cooked and eaten by the household and the ritual specialist at the riverside. The ritual specialist cuts a lot of small white paper figures, hand in hand, which are each put on a stick, and placed upright surrounding the indigo vat. The woman puts a bowl beside the figures, with a boiled egg in it to appease ghosts that Shidong Miao believe may come to bother the woman, affecting the beauty of the dyed cloth. The bowl also contains some fresh chili, and a pair of scissors is put on the top. These serve as a deterrent. If any ghosts do try to cause trouble, they can be made uncomfortable with the chili peppers or even harmed with the scissors, so that they stay away from the women who are dyeing the cloth.

In terms of identity, traditionally Shidong Miao people believe that the skills of weaving and dyeing are women's duties and vocations. If a Shidong girl can't do embroidery, she will be considered lazy or not suitable for marriage. If a Shidong woman can't weave and dye, her family will be considered impoverished and unsuitable for marriage. Yet, most Shidong people who grew up in the 1990s have very different attitudes to education and occupations compared with those of the older generation.

Young girls have been able to go to big cities to pursue education or find jobs, and this has changed their traditional ways of living and learning. Many households no longer have time to make cloth from scratch, doing the weaving and dyeing. They therefore now skip some of the steps; for example, they no longer weave cloth and instead buy it in the market, especially *dob*, the plain woven cloth.

Some take this 'white cloth' (i.e. plain, undyed cloth) to the market and have it dyed commercially using chemical dyes. This produces still unfinished dyed cloth which Shidong Miao call 'semi-cooked.' Local women told me that initially (in the early 1990s) they felt ashamed about preparing cloth this way to achieve a quick result but after many years people have become used to it. They have developed a new process in response to the demands of modern society. The main difference is that they have given up the weaving and indigo dyeing. They still maintain the last two steps: adding the flesh and blood, and making the skin. The commercial chemical dyes allow them to get dark or black cloth more quickly, but this semi-cooked cloth is considered rough and vulgar. People say it is immature and incomplete 'semi-cloth' which lacks flesh and blood and skin, so this semi-cooked cloth is also beaten, as described above.

The new way of doing things uses an 'equivalent exchange' principle: using money instead of labor as a workable exchange. I heard some women waiting for cloth to be chemically dyed in the market chatting. One, a part-time worker in a distant factory, explained that she did not have time to weave and dye. Her income working was higher than what she might earn if she stayed at home making cloth. She therefore thought it was reasonable to spend a little money having the dyeing done in exchange for the time to make more money working.

The overheard conversation indicates women are now considering monetary factors when deciding how to allocate their time. The mother traditionally used her labor and made the fabric to produce clothes for everyone in the household, but even traditional indigo dyeing still involved a lot of costs for items such as the warp and weft threads, and the cowhide glue. Plain fabric involved costs of about RMB 1.5 for each *chi*, patterned fabrics about RMB 2–3 per *chi*. Adding the value of the labor, a *chi* of fabric would cost at least ten times as much. So, based on the amounts of different cloth used, a woman's jacket was worth about RMB 260 in 2007.

As social change occurred, the Shidong Miao began using chemical dyes to help speed up the process of making cloth. The critical factor is that they consider the core procedure to be the last stage, making the skin. Currency is something which flows, something alienable, but it is still the mother's labor which transforms semi-cooked cloth from a mere possession into something inalienably connected with her. The labor of making fabric and embroidery is traditionally female. Nevertheless, every outlay of money to buy material for weaving and dyeing is taken from the household and seen as male. Materials from the wild and the market are all considered male and need to be transformed by currency acquired through the mother's outside labor to make the cloth cooked.

So perhaps a critical question as Shidong Miao society interacts with modernity is whether male money can also be seen as female when it is earned by women, and thus constitute the essential transformative female contribution to this stage creating cooked cloth. This remains to be seen. I once went to a ritual specialist with some Shidong Miao women who told me I must use my own money to buy the paper money and incense offerings. They explained that by buying them with my own money, the objects would then be transformed into mine. This indicates that, in this context at least, they saw money as constituting a way to put something of oneself into a spiritual energy transaction – a monetary parallel for how they put something of themselves into cloth through their sweat and labor. This invests cloth with substantial cultural agency in Shidong.

Conclusion

Shidong Miao use the concept of *yenb* and *yangx* to construct the body and gender of cloth. This is not done through technology, as traditional dyeing practices are being replaced by chemical process, but as a result of human and cosmological engagement which takes place through the beating of cloth as a means of educating it. From the weaving, dyeing, and finishing processes, Shidong Miao use human aspects to cultivate cloth, from a material object to one embedded with personhood. This is quite different from the Indonesian research of cloth.[19] In Shidong, cloth is the result of *yenb–yangx* fusion. The father's side provides the skeleton of the cloth and the mother gives it flesh, blood, and fat. Moreover, beating cloth makes it become well educated, and, as with children, this duty is counted as a mother's responsibility.

I found that most women in the Shidong area aged over forty-five could weave and dye fabrics and make clothes in the traditional way. The entire progression requires cooperation between matrilineal and patrilineal kin. The reason is quite simple. Marriage demonstrates that it is important to have a constant exchange of women between *ghaib* (host) and *khat* (guest), the wife takers and wife givers. The woman marrying in from the *khat* side will become a container for the *ghaib* side. When a daughter marries out, she is no longer sharing the house with her brother. Her brother-in-law is the host, and she is a guest. However, she still shares her mother's indigo dyeing container, and will not share with her brother-in-law. She has to go back to her natal home for indigo dyeing.

The plain undyed cloth is raw and immature; the dyeing and finishing process transforms the raw fabric into a well-cooked, mature cloth. Here the concept of maturity is more than biological or material; it also encompasses cultural and moral aspects. The finished fabric has flesh and blood, skin, and personhood. The finished product is metaphorically seen as a daughter. Cloth and women are, of course, different material objects; but traditionally they are both expressions of one fundamental cosmological entity.

From this we can see that Shidong personhood is not just about blood or biology. It is more important to be a social and cultural Shidong person. In the gender classification of the Shidong Miao people, marring out daughters act as a cohesive link in the relationship between host and guest. By making the cloth skeleton with the patrilineal side and making skin and blood with the matrilineal side, she completes the social reproduction process. By making embroidery, weaving, dyeing, and making clothes, Shidong Miao people not only set up a visible boundary, but also complete an invisible social ideal of reproduction (Figure 5.7).

Acknowledgments

I sincerely thank James Russell Wilkerson for his inspiration and guidance in kinship research so that I could understand the society, culture, and cosmology of Shidong Miao. I would also like to thank Eveline Bingaman

5.7 Young women dressed in silver, displaying their households' wealth, Nangl Hlinb village, 2 May 2007

for her editing and revision suggestions, so that I could express my ideas more clearly and succinctly.

Notes

1. This chapter is an ethnographic study of the cloth and clothing of the Shidong Miao society in southeastern Guizhou province. My fieldwork took place in three stages: summer pre-fieldwork in 2002, intensive fieldwork from 2006–2007, and additional fieldwork in the summer of 2008. I also went to the Jishou University library to check historical documents at the beginning of October 2006. I also reviewed the collections on Shidong Miao at Fu Jen University between different stages of fieldwork.
2. The Miao people are an ethnic group with various dialects and self-designations. For example, in the Miao language of the Western Hunan province region, they may refer to themselves as Ghab Xongb, Deb Xongb, or Deb Nceut. In the Eastern Guizhou dialect, they self-designate as Hmub or Ghab Nes. In the Sichuan-Guizhou-Yunnan dialect, they refer to themselves as Hmongb. After China's ethnic identification efforts in the 1950s, these different self-designated groups were collectively referred to as "Miao."
3. Nicholas Tapp, *The Hmong of China: Context, Agency, and the Imaginary* (Boston and Leiden: Brill Academic Publishers, Inc., 2003), p. 7.
4. Inez De Beauclair, *Ethnographic Studies: The Collected Papers of Inez de Beauclair* (Taipei: Western Books Anthropology, Southern Materials Center, 1986); Zhengwen Yang 楊正文, Miaozu fushi wenhua (苗族服飾文化 Miao Costume Culture) (Guizhou minzu chubanshe 貴州民族出版社, 1998).
5. Located in Taijiang county, Southeastern Guizhou Miao and Dong autonomous prefecture (qian dongnan miaozu dongzu zizhizhou 黔東南苗族侗族自治洲). According to the fifth population census (2000), the population of Shidong is 12,332. More than 94.9% are ethnic Miao; the remainder are Han, Tung-Chia (Dong), or Chung-Chia (Buyi).
6. James C. Scott, *The Art of Not Being Governed: An Anarchist History of Upland Southeast Asia* (New Haven and London: Yale University Press, 2009).
7. Zhaohua Ho, 'Gifts to Dye For: Cloth and Person among Shidong Miao in Guizhou Province (染之成禮：貴州施洞苗族的布與人).' PhD dissertation (National Tsing Hua University 國立清華大學人類學博士論文, 2011).
8. Herold J. Wiens, *China's March toward the Tropics: A Discussion of the Southward Penetration of China's Culture, Peoples, and Political Control in Relation to the Non-Han-Chinese Peoples of South China and in the Perspective of Historical and Cultural Geography* (Hamden: Shoe String Press, 1954), pp. 232–233.
9. Ho, 'Gifts to Dye For,' ch. 3.
10. In Miao society, the practice of exchanging betrothal gifts and engaging in bilateral marriage allows women to move within the community, maintaining the cultural ideal of "a head coming, a head going." This is achieved through restricted intermarriage and a system of gift exchange, which helps preserve the boundaries of the community and ensures the transmission and continuity of social relationships and cultural representations.
11. Ibid., ch. 2.
12. The extensive range and variety of visual styles have long been a renowned function of the clothing worn by Shidong Miao women, particularly their embroidered jackets. Through embroidery, Shidong Miao women express themselves creatively. On the one hand, embroidery holds significant collective social representation, and on the other, it serves as a vehicle for individual artistic expression. Besides showcasing a woman's design flair, possessing high-quality embroidery skills elevates

a woman's status within the community. Women's jackets in Shidong Miao can be categorized into two types: festival jackets, reserved for special occasions, and ordinary daily wear jackets. Festival jackets usually incorporate embroidery created using stencils bought from the market, while some combine elements from the two major embroidery categories. These festival jackets can be further differentiated into four types, primarily based on their distinct sleeve designs: *hob mongl, ob ait, khait mongl*, and *hob jub*. Additionally, each type can be further subdivided into blue (dark) and red (bright) variations.

13 Even so, a daughter is considered to be of great value to a family, and especially to the mother. Among Shidong Miao, it is considered a great pity for a woman to be without a daughter. Not only will that mother have no one to pass her clothes and silver to in the next generation, but also there will be no one to listen to her, accompany her, and cry for her when she dies.

14 James Wilkerson, 'The Case of "The Returning Sleeve": A Preliminary Description of the Classification of Shidong Miao Kin Terms,' Paper presented at the Conference in the Sixteenth Meeting of the International Union of Anthropological and Ethnological Sciences, Kunming, Yunnan, July 2009.

15 The Thunder God is the highest deity that Shidong Miao interact with in the spiritual realm. They believe that the Thunder God was assigned by the Chinese emperor to control the Miao people. This is analogous to the imperial paradigm of 'using barbarians to control barbarians' (Ch. *yiyi zhiyi* 以夷制夷), more particularly 'using a Miao deity to control the Miao people.' The emperor delegated his power to the Thunder God to manage the fate of the Miao people, but Miao men still have control over both pregnancy and women, both in the living world and in the garden of the Thunder God.

16 The pattern threads are usually dyed beforehand.

17 This diamond in weaving contexts is also referred to as a 'rhombus.'

18 One *jin* equals 500 grams.

19 According to the Leiden school and Van Wouden's approaches, cloth is closely connected to symbolic and cosmological aspects. Regarding reproduction, making and using cloth represents the kinship system and the ideal of society. For example, the research mentioned, like that of J. H. Jager Gerling and Niesson, is based on kinship studies. In Niesson's study of Batak cloth, during weddings, Batak families keep careful count of which clans donate what type of large woven cloths, called *ulos*, and give certain cloths back in exchange in a very formal, ritualized set of ceremonies. Niesson (1985, 1994, 2009), Drake (1991), Gavin (2004) and Hoskins (1989) illuminate a dynamic relationship between social groups and their representation in material culture. Moreover, Niessen's long-term research on the woven cloth of the Toba Batak offers a definitive study. The Toba Batak submit to a dualistic worldview of opposing male and female, which are expressed in the terms *ulso* and *piso* (similar to the Shidong Miao concepts of *yenb* and *yangx* that are elaborated in this chapter). Gifts for Toba Batak are gendered; female gifts pass from mother to daughter, and male gifts pass from father to son (Niesson 1985). With regards to cosmology, what is needed for a full understanding of this materiality is not only an elucidation of the social metaphor aspect, but additionally a cultural investigation of religion and reproduction.

Bibliography

De Beauclair, Inez. *Ethnographic Studies: The Collected Papers of Inez de Beauclair*. Taipei: Western Books Anthropology, Southern Materials Center, 1986.

Ho, Zhaohua. 'Gifts to Dye For: Cloth and Person among Shidong Miao in Guizhou Province (染之成禮：貴州施洞苗族的布與人).' PhD dissertation, National Tsing Hua University 國立清華大學人類學博士論文, 2011.

Scott, James C. *The Art of Not Being Governed: An Anarchist History of Upland Southeast Asia*. New Haven and London: Yale University Press, 2009.

Tapp, Nicholas. *The Hmong of China: Context, Agency, and the Imaginary*. Boston and Leiden: Brill Academic Publishers, 2003.

Wiens, Herold J. *China's March toward the Tropics: A Discussion of the Southward Penetration of China's Culture, Peoples, and Political Control in Relation to the Non-Han-Chinese Peoples of South China and in the Perspective of Historical and Cultural Geography*. Hamden: Shoe String Press, 1954.

Wilkerson, James. 'The Case of "The Returning Sleeve": A Preliminary Description of the Classification of Shidong Miao Kin Terms.' Paper presented at the Conference in the Sixteenth Meeting of the International Union of Anthropological and Ethnological Sciences. Kunming, Yunnan, 15–23 July 2009.

Yang Zhengwen 楊正文. Miaozu fushi wenhua [苗族服飾文化 Miao clothes and culture]. Guizhou minzu chubanshe 貴州民族出版社, 1998.

PART II

Gendering creative agency: women fashion designers, textile makers, and entrepreneurs

6

Soft power: Guo Pei and the fashioning of matriarchy

Kristen Loring Brennan

When the Chinese designer, Guo Pei 郭培 (b. 1967), catapulted into the world of Parisian *haute couture*, critics embraced her embellished styles and grand scale of production – a match of materials and labor that seemed possible only in China. They pondered Guo Pei's bold leap back over the austerity of the Mao years to the iconography and materiality of imperial China, seen in ornate applications of crystals and gold thread, with embroidered symbols on lavish surfaces of silk and fur. Celebrity clients and museum exhibitions further amplified the romantic Orientalism of designers, as seen in the red carpet pageantry of Guo Pei's *Yellow Queen*, worn by the singer Rihanna at the 2015 Met Gala (Figure 6.1). The gown represents two years of labor and materials so elaborate that it could be lifted only with the help of several assistants. Significantly, the warm, golden yellow hue of the robe, and its expansive, scalloped form, prompted its characterization in Western media as a French omelette, rather than as the ceremonial robe of Qing dynasty (1644–1912) emperors and their consorts, thereby obscuring Guo Pei's poignant statement about gender and power in Chinese history.

Recent exhibitions, such as *China: Through the Looking Glass* at The Metropolitan Museum, New York, have examined the mechanisms of chinoiserie, further probing Guo Pei's identity as a Chinese designer and her works as emblems of a radically different social era. Andrew Bolton has observed appropriately that Western designers' focus on fashion over politics privileges an aesthetic of surfaces, one that is less concerned with cultural conventions.[1] Nevertheless, the visual histories of Guo Pei's designs, communicated through their materiality, forms, and emblems, appear to resonate with her Chinese clientele who embrace these marks of imperial grandeur and associate them with their own cultural heritage.

6.1 Guo Pei, *Yellow Queen. One Thousand and Two Nights* collection, 2010. Silk cloak embroidered with metal thread and silk and 24-carat-gold-spun thread and adorned with silk bows and fox fur. Collection of Guo Pei. Photo in Guo Pei, *Couture and Beyond*, p. 12

With her debut in Paris, Guo Pei came to operate within the construct of transorientalism, which Adam Geczy has described as 'a continual process of intervention involving appropriation, reclaiming, and reshaping.'[2] Indeed, one could argue that the project of disentangling Guo Pei's work from its audiences, whether in Beijing, Hong Kong, New York, or Paris, has obscured a broader issue: her pivotal role as a woman designing *haute couture*.

As the first Chinese designer invited into the official Chambre Syndicale de la Haute Couture, Guo Pei joined a handful of female designers at the helm of Parisian *haute couture*. Women now direct three of the most famous French *couture* houses, Chanel, Givenchy, and Dior, bringing techniques and concepts to rethink common approaches of their former patricians. As fashion critic Vanessa Friedman recently observed, 'Couture, after all, is traditionally considered the most hidebound part of an industry latterly famous for being built on the practice of men dictating to women how they should look. Not anymore. Not now.'[3] Guo Pei similarly engages with the long-standing patriarchy of French *couture* houses through her designs, though it is not through the authoritative trousers of Chanel's Virginie Viard or the element of personal choice presented by Dior's Maria Grazia Chiuri. Nor does she indulge the drab palette and gender-neutral suits of China's Mao era – a wardrobe praised for its revolutionary, egalitarian agenda. Rather, her works bypass recent history, and instead recapture the traditional handwork and lavish materials of the late Qing dynasty, capturing an aspect of the early modern era that is fresh, incisive, and remarkably forward thinking.

Recalling the observations conveyed by her grandmother, Guo Pei's designs point to powerful matriarchs like Empress Dowager Cixi (1835–1908), who used fashion and international diplomacy to shape public opinion and shepherd the role of China in the modern world. Like Cixi, Guo Pei's designs visualize power as an amassing of resources and relationships through cultural diplomacy, specifically soft power. A term coined by political scientist Joseph Nye to describe the influence exerted through international relations, soft power utilizes the seduction of a country's culture, political ideals, or policies, and the perception of their legitimacy; it is 'the ability to get what you want through attraction rather than coercion or payments.'[4] Identifying the relevance of this concept in the arts, Gail Dexter Lord and Ngaire Blankenberg have explored the role of museums in civil society, defining the resources of soft power as 'intangibles,' such as ideas, knowledge, values, and culture.[5] Guo Pei exemplifies this notion of soft power by exercising gender and ethnicity as a means of allure in the world of *haute couture*.

This chapter explores Guo Pei's fascination with the Qing dynasty Empress Dowager Cixi and the contemporary American model, Carmen Dell'Orefice (b. 1931), as an alternative to the femme fatale presented in fashion from the nineteenth century through the present. Andrew Bolton has described the femme fatale as a highly educated woman who enjoyed the accoutrements of wealth and social standing, yet was also a libertine, challenging the constraints of contemporary sexual practice.[6] Often intertwined with the *fashionista au courant*, the femme fatale represents the celebration of the barren, sterile, and childless woman. As Valerie Steele pointedly described, she was regarded as 'a dangerous individual who selfishly ignored her familial duties in pursuit of her own pleasures.'[7] The matriarch, in contrast, is defined by her obligations to her world, whether familial, social, or institutional, and further revered for age and lineage. Although her position is in large part due to her fertility, as Julia Twigg has observed, nonetheless older women are regarded in contemporary fashion as 'beyond the erotic,' and even 'beyond sex itself.'[8] Guo Pei suggests that rather than the contingency of the femme fatale, who is defined by the absence of maternal duty, the roles of Cixi and Dell'Orefice are intimately and consequentially linked to life cycle rites, thereby displacing the seduction of the erotic with the allure of soft power.

Rather than portraying women as a sexualized commodity or cunning consumer, Guo Pei inverts the ephemerality of the femme fatale and challenges notions of age and tradition as antiquated. Empress Dowager Cixi offers a precedent – a well-connected matriarch whose theatrical imagery articulated and extended her worldly power both within China and beyond. For the runway, Guo Pei selected the iconic model, Dell'Orefice, who in her late eighties embodies regal authority and responsibility while reigning over the longest career in high fashion. Both Cixi and Dell'Orefice serve Guo Pei's vision of powerful matriarchs as crucial to the success and endurance of the institutions they serve, whether the Manchu Qing dynasty or the world of *haute couture*. By leveraging dignity and dominance through soft power, Guo Pei offers a provocative image of a woman of means – a matriarch who defines history.

Visualizing soft power in twentieth-century Beijing and Paris

At the Paris Salon of 1906, the Dutch-American artist Hubert Vos (1855–1935) presented an unauthorized portrait of Empress Dowager Cixi, picturing her seated in a three-quarter-length portrait, wearing an emerald gown and clutching a round fan displaying a peony flower.[9] A duplicate of the painting, which Vos painted a year later, accorded more closely with his sitter's specifications.[10] Rendered in full length, the authorized image portrayed Cixi clutching the peony fan once again, but with a more youthful visage and wearing an informal robe of imperial yellow silk (Figure 6.2). Reserved for empresses, empress dowagers, and second-rate court consorts, the luminous golden surface of the robe signaled Cixi's power and legitimacy as a Qing matriarch. The imperial yellow color could also be found adorning court objects, as Cixi undoubtedly was aware, for she rose to power by navigating the channels of filial piety, asserting political authority on behalf of her son and mastering ritual occasions.[11] However, to a Parisian audience, the color of her robe appears to have been less significant – an oversight that Guo Pei corrected over a century later with her debut of *Yellow Queen*.

Having rendered the peony prominently on Cixi's fan in both of his portraits, Vos also recognized the flower as an icon of Cixi that also aligned with Western perceptions of imperial China as exotic and feminine. Cixi celebrated the peony as the national flower, devoting a terrace for viewing peonies at the Summer Palace in 1903. Around that time, she commissioned several portraits of herself, including the painting by Vos, which she sent to Western dignitaries abroad.[12] Many of those portraits, both paintings and photographs, pictured Cixi beside images of peonies, drawing a close association between this powerful woman and her visual emblem. The peony thus could be intended as a message of Qing legitimacy directed towards domestic audiences, as well as an icon to captivate subjects abroad.

However, for Cixi, the peony also had dual roles – it both suggested dynastic continuity while distinguishing her reign amid a global audience. With its woody branches resplendent with paper-thin petals, the

6.2 Hubert Vos, *Empress Dowager Cixi*, 1905. Oil on canvas, 200 × 121.6 cm. Gardens of Nurtured Harmony, Summer Palace, Beijing

peony symbolized a profusion of wealth – both showy and alluring, offering the promise of spring. Regarded as the 'King of Flowers,' the peony was referred to as *fugui hua* 富貴花, or 'flower of wealth and honor.' Cixi likely identified the peony for its role in defining the reigns of several Qing emperors during the seventeenth through twentieth centuries, most notably the Kangxi (1654–1722), Yongzheng (1678–1735), and Qianlong (1711–1799) emperors.[13] One informal portrait pictures the empress dowager playing chess in a garden setting, subtly configuring her role as a matriarch through lineage and power (Figure 6.3). Wang Cheng-hua has identified her opponent as her son, the Tongzhi Emperor (1861–1875), due to the highly politicized nature of chess in imperial portraiture.[14] Cixi, poised as if waiting for his next move, is well matched to her son in this competitive game. A pine tree frames the seated Cixi, as her son rests his arm on the edge of the table. Visibly indicating Cixi's power is her blue gown, adorned with peonies, echoing both the blue robe of the emperor and the flowering pink peonies positioned centrally on the ground below. Peng Ying-chen has noted that the peonies symbolize the prosperous joint rulership of mother and son,[15] one carefully orchestrated by Cixi.

The Empress Dowager Playing Chinese Chess not only reveals how Cixi defined her power through gendered contrast with her son, the emperor, but also through ethnicity. Beneath her gown, the white platforms of her shoes prominently display her status as a powerful Manchu empress. Termed 'horse hoof' shoes, or *matidi* 馬蹄底, their imprint resembles that of the horse's hoof, formed of a wood base several inches high, wrapped in white cloth (Figure 6.4). The height of the platform, positioned directly under the arch of the foot, requires the wearer to carry her body in an upright posture, carefully balanced over the center of the shoe. Whether walking with the assistance of servants, or independently moving by swinging one's arms, the shoes evoke an image of power and responsibility through her height and strength. Such a vision contrasted with the footwear and posture of Han Chinese women, whose bound feet often measured only a few inches long, dramatically abbreviating their range of movement and forming their posture into a gesture of subjugation.

The crippled demeanor of Han women with bound feet not only contrasted with Manchu palace women, who strode upright, but also highlighted gender differences between the two cultures. Forbidden to bind their feet, Manchu women rode horses, practiced archery and hunting, and walked in public places.[16] They occupied significant positions in court rituals and politics as shamans and lieutenants on the battlefield. Well-to-do Han women, limited in their mobility, circulated within the inner chambers of their residences where activities included embroidery, painting, music, and literary arts. Their stature, as well as their shoe size, was visibly reduced in comparison to both Han men and Manchu women, and so defined their roles in both gender and ethnic realms.

6.3 Court painters in Beijing, *Empress Dowager Cixi Playing Chinese Chess (Weiqi)*. Tongzhi or Guangxu period, 1862–1908. Hanging scroll, ink and color on silk, 231.1 × 142.6 cm. Photograph by Zhang Yuntian

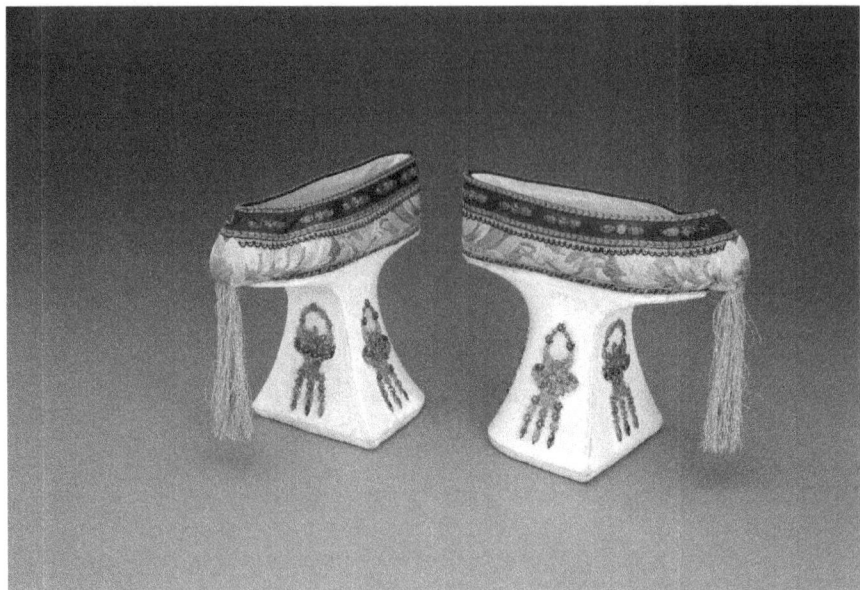

6.4 Platform shoes. China, Guangxu period, 1875–1908. Embroidery, polychrome silk threads on silk satin with silk tassels; platforms: wood core covered with cotton and glass beads. Photograph by Li Fan

The floral motif embroidered on Cixi's shoes further conveys a gendered representation of her imperial power. Alternately known as 'flowerpot' shoes, or *huapenxie* 花盆鞋, slippers rest atop the square platforms, embroidered with flowers such as peonies and adorned with silk tassels. The shoes resemble the shape and motif of a porcelain flowerpot that was in production at the time of the Tongzhi Emperor's death in 1874, amid his ambitious plan to construct Yuanmingyuan, the Garden of Perfect Brightness, for his mother, the Empress Dowager Cixi (Figure 6.5). Cixi approved the design of this flowerpot, a vibrant display of peonies on a white background, for use in her future garden palace in the Garden of Myriad Springs.[17] The title of her intended palace, 'Whole world celebrating as one family' (*Tiandi yijiachun* 天地一家春), indicates how each of these elements – the flowerpot shoes, the flowerpot, and the peonies embroidered on her gowns, together convey a vision of Cixi as a matron of China and embodiment of worldly power.

Paintings and photography were part of Cixi's larger effort to wield soft power through diplomacy, complemented by gifts distinguished by her preferred visual currency: the peony. In a notable example, Cixi gifted a photograph of herself to Sarah Pike Conger (1843–1932), the wife of the first United States ambassador to imperial China, who served during the Boxer Rebellion.[18] Another photograph depicts Conger and other foreign

6.5 Flowerpot with peonies and birds. Imperial Porcelain Factory, Jingdezhen, Guangxu period, 1875 or 1876, porcelain with enamels over colorless glaze, 23 × 27 × 21.9 cm. Photograph by Wang Jin

envoys' wives alongside the empress dowager in the Hall of Happiness and Longevity (Leshou tang 樂壽堂).[19] Conger later wrote that along with photographs, the empress dowager specifically sent gifts of peonies to the diplomatic ladies in Beijing. One season, Cixi sent eight painted porcelain pots with fine black stands, 'filled with most thrifty bush peonies bearing exquisite pink blossoms and buds.' Ms. Conger then created a pillow for its petals, covered in unfading flowers embroidered in the 'imperial Yellow.'[20] Such gifts – which we also may understand as visual exchanges – clearly expedited the association between peony imagery and Cixi's regency in the early twentieth century.

Cixi's command of both material wealth and social resources formed an expansive, global network of relationships between women. Marked by the golden hue of imperial yellow, and the voluptuous blossoms of the peony, the objects and imagery of the empress dowager exuded royalty and grace. In shrewdly expanding and redirecting patriarchal practices, such as the use of visual imagery to promote filial piety and glorify her reign as a Manchu empress, Cixi brought attention to matriarchal power both at home and abroad. Her message of soft power and grand-scale responsibility resonated with contemporaries, including Guo Pei's grandmother, whose experience of bound feet and appreciation of embroidery presented a mandate to her granddaughter.

Queenship and courtly costume: Guo Pei's *Palace Flowers*

Although the concept of queenship rarely enters into our vocabulary today, Guo Pei's approach to *haute couture* centers upon the roles of formidable matriarchs in visual history. Matriarchs include queens and empresses, the most aspirational of whom become queen mothers or empress dowagers. As Michelle Beer has explained, the bodies of queens were invested with enormous political potential, due to their intimate relationship with the king and their potential role as mothers of the heir to the throne. Their bodies, and the material culture that clothed and surrounded those bodies, defined their honor and identities.[21] A matriarch demonstrates the use of soft power through extensive interpersonal connections and articulates her values through clothing and adornment rather than by hard-power values of competition or force. Consequently, she who emerges at the top of her lineage as a queen or empress is defined by her legacy of relations rather than her liberation from them.

Guo Pei's *Palace Flowers*, from the *Legend of the Dragon* collection (2012), invokes the aesthetic surfaces favored by Empress Dowager Cixi, kept alive through the memories transmitted to Guo Pei by her grandmother (Figure 6.6). Drawing on the celebratory attire of the Qing court, or 'flowery costume' (*huayi* 花衣), the robe is embroidered with silver and twenty-four carat gold thread, a silk jacquard robe in a vibrant fuchsia hue embroidered with peonies and waves, established symbols of wealth and Manchu kingship. The billowing gown beneath is covered in three-dimensional silk flowers, roundels that contrast with gold-embroidered ornaments resembling the tail feathers of a phoenix, a symbol of the empress. Flowers such as these were popular at the Qing court, as Cao Xueqin described in the late eighteenth-century novel, *Dream of Red Chambers*. Bearing the precious gift of silk flowers for the girls of the noble Jia family to wear in their hair, Aunt Xue notes that they are 'exquisitely fashioned by Palace craftsmen out of silk gauze.'[22] The term 'palace flowers' thus refers not only to the flowers on Guo Pei's gown, but also to the palace women who epitomize the fresh romance of springtime.[23] Recalling the splendor of the adornments and festivities enjoyed by the highest-ranking women of the Manchu court, the robe thus intertwines symbols of gender with imperial power.

The production of Guo Pei's works, such as *Palace Flowers*, represents a vast command of resources and materials. Guo Pei employs several hundred embroiderers and tailors at her workshop in the suburbs of Beijing, who spend between months and years constructing each ensemble by hand. She further procures large quantities of obscure materials, such as the silk flowers on the gown, from private collections in the countryside where they were formerly used for the lavish adornment of Qing headpieces and other accessories. Such remarkable amounts of labor, materials,

6.6 Guo Pei, *Palace Flowers*. *Legend of the Dragon* collection, 2012. Silk, jacquard, silver-spun thread, gold-spun thread, beads, Swarovski crystals, fur, silk peonies salvaged from private collections in the countryside. Collection of Guo Pei. Photo in Guo Pei, *Couture and Beyond*, p. 76

knowledge, and specialized skills could be likened to the production of Manchu court robes, such as those worn by the empress dowager. In the Qing dynasty, embroidery of the finest materials took place at the Imperial Silk Manufactory in Suzhou, while tailors in the Imperial Workshop in Beijing stood ready to fashion each robe to appropriate size.[24] As Manchu court attire denoted the power of the empress through this tremendous web of resources, Guo Pei's *Palace Flowers* similarly contextualizes the woman who wears it in light of prominent matriarchs of the past.

Peonies and phoenixes adorn the robes and footwear of *Palace Flowers*, seamlessly incorporating the iconography prized by Empress Dowager Cixi in the late Qing dynasty. Embroidered in deep red and pink hues atop a gold and silver motif of billowing clouds, peony blossoms surround the heel of the platform shoes, physically supporting the wearer in a gesture of power and responsibility while evoking the flowerpot form of Manchu footwear (Figure 6.7). Golden feathers adorn the embroidered uppers of the shoes, again simulating the feathers of a phoenix. As Evelyn Rawski has pointed out, both court ladies and specialist sewing women in the palace might have engaged in the embroidery of the uppers of shoes[25] – a domestic activity of the Qing court captured in Guo Pei's design.

Further referencing the upright postures of Qing palace women, Guo Pei created a headpiece dripping with golden tassels, inlaid with precious stones, and encased within an elaborate metal fillet. The headdress recalls the mesmerizing decorations affixed to the horizontal *bianfang* 扁方, or non-official headdress worn by married Manchu palace women and rendered in Vos's *Empress Dowager Cixi*. Moreover, the exaggerated vertical flanges also recall the golden embellishments and precious stones adorning the official court hat, or *chaoguan* 朝冠, of Manchu consorts. Such hats displayed ornaments and finials carefully prescribed for each rank, set atop a crown of luxurious fur, satin, or velvet.[26] By extending the surface decoration of metalwork and precious materials to the entire headpiece, Guo Pei created a towering illusion that closely aligned with the luminous materiality of royal crowns throughout world histories.

Although contemporary viewers may associate the voluptuous forms and decadent materials of *Palace Flowers* with imperial China more broadly, they may overlook notable distinctions between Manchu and Han dress. The Qianlong Emperor sought to define Manchu court attire in 1759 through guidelines presented in *Illustrated Precedents for Ritual Paraphernalia of the Imperial [Qing] Dynasty*, or *Huangchao liqi tushi* 皇朝禮器圖式.[27] Significantly, the A-line silhouette of *Palace Flowers* follows the shape of Qing imperial costumes, as seen in the portrait of Cixi by Vos. However, Guo Pei departed from formal women's court attire by replacing the requisite outermost garment, a detachable collar, with a full-length robe constructed by inserting seams that attach sleeves at the shoulders.

Guo Pei and the fashioning of matriarchy 147

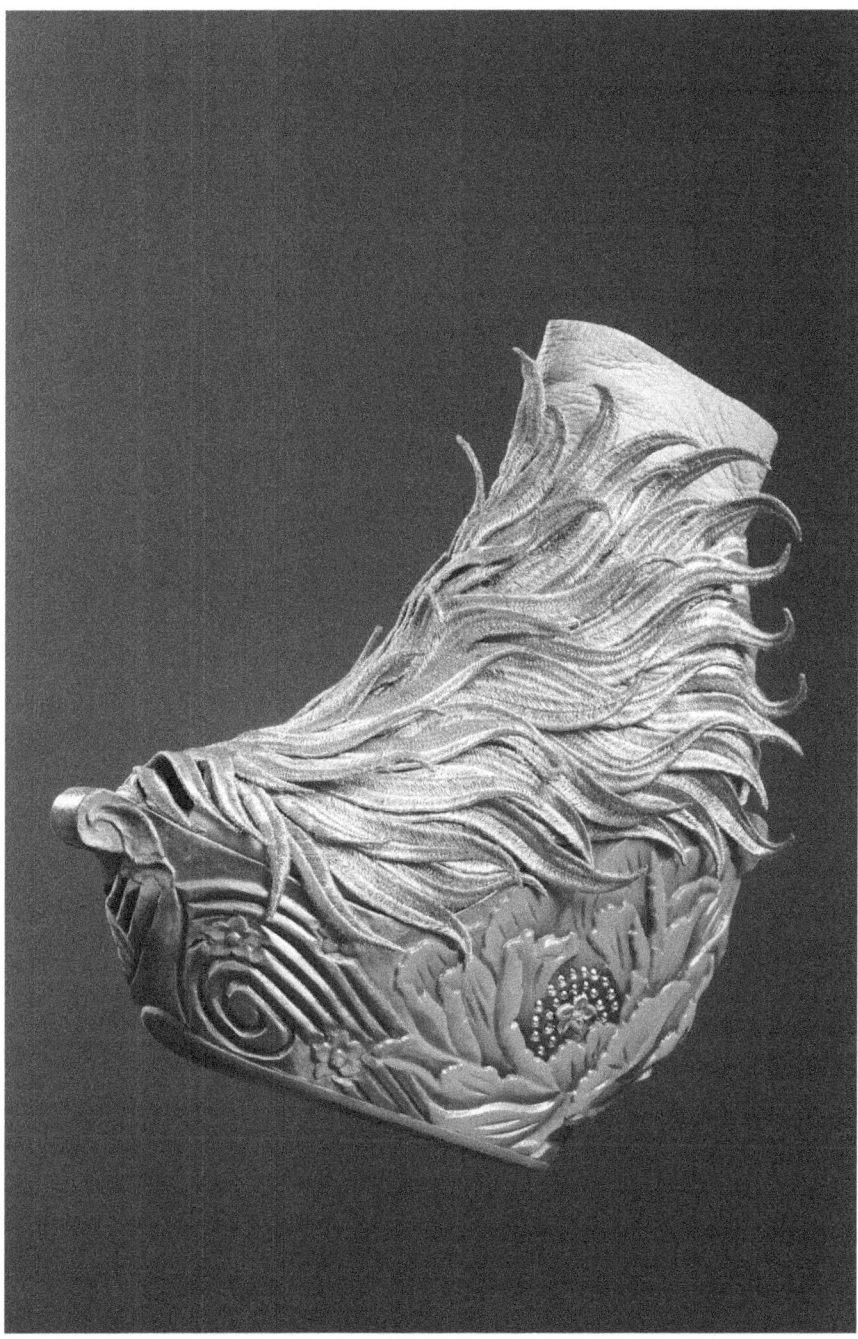

6.7 Guo Pei, *Palace Flowers*, detail of shoes. *Legend of the Dragon* collection, 2012. Collection of Guo Pei. Photo in Guo Pei, *Couture and Beyond*, p. 81

Narrow and elegant, the sleeves of *Palace Flowers* end in a slight V-shaped diagonal below the wrist, recalling the sleeves of Manchu women's robes that taper from the shoulder and end in a cuff shaped like a horse's hoof. As Jan Stuart and Qu Weixun have observed, the horse-shaped cuff is generally recognized as a reference to the hand coverings worn by semi-nomadic horsemen and hunters from whom the Manchu are descended.[28] Signaling distinction from the wide sleeves of Han women's robes, tapering sleeves reiterate the Manchu heritage of the reigning Qing court. Moreover, Guo Pei's adjustments to the robe allow the silk flowers and golden phoenix tails adorning the gown to billow forth in a frontal view, reserving the full length of the back of the robe for its mesmerizing pattern of embroidered waves and peonies.

In keeping with the propriety of the Manchu court, Guo Pei's *Palace Flowers* obscures the figure beneath, denying any curves or distinctive physical features that might denote the gender, age, or ethnicity of its wearer. One may contrast the design of *Palace Flowers* with the attenuated shapes that fashion queenship in early modern Europe, such as the corset. Although the silhouette of the form-shaping corset seems antithetical to the concealing impulse of the A-line gown, both project power through an imposing display of self-control. Initially a fashion among the ruling class, the corset denoted cultural ideals including, as Valerie Steele has noted, 'social status, self-discipline, artistry, respectability, beauty, youth, and erotic allure.'[29] Thus, while the technology differed – corsets and hoop skirts rather than platform shoes beneath an A-line robe, for instance – uprightness in posture conveyed wealth and social standing in both early modern Europe and China. Consequently, Guo Pei's *Palace Flowers* suggests that a matriarch seduces with a powerful, upright form, one that embodies the stable footprint of a horse, the glistening feathers of a phoenix, and the exuberant blossoms of a peony.

Thus, *Palace Flowers* demonstrates Guo Pei's characterization of queenship in light of qualities embodied by the Qing Empress Dowager Cixi. Through the use of soft power in diplomacy, whether by the gifting of peonies that mirrored her court dress or obliging Western traditions of photographic and painted portraits, Cixi cultivated a global network of supporters. In one notable encounter, the diplomatic wife, Sarah Pike Conger, encouraged Cixi to commission the portrait painter Katherine Carl (1865–1938) to create images of the empress dowager as a means to mediate negative press in the West.[30] These three women formed a concerted vision of Cixi as an alternate image of royalty, one neutralized by the feminine associations of the peony and contextualized by European approaches to picturing royalty. Furthering their collaborative impulse, Guo Pei harnessed the allure of queenship by re-envisioning the palace flowers and yellow robes of the empress dowager for the world of *haute couture*.

Crowning a matriarch in Beijing and Paris

In presenting her muse, Carmen Dell'Orefice, an unmistakable face in fashion and the oldest living model to walk the runway, Guo Pei further posited that the future of fashion is not found in youth or consumerism. Shunning the sexual liberation of the childless femme fatale and the consumerist fantasy of a fashionista, she rendered Dell'Orefice as an aspirational icon who possesses the confidence and poise of over seven decades of a career in fashion. In doing so, Guo Pei emphasized age and endurance as intrinsic components of the lineage and ancestry that undergird matriarchal power. Drawing on the visual lexicon of queenship in China and Europe, Guo Pei designed works for Dell'Orefice that generate soft power through bold forms and lavish materials. Moreover, in casting Dell'Orefice as a queen at shows in both Beijing and Paris, Guo Pei recentered cultural ideals regarding age, beauty, and power in the contemporary moment.

In the debut of Guo Pei's *One Thousand and Two Nights* collection (2009) in Beijing, Dell'Orefice strode the runway with the assistance of four young men, her white hair fanning out from beneath a brass crown inflected with crystals and glistening gems. Her gown, weighing ninety pounds, has been referred to as *White Queen* (Figure 6.8).[31] In contrast to the A-line silhouette of *Palace Flowers*, *White Queen* is cut close to the model's body, emphasizing her elongated form while glistening golden ornaments and dangling pearls accentuate the curvature of her breasts, waist, and hips. Resembling neither a Manchu empress nor a French queen, the columnar silhouette nonetheless emphasizes upright posture – indexing power through self-discipline. Moreover, the gown reveals the sensual curves of Dell'Orefice's female figure to honor crucial aspects of queenship: fertility and piety. In doing so, Guo Pei reiterated that fashion and material culture articulate the queen's position in relation to the king, future kings, and the people of her nation or empire.[32]

Dell'Orefice, modeling for the first time for Guo Pei in Beijing, appeared to embody a notion of Parisian high *couture* formed from the legacy of European queenship. In *White Queen*, the pale blue tones of the silk, golden ornamentation, and scrolling curves are reminiscent of the French Rococo. The cool palette marks a distinct contrast with the Qing imperial overtones of Guo Pei's *Yellow Queen*, which appears bold and decisive in contrast. The robe of *White Queen* requires the model to extend her arms to either side, positioning them as a frame for the floor-length silk sleeves. The entire robe is embroidered with gold and bordered in fox fur. While Guo Pei may have favored pastel hues for her stately muse, her use of fur in both *White Queen* and *Yellow Queen* intersects with myriad cultural contexts. At various times throughout European history, sumptuary laws regulated the use of fur, recognizing its association with wealth and status in society. More recently, fur has been associated with sexuality – a

6.8 Guo Pei, *White Queen*. *One Thousand and Two Nights* collection, 2010. Silk mesh gown embroidered with silk-, 24-karat gold- and silver-spun thread, and embellished with crystals, gems, beads, sequins, and pearls; embroidered silk cape trimmed in fox fur; brass crown embellished with gems, Swarovski crystals, diamonds, and pearls. Collection of Guo Pei. Photo in Guo Pei, *Couture and Beyond*, pp. 46–47

reading furthered by the shapely silhouette modeled by Dell'Orefice.[33] Although fur represents a coveted resource throughout world history, it bears especial significance in Qing imperial dress as a marker of Manchu identity. As Jonathan Schlesinger has observed, 'To be Manchu was to wear fur,' in contrast to Han Chinese, who wore silk during the early years of the dynasty.[34] As the Manchu assimilated over the following centuries, Chinese elites also came to wear fur, and gradually this luxurious material came to signify a broader imperial sensibility. Dell'Orefice, tasked with modeling this confluence of French royalty and Qing imperial aesthetics in Beijing, acknowledges what Geczy has described as 'the impossibility of saying where the Orient begins and where the West starts.'[35] The project of unpacking the transorientalism of Dell'Orefice modeling Guo Pei's regal, Rococo-inflected gown in Beijing, therefore, is also an act of acknowledging our postglobal stance in this present moment.

Guo Pei's creation further transcends geopolitical, cultural, and even historical boundaries in its staging at the Beijing National Stadium, popularly nicknamed the 'Bird's Nest.' Jointly designed by architects Jacques Herzog, Pierre de Meuron, and project architect Stefan Marbach of Herzog & de Meuron in Basel, Switzerland, along with Li Xinggang of

China Architectural Design & Research and the artist Ai Weiwei, the structure represents international coordination in its construction and use as an Olympic stadium. The curved steel frame, shaped into an enormous web of metal, is rendered with the quaint associations of a bird's nest and repurposed as a cradle for humanity. Its design has been likened to crazing, a random patterning of fine cracks seen on the glaze of fine Chinese porcelains. To others, it recalls the Chinese delicacy of bird's nest soup. Regardless, Guo Pei's presentation of Dell'Orefice modeling *White Queen* in the Bird's Nest has the visual effect of dignifying those who navigate power structures to form enduring cultural institutions.

Guo Pei later selected Dell'Orefice to model her *Legend Collection* (2017) at the Conciergerie in Paris, a marked contrast with the audience and setting she occupied in Beijing. Having recently gained an invitation from the Haute Couture Commission, Guo Pei presented Dell'Orefice in her mid-eighties, wearing a luminous gown created specifically for her. Draped in red from her crown to her gloves, and accompanied by two male assistants dressed in gold, Dell'Orefice conveyed a vibrant and regal image of an empress.[36] The red lace of her robe simulated the feathers of a phoenix, set against a textured, columnar gown. Her white hair and porcelain face punctuated the crisp crepe that fanned out in a red halo behind her head. Guo Pei's vivid imagery of the phoenix recalls the power of an empress, then reasserted by Dell'Orefice as a matriarch of the global fashion enterprise. Guo Pei thus presented a cultural equivalency, positioning queenship as a mobile identity defined by a matriarch's endurance within a gendered power structure.

Guo Pei selected the Conciergerie as the site of her Paris show, further articulating the shifting boundaries of her work through emotional content and cultural lore. The Conciergerie, the site of the Revolutionary Court and a center for detention during the French Revolution (1789–1799), sits prominently between the Cathédrale Notre-Dame de Paris and Sainte-Chappelle on the Île de la Cité. It also represents the site where Marie Antoinette (1755–1793), the last queen of France, remained imprisoned for the seventy-six days prior to her execution. Intriguingly, Guo Pei has remarked that she sought models for the show that could convey the air of death with grace and nobility, which she likened to 'the last queen of an era about to be beheaded … wearing her most beautiful outfit in her last moment of life.'[37] As Marie Antoinette wore a plain white dress to the guillotine, Guo Pei appears to be referencing the image of Dell'Orefice as an empress in red, a stunning conclusion to the *Legend Collection* show in the Conciergerie. The vital red hue of her gown, phoenix imagery, and ghostly white hair convey an air of life and death, characterizing a queen as a formidable matriarch in life with an unyielding legacy in death. Guo Pei presents Dell'Orefice as a noble ancestor, neither French nor Chinese.

Guo Pei's reference to Marie Antoinette by way of situating her show at the Conciergerie signified her distinctive stance towards global fashion. Zoya Nudelman has noted that the first French fashion designer was Rose Bertin (1747–1813), a milliner and designer for Marie Antoinette, and credited her with bringing *haute couture* to French culture.[38] Upon joining the Haute Couture Commission, Guo Pei affirmed this heritage, and so revived Georg Simmel's top-down view of the upper class as the tastemakers of fashion.[39] Diana Crane has noted that in recent years, demographic and economic factors have replaced Simmel's model with one in which age replaced social status as the variable that conveys prestige.[40] However, in confronting the ephemerality of fashion with the dignity of age and endurance of tradition, Guo Pei repositioned the matriarch as aspirational – envisioning her as a queen, and so displacing the young and liberated who constitute the driving forces of contemporary fashion. The rarefied allure of Dell'Orefice demonstrates how Guo Pei's designs signal the iconic moments in one's life, including marriage and death, and so define age as not only biological, but also social and generational. These moments form a certain vision of matriarchy, one that is a kind of immortality seen in the rebirth of a phoenix or the legacy of ancestorhood.

Haute couture as soft power

A rare combination of material wealth and enduring relationships defines Guo Pei's unique stance towards *haute couture*, marvelously superseding the worlds from which both the designer and *haute couture* have emerged. On the one hand, Guo Pei's work denies the egalitarianism and austerity of the Mao era, so often the foundation for contemporary fashion from China. On the other hand, her designs deny the weightless, liberated image of the femme fatale and the obsessive consumption of the fashionista seen in the West – replacing their charms with the endurance and responsibility of age and lineage. Rather, Guo Pei recast notions of queenship in both China and Europe as the natural conclusion of a powerful matriarch, one who demonstrates soft power through the harnessing of resources and relationships.

Uniquely positioned as a woman designing *haute couture*, Guo Pei's work recenters fashion through her fascination with imagined cultures and visual traditions. While borrowing the fantasy and allure of the past, her work replicates, trades, reflects, and responds to the impulses of the present. Two muses, Cixi and Dell'Orefice, embody Guo Pei's vision. The Empress Dowager Cixi, in presenting herself as a prominent figure among Manchu, Han, European, and American women, masterfully used costume to reinforce her global network as the ruling matriarch of the Qing Empire. Carmen Dell'Orefice, in investing the institutions of *haute couture* with age, experience, and legacy, transcends the cultural distinctions of Paris,

Beijing, and New York – replacing them instead with a culture of royal matriarchy. Thus, as a woman working in the rarefied realm of *haute couture*, Guo Pei designs fashion that attests to the lasting power of duty and heritage – a vision for soft power in a postglobal world.

Notes

1. Andrew Bolton with John Galliano et al., 'Toward an Aesthetic of Surfaces,' in *China: Through the Looking Glass* (New York: The Metropolitan Museum of Art, 2015), p. 19.
2. Adam Geczy, 'A Chamber of Whispers,' in *China: Through the Looking Glass*, pp. 27–28. See also Adam Geczy, *Transorientalism in Art, Fashion, and Film* (London: Bloomsbury, 2019), p. 5.
3. Vanessa Friedman, 'Women are Defining Paris Couture,' *New York Times*, 2 July 2019, Fashion Review.
4. Joseph S. Nye, Jr, *Soft Power: The Means to Success in World Politics* (New York: Public Affairs, 2004), p. x.
5. Gail Dexter Lord and Ngaire Blankenberg, 'Why Cities, Museums, and Soft Power,' in *Cities, Museums, and Soft Power* (Washington, D. C.: The American Alliance of Museums, 2015), p. 9.
6. Andrew Bolton, *Wild: Fashion Untamed* (New York: Metropolitan Museum of Art, 2004), p. 173. See also Julia M. White, 'Educated and Probably Dangerous Women in Seventeenth- and Eighteenth-Century Chinese Painting,' in James Cahill, Chen Fongfong, Sarah Handler, and Julia M. White, *Beauty Revealed: Images of Women in Qing Dynasty Chinese Painting* (Berkeley: University of California, Berkeley Art Museum and Pacific Film Archive, 2013), pp. 23–33.
7. Valerie Steele, 'Femme Fatale: Fashion and Visual Culture in Fin-de-Siècle Paris,' *Fashion Theory*, 8, no. 3 (2004): 315–328, at 322.
8. Julia Twigg, *Fashion and Age: Dress, the Body and Later Life* (London: Bloomsbury Academic, 2013), p. 11.
9. Hubert Vos, *Empress Dowager Cixi*, 1906. Oil on canvas, 196 × 123.6 cm. Fogg Museum at Harvard University, Boston.
10. Ying-chen Peng, 'Staging Sovereignty: Empress Dowager Cixi (1835–1908) and Late Qing Court Art Production,' PhD dissertation (University of California, Los Angeles, 2014), pp. 1–2.
11. One such example is an informal court robe embroidered with a motif of peonies on imperial yellow silk, which combined the yellow of royalty with a floral emblem specifically favored by Cixi and celebrated by her Han subjects in the south. *Informal robe with peonies and the character for longevity*, Guangxu period, 1875–1908, embroidery, polychrome and metallic-wrapped silk threads on silk tabby, 136.5 × 132 cm. Palace Museum, Gu45925.
12. For more on the reception of portraits of Cixi, see Ying-chen Peng, 'Lingering between Tradition and Innovation: Photographic Portraits of Empress Dowager Cixi,'*Ars Orientalis*, 43 (2014): 157–174; Cheng-hua Wang, '"Going Public": Portraits of the Empress Dowager Cixi, Circa 1904,' *Nan Nü*, 14, no. 1 (January 2013): 119–176.
13. Kristen L. Chiem, 'Possessing the King of Flowers, and Other Things at the Qing Court,' *Word & Image*, 34, no. 4 (2018): 388–406; see also Kristen Chiem, 'Painting, Peonies, and Ming Loyalism in Qing Dynasty China, 1644–1795,' *Archives of Asian Art*, 67, no. 1 (2017): 83–109.
14. Wang Cheng-hua, 'Zouxiang "gongkaihua": Cixi xiaoxiang de fengge xingshi zhengzhi yunzuo yu xingxiang suzao' 走向'公開化'：慈禧肖像風格形式，政治運作與形象塑造 [Going public: the stylistic form, political function, and image construction in

Cixi's portraits], 239–316, 320. *Guoli Taiwan daxue meishushi yanjiu jikan* 國立台灣大學美術史研究集刊 [*Taida Journal of Art History*] 32 (2012): 239–299.

15 Ying-chen Peng, 'Empresses and Qing Court Politics,' in Daisy Yiyou Wang and Jan Stuart, eds, *Empresses of China's Forbidden City: 1644–1912* (Salem and Washington, D. C.: Peabody Essex Museum and Arthur M. Sackler Gallery, Smithsonian Institution, distributed by Yale University Press, 2018), p. 132.

16 Evelyn S. Rawski, *The Last Emperors: A Social History of Qing Imperial Institutions* (Berkeley: University of California Press, 1998), p. 129. See also Valerie Steele and John S. Major, *China Chic: East Meets West* (New Haven: Yale University Press, 1999), pp. 37–44.

17 Ying-chen Peng, 'Flowerpot with peonies and birds,' catalog entry in Wang and Stuart, eds, *Empresses of China's Forbidden City*, p. 218.

18 Her Imperial Majesty, the Empress Dowager of China. Photographed by Yu Xunling (1847–1943). Guangxu period, about 1903, hand-colored silver gelatin print, Museum of Fine Arts, Boston.

19 Empress Dowager Cixi with foreign envoys' wives in the Hall of Happiness and Longevity (*Leshou tang*) in the Garden of Nurturing Harmony (*Yihe yuan*). Photographed by Yu Xunling (1874–1943), Guangxu period, 1903–1905, print from glass-plate negative, 24.1 × 17.8 cm. Freer Gallery of Art and Arthur M. Sackler Gallery Archives, FSA A.13 SC-GE-249. Smithsonian Institution, Washington, D. C., purchase.

20 Sarah Conger, *Letters from China: With Particular Reference to the Empress Dowager and Women in China* (Chicago: A. C. McClurg, 1909), p. 274, https://archive.org/details/lettersfromchina00cong/page/274 (accessed 7 August 2023).

21 Michelle L. Beer, 'Material Magnificence, Royal Identity, and the Queen's Body,' in *Queenship at the Renaissance Courts of Britain: Catherine of Aragon and Margaret Tudor, 1503–1533* (Rochester: Boydell Press, 2018), p. 46.

22 Cao Xueqin, *Story of the Stone*, vol. 1, trans. David Hawkes (Harmondsworth: Penguin Books, 1982), p. 174.

23 For more on the association between palace ladies and flowers, see Hans H. Frankel, *The Flowering Plum and the Palace Lady: Interpretations of Chinese Poetry* (New Haven and London: Yale University Press, 1976), pp. 1–19.

24 Jan Stuart with Qu Weixun, 'Qing Court Women's Dress and Notions of Auspiciousness and Antiquity,' *Arts of Asia*, 49, no. 1 (2019): 34–47, at 39.

25 Evelyn S. Rawski, 'Pair of shoes with phoenixes,' catalog entry in Wang and Stuart, eds, *Empresses of China's Forbidden City*, p. 171.

26 Valery Garrett, *Chinese Dress: From the Qing Dynasty to the Present Day* (Tokyo: Tuttle Publishing, 2019), pp. 38–40.

27 Yunlu (1695–1767), comp., *Huangchao liqi tushi* 皇朝禮器圖式, in a modern edition, Mu Dong, ed. (Yangzhou: Yangzhou Guangling shushe, 2004).

28 Stuart with Qu, 'Qing Court Women's Dress,' 38.

29 Valerie Steele, *The Corset: A Cultural History* (New Haven: Yale University Press, 2001), pp. 1–2.

30 Peng, 'Lingering between Tradition and Innovation,' 159.

31 Mary Logan Bikoff, 'Guo Pei's Extravagant Gowns Land at SCAD FASH,' *Atlanta Magazine*, 22 August 2017, www.atlantamagazine.com/style/guo-peis-extravagant-gowns-land-scad-fash/ (accessed 7 August 2023).

32 For discussion of images of queenship in medieval Europe, see Lisa Benz St. John, *Three Medieval Queens: Queenship and the Crown in Fourteenth-Century England* (New York: Palgrave Macmillan, 2012), pp. 19–32; and Jill Hamilton Clements, 'The Construction of Queenship in the Illustrated Estoire De Seint Aedward Le Rei,' *Gesta*, 52, no. 1 (2013): 21–42.

33 Andrew Bolton, 'The Lion's Share,' in *Wild: Fashion Untamed* (New York: Metropolitan Museum of Art, 2004), p. 43.

34 Jonathan Schlesinger, *A World Trimmed with Fur: Wild Things, Pristine Places, and the Natural Fringes of Qing* (Stanford: Stanford University Press, 2017), pp. 17–18.
35 Adam Geczy, *Fashion and Orientalism: Dress, Textiles, and Culture from the 17th to the 21st Century* (London: Bloomsbury, 2013), p. 157.
36 Amy Verner, 'Guo Pei: Spring 2017 Couture,' *Vogue*, 27 January 2017, Look 19, https://www.vogue.com/fashion-shows/spring-2017-couture/guo-pei (accessed 7 August 2023).
37 古代的是要上斷頭台的王后 … 只在生命一刻穿著最美的一件衣服. *Yellow is Forbidden*, directed by Pietra Brettkelly (New Zealand Film Commission, Libertine Pictures, Gaumont-Pathe Archives, 2019), streaming.
38 Zoya Nudelman, *The Art of Couture Sewing* (New York and London: Bloomsbury Publishing Inc., 2016), p. 4.
39 Georg Simmel, 'Fashion,' *American Journal of Sociology*, 62, no. 6 (1957): 541–558, at 545.
40 Diana Crane, *Fashion and Its Social Agendas: Class, Gender, and Identity in Clothing* (Chicago: University of Chicago Press, 2000), p. 14.

Bibliography

Beer, Michelle L. 'Material Magnificence, Royal Identity, and the Queen's Body.' In *Queenship at the Renaissance Courts of Britain: Catherine of Aragon and Margaret Tudor, 1503–1533*. Rochester: Boydell Press, 2018.

Bikoff, Mary Logan. 'Guo Pei's Extravagant Gowns Land at SCAD FASH.' *Atlanta Magazine*, 22 August 2017. www.atlantamagazine.com/style/guo-peis-extravagant-gowns-land-scad-fash/ (accessed 7 August 2023).

Bolton, Andrew. 'The Lion's Share.' In *Wild: Fashion Untamed*. New York: Metropolitan Museum of Art, 2004.

Bolton, Andrew. *Wild: Fashion Untamed*. New York: Metropolitan Museum of Art, 2004.

Bolton, Andrew, with John Galliano et al. *China: Through the Looking Glass*. New York: Metropolitan Museum of Art, 2015.

Cao Xueqin. *Story of the Stone*. Vol. 1. Translated by David Hawkes. Harmondsworth: Penguin Books, 1982.

Chiem, Kristen. 'Painting, Peonies, and Ming Loyalism in Qing Dynasty China, 1644–1795.' *Archives of Asian Art* 67, no. 1 (2017): 83–109.

Chiem, Kristen L. 'Possessing the King of Flowers, and Other Things at the Qing Court.' *Word & Image* 34, no. 4 (2018): 388–406.

Clements, Jill Hamilton. 'The Construction of Queenship in the Illustrated Estoire De Seint Aedward Le Rei.' *Gesta* 52, no. 1 (2013): 21–42.

Conger, Sarah. *Letters from China: With Particular Reference to the Empress Dowager and Women in China*. Chicago: A. C. McClurg, 1909. https://archive.org/details/lettersfromchina00cong/page/274 (accessed 7 August 2023).

Crane, Diana. *Fashion and Its Social Agendas: Class, Gender, and Identity in Clothing*. Chicago: University of Chicago Press, 2000.

Frankel, Hans H. *The Flowering Plum and the Palace Lady: Interpretations of Chinese Poetry*. New Haven and London: Yale University Press, 1976.

Friedman, Vanessa. 'Women are Defining Paris Couture.' *New York Times*, 2 July 2019.

Garrett, Valery. *Chinese Dress: From the Qing Dynasty to the Present*. Tokyo: Tuttle Publishing, 2008.

Geczy, Adam. 'A Chamber of Whispers.' In *China: Through the Looking Glass*. New York: The Metropolitan Museum of Art, 2015.

Geczy, Adam. *Fashion and Orientalism: Dress, Textiles, and Culture from the 17th to the 21st Century*. London: Bloomsbury, 2013.

Geczy, Adam. *Transorientalism in Art, Fashion, and Film*. London: Bloomsbury, 2019.

Guo Pei, Paula Wallace, Lynn Yaeger, Howl Collective, and Savannah College of Art and Design. *Guo Pei: Couture Beyond*. New York: Rizzoli Electa, 2018.

Lord, Gail Dexter and Ngaire Blankenberg. 'Why Cities, Museums, and Soft Power.' In *Cities, Museums, and Soft Power*. Washington, D. C.: The American Alliance of Museums, 2015.

Nudelman, Zoya. *The Art of Couture Sewing*. New York and London: Bloomsbury Publishing Inc., 2016.

Nye, Jr., Joseph S. *Soft Power: The Means to Success in World Politics*. New York: Public Affairs, 2004.

Peng, Ying-chen. 'Empresses and Qing Court Politics.' In *Empresses of China's Forbidden City: 1644–1912*. Edited by Yiyou Wang and Jan Stuart. Salem: Peabody Essex Museum and Arthur M. Sackler Gallery, Smithsonian Institution, distributed by Yale University Press, 2018.

Peng, Ying-chen. 'Lingering between Tradition and Innovation: Photographic Portraits of Empress Dowager Cixi.'*Ars Orientalis* 43 (2014): 157–174.

Peng, Ying-chen. 'Staging Sovereignty: Empress Dowager Cixi (1835–1908) and Late Qing Court Art Production.' PhD dissertation, University of California, Los Angeles, 2014.

Rawski, Evelyn S. *The Last Emperors: A Social History of Qing Imperial Institutions*. Berkeley: University of California Press, 1998.

Schlesinger, Jonathan. *A World Trimmed with Fur: Wild Things, Pristine Places, and the Natural Fringes of Qing*. Stanford: Stanford University Press, 2017.

Simmel, Georg. 'Fashion.' *American Journal of Sociology* 62, no. 6 (1957): 541–558.

Steele, Valerie. 'Femme Fatale: Fashion and Visual Culture in Fin-de-siècle Paris.' *Fashion Theory* 8, no. 3 (2004): 315–328.

Steele, Valerie. *The Corset: A Cultural History*. New Haven: Yale University Press, 2001.

Steele, Valerie and John S. Major. *China Chic: East Meets West*. New Haven: Yale University Press, 1999.

St. John, Lisa Benz. *Three Medieval Queens: Queenship and the Crown in Fourteenth-Century England*. New York: Palgrave Macmillan, 2012.

Stuart, Jan, Evelyn Sakakida Rawski, Freer Gallery of Art, and Arthur M. Sackler Gallery (Smithsonian Institution). *Worshiping the Ancestors: Chinese Commemorative Portraits*. Washington, D. C.: Freer Gallery of Art, 2001.

Stuart, Jan with Qu Weixun. 'Qing Court Women's Dress and Notions of Auspiciousness and Antiquity.' *Arts of Asia* 49, no. 1 (2019): 34–47.

Twigg, Julia. *Fashion and Age: Dress, the Body and Later Life*. London: Bloomsbury Academic, 2013.

Verner, Amy. 'Guo Pei: Spring 2017 Couture.' *Vogue*, 27 January 2017, Look 19. www.vogue.com/fashion-shows/spring-2017-couture/guo-pei (accessed 7 August 2023).

Wang Cheng-hua. '"Going Public": Portraits of the Empress Dowager Cixi, Circa 1904.' *Nan Nü* 14, no. 1 (January 2013): 119–176.

Wang Cheng-hua. 'Zouxiang "gongkaihua": Cixi xiaoxiang de fengge xingshi zhengzhi yunzuo yu xingxiang suzao' 走向'公開化': 慈禧肖像風格形式，政治運作與形象塑造 [Going public: the stylistic form, political function, and image construction in Cixi's portraits]. *Meishushi yanjiu jikan* 美術史研究集刊 32 (2012): 239–316, 320.

Wang, Daisy Yiyou and Jan Stuart, eds. *Empresses of China's Forbidden City: 1644–1912*. Salem and Washington, D. C.: Peabody Essex Museum and Arthur M. Sackler Gallery, Smithsonian Institution, distributed by Yale University Press, 2018.

White, Julia M. 'Educated and Probably Dangerous Women in Seventeenth- and Eighteenth-Century Chinese Painting.' In *Beauty Revealed: Images of Women in Qing Dynasty Chinese Painting*. By James Cahill, Chen Fongfong, Sarah Handler, and Julia M. White. Berkeley: University of California, Berkeley Art Museum and Pacific Film Archive, 2013.

Yellow is Forbidden. Directed by Pietra Brettkelly. New Zealand Film Commission, Libertine Pictures, Gaumont-Pathe Archives, 2019.

Yunlu (1695–1767), comp. *Huangchao liqi tushi* 皇朝禮器圖式. Edited by Mu Dong. Yangzhou: Yangzhou Guangling shushe, 2004.

7

Investigating female entrepreneurship in silk weaving in contemporary Cambodia

Magali An Berthon

Introduction

In Cambodia, silk weaving is an ancient textile practice dating back as early as the thirteenth century. Structured as a cottage activity, it was almost exclusively run by women in rural areas, the cloth and clothes produced mostly destined for domestic consumption. In the mid-1970s, the Khmer Rouge regime nearly destroyed the entire local silk production. Since the country's pacification process in the early 1990s, the sector has reopened to international investment and restructured under the leadership of local non-governmental organizations (NGOs) and foreign-owned craft companies. Focusing on Cambodian initiatives offers the possibility of examining the agency of national approaches and their influence in a global-economic framework. To advance towards an exploration of Cambodian voices involved in the silk market, this chapter discusses several initiatives founded by women, from the pioneering NGO Khemara directly supported by international funders to more recent independent entrepreneurial projects such as Silk Associations Cambodia and Color Silk. Silk Associations Cambodia is located in Takeo province, the historical center for silk weaving in Cambodia. It is led by Chin Koeur, a silk weaver turned business owner, who was trained in 1995 in one of the first UNESCO grassroots weaving programs. Color Silk was founded in 2009 by Ngorn Vanntha, also from Takeo, operating under the social enterprise model and focusing on silk products for export.

Female leadership in silk weaving is examined through ethnographic research methods, looking at the ways in which women entrepreneurs have embraced a Cambodian hybrid model of production and distribution navigating foreign and domestic incentives. These perspectives are anchored within the silk industry, which is treated as a hub of policy makers, organizations, and makers, but also of materials and commercial exchanges. Given this, this chapter offers a polyphonic exploration of the Cambodian weaving sector, which integrates the company owners' stories and approaches, as well as their projects' marketing strategies and typologies of handcrafted goods. It examines, in particular, the themes of ownership, women's agency, and empowerment, and their ramifying effects on silk production.

Revitalizing silk-weaving production in a post-conflict globalized context

Following two destructive decades of civil war and isolation from the international community, the revitalization of silk craft practices has been linked to the exponential growth of foreign NGOs coming to Cambodia by 1992, especially from the United States, Japan, and Europe, which supported the reformation of the silk network locally. To identify gendered social codes in Cambodia in regards to themes of silk-weaving production and workforce, this chapter chooses a form of ethnographic micro-level research and confronts it with a macro-perspective on the silk-weaving sector which includes all the actors involved in the production chain.[1] The data and semi-structured interviews presented here come from two periods of fieldwork in the southern parts of Cambodia in July 2017 and March 2018, especially in Phnom Penh and Takeo province, about forty kilometers south of the capital city (Figure 7.1).[2] In Phnom Penh, research has centered on visits to UNESCO archives and Color Silk's showroom to interview Ngorn Vanntha, its founder. Fieldwork in Takeo province was dedicated to visiting Silk Associations Cambodia and interviewing its founder, as well as a visit to Color Silk's weaving training center. The analysis also involves tracing the companies' structure from genesis to production and distribution models, including biographies of the organizations' founders, and commercial communication and marketing strategies.

The political changes affecting Cambodia in the second half of the twentieth century strongly inform the structural imbalances of the country's economy and society at the turn of the twenty-first century. Between 1975 and 1979, the Khmer Rouge regime turned the country into a communist peasant dictatorship, ruled with economic quasi-autarky.[3] The dictatorship instituted mass collectivization, separating families, displacing people across the country, and engaging them in forced work. These mass purges and disastrous policies left starving populations facing penury and a major sanitary crisis that claimed an estimated 1.7 million victims, about a quarter of the population at the time. By the late 1970s, silk production and weaving practices were massively affected by the destruction of mulberry tree fields, the sacking of villages, and the displacement of craftspeople.[4]

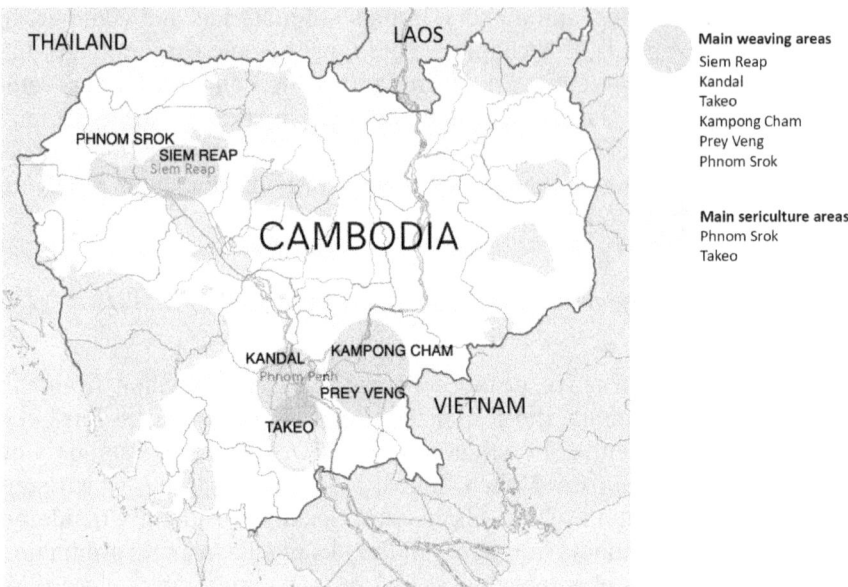

7.1 Map of the main sericulture and weaving areas in Cambodia in 2016, based on data from the National Silk Strategy, 2016–2020

There are no data available about the number of weavers still active in the aftermath of the genocide, until silk production became a more salient concern for Cambodian officials in the early 2000s. Estimates show that the overall number of silk weavers grew exponentially to twenty thousand in 2005, declining again at an alarming rate from the 2010s to an estimate of five thousand in 2016.[5] The largest silk-weaving workforce is concentrated in Takeo, especially in the Prey Kabas and Bati districts, which is the area represented in more depth in this chapter.[6] Silk weavers from Takeo are especially experienced in the art of *hol*, the Khmer term for the polychromic weft ikat silk technique. Silk weavers are still predominantly women, about 66–87% of the workforce.[7] Weaving is often practiced in addition to rice farming. In villages, Cambodian women generally carry the '"double duty" [of] engaging in agricultural labor or wage employment, and taking care of the household tasks.'[8] Women are also often the only wage earner in the household. As the primary carers for their children, they use their income, an average of fifty to seventy USD per month, in particular to buy medical supplies and send the children to school. When the families are too poor, they will only send their boys to school and girls will drop out to take over household tasks.[9] Recognized as an acceptable activity for women in rural areas, weaving strongly reproduces gendered positions within Cambodian society. The price of silk fiber and consistency of sales regulate the extent to which weaving enhances or limits women's agency.

Subsidized domestic sericulture farming resumed and peaked at ten metric tons of annual silk yarn production in 2008, to decline again in the 2010s to an average of one to three metric tons of yarn annually, returning to its lowest levels since the early 1990s.[10] To compensate for this low indigenous silk production, about four hundred metric tons of fiber annually – often of lower quality – is imported from Vietnam and China (Figure 7.2).[11]

With the Paris Peace Accords in 1991 and the national elections in 1993, Cambodia formed new alliances with foreign investors and humanitarian aid, which expressed interest in relaunching the silk sector. The collapse of indigenous fiber production was a fundamental argument for the involvement of foreign sponsors. Moreover, the local market lacked a locally produced high-end silk offer, privileging instead imported styles such as Indonesian cotton batiks and Lao silk *sarung*.[12] UNESCO, followed by a majority of European and Japanese-sponsored NGOs, were able to access new economic ventures by securing funding and implementing ambitious capacity-building training programs with rural communities. The UNESCO office in Cambodia played an essential role in creating synergies with local and international actors. One of these was Khemara, which is considered the first Cambodian-founded NGO. A pioneering

7.2 Qualities of silk yarn: from raw silk on the left to fine silk on the right before degumming, Koh Dach island. December 2016

model at the time, Khemara was started in 1991 in Phnom Penh with a staff almost entirely comprising women.[13] The organization relied on external funding and networking to implement programs improving women's rights and supporting their advancement in leadership positions, 'drawing upon Western concepts of feminism in its approach.'[14] In 1995 it received funding from the United Nations Development Programme (UNDP) and Princess Marie Ranariddh for a five-year plan to revitalize sericulture and weaving and support rural women. Established via the international organization Oxfam, Khemara benefited from direct connections between its founder, Mu Sochua Leiper, and her husband, Scott Leiper, former UNDP Advisor in Cambodia. Mu Sochua Leiper was born in Phnom Penh in 1954. She was sent to Paris to study in the early 1970s before relocating to the United States, where she earned a Bachelor's degree in Psychology from San Francisco State University and a Master's in Social Work from the University of California, Berkeley.[15]

Focused on women's welfare, Khemara aimed to serve marginalized communities with little to no access to education or work opportunities. The silk scheme implemented weaving training for women based in the Kampong Speu and Phnom Penh areas while providing them with basic literacy and numeracy education, partnering with regional women's associations.[16] The NGO recruited young women not necessarily with prior knowledge of silk, such as Srey Mom cited in a 1995 *Phnom Penh Post* article: 'Before I wasn't interested in the job, but when I learned how to do it, I liked it.'[17] In *Soul Survivors*, which gathers oral histories from Khmer Rouge regime survivors, Thavery exemplifies the type of women who benefited from Khemara's program. She recalled witnessing her mother and older sister weaving *sampot hol* (ikat hip wrap) and *phamaung* (solid silk twill cloth) at home when she was a child. It was only in late 1979 that she learned the technique with experienced female weavers when she finally returned to her home village in Takeo province, after the fall of the Khmer Rouge regime. She explained: 'the women in my village wove silk skirts, and I wanted to learn how to weave, so I volunteered to help them.'[18] Thavery eventually moved to Phnom Penh and in 1993 started working as a weaving instructor and *pidan* (pictorial ikat) weaver for Khemara, which gave her a sense of purpose.[19] The NGO supported weavers by reaching international markets in the United States, Hong Kong, Africa, and France with their silk products. Silk-weaving activities continued until the 2000s and have now stopped. Khemara now focuses mainly on social services and advocacy for children's care and access to education. Founder Mu Sochua moved to politics, becoming the first woman to head the Ministry for Women's and Veterans' Affairs from 1998 to 2004 in Hun Sen's coalition government. She then joined the opposition, acting as the Vice-President of the (now-dissolved) Cambodia National Rescue Party until 2017.

Benefiting from the early investment of UNESCO and other transnational agencies, as well as the reputation of its founder, Khemara fits into the model of other silk craft NGOs active in the 1990s. While it cultivated a woman-centric focus and strong female governance, the organization did not foster lasting changes in the silk sector into the 2000s in terms of women's empowerment and leadership.

The high dependence of the country on humanitarian aid and transnational sponsors has reconfigured the silk sector paradigm in the post-conflict era, creating a major rupture in the continuation and significance of silk practices. Looking at two projects, Silk Associations of Cambodia and Color Silk, owned by Cambodian women and established in the early developments of the 1990s, described above, helps to explore how gender is part of the distribution of agencies in the silk network in friction between local anchoring and global markets, and self-sufficiency and international philanthropy.

Chin Koeur from Silk Associations of Cambodia

Since the early 2000s, the silk sector has been marked by two overlapping movements of expansion and segmentation, divided between larger membership associations, foreign-owned actors, and Cambodian-owned enterprises. According to a governmental report dating from 2016, the majority of the weaving workforce in Cambodia operates in about two hundred and fifty small and medium enterprises and NGOs.[20] This fragmented landscape suffers from a lack of cooperation between these various actors, who often compete for funding and customers. In this competitive landscape, despite the prominence of women in the Cambodian craft sector, they have struggled to access entrepreneurship and higher levels of management.[21] Chin Koeur provides an example of a female owner whose business originates in a UNESCO-funded silk project in Phnom Chisor commune in Takeo province. This program, 'Revival of Traditional Silk Weaving,' was launched in August 1992 for five years, recruiting Leav Sa Em, a renowned sixty-year-old male master weaver who had survived the Khmer Rouge regime and was working for the Royal Court, as the training leader.[22] Originally from Prey Kabas commune in Takeo province, Leav Sa Em learned the art of polychromic *hol* from his mother, which was uncommon for a boy.[23] Between 1992 and 1996, seventy-two women from the area undertook semester-long training before returning to their hometowns to become independent weavers.[24] Weavers would come to the UNESCO office to drop off their products, which would, in turn, be sold on site. Chin Koeur is the only weaver stemming from this program who is known to have succeeded in developing her activity on a larger scale. While UNESCO continued to let the weavers who were still active sell their products at the Phnom Penh branch until the mid-2010s, there was no follow-up from the agency to determine the continuity of practice and the long-term impact of the training.

I met Chin Koeur in March 2018 during a field trip in Takeo province, introduced by Prom Chak, a Program Officer Assistant at UNESCO in Phnom Penh, originally from Phnom Chisor. The two had known each other since the UNESCO weaving project and had built a relationship of trust. The former trainee, in her mid-forties in 2018, opened her business in 1996 in her home village of Kanhjang in Takeo province. Chin Koeur showed me her laminated certificate which attested, with her name and picture, to a period of training conducted from May to October 1995 in Phnom Penh under Leav Sa Em's apprenticeship, whom she considered an 'easy going' master supportive of 'someone who really wants to learn' (Figure 7.3).[25] She had kept the certificate in a translucent plastic folder in pristine condition for more than twenty years, within range of the warehouse where she had set up her business. The space had a desk and a few chairs, one loom, some weaving and tying supplies, stored products on shelves, and motorbikes.

The UNESCO training program recruited individuals from impoverished families, uneducated backgrounds, and orphans. When she started

7.3 Chin Koeur's certificate, dated October 1995, for training under master weaver Leav Sa Em, next to tie-dyed silk threads, Kanhjang village, Takeo, 17 March 2018

in 1995, Chin Koeur had only a rudimentary knowledge of weaving, learned at school. She found it 'difficult to prepare the threads, as I had no experience before. And learning was hard for me.' This program provided her with the foundation skills to undertake all the stages of Cambodian silk weaving, especially the *hol* (ikat) and *pidan* (pictorial ikat) techniques, from designing patterns for weft threads to tying and dyeing them with natural and chemical dyes, preparing the warp, and weaving on the loom. At the final ceremony marking the end of her training, in addition to the certificate, she 'got a gift from the training plus one *kbun*' (three and a half meter silk hip wrap). And then she 'sold that *hol* (ikat) at the closing ceremony at the UNESCO office.'[26] Chin Koeur continued: 'After I got that money, I asked my brother to take me to the Central Market and I bought silk material.'[27] Each time she finished a new piece, she would take it to the UNESCO office to sell it on site and would use the money to create a rolling fund.

Pragmatic and proactive, Chin Koeur realized she needed to expand her practice. UNESCO encouraged her to develop an association and supported her commercially in the beginning. She contended that the association model did not work and tried to self-fund. She turned to other resources available to her provided by the already established network of foreign-owned craft NGOs. She learned business development through the Cambodian Ministry of Women's Affairs. She pursued additional training on natural dyes at Caring for Young Khmer, a well-known Japanese-led NGO which had operated weaving programs for Cambodian youth and women in Trapaing Krasaing village, Bati district, Takeo province, since 2003. Then she started working with her sister and mother, managing to build more capital and launch her own business, Silk Associations of Cambodia, in her home village of Kanhjang, Sla commune, Takeo province in 1996. To produce more, she hired weavers based in her area, whom she paid by the piece. She progressed from weaving to designing, training, management, and distribution. Twenty years later she was working with 'fifty looms,' which meant fifty weavers, who worked from home and could produce up to three *kbun* per loom – about one hundred and fifty pieces monthly (Figure 7.4). Chin Koeur said that 'I have now no time to weave, just focus on designing. ... I hire my mother to start to do the tying, and then I will send this pattern to other persons to design, and then I simply check it to correct the design. And after that, I send it to the person who does the dyeing.'[28]

To sell her products at a competitive price, Chin Koeur also kept an eye on raw material costs. She expressed concern about the price of imported silk from Vietnam or Thailand, and what it meant for profitability. She could not understand why it had doubled in recent years: 'I don't know why it's so expensive like that,' costing seventy USD for one kilo, despite the Cambodian government's statement that 'to import [silk] there

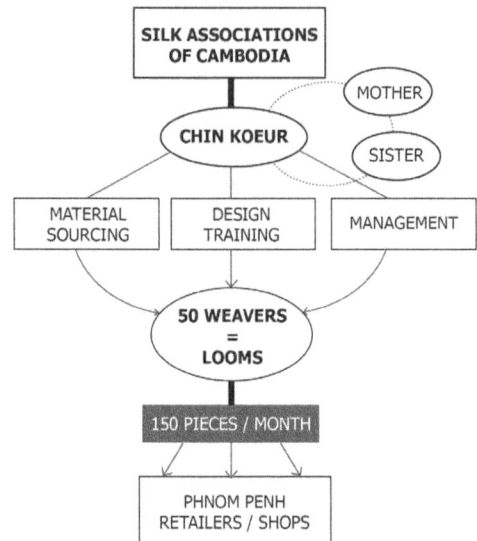

7.4 Silk Associations of Cambodia's business model, based on an interview with Chin Koeur

is no tax.' She explained that 'I always complain to the people who sell the silk. But … and the government said they don't charge the import tax, but that's still expensive.'[29] This situation has forced her to raise the price of her products to a minimum of two hundred USD for one *hol kbun*. From other testimonies collected in the field, these are slightly high prices for complex multicolored handwoven silk textiles, if one includes the markup applied by the final seller.

Within the silk network, despite bearing the title of 'association', Chin Koeur's business has relied on her sole ownership. Her positioning retains the characteristics of the traditional role of a middlewoman, which is how UNESCO officer Prom Chak referred to her when he introduced us. Middlemen (or women) are central actors in domestic silk-weaving production and trade. They source the raw material, loan it to the weavers, pass them specific orders, and collect the finished pieces to sell them to retailers in city centers. Middlemen set up the price paid to weavers minus the cost of silk fibers and dyes they have loaned, which keeps weavers in a position of dependence.[30] Chin Koeur passes orders to weavers, providing them with raw materials on credit, and receives the finished products before selling them to shops. While she has been working on a larger production scale, she has continued to purchase raw materials in Phnom Penh, including pre-dyed silk threads.

However, her role also entails developing colorful silk designs in the *hol* resist-dye technique. For her textile products, Chin Koeur has moved from copying ikat patterns from different villages, a practice common to middlemen choosing styles and bringing them to weavers, to designing new motifs, for which she has been recognized nationally. Chin Koeur positions herself as a designer, and not simply a buyer, delivering original models each month. To find ideas and interesting color combinations she has relied on her sellers' feedback in Phnom Penh, who communicate customers' tastes, comments, and various requests. As a business owner, she has engaged in a dynamic set of relations. Her mobility between the countryside and the capital city indicates how she had shifted from her original position of weaver, a more static role assigned to a loom that relies on middlemen for materials sourcing, orders, and sales. With the help of her mother, she has provided sets of pre-tied and dyed weft yarn to weavers who are paid sixty USD to weave a *kbun* for her. In rural areas, middlemen usually pay weavers about ninety USD to make a piece from start to finish, including tying and dyeing, and the weavers have to deduct the cost of raw materials. Depending on the complexity of the pattern, for a two-color ikat piece, this whole process of dyeing and weaving may take between two and three weeks for a weaver. It would take a minimum of a month to complete a polychromic silk ikat. By paying them only for weaving, without dyeing, Chin Koeur has accelerated production and ensured control over the designs. Moreover, she has trained a selection of weavers in tie-dye techniques to secure a skilled workforce able to fulfill her company's orders. This speaks to her creative mindset: she has positively utilized her UNESCO training and expanded her skills from solo weaver to design and production manager.

While she has operated without a website or Facebook page, Chin Koeur has won several regional awards for the best ikat designs. In December 2015, her organization was recognized by the Cambodia Silk Sector Promotion and Development Commission for its products. As part of a tour of the main textile initiatives operating in Takeo province, she received a visit from Mao Thora, Secretary of State for the Ministry of Commerce and Chairman of this silk commission, with industry representatives.[31] For sales, she has worked with shops in Phnom Penh, which in turn sell to local buyers, as well as Cambodians who live abroad, and Cambodians exporting to Europe and the United States. She works on these orders immediately, subcontracting the weaving and shipping the pieces back to Phnom Penh, using the flexibility of artisanal production to her advantage. Aware of the need to bypass shop sellers to increase profit, Chin Koeur has thought about how to distribute her products directly to customers. She explained she has 'just bought a house in Phnom Penh [to] open a shop just in the house' with her daughters and travels to sell in person in Thailand.[32]

Silk Associations of Cambodia has remained organically a family business, rather than an association, cooperative, or NGO. Chin Koeur offers a rare example of a female weaver who has directly benefited from UNESCO-sponsored training to build regular sources of income and produce elaborate marketable silk textiles. Nevertheless, her business model has not, in turn, provided possibilities of social transformation and autonomy for the fifty weavers it employs. She perpetuates the hierarchical patron–client system of *khsae* (threads), which had cemented Cambodian society long before the Khmer Rouge regime and resumed in the post-conflict era.[33] Within power relationships that imply loyalty and obligation, one person is indebted to another within a family or a business. Chin Koeur has kept her weavers outside of leadership decisions. By paying by the piece, she has maintained pressure on them to produce rapidly, without the security of a salary. Chin Koeur sounded more concerned with securing her family legacy by expanding her reach within domestic and regional markets. Her husband has been involved in sales and deals with merchants in Phnom Penh. She expressed the hope that, when she retires, her daughters will take over and manage Silk Associations of Cambodia.

Ngorn Vanntha from Color Silk

Color Silk, a venture founded in Phnom Penh by Ngorn Vanntha, fosters a different approach grounded in social entrepreneurship, digital communication, and export-oriented production. The roots of this organization are also in Takeo province, where the founder grew up in a family of silk weavers (her mother) and traders.[34] Ngorn Vanntha went to high school in Phnom Penh and earned a Master's in Business Administration at the Royal University of Law and Economics. She worked as an IT analyst for a private company until she won, with two other students, the National Business Plan Competition in Phnom Penh, organized by the National University of Management in partnership with the international consulting firm McKinsey. Her proposal was inspired by her youth spent in Takeo surrounded by weavers. Based on the observation that looms were disappearing from villagers' houses due to rural exodus, she planned to create employment opportunities for female weavers in Takeo by undercutting middlemen and expanding distribution channels.

Ngorn Vanntha started Color Silk in 2009 with personal funds. For her first order, she recruited ten weavers from Prei Kabas district in Takeo to develop silk samples destined for the US market. She reached out to older female weavers in her hometown to encourage them to continue. Some of them told her: 'If you find a market for me, I will continue weaving.'[35] Color Silk has progressively adopted the codes of social entrepreneurship, another craft company model alongside the NGO model, which gained more prominence in Cambodia in the 2000s with the erosion of the foreign-donor funding system.[36] Ngorn Vanntha, now in her mid-thirties, has operated as Color Silk's Managing Director and Chairman of the Board.[37] In interview in August 2017, she confided that she experienced pressure and doubts from her own family and in-laws: 'Nobody listened to me in the beginning.' She added: 'My husband was my only support. He works in corporate but never had a say in my work.'[38] This illustrates the prevalence of gendered cultural norms, even among educated Cambodian women, who are still relegated to the domestic role of homemaker and mother. In the post-conflict era, gender stereotyping discourses have re-emerged at the same time as the rise of the first women's associations encouraged by the return of exiled Cambodian women from refugee camps and Western countries.[39] The resistant attitude towards women working in management roles has persisted in Cambodian society and is only slowly changing in the younger generation.

To gain recognition and support locally and internationally, Ngorn Vanntha strategically entered a series of US competitions for social innovators, which successfully put Color Silk on the map of silk organizations in Cambodia. In 2010, Ngorn Vanntha was honored by the YouthActionNet® Global Fellowship program launched by the International Youth Foundation, a Baltimore-based non-profit organization supporting global youth empowerment since 1990. She was offered a twelve-month fellowship and was invited to a week-long networking program in Washington, D. C., and received a grant acknowledging her project's social impact in the Phnom Penh area. In 2011 she received the support of the International Youth Foundation–Starbucks Shared Planet Youth Action Grant.[40] One of Color Silk's board members, Reagan Hudgens, is an American digital specialist acting as an advisor for the silk company on optimizing distribution and client relationships, which could explain the company's US positioning.[41] Ngorn Vanntha was then honored nationally at the Cambodian Young Entrepreneur Awards 2015, organized by JCI Cambodia and the Young Entrepreneurs Association of Cambodia.[42] In a matter of a few years, these awards made Ngorn Vanntha's project attractive to funders interested in advancing their Corporate Social Responsibility agenda. Conversely, these different fellowships and sources of funding also helped develop Color Silk's frame of action as a social business.[43]

Approximately 65% of Color Silk's products are made to order for a wholesale market, with a roster of clients who are mostly based in the EU (Germany, in particular), Japan, the United States, and Singapore; the rest is sold to retailers in Phnom Penh and Siem Reap, a strategy which differs from that of other players in the sector focused on the tourist or local market.[44] While facing strong competition from Asian producers in China, Vietnam, and Thailand, Ngorn Vanntha has succeeded in exporting products and integrating international consumers into the company's distribution network. Clients, including buyers and fashion designers, can make custom orders and select styles online. As advertised on Color Silk's website, weavers produce a wide range of silk products such as yardage in solid colors and patterned using the *hol* technique, *sarung*, scarves, bags, and clothes, including face masks in 2020.[45] New styles are presented to customers each month on the company's Facebook page of 13,354 followers to encourage direct sales (Figure 7.5).

In parallel with its commercial structure, with a showroom and office in Phnom Penh, Color Silk set up a foundation in 2011, providing free

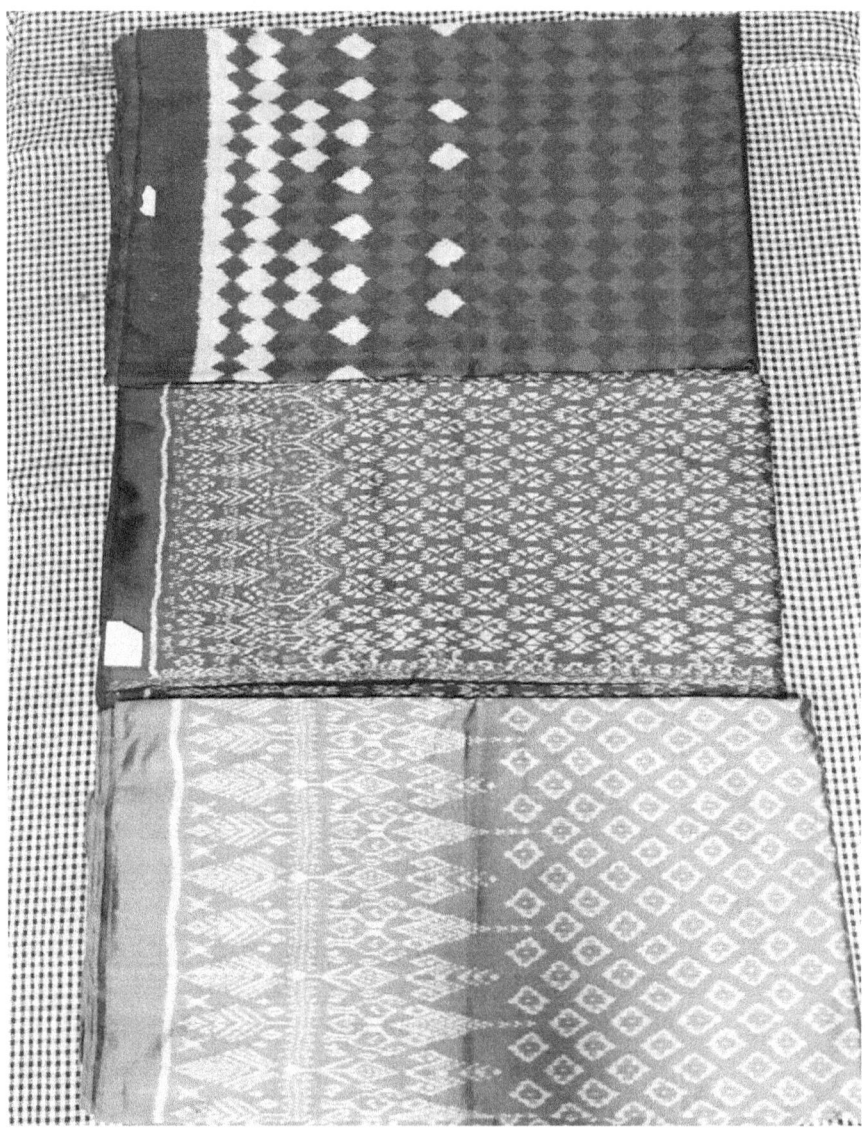

7.5 Polychromic *hol* (ikat) silk scarves in a variety of patterns, Color Silk Facebook page, 7 September 2020

training workshops in silkworm farming, yarn processing, weaving, and dyeing for low-income, vulnerable, disabled, and illiterate young women. This development has been strongly tied to the involvement of the Maybank Foundation, the philanthropic branch of the Malaysian bank. The Maybank Women Eco-Weavers program aims to 'promote traditional textiles globally in a sustainable manner, whilst creating economic independence and financial inclusion for women across the ASEAN region' in Laos, Cambodia, Indonesia, and Brunei.[46] Supporting Color Silk, therefore, fulfills objectives around the economic sustainment of Cambodian women through artisanal textile production. The project started with a weaving center in Sla commune in Takeo, followed by a larger construction near Phnom Chisor built in March 2016 with the support of the Maybank Foundation (Figure 7.6). The center was ceremonially opened in August 2017 by Chan Sorey, Secretary of State, Ministry of Women's Affairs, and Datuk Mohaiyani Shamsudin, Maybank's Chairman. On this occasion, Maybank's communication portrayed Ngorn Vanntha as a 'vision weaver' who is 'crafting futures on a forgotten way of life,' constructing a narrative linking innovation to textile practices and rural traditions.[47] A second center opened in Siem Reap in 2019 with the Maybank Women Eco-Weavers program and the ASEAN Wise Program.[48]

One of the key markers of Color Silk's success is its quantifiable outreach and community engagement. By 2017 Color Silk had worked with three hundred and fifty household farmers who grow mulberry trees to help increase domestic sericulture. About five hundred weavers received training for a minimum of five months, integrating them as 'members' who operate from home with the status of micro-entrepreneur in seven villages in Takeo province, which allows them to tend to their families. As part of its normal practice, the organization provided the weavers with materials at no cost, loaned money to set up looms, and paid piece rates above the market price.[49] Weavers have managed to earn an income up to two hundred USD per month.[50] While they are offered skills-building training, access to raw materials, and higher wages, they are on a yearly contract and only sell their final silk products to Color Silk enterprise, which may limit their possibility of autonomy.[51] There are, however, signs that members benefit from some more direct representation within the organization's management. Hok Sok Ny, an experienced weaver recruited by Color Silk, joined the Board of Directors. She has been in charge of training new members in silk weaving, ikat tying, and dyeing. Two other female members occupy management positions: Hok Changy is Production and Community Development Coordinator and Yeiy Chreng is Training Coordinator.[52]

Grounded nationally and internationally with this two-part structure, Color Silk is firmly established within the codes of social business and champions discourses on gender equality and women's empowerment. The company's approach to transparency and goal-oriented problem

7.6 Weaving training program with founder Ngorn Vanntha (in blue) at the Maybank Silk Weaving Training Center, Sla commune, Takeo province, n. d.

solving with clear impact objectives overlaps with funders' main goals to address challenges for women in rural areas, from poverty to internal migration. For instance, in 2015 Color Silk provided details of its salary levels, business plan, expected growth, anticipated increase in the number of trainees, and the content of its training on its online application for the leading social innovation network Ashoka.[53] The open sharing of this information differs from other craft companies and foreign NGOs focusing primarily on safeguarding Cambodian silk-weaving traditions or Chin Koeur's more informal model. On the 'About' page of Color Silk's website, 'preserving a Cambodian silk heritage' comes last in the company's target objectives to emphasize the imperatives for quantifiable social impact.[54] Furthermore, Color Silk has joined the global conversation on labor and ethical textile production. In 2017 the organization participated in the online campaign 'Who Made my Clothes?' for more transparency in the garment-manufacturing supply chain, an initiative of the UK-based international movement Fashion Revolution, founded in the aftermath of the Rana Plaza factory disaster in 2013. Color Silk promoted the Cambodian origins of its products and its artisanal approach, sharing pictures of weavers holding signs stating in English 'I made your clothes' (Figure 7.7).[55]

Through a range of strategic decisions, Color Silk has entered specific networks, thus elevating its status and access to development and funding opportunities. The number of awards, fellowships, and partnerships earned over the years is testament to Ngorn Vanntha's deep

7.7 Color Silk weavers for the Fashion Revolution 2017 campaign, April 2017, Color Silk Facebook page

understanding of the silk market and the philanthropic landscape. Thanks to important contributions from transnational sponsors, the organization has managed to scale up the number of beneficiaries from ten to several hundreds over a decade. As Color Silk's founder, Ngorn Vanntha faces the delicate task of navigating between her partners' agendas and discourses, profitability goals, and the implementation of women- and rural-centric actions at a grassroots level. Helping communities reach financial autonomy is the first crucial step. To circumvent structural inequalities and foster gendered agency, the continued development of skills building in entrepreneurship and leadership for Color Silk's members would open women to a broader range of careers beyond the sole roles of home-based weavers and farmers currently provided by the organization.

Conclusion

In Cambodia women entrepreneurs disrupt persistent discourses on gender representation which are linked to ideas of nostalgia and virtue and limit women in their roles, casting them as figures of a pre-Khmer Rouge traditional family and social order. Chin Koeur and Ngorn Vanntha, respectively a weaver and the daughter of a weaver, have successfully reached leadership positions going against gender norms through two different strategies. Silk Associations of Cambodia has focused on producing for the domestic market, finding recognition nationally for its creative designs by pursuing a middleman–weaver relationship on a larger scale without investing in fair-trade practices. Color Silk, on the other hand, has capitalized on a Western-inspired model of social entrepreneurship to sign international partnerships and reach global fashion markets. In both cases, training local communities aims to increase textile production and the marketability of silk products within a consumer-oriented framework. Their strategies and paths point to the heterogeneity of the Cambodian sector's realities and interrogates the position of weavers, not simply as objects of economic policies but as active subjects of their practice, taking in charge the transmission of their skills in silk production.

From Khemara to Silk Associations of Cambodia and Color Silk, Cambodian organizations involved in the revitalization of silk crafts have developed in the post-conflict era with a strong reliance on international donors under different forms of sponsorship, training, and partnership. This chapter has touched upon the power differentials between local structures and transnational funding sources and how it affects development strategies for the populations they aim to serve. Chin Koeur used UNESCO's support as seed funding to launch her activity, consequently leaving behind the non-profit model and focusing only on expanding her production capacity. For Color Silk, supporting feminist agendas means aligning with corporate foundations to implement impact-oriented actions such as opening two training centers in Takeo and Siem Reap under the Maybank Foundation's tutelage. The examination of the Cambodian silk sector from the perspectives of the company founders reveals blurred distinctions between commercial, philanthropic, local, regional, and transnational incentives.

Cambodian women from the countryside are simultaneously the main beneficiaries and workforce of these silk initiatives. With Color Silk, Ngorn Vanntha has specifically targeted fragile segments of the female population. Her foundation branch incorporates a variety of social benefits for weavers such as vocational training, access to primary education, and health care. Chin Koeur recruits weavers in her village and close surroundings, offers some training in ikat techniques, and pays them by the piece. Weaving provides new skills and, more importantly, regular sources of income and more financial independence. However, championing these approaches continues to feed into stereotypical representations of Cambodian rural women as static recipients with limited agency. Women remain heavily dependent on these organizations for their livelihoods. Diversifying and expanding what has been recognized and promoted as women's empowerment would increase the range of possibilities for women in terms of skillset, leadership, and equality, in silk craft organizations and beyond.

Acknowledgements

I would like to thank Dr Sarah Cheang and Martina Margetts for their thoughtful read of the examination of gender and power dynamics within the contemporary Cambodian silk craft sector. I would also like to extend my gratitude to Prom Chak, officer at UNESCO Phnom Penh, for supporting me in the field in Phnom Chisor, Takeo province. This work was made possible with the support of TECHNE – Arts and Humanities Research Council and the Marie Skłodowska-Curie Actions/European Union Horizon 2020 programs.

Notes

1 See Bruno Latour, *Reassembling the Social: An Introduction to Actor-Network-Theory* (Oxford: Oxford University Press, 2005), p. 5; Madeleine Akrich, 'The De-scription of Technical Objects,' in W. Bijker and J. Law, eds, *Shaping Technology/Building Society* (Cambridge: MIT Press, 1992), p. 208.
2 See geographer Katherine Brickell's invaluable model of micro-level research combining historical study with 'empirical material' taken from group discussions and interviews. Katherine Brickell, 'We Don't Forget the Old Rice Pot When We Get the New One,' *Signs*, 36, no. 2 (Winter 2011): 443–444.
3 Charles H. Twining, 'The Economy,' in Karl D. Jackson, ed., *Cambodia, 1975–1978: Rendez-vous with Death* (Princeton: Princeton University Press, 1989), p. 121.
4 Bernard Dupaigne, 'L'élevage des vers à soie au Cambodge,' *Revue d'ethnoécologie*, 14 (2018): 1–29, at 4.
5 Cambodia Ministry of Commerce and International Trade Center (ITC), *Cambodia National Silk Strategy* (Phnom Penh: Cambodia Ministry of Commerce and ITC, 2016), p. 1.
6 John ter Horst, *Weaving into Cambodia: Trade and Identity Politics in the (Post)- Colonial Cambodian Silk Weaving Industry* (Amsterdam: Eigen Beheer, 2008), pp. 131–133.
7 Cambodia Ministry of Commerce and ITC, *National Silk Strategy*, p. 5.
8 Judy Ledgerwood, 'Women in Cambodian Society,' Center for Southeast Asian Studies, Northern Illinois University, www.seasite.niu.edu/khmer/ledgerwood/women.htm (accessed 2 November 2020).
9 Mary N. Booth, 'Education and Gender in Contemporary Cambodia,' *International Journal of Humanities and Social Science*, 4, no. 10 (August 2014): 42–50, at 44.
10 Cambodia Ministry of Commerce and ITC, *National Silk Strategy*, p. 1.
11 Rann Reuy, 'Imported Raw Silk Gets Cheaper,' *Phnom Penh Post*, 11 September 2012, www.phnompenhpost.com/business/imported-raw-silk-gets-cheaper (accessed 10 September 2019).
12 Barbara Crossette, 'An Ancient Silk Trade Is Reborn,' *New York Times*, 20 April 1997, www.nytimes.com/1997/04/20/travel/an-ancient-silk-trade-is-reborn.html (accessed 12 October 2019).
13 Maeve Donelan, 'Khemara Builds Leaders,' *Phnom Penh Post*, 31 December 1993, www.phnompenhpost.com/national/khemara-builds-leaders (accessed 12 January 2021).
14 Trudy Jacobsen, 'Riding a Buffalo to Cross a Muddy Field: Heuristic Approaches to Feminism in Cambodia,' in Mina Roces and Louise Edwards, eds, *Women's Movements in Asia: Feminisms and Transnational Activism* (London: Routledge, 2010), pp. 215–216.
15 Helen O'Connell, *Oxfam Focus on Gender: Women and Conflict* (Oxford: Oxfam, 1993), pp. 45–47.
16 Heng Sok Chheng, 'Reviving the Traditions of Khmer Weaving,' *Phnom Penh Post*, 3 November 1995, www.phnompenhpost.com/national/reviving-traditions-khmer-weaving (accessed 1 January 2018).
17 Ibid.
18 Carol Wagner, *Soul Survivors: Stories of Women and Children in Cambodia* (Eugene: Wild Iris Press, 2008), p. 198.
19 Ibid., pp. 190–201.

20 Cambodia Ministry of Commerce and ITC, *National Silk Strategy*, p. 11.
21 OECD, 'Aid for Trade Case Story World Bank: Women Entrepreneurs in Cambodia,' OECD World Trade Organization, 2010, www.oecd.org/aidfortrade/47803414.pdf (Accessed 2 May 2020).
22 UNESCO Cambodia, internal report, 1993, UNESCO Phnom Penh Archives.
23 Lon Nara, 'Silk Weaving Trade of Liv Sa Em Under Threat,' *Phnom Penh Post*, 26 October 2001, www.phnompenhpost.com/national/silk-weaving-trade-liv-sa-em-under-threat (accessed 12 November 2019).
24 Noella Richard, *Handicrafts and Employment Generation for the Poorest Youth and Women* (Paris: UNESCO, 2007), p. 64.
25 Chin Koeur, interview with Magali An Berthon, trans. Prom Chak, 17 March 2018, Kanhjang, Cambodia.
26 Ibid.
27 Ibid.
28 Ibid.
29 Ibid.
30 John Ballyn, 'A Cultural Economic Analysis of Crafts: A View from the Workshop of the World,' in Anna Mignosa and Priyatej Kotipalli, eds, *A Cultural Economic Analysis of Craft* (New York: Springer, 2019), pp. 191–192.
31 CEDEP I Cambodia High Value Silk, 'Study Tour of SDC on Silk Sector to Takeo Province,' *Facebook*, 2015 (accessed 1 May 2020).
32 Chin Koeur, interview with Magali An Berthon.
33 Trudy Jacobsen, *Lost Goddesses: The Denial of Female Power in Cambodian History* (Copenhagen: NIAS Press, 2008), p. 5.
34 Prom Chak, UNESCO Office Program Assistant, from the same area in Takeo, told me that Ngorn Vanntha's family were known as local middlemen trading silk. In her interview (see below), Ngorn Vanntha also described her family as silk weavers.
35 Ngorn Vanntha, interview with Magali An Berthon, 2 August 2017, Phnom Penh, Cambodia.
36 In Cambodia the term 'social enterprise' does not correspond to a specific legal status. Social enterprises in Cambodia may be branches of NGOs, registered as associations with Cambodia's Interior Ministry, or as businesses with the Ministry of Commerce. It is the owner's responsibility to declare the enterprise as social and provide factual elements supporting this claim.
37 Stephen Paterson and Keorithy Yim, 'Developing an Innovative Business Model: The Case of Color Silk Enterprise in Cambodia,' *ASEAN SME Case Study Project*, unpublished report, 21 June 2013, pp. 18–19.
38 Ngorn Vanntha, interview with Magali An Berthon.
39 Jacobsen, *Lost Goddesses*, p. 278.
40 International Youth Foundation, 'International Youth Foundation & Nokia Honor 20 Youth Leaders,' 2010, www.iyfnet.org/blog/international-youth-foundation-nokia-honor-20-youth-leaders (accessed 3 January 2018).
41 Changemakers Ashoka, 'Color Silk Enterprise: Silk Weaving,' 2015, www.changemakers.com/globalgoals2015/entries/color-silk-enterprise (accessed 2 May 2020).
42 Junior Chamber International Cambodia (JCI Cambodia) is a membership-based non-profit organization, which focuses on providing development opportunities for young Cambodian people in business leadership, community engagement, and networking.
43 Victoria Bernal and Inderpal Grewal, eds, *Theorizing NGOs: States, Feminisms, and Neoliberalism* (Durham: Duke University Press, 2014), p. 5.
44 Sok Chan, 'Traditional Silk Industry Struggles to Keep its Shine,' *Khmer Times*, 10 March 2016, www.khmertimeskh.com/news/22615/traditional-silk-industry-struggles-to-keep-its-shine/ (accessed 15 December 2017).

45 'Weavers Chip In to Fight COVID-19 Pandemic,' *Khmer Times*, 29 May 2020, www.khmertimeskh.com/50728077/weavers-chip-in-to-fight-covid-19-pandemic/ (accessed 8 January 2021).
46 Maybank Foundation, 'Our Programmes: Maybank Women Eco-Weavers', www.maybankfoundation.com/index.php/our-impact/eco-weavers/women-eco-weavers-overview (accessed 10 June 2022).
47 Ngorn Vanntha was featured on the Maybank Silk Weaving Training Center for the Maybank Foundation Facebook page, 26 July 2017. Source: Maybank Foundation (Facebook), www.facebook.com/Maybank/photos/a.168159803216857/1640555265977296 (accessed 10 June 2022).
48 Post Staff, 'Maybank's Silk Weaving Centre Aims to Provide Economic Lifeline for Women,' *Phnom Penh Post*, 12 December 2019, www.phnompenhpost.com/post-focus/maybanks-silk-weaving-centre-aims-provide-economic-lifeline-women (accessed 10 June 2022).
49 'About Us,' Color Silk, https://colorsilkcommunity.wixsite.com/colorsilk-cambodia/color-silk-enterprise (accessed 2 May 2020).
50 Robin Spiess, 'Silk Training Centre Weaves an Opportunity for Rural Women,' *Phnom Penh Post*, 2 August 2017, www.phnompenhpost.com/business/silk-training-centre-weaves-opportunity-rural-women (accessed 28 January 2021).
51 Paterson and Yim, 'Developing an Innovative Business Model,' p. 17.
52 Ibid., p. 23.
53 Changemakers Ashoka, 'Color Silk Enterprise: Silk Weaving', 2015, www.changemakers.com/globalgoals2015/entries/color-silk-enterprise (accessed 2 May 2020).
54 'About Us,' Color Silk.
55 Color Silk Cambodia, 'Story,' www.facebook.com/pg/colorsilkcambodia/about/?ref=page_internal (accessed 8 October 2017).

Bibliography

Akrich, Madeleine. 'The De-scription of Technical Objects.' In *Shaping Technology/Building Society*. Edited by W. Bijker and J. Law. Cambridge: MIT Press, 1992.

Ballyn, John. 'A Cultural Economic Analysis of Crafts: A View from the Workshop of the World.' In *A Cultural Economic Analysis of Craft*. Edited by Anna Mignosa and Priyatej Kotipalli. New York: Springer, 2019.

Bernal, Victoria and Inderpal Grewal, eds. *Theorizing NGOs: States, Feminisms, and Neoliberalism*. Durham: Duke University Press, 2014.

Booth, Mary N. 'Education and Gender in Contemporary Cambodia.' *International Journal of Humanities and Social Science* 4, no. 10 (August 2014): 42–50.

Brickell, Katherine. 'We Don't Forget the Old Rice Pot when We Get the New One.' *Signs: Journal of Women in Culture and Society* 36, no. 2 (Winter 2011): 437–462.

Cambodia Ministry of Commerce and International Trade Center (ITC). *Cambodia National Silk Strategy*. Phnom Penh: Cambodia Ministry of Commerce and ITC, 2016.

CEDEP I – Cambodia High Value Silk. 'Study Tour of SDC on Silk Sector to Takeo Province.' *Facebook*. 2015 (accessed 1 May 2020).

Chan, Sok. 'Traditional Silk Industry Struggles to Keep its Shine.' *Khmer Times*, 10 March 2016. www.khmertimeskh.com/news/22615/traditional-silk-industry-struggles-to-keep-its-shine/ (accessed 15 December 2017).

Change Makers Ashoka. 'Unilever Sustainable Living Young Entrepreneurs Awards 2015: Color Silk Enterprise: Silk Weaving.' 2015. www.changemakers.com/globalgoals2015/entries/color-silk-enterprise (accessed 2 January 2018).

Cheang Sokha and Duncan O'Brien. 'UNESCO Promotes Phnom Chisor.' *Phnom Penh Post*, 13 August 2004. www.phnompenhpost.com/national/unesco-promotes-phnom-chisoh (accessed 1 May 2020).

Chin Koeur. Interview by Magali An Berthon. Trans. Prom Chak. 17 March 2018. Kanhjang, Cambodia.

Color Silk Cambodia. 'Story.' *Facebook*. www.facebook.com/pg/colorsilkcambodia/about/?ref=page_internal (accessed 8 October 2017).

Color Silk Community. 'About Us.' 2017. http://colorsilkcommunity.wixsite.com/colorsilk-cambodia/color-silk-enterprise (accessed 3 January 2018).

Crossette, Barbara. 'An Ancient Silk Trade Is Reborn.' *New York Times*, 20 April 1997. www.nytimes.com/1997/04/20/travel/an-ancient-silk-trade-is-reborn.html (accessed 12 October 2019).

Donelan, Maeve. 'Khemara Builds Leaders.' *Phnom Penh Post*, 31 December 1993. www.phnompenhpost.com/national/khemara-builds-leaders (accessed 12 January 2021).

Dupaigne, Bernard. 'L'Élevage des vers à soie au Cambodge.' *Revue d'ethnoécologie* 14 (2018): 1–29.

Heng, Sok Chheng. 'Reviving the Traditions of Khmer Weaving.' *Phnom Penh Post*, 3 November 1995. www.phnompenhpost.com/national/reviving-traditions-khmer-weaving (accessed 1 January 2018).

International Youth Foundation. 'International Youth Foundation & Nokia Honor 20 Youth Leaders.' 2010. www.iyfnet.org/blog/international-youth-foundation-nokia-honor-20-youth-leaders (accessed 3 January 2018).

Jacobsen, Trudy. *Lost Goddesses: The Denial of Female Power in Cambodian History*. Copenhagen: NIAS Press, 2008.

Jacobsen, Trudy. 'Riding a Buffalo to Cross a Muddy Field: Heuristic Approaches to Feminism in Cambodia.' In *Women's Movements in Asia: Feminisms and Transnational Activism*. Edited by Mina Roces and Louise Edwards. London: Routledge, 2010.

Latour, Bruno. *Reassembling the Social: An Introduction to Actor-Network-Theory*. Oxford: Oxford University Press, 2005.

Ledgerwood, Judy. 'Women in Cambodian Society.' Center for Southeast Asian Studies, Northern Illinois University. www.seasite.niu.edu/khmer/ledgerwood/women.htm (accessed 2 November 2020).

Lon Nara. 'Silk Weaving Trade of Liv Sa Em under Threat.' *Phnom Penh Post*, 26 October 2001. www.phnompenhpost.com/national/silk-weaving-trade-liv-sa-em-under-threat (accessed 12 November 2019).

Ma, Laura. 'The Struggle for Gender Equality.' *Phnom Penh Post*, 30 August 2013. www.phnompenhpost.com/business/struggle-gender-equality (accessed 24 December 2017).

Maybank Foundation. 2017. 'Launching of the Maybank Silk Weaving Training Centre, Cambodia.' [Press release.] Maybank Foundation. http://maybankfoundation.com/index.php/how-we-work/press-releases/item/launching-of-the-maybank-silk-weaving-training-centre-cambodia (accessed 12 December 2017).

Ngorn Vanntha, informal interview with Magali An Berthon, 2 August 2017, Phnom Penh, Cambodia.

O'Connell, Helen, ed. *Oxfam Focus on Gender: Women and Conflict*. Oxford: Oxfam, 1993.

OECD. 'Aid for Trade Case Story World Bank: Women Entrepreneurs in Cambodia.' OECD World Trade Organization. 2010. www.oecd.org/aidfortrade/47803414.pdf (accessed 26 December 2017).

Paterson, Stephen and Yim Keorithy. 'Developing an Innovative Business Model: The Case of Color Silk Enterprise in Cambodia.' *ASEAN SME Case Study Project.* Unpublished report. 21 June 2013.

Post Staff. 'Maybank's Silk Weaving Centre Aims to Provide Economic Lifeline for Women.' *Phnom Penh Post*, 12 December 2019. www.phnompenhpost.com/post-focus/maybanks-silk-weaving-centre-aims-provide-economic-lifeline-women (accessed 10 June 2022).

Rann, Reuy. 'Imported Raw Silk Gets Cheaper.' *Phnom Penh Post*, 11 September 2012. www.phnompenhpost.com/business/imported-raw-silk-gets-cheaper (accessed 10 September 2019).

Richard, Noella. *Handicrafts and Employment Generation for the Poorest Youth and Women*. Paris: UNESCO, 2007.

Spiess, Robin. 'Silk Training Centre Weaves an Opportunity for Rural Women.' *Phnom Penh Post*, 2 August 2017. www.phnompenhpost.com/business/silk-training-centre-weaves-opportunity-rural-women (accessed 28 January 2021).

ter Horst, John. *Weaving into Cambodia: Trade and Identity Politics in the (Post)-Colonial Cambodian Silk Weaving Industry*. Amsterdam: Eigen Beheer, 2008.

Twining, Charles. 'The Economy.' In *Cambodia, 1975–1978: Rendez-Vous with Death*. Edited by Karl D. Jackson. Princeton: Princeton University Press, 1989.

UNESCO Cambodia. Internal report. UNESCO Phnom Penh Archives, 1993.

Wagner, Carol. *Soul Survivors: Stories of Women and Children in Cambodia*. Berkeley: Creative Arts Book Company, 2002.

'Weavers Chip In to Fight COVID-19 Pandemic.' *Khmer Times*, 29 May 2020. 2021. www.khmertimeskh.com/50728077/weavers-chip-in-to-fight-covid-19-pandemic/ (accessed 8 January 2021).

8

(Re)crafting distribution networks for contemporary Philippine textiles: women's advocacy and social enterprise

B. Lynne Milgram

Introduction

Throughout the Philippines, as in many global south countries, traveling neoliberal development policies privileging large-scale projects (e.g. malls, condominiums) have meant that those involved in artisanal production such as weaving, ceramics, basketry, and woodcarving cannot depend solely on income from this work to meet their families' subsistence needs. Instead, artisans must engage in a variety of part-time alternative income-generating activities to secure their livelihoods. Artisans living in rural areas usually work in farming by cultivating commodities such as rice and vegetables for home use and for sale. Artisans residing in both rural and urban areas may also work in periodic wage labor, while women, in particular, often perform personal grooming, cleaning, and laundry services. To better promote their artisanal enterprises, artisans throughout the Philippines have thus self-organized into associations to gain the equipment, skills training, and marketing assistance that can enhance their practices.

Such collaborative initiatives are particularly evident in the number of weaving collectives that artisans and social entrepreneurs have organized in Luzon, northern Philippines, where weaving continues as a viable livelihood option practiced within households as well as in small workshop settings. While the majority of artisans and entrepreneurs engaged in textile production and marketing are women, some men, as I discuss later, are starting to weave using upright floor looms rather than backstrap (body-tension) looms which are more commonly used by women in household production. Drawing on case studies in Ifugao province and in Manila, this chapter focuses on two smaller-scale, social welfare-mandated enterprises that have emerged within the past ten to fifteen years to operationalize alternative marketing channels for local textile production. These include Save the Ifugao Terraces Movement (SITMo)[1] located in Kiangan, Ifugao province, and Rags2Riches (R2R) located in Manila. Adhering to a model of business transparency, both social enterprises promote not only income generation for makers, but also social welfare projects that invest in community well-being (e.g health insurance, education), foster long-term producer–buyer relations, and ensure that artisans' designs can compete in global markets while simultaneously maintaining local knowledge and technology. To this end, these social enterprises have recently harnessed the marketing potential of information and communication technology (ICT) platforms that promise wider distribution options for artisans' textile production.

In this chapter, I thus explore the channels through which artisans and the entrepreneurs engaged in these social enterprises can realize the potential of ICT and negotiate market precarity given shifts in the availability of raw materials, conditions of labor, market demand, and the degree to which products are required to represent markers of local cultural identity. I also question the extent to which these social enterprises can use ICT outreach to scale up from their smaller-scale origins and still maintain their social welfare mandate. Given the context of minimal social welfare support from the Philippine government,[2] I suggest that the personal initiatives of artisans and social entrepreneurs emerge as the major drivers fashioning these enterprises' constant reshaping and perseverance across a range of distribution channels. Their efforts, in turn, can facilitate artisanal stakeholders to achieve autonomy more on their own terms in today's locally grounded yet globally connected world.

To understand the nuanced dynamics of such transnational Philippine textile distribution, I first review studies on ICT and its implications for women's empowerment as applied to textile production, in particular. I then discuss the field of social entrepreneurship and alternative economies to contextualize how the socially mandated entrepreneurs I discuss here enhance artisans' economic and social security.

Information and communication technology: an avenue for change?

The interdisciplinary field of feminist technology studies fruitfully addresses the degree to which women's increasing access to ICT can enhance their power and agency. To this point, Francesca Bray notes that 'Technical skills and domains of expertise are divided between and within the sexes,' shaping not only gender identities, but also access to socio-economic opportunities.[3] Güney-Frahm thus points out that international development practitioners predictably consider training in ICT as a solution for women's restricted access to capital and business skills.[4] Thus, development practitioners seeking to open more economic options for small-scale producers, advocate that with increased access to the internet, artisans, and women in particular, will finally have the competitive market tools they require to gain broader financial inclusion and assume more entrepreneurial roles.[5] In practice, however, studies document both advantages and shortcomings of ICT access, such that the extent to which online selling platforms affect gender equality and women's empowerment for home-based female workers remains contentious.

On the one hand, some female entrepreneurs with ICT access and skills have been able to expand their businesses especially with regard to online product marketing.[6] In this light, Susan Davis's study of the 'Women Weavers OnLine' project in Morocco demonstrates that, with Davis's personal hands-on assistance and that of educated and trained community assistants, rural Moroccan women weavers have been successfully selling their handwoven rugs via the internet since the project's inception in November 2000. Davis, a digital development practitioner, concedes however, that on-the-ground hand holding may be necessary at a project's outset to mitigate the rural constraints of variable electricity and hence unreliable internet access. Related challenges also emerge regarding some rural women's low level of education and financial training, and artisans' lack of knowledge about, and the cost of, international currency conversions and fund transfers.[7]

Rather than applying an e-commerce business model to marginalized craft communities that lack the infrastructure to ensure an early positive start, Thomas Molony suggests providing more support to women entrepreneurs who already have access to the basic ICT resources required for success. In so doing, the systems that these entrepreneurs establish can benefit others. Molony's study of three successful Tanzanian businesswomen who export African ebony carvings illustrates the innovative ICT channels these women use to leverage resources, ideas, and information from contacts outside their own social milieu.[8] ICT, including e-mail, is essential to their business strategies, not only for economic exchanges, but more importantly to build long-term 'networks of working relationships' grounded in trust – what Molony terms establishing 'social-technical capital.'[9] Nurcan Törenli similarly identifies that women artisans and entrepreneurs, including home-based workers, who effectively operationalize ICT for marketing can additionally use this resource to foster socially supportive networks for future initiatives through what she terms 'solidaristic practices.'[10] Meera Joseph's research in India cautions, however, that while ICT has the potential to provide women with new opportunities, given the logistic challenge to overcome socio-economic infrastructure shortcomings inherent in many global south communities, there is also a need to use ICT resources in more locally viable ways.[11]

In countries where there has been more government support for ICT access, for example, projects have yielded new opportunities for home-based workers. The Malaysian platform, E-Entrepreneurs Women Trade Center, carries products that range from hijab clothing to bakery goods,[12] while a Turkish initiative provides government-sponsored training workshops for women and subsequently enables them to produce and sell goods on a government-supported platform.[13]

Simultaneously, as noted, studies also document that for women to realize ICT's potential means overcoming limitations. In contrast to Davis's findings, Brie Rehbein argues that the artisans with whom she worked in Mexico's silver jewelry industry had less internet-marketing success with their production.[14] Rehbein outlines that while e-commerce is repeatedly recommended as an alternative business strategy to traditional in-person means of selling, the barriers to operationalizing expanded market access (e.g. IT infrastructure, transportation), human deficiencies (e.g. education, lack of training), and insufficient government support structures, as Davis also noted, remain too great for most financially undercapitalized rural Mexican artisans to overcome.[15]

As I have argued in earlier research on microfinance development in the Philippines, and as ICT-focused studies assert, although the latter projects aim for female empowerment and gender equality, their interventions do not necessarily challenge the existing structures of inequality but rather may prefer to operate within them.[16] To this point, Güney-Frahm identifies three 'blind spots' that ICT-based projects such as e-commerce platforms overlook for home-based workers: the importance of encouraging artisans to produce high-quality work; the degree to which ICT use can increase female visibility in the public sphere; and the extent to which ICT can promote gender identity beyond the domestic sphere.[17] Güney-Frahm argues, as evidenced in the aforementioned study by Rehbein, that it is questionable to what extent women's ICT-supported income-generating activities can transform the situation in which these women are mostly home-based workers selling products with a low profit margin in highly competitive markets while continuing to be expected to fulfill domestic responsibilities.[18] The question I explore in the following case studies, then, is, does access to ICT simply address symptoms rather than root causes of inequality to reproduce the discriminatory systems it proffers to alleviate?

Social entrepreneurship and alternative economies

One avenue through which craft artisans, and women in particular, can use ICT options to address this question is by working within an alternative economic structure such as that of social enterprise. The social entrepreneurs who have founded the viable textile-marketing initiatives I highlight here are pragmatic and visionary social activists whose enterprise models borrow from an eclectic mix of business, charity, private, and social movement models to reconfigure solutions to community problems while facilitating the security of artisans' livelihoods.[19] As Alex Nicholls suggests, social entrepreneurship represents an 'umbrella term' for a range of pioneering practices that champion social and environmental sustainability, business transparency, and high-quality production[20] – issues Güney-Frahm identifies as priorities for women to gain more market control and visibility outside the household.[21]

Social entrepreneurs thus work towards a 'combined value proposition' that dispels the traditional view that the creation of economic value is separate from its social equivalent.[22] Embracing an alternative economy approach, such as that of social entrepreneurship, dislodges our taken-for-granted organizational structure privileging profit maximization to foreground, instead, relationships rooted in care and altruism, labor that is volunteered, transactions that require no money, and organizations that seek to benefit collective members rather than owners.[23] Indeed, this blurring of socio-economic boundaries foregrounds the significance and usefulness of building long-term social networks, as is clearly evidenced in the successful cross-sector business strategies of the Tanzanian women entrepreneurs in Molony's research.

Thus, value creation for the Philippine weaving enterprises I analyze in this chapter – SITMo and R2R – includes not only designing high-quality textiles and improving market access, but also achieving more nuanced empowerment initiatives such as increasing artisans' access to crop or house insurance, or education, and revitalizing depleted community resources such as water and sanitation – initiatives that can potentially shake the foundation of infrastructure inequities.[24] When these activities are valorized, they open an ontological space in which a range of alternatives to mainstream capitalist logic is 'not only achievable, but already existing.'[25] As J. K. Gibson-Graham argues, this other economy is fundamental to our economic well-being and yet is undervalued precisely because it often works outside conventional economic systems.[26]

Despite the rhetoric proffering technology support for disenfranchised groups, government and private funding in the Philippines still fall short of matching the growth of new social ventures, resulting in keen competition for limited funds.[27] In response to the mismatch between resource supply and demand, Nicholls identifies that social entrepreneurs need to 'consider strategic moves into new markets to subsidize their social activities either through exploiting profitable opportunities in the core activities of their not-for-profit venture or via for-profit subsidiary ventures and cross sector partnerships with commercial corporations'[28] – a strategy used by Rags2Riches in its recent partnership with Swedish furniture leader, IKEA.[29] In the following case studies of northern Philippine textile production, I explore the extent to which trickle-down benefits generated

Women's contemporary Philippine textile production and marketing

Since the restoration of democratic government in the Philippines in 1986, state policies have continued to promote anti-poverty programs that rarely come to fruition and to support initiatives that tend to benefit more well-off residents.[30] Of particular relevance to the issue of women's work in textile production and marketing is that government-sponsored programs supporting craft production tend to benefit larger export-oriented enterprises (e.g. rattan and bamboo furniture), leaving most home-based artisan trades to fend for themselves.[31] Despite this lack of ongoing government assistance across sectors, Philippine women have persistently engaged in small-scale craft businesses by drawing on alternative community practices and values that support women's parity within households and their right and access to extra-household social and economic opportunities. Although women in the Philippines most often assume the major role for domestic and childcare responsibilities, their long-standing positions as primary household financial managers and public market traders enable them to pursue potential extra-household work and education options. In northern Luzon men often assume domestic responsibilities when women are successful in business.[32] In this way, as Wazir Karim argues for Southeast Asia generally, women secure a 'continuous chain of productive enterprises' for family and personal well-being by establishing 'a repertoire of social units' linked to household and market; and they 'unlink' themselves in an 'open-ended' and 'multi-focal' system when situations change.[33] However, while women find household production and market vending to be occupations they can activate as extensions of their households in a non-dualistic public–private manner, the fact remains that women's cross-sector work can yield a 'double burden' that potentially precludes them from pursuing further work opportunities. Although artisans' income from their part-time weaving may seem minimal – about US$ 45.00–50.00 a month – these earnings significantly contribute to overall rural household income, as evidenced in the social enterprises I outline here.

Rematerializing discarded cloth: the Rags2Riches journey

Rags2Riches, founded in 2008, started as a project for urban poor communities in Payatas, southern Luzon, the location of one of the largest dumpsites in the Philippines. Many of the families living in this urban community continue to earn their income through scavenging materials from the site's trash. Some women used the cloth scraps they had collected to weave loosely constructed plain weave rag rugs and household items (e.g. potholders), which they sold at local markets in what developed into an informal cottage industry. This production, however, was dependent upon artisans securing ongoing supplies of discarded textile remnants. To assist these women to obtain regular supplies of cloth scraps, Sarah,[34] the founder and current Director of R2R, drew on her work in development to link producers directly to factory suppliers, and subsequently established the R2R social enterprise. To develop better-quality products that can respond to contemporary consumer demands, Sarah also enlisted the assistance of a professional designer. In late 2020, to offset material shortages caused by the COVID-19 pandemic, R2R added a limited range of clothing to its product line. Its core and signature production, however, remains re- and upcycled, high-quality handwoven functional home products which comprise the focus of this case study (e.g. bags, place mats, rugs, coasters) (Figures 8.1–8.3).

As I observed while visiting R2R's Manila workshop, each woven textile piece carries a well-documented label identifying the name of the artisan and the circumstances of production, which are more fully explained on R2R's website:

> We are a fashion and design house empowering community artisans. … We partner with local artisans across the Philippines to create eco-ethical fashion and home accessories out of upcycled, overstock cloth and indigenous fabrics.

8.1 A display of plain weave bags woven from re- and upcycled fabric in the Rags2Riches showroom. Quezon City, Manila, Philippines, 2018

8.2 A display of plain weave bags and cushions woven from re- and upcycled fabric in the Rags2Riches showroom, Quezon City, Manila, Philippines, 2018

> ... A big and constant part of our design is the signature R2R weave. Our community artisans weave these and since most of them are mothers, we have created a unique system that allows them to work from their homes. ... We are intentional about creating a super integrated, opportunity-providing social enterprise from the beginning.[35]

As R2R's website mandate thus evidences, the company supports long-term community sustainability by enhancing artisans' income opportunities and establishing social welfare projects for artisans, such as better health insurance, skills training, and socio-economic mobility through enhanced education. To best facilitate artisans' production capacity, given that women artisans remain responsible for most domestic tasks, the project is designed to remain at the household level. Artisans receive small wood-frame looms that are easily accommodated in their homes and easy to store when not in use.

The heading on the R2R website reads 'Things that Matter' as R2R represents itself as a 'brand with a cause.'[36] Currently working with ten local Manila-area communities and about two hundred weavers, R2R's signature products, as noted, continue to feature plain weave panels grounded in its earlier use of recycled fabrics (see Figures 8.1–8.3). In order to maintain high-quality production and foster collaborative teamwork while developing new designs, R2R continues to mount design workshops for

8.3 Detail of a Rags2Riches woven panel on a simple wood-frame loom, Quezon City, Manila, Philippines, 2019

weavers, employ full-time designers, organize periodic contracts with freelance designers for special projects, and has founded a formal two-year training program for weavers in the R2R 'Artisan Academy.'[37]

As Sarah, the Director, explained, R2R's household weavers are paid in a flexible putting-out system in which artisans' income depends upon the technical difficulty of, and hence the time taken to complete, their weavings. Weavers receive the materials they require for each order plus 50% of the anticipated labor costs. When weavers submit their woven panels, the pieces are weighed such that the material advanced equals the material woven, including cloth scraps which are then returned to the weavers for their own use. For each community order completed by the deadline, the weaving group receives a bonus payment which R2R deposits to the community's communal bank account. Artisans can borrow these funds at low interest rates or vote to designate the funds to community infrastructure development. In order to consistently support weavers, R2R maintains a database of woven panels for general stock. Thus, if weavers do not have specific orders to fill, they can earn additional income by weaving the most in-demand, patterned panels that are held for future orders.[38]

To streamline final production, four in-house teams or twenty artisans work full time on site with full benefits to oversee pre- and post-production tasks (Figure 8.4). The Cutting Team pre-cuts the non-woven

8.4 Artisans work on assembling bags and household products in the Rags2Riches workshop, Quezon City, Manila, Philippines, 2018

parts (e.g. cloth panels, linings, seam binding) for all ordered products; once artisans deliver their woven panels to the workshop, the Assembly Team organizes the different components for each type of piece. Other artisans working in the Sewing Team then sew together the components to complete each product, which then travels to the Quality Control Team for its final inspection. Within this operational model, R2R's social enterprise mandate integrates 'collaborative conscientious' and 'human-centered design' to 'professionalize home-based community artisans' with the goal that artisans' increased access to enterprise opportunities will facilitate their socio-economic mobility.[39]

To realize efficient operation, R2R maintains a digital database in which weavers make a commitment to their community project by confirming with their group coordinator how many hours a day they can weave, depending upon their other responsibilities. When R2R receives an order, staff submit the order to a specific community of weavers whose capacity is sufficient to complete the required woven panels by the delivery deadline. As Sarah explained, 'We also conduct collective bargaining with weavers to negotiate their rate of pay, building in potential for higher earnings as artisans can earn more as their speed increases.' She continued, 'In so doing we work to de-center production control and professionalize the system to promote collaborative teamwork.'[40]

While Sarah, as the R2R Director, retains responsibility for overseeing the enterprise's daily operations, she works collaboratively with the Executive Board and with managers, the latter of whom includes artisans who have moved into supervisory positions. Cynthia, for example, one of the first artisans employed by R2R from the Payatas community, is currently a R2R senior leader responsible for community development and purchasing. Juliette, originally from a marginalized community in Caloocan, first worked as an embroiderer. After receiving computer training, she then assumed a position as one of R2R's Inventory Officers supervising the digital data repository of available raw materials and woven panels. Women also assume leadership roles as Community Coordinators and Leaders in charge of allocating work and providing mentorship and training to artisans, organizing community meetings, and coordinating deliveries of completed woven panels to the Manila workshop.[41] Such varied work responsibilities provide artisans with avenues of upward mobility similar to the initiatives that artisans have pursued in the following case study.

Save the Ifugao Terraces Movement and Ifugao Nation[42]

The Save the Ifugao Terraces Movement, established in Kiangan, Ifugao province, northern Luzon in the early 2000s, is a grassroots non-governmental organization (NGO) bringing together public and private sector institutions to implement sustainable provincial development. Within the last ten years SITMo has expanded its initial mandate to conserve Ifugao's unique environmental resources – its dramatic rice terraces and water supplies. To this end, SITMo has established the Indigenous Peoples Education Center, which is devoted to preserving Ifugao cultural traditions through educating youth, and actively promotes local sustainable livelihoods through the arts, facilitated by its new website presence, Ifugao Nation. As the Ifugao Nation website reads,

> We are involved in rice research, documentation of traditional practices, heritage education, ecotourism, and weaving. As the social enterprise arm of SITMo, Ifugao Nation helps in our conservation work by supporting traditional economic opportunities in our communities and raising awareness of the Ifugao culture through advocacy.[43]

The town of Kiangan, the home of SITMo, was formerly the provincial administrative and spiritual hub, where a vibrant community of weavers continue to produce the region's distinctive 'traditionally' patterned textiles which remain in demand for local religious events and for general cultural occasions. As the SITMo Director, Michael, explained, 'One of our organization's objectives is to ensure the integrity of Kiangan's extensive history of fine weaving by working with older weavers to transfer their knowledge to the next generation of younger artisans.'[44] Although Michael is director, the organization is collaboratively administered by an Executive Committee in which women play prominent roles and which, in turn, represents SITMo's approximately fifty active members, most of whom are women. With the enterprise's expansion, some men are starting to weave at the SITMo workshop using the upright floor looms which, along with a few backstrap looms, are available for members' general use (Figure 8.5). Most women artisans however, as members of the Kiyyangan Weavers' Association, weave on backstrap looms in their homes. Weavers produce a variety of textiles that include Ifugao's characteristic or 'traditionally' patterned blankets, women's skirts and blouses, and shoulder cloths, but also alternative format pieces such as table runners, scarves, and shawls that can meet emergent consumer demands (Figures 8.6 and 8.7).

The SITMo production system, like that of R2R, operates a flexible putting-out system in which the SITMo Executive Committee functions as the linchpin in the local-to-global flow of the enterprise's woven textiles. Since the wholesale suppliers of high-quality cotton yarn – the raw material most weavers prefer to use – usually accept only large-scale bulk orders, individual artisans have limited access to this thread. Consequently, SITMo, like R2R, supplies the raw materials to artisans, deducting the cost of the yarn from the amount artisans receive for their labor. Producers are

8.5 Two artisans weave in the workshop of the social enterprise, Save the Ifugao Terraces Movement, Kiangan, Ifugao, Philippines, 2018

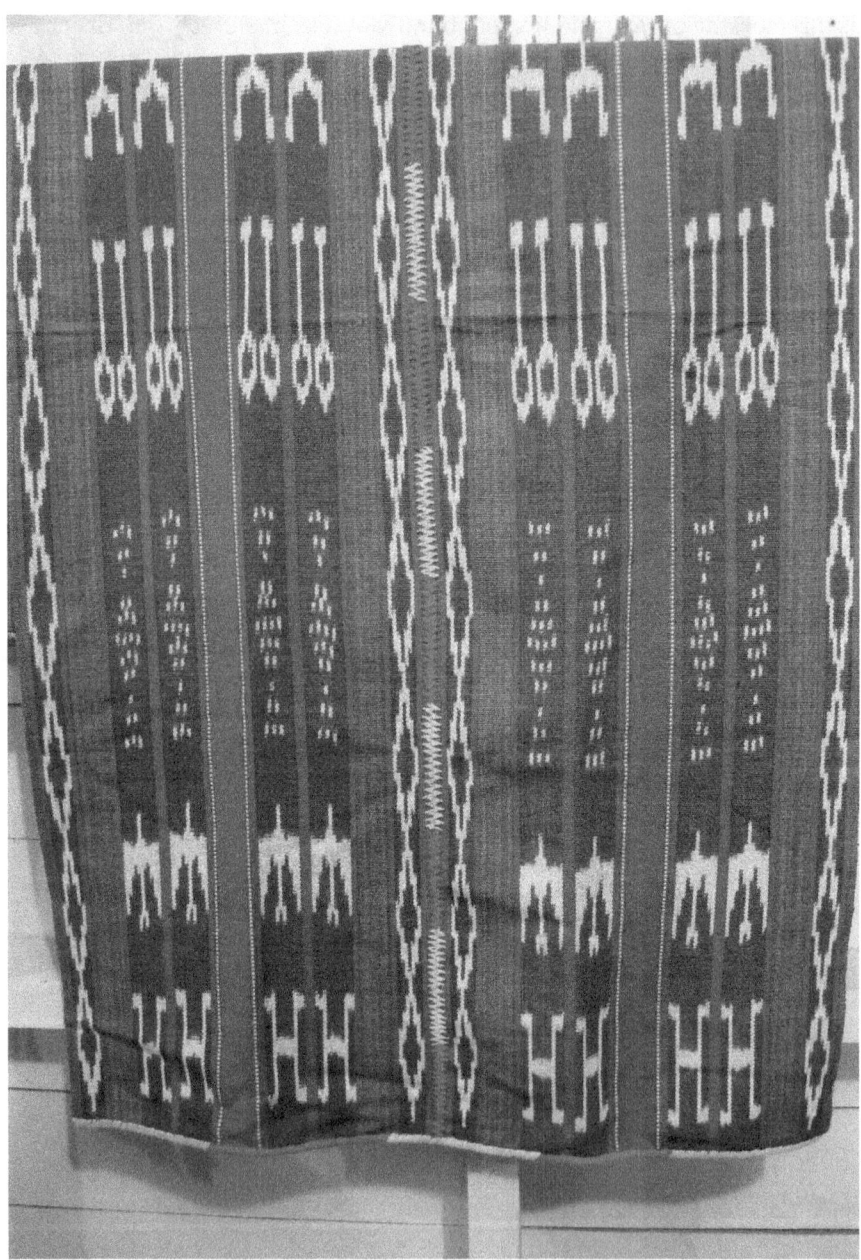

8.6 A naturally dyed ikat (resist tied and dyed) textile panel woven by artisans for the NGO, Save the Ifugao Terraces Movement/Ifugao Nation, Kiangan, Ifugao, Philippines, 2018

8.7 A naturally dyed ikat (resist tied and dyed) textile panel woven by artisans for the NGO, Save the Ifugao Terraces Movement/Ifugao Nation, Kiangan, Ifugao, Philippines, 2018

paid for their work based on the technical difficulty of the weaving and on the time required to complete the piece. For specific orders, the Director along with committee members will identify the designs that weavers execute and generally supervise the weaving quality. Within this social entrepreneurship model, however, as with that of R2R, Michael explained that SITMo prioritizes working collaboratively with artisans to enhance producers' social welfare. This includes ensuring not only increased income, but also food security, better banking access, and general social support in the form of health and crop insurance. Assistance may also include facilitating access to design-training workshops such as those regularly offered by the Department of Trade and Industry as well as capacity building such as financial literacy training.

SITMo actively markets its textiles by responding to specific local-to-transnational customer orders facilitated by Facebook and Instagram posting, and as of December 2020, on its newly launched website, Ifugao Nation. While artisans produce pieces for specific requests, as weaver, Patricia, explained, 'Even when buyers suggest we use specific colors or patterns, we still weave the cloth the Ifugao way. Our textiles are personalized as I play a part in creating even a preordered pattern.'[45] To thus ensure that SITMo's contemporary woven textiles continue to speak of Ifugao design heritage, the newly woven blankets each have 'traditionally' patterned selvedge end bands sewn to two blanket edges to complete the spirit of the cloth; and consumers are informed of this textile detail in the cloth's accompanying label, as I outline below for the posted *Kinattibanglan ya Hinulgi* piece. Yet, simultaneously SITMo contemporizes its woven blankets by marketing them as 'wraps' with website photos depicting the blankets fashionably draped around models' bodies (Figure 8.8).[46]

'The challenge,' SITMo Director Michael explained, 'is to modernize and diversify the character of Ifugao weavings to appeal to consumers in global locations while ensuring pieces still suggest our Ifugao identity.' As Aida, an Executive Committee artisan continued, 'We know there is a thin line between appreciation and cultural appropriation' and we are 'very conscious' of this fact.[47] Thus, as the Ifugao Nation website notes about the contemporary pieces they post,

> While we still make and use the traditional blankets described here [on the product labels], most of what we put online are new creations inspired by these textiles. With blessings from the elders, we have switched the colors and patterns to innovate and bring new life into the weaves that we make. ... When we do upload traditional textiles and garments, we'll make sure to write about the cultural context of these weaves to create learning opportunities for everyone.[48]

To inform consumers of the context of Ifugao Nation's contemporary production, each piece posted on the website is thus accompanied, as with

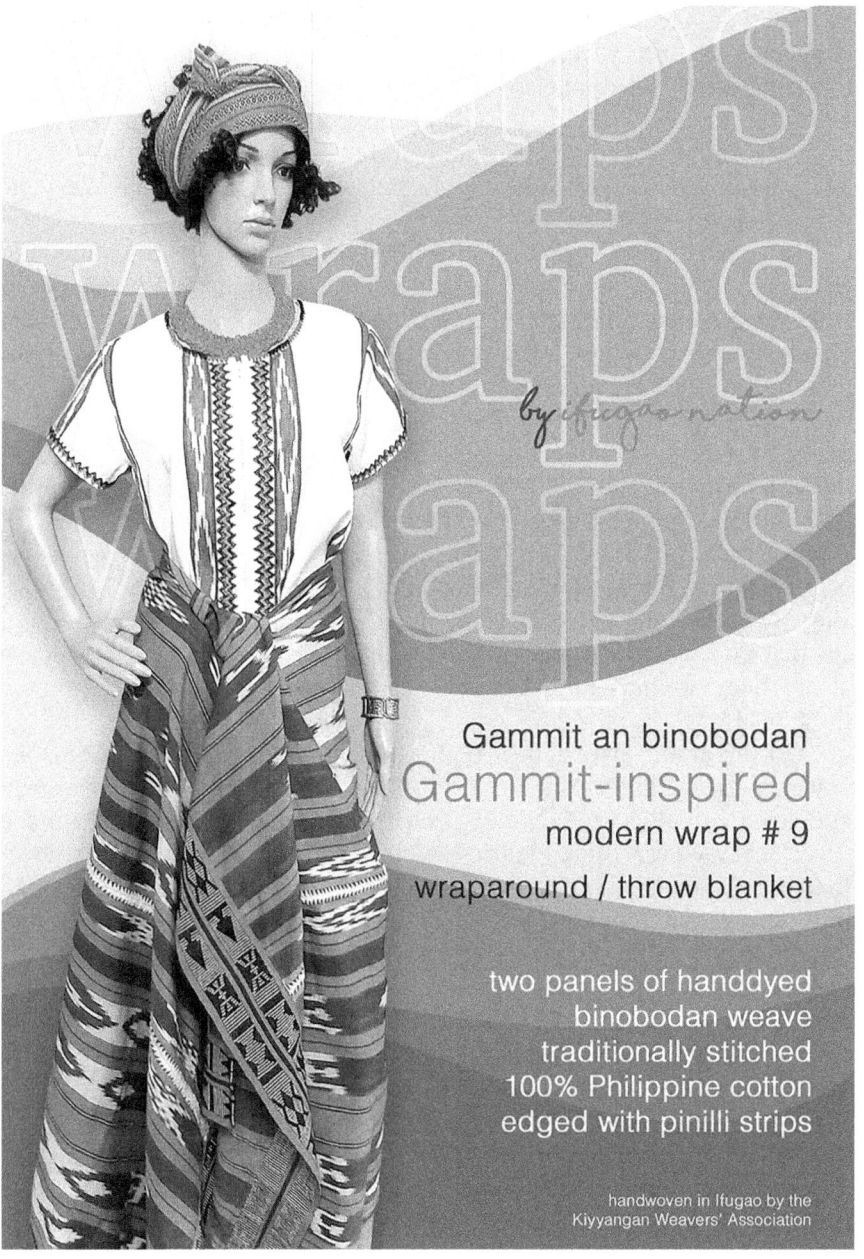

8.8 Woven textile 'wrap' using the ikat (resist tied and dyed) technique is displayed for sale on the SITMo/Ifugao Nation website

R2R, by a detailed label. The following label example is typical of SITMo's educational effort: '*Kinattibanglan ya Hinulgi*, 31 × 68 inch wrap/throw blanket, single wide panel of hand dyed *binobodan* weave (ikat) handwoven by men weavers on upright looms edged with *pinilli* strips made from raw Philippine cotton.'[49] Other featured pieces will additionally credit producers by noting, 'Handwoven in Ifugao by the Kiyyangan Weavers' Association.'[50]

The question that then arises for SITMo's production is not how accurately its woven textiles duplicate an assumed tradition, but rather to what extent can weavers stretch the representation of local design such that pieces still maintain their local caché? On this issue, Edward Bruner argues that the so-called authenticity of material culture generally is a 'contested site' that 'plays itself out in a soft struggle over meaning' between the intent of makers and the perception of consumers.[51] Bruner's conceptualization highlights that 'We all enter society in the middle' to reveal 'the tensions that exist in cross-cultural coproductions of authenticity.'[52] The comment of Carolyn, a SITMo weaver, illustrates this issue when she pointed to two Ifugao women's woven blouses posted to the SITMo website: 'If you say to me that these newly woven blouses are not authentic, I say that the authentic Ifugao women's upper body covering was no blouse at all. Today, we have to be flexible such that people do not say we are too traditional.'[53]

Indeed, at the onset of the COVID-19 pandemic in spring 2020, SITMo advantageously fulfilled the need for protective masks by asking weavers and sewers to shift production to constructing high-quality masks made from locally woven Ifugao fabrics. With donations from patrons to cover the cost of materials and artisans' labor, SITMo's masks were distributed free to local communities and 'donated to medical personnel and other frontliners in neighboring communities.'[54] The success of these early mask donations led, in the autumn of 2020, to masks being sold and shipped throughout the Philippines. The fluidity of internet communication paved the way for subsequent wholesale mask sales transnationally to Filipino social enterprises such as Cambio & Co., Inc. in Toronto, Canada, an online social enterprise that imports a range of Philippine artisanal production.[55]

Given their early successes, then, how can social enterprises such as Rags2Riches and Save the Ifugao Terraces Movement further leverage the potential of information and communication technology to expand their businesses while maintaining their social mandates?

Information and communication technology opportunities and constraints

Rags2Riches has developed a dynamic interactive website that simultaneously builds community among consumers while product sales ensure the sustainability of the company. In addition to the online shopping options, R2R's website provides extensive background on the circumstances of its founding and outlines how its social welfare goals impact artisans and their partner communities, and how the organization's future initiatives will ensure socio-economic sustainability for makers. In so doing, R2R creates a sense of belonging. It invites those who visit the site to become an ongoing part of its 'imagined community'[56] by encouraging consumers to contribute reviews of the products they buy and post stories and photos about themselves and their purchases. To facilitate its global reach, R2R has established easily facilitated sales through PayPal and credit card payment options. Yet, even with R2R's extensive experience, the heading on its website on 15 February 2021 read: 'We now ship nationwide and internationally. But we ask for your patience and understanding for possible delays in shipping.'[57]

My conversations with Sarah, the Rags2Riches Director, indicated that although sales are increasing, the enterprise needs to consistently canvass for sponsorship in order to support more makers. As Sarah noted, 'We are continually seeking potential partners and patrons and our internet access is essential to achieve the outreach we need. One source of growing investors who have found us via the internet are corporate accounts in which corporations place large orders, such as for a thousand pieces, which they distribute as gifts to employees and to clients.'[58] 'Since 2019,' Sarah continued, 'Canada's Cambio & Co., Inc., has become a reliable and collaborative partner.'[59] To this end, effective 1 October 2020, Cambio & Co., Inc. launched a separate digital R2R store on its website as well as videos from earlier Webinar conversations with Sarah about R2R's socially mandated operation. As Sarah noted in R2R's press release, 'Building this online store will allow us [R2R] to continue creating livelihood opportunities for artists from the Philippines while making things that matter to our advocates from North America.'[60]

While maintaining its digital presence remains paramount, especially during the constraints created by the COVID-19 pandemic, Sarah explained that R2R 'identified the advantages of also establishing a physical presence for consumers in the Philippines who may not consistently shop online.' To this end, in mid-2020 Rags2Riches enabled customers to pick up their orders at its Quezon City, Manila showroom and the company mounted product displays at both the UP Town Center, a shopping venue on the campus of the University of the Philippines Diliman, and the retail outlet, Anthropologie. Sarah explained, 'Our customers will again have access to our in-store products with the easing of COVID-19 restrictions.'[61] Indeed, R2R's recent partnership with IKEA, in which R2R operates its own in-house store within the latter's new outlet in Manila's Mall of Asia, highlights the paradoxical situation in which even with a global online presence, medium-sized social enterprises still see the advantage of maintaining a physical presence.⁶² In what ways, then, do smaller-scale Philippine social enterprises with less secure internet access balance their digital and physical entities?

Unlike R2R's established digital presence, smaller social enterprises such as Save the Ifugao Terraces Movement struggle to realize the global reach offered by ICT. Until November 2020, SITMo's market was confined to local and national sales which it advertised through Facebook and Instagram with payments facilitated largely through local Philippine money transfer agents or cash sales. To enable the December 2020 launch of the Ifugao Nation website given the limited bandwidth available in the small town of Kiangan, SITMo had to enlist the services of Manila volunteers to host the website.

Consistent with its social enterprise mandate, as with R2R, a key intent of SITMo's digital presence through Ifugao Nation is to promote education about Ifugao history, culture, resources, and artisanal practice. Thus, upon accessing the Ifugao Nation website, one is met with a spectacular view of the Ifugao rice terraces, a row of mountain-side onlookers each draped in Ifugao ikat patterned (resist tied and dyed) woven blankets, and text scrolled over the mountain imagery that reads – 'Each Strand is a Story.' An invitation to web visitors to 'Read' further introduces viewers to the weavers and to the region's weaving history. Detailed label information is provided for each of the featured pieces vis-à-vis weaving technology, as well as the indigenous names for each textile type, as noted in the aforementioned label for the *Kinattibang ya Hinulgi* piece.⁶³

Like other social entrepreneurs who promote contemporary Philippine textiles, SITMo's expansion is also constrained by the fact that artisans weave only part time given the other domestic and cultivation responsibilities in which they engage to earn sufficient income. SITMo Director, Michael explained that 'If we obtain orders we cannot fill because weavers are not available or because the ikat [tied and dyed threads] technique is time consuming to complete, SITMo risks alienating its buyers.'⁶⁴ Michael continued, 'SITMo seeks a balance between obtaining the volume of orders we know we can complete and encouraging weavers to spend more time weaving.'⁶⁵ A committee member added that 'We say to buyers, this is a handwoven product; you want to purchase these textiles because they are artisanal, high quality, and ethically produced, but you want them delivered according to a commercial distribution schedule.'⁶⁶ Thus, while the new Ifugao Nation website fruitfully informs consumers about the cultural background of their purchases and professionally enables consumers to complete their sales transactions online, the task of delivering products to clients in a timely manner remains problematic.

Indeed, Philippine development practitioners promoting the businesses of micro, small, and medium enterprises (MSME) note the challenges such enterprises face in navigating the export process. As one Head of a Philippine NGO explained,

> The only ones I see who are able to operationalize the system are companies whose established brands and longer histories and experience enable them to raise additional funds – privately or through business connections – to establish accounts with transnational shippers such as DHL or FedEx. The paperwork required to ship internationally is often too costly and the system too complicated for most MSMEs to figure out.[67]

These observations capture the situation of even fairly well-established enterprises such as SITMo, which still struggles to fulfill domestic orders, its primary market. An Ifugao Nation website posting in 2021 asked for patrons' patience, explaining that the NGO has no full-time sales staff and thus filling orders takes time.[68] Customers are invited to pick up their orders in person if they are near Kiangan – an unlikely option given Kiangan's rural location a ten-hour drive from Manila. Thus, orders are sent to a volunteer in Manila via a private van service; the volunteer then enlists DHL for local deliveries. When Cambio & Co., Inc. ordered SITMo's COVID-19 masks in late 2020, the former devoted substantial time to mentor the Manila volunteer on how to complete the transnational shipping documents to Toronto, efforts the Cambio & Co., Inc. directors explain they have repeatedly had to make with their other smaller-scale Philippine suppliers.[69]

Given the disjuncture between achieving a successful online presence and the on-the-ground logistics of shipping products globally, alternative economy systems anchored in trust and mentorship have emerged to achieve the latter task. Rags2Riches, for example, has agreed to receive products in Manila that Cambio & Co., Inc. has ordered from more rural-based Philippine artisans. R2R simply includes the latter artisans' pieces in its FedEx shipments to Canada, considering their volunteer labor as an expression of goodwill in their Cambio & Co., Inc. partnership. SITMo is currently discussing the potential of a similar arrangement with R2R for its next Cambio & Co., Inc. shipment to Toronto, given that SITMo now has a Manila volunteer who can receive provincial shipments from Ifugao.

While these specific mentoring arrangements solve the challenge of facilitating global shipping, the wider socio-economic infrastructure that hinders smaller-scale social enterprises from sustainably scaling up remains largely in place. Recall that the Moroccan women artisans and entrepreneurs responsible for the ongoing export of handwoven rugs via the Women Weavers OnLine project, owe much of their export success to Susan Davis's and trained community coordinators' continuing on-site assistance.[70]

As a development practitioner working in the Asia-Pacific region suggested, in order to facilitate MSME's initial outreach capacity in countries where government support is minimal, transnational development organizations such as APEC (Asia-Pacific Economic Cooperation) need to 'step in' to formulate a coordinated cross-sector plan that can train MSME's on export document completion and enable accessible and efficient discounts for shipping.[71]

Conclusion

To realize their alternative community economy enterprises,[72] Save the Ifugao Terraces Movement and Rags2Riches have, to a degree, harnessed the social and economic potential of artisans' transnational trade of Philippine textiles. They have built on weavers' skills to design innovative textiles that privilege local cultural heritage, and by facilitating access to ICT they have mobilized a broad range of networks to support a sustainable socio-economic practice. Yet, their vision continues, in some arenas, as a project-in-process.

International development practitioners, for example, often consider that providing women with better ICT access results in broader financial inclusion, but the advantages of such engagement cannot be assumed, as the case studies here suggest. As evidenced in the 2020 launch of the Ifugao Nation retail website, although SITMo can now market artisans' textiles online, given that its local digital capacity is limited, the organization has an ongoing dependence on enlisting Manila volunteers for sufficient technology capability. Indeed, although R2R has a long and successful business history and employs artisans with financial literacy skills, it must continually recruit new funding partners to ensure that the enterprise's online presence as well as its new physical sites can be financially maintained.

The dilemma that persists in many cases, as Güney-Frahm argues, is that online selling platforms, especially those for textiles – a sphere dominated by women – hardly contribute to an increased female presence in the offline public sphere, where men's activities often take precedence.[73] While women who have attained management positions in R2R and SITMo achieve some degree of middle-class standing, the majority of textile artisans in both enterprises still weave only part time, combining their artisanal work, as noted, with farming, household responsibilities, and/or part-time contract jobs. Although artisans can move horizontally across production jobs and even vertically up to the level of department head and manager, fewer women have been able to start their own businesses. Over the past few years, however, this situation has slowly begun to change as SITMo and Rags2Riches, for example, have enabled more vertical mobility for artisans to assume roles in Executive Committees as well as positions of more responsibility in production and enterprise supervision. In this light, as Sarah, the Rags2Riches Director noted, 'Our way of scaling up looks very different. We go deep [to ensure artisans receive the skills they request] because we want to ensure people are positively impacted for life.'[74]

In addition to facilitating ICT access, then, development programs might simultaneously institute broader goals to include, for example, the 'creation of new types of economic activity, employment opportunities, improvements in health-care delivery and other services and the enhancement of networking, participation and advocacy within society' that can broaden 'the potential to improve interaction between Governments and citizens, fostering transparency and accountability in governance.'[75] Only by supporting such cross-sector approaches can we challenge internalized gender norms that often keep women less visible.[76] As Nancy Fraser perceptively argues, to address 'inequitable outcomes of social arrangements without disturbing the underlying framework that generates them,' not only leaves intact ideological structures that produce gender and class marginalization, but also marks women as deficient as system adjustments must be repeatedly administered.[77]

While these case studies may prompt questioning the efficacy of social entrepreneurial approaches and of increased ICT access to realize social change, the new opportunities Rags2Riches and Save the Ifugao Terraces Movement have created are unquestionably positive outcomes. By giving artisans a voice in their social enterprise operations, both SITMo and R2R relevantly incorporate women's knowledge and experience into locally appropriate and potentially empowering livelihood enterprises to challenge the institutionalization of women's domestic work. Their accomplishments to date thus encourage such social enterprises to tinker with their approach – to continue to mobilize forms of ordering, particular technologies, and interdependent socio-economic practice that can resist and indeed compromise the singular model of global capitalist enterprise. In so doing, artisans and social entrepreneurs can gain growing control over the conditions of where they live, where and how they work, and their engagement in global market flows.

Acknowledgments

Research for this chapter was conducted between 2018 and 2022, with personal visits to SITMo and R2R in the Philippines in 2018, and follow-up communication via e-mail through 2022. Financial support has been provided by the Social Sciences and Humanities Research Council of Canada (SSHRC) (2015–2019 and 2020–2024). In the Philippines, I am affiliated with the Cordillera Studies Center, University of the Philippines Baguio. I thank my research assistant, Marie Joy Lumiwes, and my UP Baguio colleagues for their support. To the artisans and social entrepreneurs who answered my questions, I owe a debt of gratitude.

Notes

1. The SITMo and R2R Directors wished to feature their organizations' formal names.
2. Paul D. Hutchcroft and Joel Rocamora, 'Patronage-Based Parties and the Democratic Deficit in the Philippines: Origins, Evolution, and the Imperatives of Reform,' in Richard Robinson, ed., *Routledge Handbook of Southeast Asian Politics* (London and New York: Routledge, 2012); David G. Timberman, 'Persistent Poverty and Elite-Dominated Policymaking,' in Mark R. Thompson and Eric Vincent C. Batalla, eds, *Routledge Handbook of the Contemporary Philippines* (London and New York: Routledge, 2018).
3. Francesca Bray, 'Gender and Technology,' *Annual Review of Anthropology*, 36 (2007): 37–53, at 38.
4. Irem Güney-Frahm, 'A New Era for Women? Some Reflections on Blind Spots of ICT-Based Development Projects for Women's Entrepreneurship and Empowerment,' *Gender, Technology and Development*, 22, no. 2 (2018): 130–144, at 135.
5. Ibid., 135.
6. L. M. Martin and L. T. Wright, 'No Gender in Cyberspace? Empowering Entrepreneurship and Innovation in Female-Run ICT Small Firms,' *International Journal of Entrepreneurial Behavior & Research*, 11 (2005): 162–178; B. D. Motilewa, O. A. Onakoya, and A. O. Oke, 'ICT and Gender Specific Challenges Faced by Female Entrepreneurs in Nigeria,' *International Journal of Business and Social Science*, 6 (2015): 97–105.
7. Susan Schafer Davis, 'Women Weavers OnLine: Rural Moroccan Women on the Internet,' *Gender, Technology and Development*, 8, no. 1 (2004): 53–74, at 73.
8. Thomas Molony, 'Carving a Niche: ICT, Social Capital, and Trust in the Shift from Personal to Impersonal Trading in Tanzania,' *Information Technology for Development*, 15, no. 4 (2009): 283–301, at 297.
9. Ibid., 296–297.
10. Nurcan Törenli, 'The Potential of ICT to Generate "Solidaristic" Practices among Women Home-Based Workers in Turkey,' *New Technology, Work and Employment*, 25 (2010): 49–62.
11. Meera Kenkarasseril Joseph, 'Critical Theory for Women Empowerment through ICT Studies,' *Qualitative Research Journal*, 13 (2013): 163–177.
12. E-Entrepreneurs Women Trade Center. Last modified 2017. Facebook, www.facebook.com/pg/ewtcmy/about/?ref=page_internal (accessed 17 February 2021).
13. Güney-Frahm, 'A New Era for Women?' 136.
14. Brie Rehbein 'Rural Livelihoods and e-Commerce: A Case Study of Artisans in Guerrero, Mexico,' Master's thesis (St. Mary's University, Halifax, NS, 2013).
15. Ibid.
16. Güney-Frahm, 'A New Era for Women?' 137; Lynne Milgram, 'From Margin to Mainstream: Microfinance, Women's Work and Social Change in the Philippines,' *Urban Anthropology and Studies of Cultural Systems and World Economic Development*, 34, no. 4 (2005): 45–84.
17. Güney-Frahm, 'A New Era for Women?' 137.
18. Ibid., 137.
19. Johanna Mair, Jeffrey Robinson, and Kai Hockerts, 'Introduction,' in Johanna Mair, Jeffrey Robinson, and Kai Hockert, eds, *Social Entrepreneurship* (Houndmills: Palgrave Macmillan, 2006).
20. Alex Nicholls, 'Introduction,' in Alex Nicholls, ed., *Social Entrepreneurship: New Modes of Sustainable Social Change* (Oxford: Oxford University Press, 2006), p. 5.
21. Güney-Frahm, 'A New Era for Women?'
22. Nicholls, 'Introduction,' p. 18.
23. J. K. Gibson-Graham and G. Roelvink, 'The Nitty-Gritty of Creating Alternative Economies,' *Social Alternatives*, 30, no. 1 (2010): 29–33; J. K. Gibson-Graham,

J. Cameron, and S. Healy, *Take Back the Economy: An Ethical Guide for Transforming Our Communities* (Minnesota: University of Minnesota Press, 2013).

24 See Chris Stevaert and Daniel Hjorth, 'Introduction: What is Social in Social Entrepreneurship,' in Chris Steyaert and Daniel Hjorth, eds, *Entrepreneurship as Social Change* (Cheltenham: Edward Elgar, 2006), pp. 1–20.
25 Sarah Wright, 'Cultivating Beyond-Capitalist Economies,' *Economic Geography*, 86 (2010): 297–318, at 301.
26 Gibson-Graham and Roelvink, 'The Nitty-Gritty'; Gibson-Graham, Cameron, and Healy, *Take Back the Economy*.
27 Timberman, 'Persistent Poverty.'
28 Nicholls 'Introduction,' p. 11.
29 ABS-CBN, https://news.abs-cbn.com/business/02/16/21/ikea-philippines-rags2riches-sewing (accessed 21 February 2021).
30 Hutchcroft and Rocamora, 'Patronage-Based Parties'; Timberman, 'Persistent Poverty.'
31 Filomena Aguilar and Virginia Miralao, *Rattan Furniture Manufacturing in Metro Cebu: A Case Study of an Export Industry*, Handcraft Paper Series No. 6. (Manila: Ramon Magsaysay Award Foundation, 1985); Lynne Milgram, 'Transforming a Global Craft Commodity Flow from Aklan, Central Philippines,' in Claire M. Wilkinson-Weber and Alicia Ory DeNicola, eds, *Critical Craft: Technology, Globalization, and Capitalism* (London and New York: Bloomsbury, 2016); Lynne Milgram, 'Recrafting Tradition and Livelihood: Women and Bast Fiber Textiles in the Upland Philippines,' in Roy W. Hamilton and B. Lynne Milgram, eds, *Material Choices: Refashioning Bast and Leaf Fibers in Asia and the Pacific* (Los Angeles: Fowler Museum at UCLA, 2007).
32 Milgram, 'Recrafting Tradition and Livelihood'; Milgram, 'Transforming a Global Craft Commodity Flow.'
33 Wazir Jahan Karim, 'Introduction: Genderising Anthropology in Southeast Asia,' in Wazir Jahan Karim, ed., *'Male' and 'Female' in Developing Southeast Asia* (Oxford: Berg, 1995), p. 28; see also Mary Beth Mills, 'Gendered Divisions of Labor,' in Lisa Disch and Mary Hawkesworth, eds, *The Oxford Handbook of Feminist Theory* (Oxford and New York: Oxford University Press, 2016).
34 All personal names of people are pseudonyms.
35 thingsthatmatter (Rags2Riches), https://thingsthatmatter.ph/pages/rags2riches (accessed 5 January 2021 and 2 January 2022).
36 Ibid.
37 Interview with Rags2Riches Director by Lynne Milgram, Quezon City, Manila, Philippines, 10 May 2018.
38 Ibid.
39 thingsthatmatter (Rags2Riches), https://thingsthatmatter.ph/pages/rags2riches.
40 Interview by Lynne Milgram, Quezon City, Manila, Philippines, 10 May 2018.
41 Cambio & Co., www.shopcambio.co/blogs/news/visiting-the-rags2riches-artisan-community-in-caloocan-philippines (accessed 6 February 2021).
42 Parts of this section build on and expand previously published research in Lynne Milgram, '(Re)Fashioning Frontiers in Artisanal Trade: Social Entrepreneurship and Textile Production in the Philippine Cordillera,' *South East Asia Research*, 28, no. 4 (2020): 413–431.
43 Ifugao Nation, https://ifugaonation.com (accessed 2 January 2022).
44 Interview by Lynne Milgram, Kiangan, Ifugao province, Philippines, 24 May 2018.
45 Ibid.
46 Ifugao Nation, https://ifugaonation.com (accessed 24 January 2021).
47 Interview by Lynne Milgram, Kiangan, Ifugao province, Philippines, 25 May 2018.
48 Ifugao Nation, https://ifugaonation.com (2021, 2022).
49 Ifugao Nation, https://ifugaonation.com (2021).
50 Ifugao Nation, https://ifugaonation.com (2022).

51 Edward Bruner, 'Abraham Lincoln as Authentic Reproduction: A Critique of Postmodernism,' *American Anthropologist*, 96, no. 2 (1994): 397–415, at 398.
52 Ibid., 407.
53 Interview by Lynne Milgram, Kiangan, Ifugao province, Philippines, 25 May 2018.
54 Ifugao Nation, https://ifugaonation.com (2021).
55 Interview with Cambio & Co. Inc., Directors, Toronto, ON, Canada, 15 September 2020.
56 Benedict Anderson, *Imagined Communities: Reflections on the Origin and Spread of Nationalism* (New York: Verso, 1991).
57 thingsthatmatter (Rags2Riches), https://thingsthatmatter.ph/pages/rags2riches (accessed 15 February 2021 and 2 January 2022).
58 Interview by Lynne Milgram, Quezon City, Manila, Philippines, 10 May 2018.
59 Cambio & Co., www.shopcambio.co/pages/rags2riches-expands-to-us-and-canada?_pos=1&_sid=3775bef66&_ss=r (accessed 5 February 2021).
60 Cambio & Co., www.shopcambio.co/blogs/news/visiting-the-rags2riches-artisan-community-in-caloocan-philippines (accessed 6 February 2021).
61 Interview by Lynne Milgram, Toronto, ON, Canada, via personal digital communication to the Philippines, 19 February 2021.
62 ABS-CBN, https://news.abs-cbn.com/business/02/16/21/ikea-philippines-rags2riches-sewing (accessed 21 February 2021).
63 Ifugao Nation, https://ifugaonation.com (2022).
64 Interview by Lynne Milgram, Kiangan, Ifugao province, Philippines, 24 May 2018.
65 Ibid.
66 Interview by Lynne Milgram, Kiangan, Ifugao province, Philippines, 25 May 2018.
67 Interview by Lynne Milgram, Toronto, ON, Canada, via personal digital communication to the Philippines, 12 February 2021.
68 Ifugao Nation, https://ifugaonation.com (2021).
69 Interview by Lynne Milgram, Toronto, ON, Canada, 18 February 2021.
70 Davis, 'Women Weavers OnLine.'
71 Interview with a Philippine development practitioner by Lynne Milgram, Toronto, ON, Canada, via personal digital communication to the Philippines, 12 February 2021.
72 Gibson-Graham and Roelvink, 'The Nitty-Gritty'; Gibson-Graham, Cameron, and Healy, *Take Back the Economy*.
73 Güney-Frahm, 'A New Era for Women?' 139, 141.
74 Cambio & Co., www.shopcambio.co/blogs/news/visiting-the-rags2riches-artisan-community-in-caloocan-philippines (accessed 6 February 2021).
75 United Nations, 'Gender Equality and Empowerment of Women through ICT,' New York: United Nations Division for the Advancement of Women, Department of Economic and Social Affairs. Last Modified September 2005, www.un.org/womenwatch/daw/public/w2000-09.05-ict-e.pdf: p. 2 (accessed 18 February 2021).
76 Güney-Frahm, 'A New Era for Women?' 138.
77 Nancy Fraser, *Justice Interruptus: Critical Reflections on the 'Postsocialist' Condition* (New York and London: Routledge, 1997), p. 23.

Bibliography

ABS-CBN. https://news.abs-cbn.com/business/02/16/21/ikea-philippines-rags2riches-sewing (accessed 21 February 2021).

Aguilar, Filomena, and Virginia Miralao. *Rattan Furniture Manufacturing in Metro Cebu: A Case Study of an Export Industry*. Handcraft Paper Series No. 6. Manila: Ramon Magsaysay Award Foundation, 1985.

Anderson, Benedict. *Imagined Communities: Reflections on the Origin and Spread of Nationalism*. New York: Verso, 1991.
Bray, Francesca. 'Gender and Technology.' *Annual Review of Anthropology* 36 (2007): 37–53.
Bruner, Edward. 'Abraham Lincoln as Authentic Reproduction: A Critique of Postmodernism.' *American Anthropologist* 96, no. 2 (1994): 397–415.
Davis, Susan Schafer. 'Women Weavers OnLine: Rural Moroccan Women on the Internet.' *Gender, Technology and Development* 8, no. 1 (2004): 53–74.
Cambio & Co. www.shopcambio.co/blogs/news/visiting-the-rags2riches-artisan-community-in-caloocan-philippines (accessed 6 February 2021).
Cambio & Co. www.shopcambio.co/pages/rags2riches-expands-to-us-and-canada?_pos=1&_sid=3775bef66&_ss=r (accessed 5 February 2021).
E-Entrepreneurs Women Trade Center. Last modified 2017. Facebook. www.facebook.com/pg/ewtcmy/about/?ref=page_internal (accessed 17 February 2021).
Fraser, Nancy. *Justice Interruptus: Critical Reflections on the 'Postsocialist' Condition*. New York and London: Routledge, 1997.
Gibson-Graham, J. K. and G. Roelvink. 'The Nitty-Gritty of Creating Alternative Economies.' *Social Alternatives* 30, no. 1 (2010): 29–33.
Gibson-Graham, J. K., J. Cameron, and S. Healy. *Take Back the Economy: An Ethical Guide for Transforming Our Communities*. Minnesota: University of Minnesota Press, 2013.
Güney-Frahm, Irem. 'A New Era for Women? Some Reflections on Blind Spots of ICT-Based Development Projects for Women's Entrepreneurship and Empowerment.' *Gender, Technology and Development* 22, no. 2 (2018): 130–144.
Hutchcroft, Paul D. and Rocamora Joel. 'Patronage-Based Parties and the Democratic Deficit in the Philippines: Origins, Evolution, and the Imperatives of Reform.' In *Routledge Handbook of Southeast Asian Politics*. Edited by Richard Robinson. London and New York: Routledge, 2012.
Ifugao Nation. https://ifugaonation.com (accessed 24 January 2021).
Ifugao Nation. https://ifugaonation.com (accessed 2 January 2022).
Joseph, Kenkarasseril Meera. 'Critical Theory for Women Empowerment through ICT Studies.' *Qualitative Research Journal* 13 (2013): 163–177.
Karim, Wazir Jahan. 'Introduction: Genderising Anthropology in Southeast Asia.' In *'Male' and 'Female' in Developing Southeast Asia*. Edited by Wazir Jahan Karim. Oxford: Berg, 1995.
Mair, Johanna, Jeffrey Robinson, and Kai Hockerts. 'Introduction.' In *Social Entrepreneurship*. Edited by Johanna Mair, Jeffrey Robinson, and Kai Hockerts. Houndmills: Palgrave Macmillan, 2006.
Martin, L. M. and L. T. Wright. 'No Gender in Cyberspace? Empowering Entrepreneurship and Innovation in Female-Run ICT Small Firms.' *International Journal of Entrepreneurial Behavior & Research* 11 (2005): 162–178.
Milgram, B. Lynne. 'From Margin to Mainstream: Microfinance, Women's Work and Social Change in the Philippines.' *Urban Anthropology and Studies of Cultural Systems and World Economic Development* 34, no. 4 (2005): 45–84.
Milgram, B. Lynne. 'Recrafting Tradition and Livelihood: Women and Bast Fiber Textiles in the Upland Philippines.' In *Material Choices: Refashioning Bast and Leaf Fibers in Asia and the Pacific*. Edited by Roy W. Hamilton and B. Lynne Milgram. Los Angeles: Fowler Museum at UCLA, 2007.

Milgram, B. Lynne. '(Re)Fashioning Frontiers in Artisanal Trade: Social Entrepreneurship and Textile Production in the Philippine Cordillera.' *South East Asia Research* 28, no. 4 (2020): 413–431.

Milgram, B. Lynne. 'Transforming a Global Craft Commodity Flow from Aklan, Central Philippines.' In *Critical Craft: Technology, Globalization, and Capitalism*. Edited by Claire M. Wilkinson-Weber and Alicia Ory DeNicola. London and New York: Bloomsbury, 2016.

Mills, Mary Beth. 'Gendered Divisions of Labor.' In *The Oxford Handbook of Feminist Theory*. Edited by Lisa Disch and Mary Hawkesworth. Oxford and New York: Oxford University Press, 2016.

Molony, Thomas. 'Carving a Niche: ICT, Social Capital, and Trust in the Shift from Personal to Impersonal Trading in Tanzania.' *Information Technology for Development* 15, no. 4 (2009): 283–301.

Motilewa, B. D, O. A. Onakoya, and A. O. Oke. 'ICT and Gender Specific Challenges Faced by Female Entrepreneurs in Nigeria.' *International Journal of Business and Social Science* 6 (2015): 97–105.

Nicholls, Alex. 'Introduction.' In *Social Entrepreneurship: New Modes of Sustainable Social Change*. Edited by Alex Nicholls. Oxford: Oxford University Press, 2006.

Rehbein, Brie K. 'Rural Livelihoods and e-Commerce: A Case Study of Artisans in Guerrero, Mexico.' Master's Thesis, St. Mary's University, Halifax, NS, 2013.

Steyaert, Chris and Daniel Hjorth. 'Introduction: What is Social in Social Entrepreneurship.' In *Entrepreneurship as Social Change*. Edited by Chris Steyaert and Daniel Hjorth. Cheltenham: Edward Elgar, 2006.

thingsthatmatter (Rags2Riches). https://thingsthatmatter.ph/pages/rags2riches (accessed 5 January 2021 and 2 January 2022).

Timberman, David G. 'Persistent Poverty and Elite-Dominated Policymaking.' In *Routledge Handbook of the Contemporary Philippines*. Edited by Mark R. Thompson and Eric Vincent C. Batalla. London and New York: Routledge, 2018.

Törenli, Nurcan. 'The Potential of ICT to Generate "Solidaristic" Practices among Women Home-Based Workers in Turkey.' *New Technology, Work and Employment* 25 (2010): 49–62.

United Nations. 'Gender Equality and Empowerment of Women through ICT.' New York: United Nations Division for the Advancement of Women, Department of Economic and Social Affairs. Last Modified September 2005. www.un.org/womenwatch/daw/public/w2000–09.05-ict-e.pdf (accessed 18 February 2021).

Wright, Sarah. 'Cultivating Beyond-Capitalist Economies.' *Economic Geography* 86 (2010): 297–318.

9

Women weaving silken identities and revitalizing various Japanese textile traditions

Millie Creighton

Ton, Ton. Ton, Ton.[1] The rhythmic sound of large looms as the shuttle shifts each row of warp (*tate ito* or lengthwise) threads following insertion of another row of weft (*yoko ito* or crosswise, woof) threads, reverberating throughout the mountains from morning till night. No longer just sounds of the residential workshops on Japanese traditional silk making; these are now part of the mountain sounds where the workshops are located. While some women work looms, others create different sounds that merge into the mountain soundscape, as their footsteps or quiet talking also become sounds of natural life in this area of Japan's Nagano Alps, while they trek the mountain for the minerals and plants that in correct combinations create natural dyes once more commonly known and used in Japan's traditional silk production.

Introduction

This chapter explores live-in silk cultivation (sericulture) and silk-weaving workshops for women in Japan's Nagano Alps, in terms of gender, tradition, and identity, interlinked themes with the last two also reiterating gender concepts. In *Ethnic and Tourist Arts*, Graburn[2] discusses difficulties maintaining traditional arts and crafts in 'Fourth World' smaller-scale societies, of once isolated peoples who have been engulfed by modern world processes. While Graburn and other contributors document resilience through which arts of small-scale pre-industrial societies have been retained, and the role of women in this, it is important to recognize that post-industrialized societies also have pre-existing traditions that have faced pressure and possible extinction from similar causes. In these societies it is often women leading the retention of cultural arts and craft traditions.

In Japan such traditions are undergoing revitalization, often a highly gendered process, with women at the forefront. This often involves women pursuing what Japanese call *shumi*, usually translated into English as 'hobby.' However, the cultural context suggests an underlying difference. Whereas similarly to hobbies, *shumi* involves a personal interest pursued in one's own time, and is not usually one's primary economic livelihood, *shumi* is accorded high cultural value in Japan as part of the lifetime work of bettering the self through self-education and pursuit of a validated cultural goal. Studying one of the martial arts (Judo, Kendo, Aikido, Karate), the Tea Ceremony, Flower Arranging, or numerous other pursuits are valued as self-education and self-development. Although they may be important to people's physical and mental health, and enhance creativity in our world, the term 'hobby' as used in Western countries accords lesser importance to such activities.

Women's involvement in traditional textiles can validate their taking 'time out' from household and family duties. There is also a sense of women's suitability, because women are accorded the larger role in raising, socializing, and educating future Japanese generations. Ever since the beginning of modern Japan with the Meiji Era and Japan's opening to the West (since 1868), women have been the embodiment of Japanese culture and tradition, at times literally, as in the typical family photograph of father in Western business suit (representing the public, business, and internationalized world) while mother and children wear kimono (representing the private sphere, domestic traditions, and Japanese identity). Revival of Japanese traditions is seen as congruent with women's role in transmitting Japanese culture, as women have become the curators of tradition, guardians of Japanese identity. This cloaking of cultural validation also allows women to engage in unspoken desires for travel and tourism. Tourism for fun does not find easy accord with Japanese values emphasizing work and obligations to others. Tourism in pursuit of education, self-development, spiritual engagement, and maintaining Japanese cultural identity legitimates touristic involvement that might otherwise seem self-indulgent.

While recapturing Japanese textile traditions, women are recreating identities on different levels. They are finding their own gendered selves, often recapturing traditional female domains of activities but gaining control of the processes and products of their involvement. They are, as suggested, involved in revitalizing Japanese identity through traditions considered to reverberate with Japaneseness. This is also often tied to regional identities. Traditional textiles are seen as part of Japanese identity and also the regional identities from where they stem. The resulting fabric of Japanese identity contains various regional identities, traditions, and histories. That there is both a cultural suggestion that forms of textile making with which women are involved project a sense of Japanese identity, while at the same time these traditions show variability by region and other factors, alludes to the reality that Japan is not a homogenized culture or society, and instead that historical processes have differentially shaped these traditions. Nonetheless, there is a projection of various textile traditions as somehow all part of the cultural background of a Japanese identity, with women expected to be the curators of that projected identity, as well as transmitting it to future generations. These silk workshops represent Japan's sericulture and silk-weaving heritage of the Nagano area, still known by its premodern appellation Shinshu, long acclaimed for its soba[3] and silk. This case study bears similarities to women studied by Hayes,[4] who in revitalizing sashiko embroidered clothing engage in retaining a Japanese textile tradition, but also a central identity icon of the Tohoku area of Japan in northeastern Honshu.

The workshops also reflect nostalgia encompassing Japan from the 1970s on, once the goal of achieving a high economic level and lifestyle similar to seemingly advanced Western nations was reached. Seeking 'traditional Japan' remained important in the 1980s, 1990s, and in the twenty-first century. The nostalgic mood involved looking backward towards the past and Japanese traditions to counter identity loss because of modernization, intensified urbanization, and Westernization. The bitter-sweet Japanese nostalgia for Japanese traditions is addressed by Kurita, who writes:

> We look at our tradition the way a foreigner does, and we are beginning to love it. ... The fact that Japanese are seeing charm and depth in their tradition reveals how alien it has indeed become. ... Tradition is something that rises in the consciousness only when it is about to be forgotten.[5]

Nostalgia for Japan's past is a cultural construction romanticizing rural and remote areas symbolizing to Japanese a sense of Japanese identity and community collectives, such as rural farming areas, coastal fishing villages, and mountain enclaves. The past became something one seemingly could connect with by leaving Japan's cities and traveling into the heartbeat of Japaneseness. Women in the silk-weaving workshops in Nagano, located on Honshu, Japan's so-called 'main island,' sought textile traditions, traveling to the remote mountain location and staying in a building of more traditional Japanese-style architecture representative of Japanese village communities, consistent with the espoused cultural logic of nostalgia gripping Japan. (See Figure 9.1 for a depiction of the building and setting.)

To explore these interwoven themes, this chapter presents the silk-weaving workshops in Nagano and how they reflect long-existing Japanese values while exploring the diversity of women involved, showing they do not represent a simplistic homogeneity nor a lack of individuality. The chapter presents short discussions of other highly gendered participatory pursuits in textile traditions on the other three of Japan's four main islands, Hokkaido, Shikoku, and Kyushu, showing how regional identity

9.1 Women stay in a traditional Japanese-style building during the silk-weaving workshops (photo by Millie Creighton)

is embedded in such activities while they are also considered Japanese traditions. Again, this shows how diversity rather than a simplistic concept of Japanese similarity is woven into these diverse textile traditions despite them together representing a sense of Japanese identity.

The nature of the weaving workshop retreats

This section describes the weekly and daily schedule of the silk-weaving workshops, where women can learn traditional silk textile making while communing with nature and a nostalgic Japanese home village experience living in the Nagano Alps. The workshops are operated by a couple, whom I and the other participants called *otoko-sensei* (male teacher) and *onna-sensei* (female teacher).[6] The husband grew up in a Nagano weaving household but left to pursue employment in a Tokyo stocks firm. Reflecting the nostalgic mood of Japan, he became disillusioned with the ultra-modern, ultra-urban Tokyo and returned to Nagano. Although this was consistent with the nostalgic mood embracing Japan, it also reflects his strong positioning as an individual, because giving up the status of being a company employee of a highly thought-of stock exchange company was a strong deviation from usual expectations in Japan when he did so. The wife was originally from Hiroshima and experienced the atomic bombing which killed her grandfather and two younger brothers. Her early experiences of atomic destruction enhanced her desire for a lifestyle amidst nature, that valued diverse life forms and their interconnectedness. Her experiences as someone from Hiroshima during the dropping of the atomic bomb, and thus experiencing directly this historic event which caused the death of three of her immediate family members, severe and long-term medical treatment for her mother, and her own issues to be dealt with, placed her in a different position from many other Japanese who did not directly experience an atomic bombing. This difference on occasion also revealed differences among Japanese, for example when a cab driver complained about her allowing the grasses to grow long near where he parked to pick up passengers. The cab driver expected greater 'orderliness,' whereas due to her own situated historic experiences with the atomic bombing, she felt a greater affinity for the life form of the grasses to which he was not attuned.[7]

The silk workshops were offered four months of the year, during the summer in July and August, one month in spring, and one month in autumn. They began on a Sunday evening and everyone was to arrive by the first dinner, on Sunday. Whereas all other meals were provided and included in workshop fees, participants were informed this was not the case for the initial Sunday dinner and they needed to bring their own food or *obento* (meal box) as no food would be provided. Participants could arrive at any time so long as it was before dinner. Participants comprised two types, 'newcomers' and 'repeaters.' The schedule of instruction for newcomers was always the same, whereas it varied for repeaters. Repeaters often arrived early on Sunday to set up their projects and get advice from the teachers. Newcomers arrived any time, but were not integrated into activities yet, and as strangers did not interact easily; they often found themselves with little to do in the remote location.

That first Sunday dinner reflected elements of Japanese culture. Like other participants, I was informed I needed to bring an *obento* dinner as no food would be provided. I had lived in Japan some years, and felt confident one could find a store, stand, or food vehicle selling *obento* just about anywhere. I doubted this when alighting the bus at the stop nearest the workshops, which truly was remote. There was a small bench, a telephone on a pole (there was no phone booth and this was prior to cell phone usage) to call a taxi, and nothing else besides tall grasses, mountains, and sky to be seen anywhere. I would discover, as some other participants, that there was no convenient place to get food. I was pregnant the first time I attended the workshop, and noticed that hiking in the mountains was increasing not diminishing my appetite.

I was not the only participant without food. The workshops typically have 20–24 women, and about a third had not brought food. In the remote mountainous location where there were no typical stores or shops I had found a small alcohol sales room operating as part of a remote farm house, where I was able to buy some nuts and an apple. As we all sat down to our meal, it became apparent that several women did not have anything, or not much, to eat. Japanese are socialized early into group processes, a socialization reiterated throughout the lifespan. Given the number of women without food, I thought the teachers would bring something in, at least cooked rice. That did not happen. *Otoko-sensei* mentioned it appeared some participants had not brought food as instructed. He explained that while places to buy food were extremely limited, there were some small stores, a bit far but within walking distance, such as the alcohol store I had found and a couple of others. The teachers still did not bring out food for us, and started eating. I was surprised the teachers really were not going to give those without food any, but clearly none of us would starve if we did not eat until breakfast.

Then something happened that reflected two Japanese cultural emphases. One was the process of group formation. Another was the idea that teachers or educators do not solve problems or act as judges in conflicts, but expect those involved to find solutions on their own.[8] Some of the women with food offered to share with someone without nearby. Then one woman indicated that would not work well. Instead all the food was redistributed by the women themselves, such that everyone got enough to eat. The teachers never stepped in or took part in the process. To orchestrate the food distribution, the women who had not talked to each other earlier due to being strangers were now talking and working with each other. Everyone was beginning to bond as workshop participants.

Commensality involves the idea that people experience ties to each other through sharing and eating food together. This formation of being part of a group at the initial meal through the redistribution and sharing of food was one of the examples of commensality and connectedness that occurred in the workshops. While initially surprised the teachers were not going to provide any food for the women without any, I could later see this as consistent with the educational concept that teachers are not there to solve everything but to teach others, including children in school settings, to work together to find solutions. As a repeat participant I would learn that the first session I was in was not atypical; each time, something similar happened with some women not bringing food and the teachers allowing the women to find a solution, in the process becoming members of a group, something seen as necessary to the learning process.

The daily workshop schedule

The workshops exemplified Japanese values of living a regularized life. At the opening dinner, the teachers presented the daily schedule for the days to follow. Male-*sensei* mentioned the workshops were chosen pursuits and participants should not feel they must wake up early, that is, by 4:30 or 5:00 a.m. If people wished to sleep in they could. Despite these comments, most participants began their daily activities by 5:00 or 5:30 a.m. Kondo[9] wrote about a spiritual retreat in which the participants had to be up by 5:00 a.m., reflecting the Japanese cultural belief that an ethical person rises early. Women are expected to rise and begin working very early, and doing otherwise might suggest laziness. Thus most women were up by 5:00 a.m. A few did 'sleep in,' which meant awaking by 6:00 a.m. or at the absolute latest 6:30 a.m. The sun assisted everyone in waking early. The sun has been analyzed by Ohnuki-Tierney[10] as a dominant Japanese identity symbol. Japan has maintained the entire country on one time-zone, and avoided daylight savings time or changing time during the yearly cycle. Particularly in the two summer months (July and August) of the workshops, sunlight streamed through our *shoji*, semi-transparent rice-papered windows. Once awake, participants went for walks, did 'radio exercises' (see below), cleaned their dwelling rooms, and worked at the looms until breakfast.

After breakfast, newcomers, divided into A-*han* (A group) and B-*han* (B group), received organized lessons, one group from male-*sensei* and one group from female-*sensei* (after which they alternated lessons and instructors), while repeaters worked on their own projects. Since organized lessons for newcomers continued throughout the day, the teachers assisted repeaters when they could, and at night when lessons for newcomers were done. There was a mid-morning break with green tea and fruit; always a seasonal product of the area emphasizing place, nature, and seasonal cycles. Then there were more lessons, lunch from 12:30–1:30, more lessons, and at 3:00 p.m. everyone went outside for 'radio exercises'. Radio exercises are broadcast twice daily throughout Japan, and households, schools, and companies often have their members participate in them. Since Japan has only one time-zone, this further orchestrates a collective national identity of people throughout the country doing the same thing at the same time. Outsiders, including Americans, have often seen radio exercises as quaint, showing a Japanese emphasis on discipline, or fitting a society emphasizing collective engagement over individualism. However, radio exercises actually developed in the United States and were brought into Japan, while few in the US now know about them. There was a mid-afternoon green tea and fruit break, more organized lessons, and dinner at 7:00 p.m.

The schedule reflects the Japanese emphasis on habituating the body for a regulated life. We were learning spinning, weaving, and other processes, involving hand, leg, and full body coordination, without having to always think about them. The workshops also reflected the idea that if engaged in something, one should know everything related to it, and how processes fit together. While a leisure activity, workshops reflected an apprenticeship-like situation. According to Goody[11] such situations provide not just an opportunity to learn, but also an opportunity to learn about learning. When I signed up for silk-weaving workshops, I expected to learn to weave silk. This was included, but was only a small part of newcomers' lessons, and only repeaters could focus on weaving.

Lessons for newcomers espoused Japanese ideals of understanding all aspects of something. If one studies calligraphy in Japan, one learns to grind ink, even if one will be purchasing ready-to-use ink. The first year of instruction in a company likely involves doing all or many of the jobs at the company, such as janitorial tasks, working in the mail room, and washing laundry, even if these are not tasks one will do later. Newcomers learned to cultivate silkworms (raising silkworms, boiling cocoons, removing worms from cocoons), transform boiled cocoons into batting, spin batting into silk thread, identify plants and minerals in the mountains to dye the silk yarns, dye them in large vats, and set the thousands of warp threads on the looms, in addition to weaving. (See Figure 9.2 showing a woman dyeing skeins of silk with mineral and other natural items gathered on the mountainside; and Figure 9.3 showing five women together setting up the warp or lengthwise threads of a loom before weaving could begin.)

Presenting on these silk-weaving workshops to my university classes, students brought up similar examples. One student had attended a basketball camp in the United States and a basketball camp in Japan. In the United States participants learned to enhance their basketball skills. In Japan, he said, they learned how the materials for the balls were made, how to stitch and stuff balls together, and had a guest lecturer explain the distribution and trucking system of basketballs around the country. Weaving silk textiles in Japan meant learning about the activity and preparing one's *kokoro* (heart/mind) for full, attentive engagement. Undergoing such a program brought participants a fuller appreciation for woven silk textiles because they understood all the processes involved, and how these were woven together.

The evening meal was from 7:00–8:00 p.m. and then it was 'free time.' During free time, newcomers could work on the placemat-sized pieces each was weaving on the collective looms. Women who were particularly interested in certain lessons, such as using natural minerals and plants for dyes, spent additional time experimenting with additional colors or shades. Free time could be used for socializing, and once participants were enmeshed in their A-group or B-group identities this became a bigger part of activities. In one session women started a beer fund, with someone going to the small alcohol store to get beer for evening chats. Conversations became quite philosophical, such as the night we discussed life's existential meaning for silkworms, and whether aesthetically women found them 'cute' (*kawaii*) or 'gross' (*kimochi warui*, or 'giving a bad/gross feeling'). There were women in both camps. This took place the night women removed the dead silkworms from the boiled cocoons to make batting. That 'free time' began late echoed Japanese first-year

9.2 In addition to weaving, women learn to dye silk skeins from natural substances collected on the mountainside (photo by Millie Creighton)

9.3 Newcomers together set up the loom's lengthwise threads (warp) before weaving their individual segments (photo by Millie Creighton)

employee-training programs. A female first-year employee of a department store corporation described how the daily schedule was set every day until 'free time', specified from 10:00 p.m. on. They were not supposed to ask questions during the daily lessons but could ask their trainers about the lessons during 'free time.'[12]

There were two notable deviations from the daily schedule. One was the anticipated occasion, women had been informed, when we would be 'eating out.' The other was the final farewell party dinner ending each workshop.

Eating out

The workshops catered to Japanese nostalgia for the seemingly lost, or vanishing Japan,[13] offering reunion with more remote areas considered more natural and more 'Japanese.' However, the workshops also reflected modern, urbanized post-industrial Japan. While some of the women were from still existing farming or fishing communities, most were city dwellers. Many signed up for the workshops through urban culture centers or large department stores, transferring payments from banks to attend. Despite romanticizing being in the Nagano Alps, after some days many women were looking forward to 'eating out.'

The special day arrived towards the end of the session. The meal time did not change but the location did. One woman told me she had been anticipating the event, and wondered where we were going. She thought that maybe even in this remote location there might be a fancy French restaurant where locals occasionally dined. On the designated day food was prepared as usual. One of the women reminded male-*sensei* this was the day we were eating out. Another asked where we were going. He told all participants, we would be 'eating out,' out. Then everyone carried food outside to picnic tables used for the meal. Even the special occasion of 'eating out' kept everyone close to the usual daily schedule, emphasizing a life lived in rhythm with natural cycles, and that at one time people did not have or need more extravagant outings to make special occasions. (See Figure 9.4 showing women 'eating out' for the special picnic-style dinner. The women are shown with head towels because it began to rain on this occasion.)

Farewell party, collectivity, and individuality

The other change in routine was the farewell party and dinner the final evening of the week-long workshops. The dinner started at the same time, but went on much later and was more elaborate, with participants joking or reminiscing about the week. The farewell dinner also signified the cutting of bonds of participants. Newcomers had woven several placemat-sized cloths on different looms. For each, the lengthwise threads had been set up collectively before weaving, then each participant

9.4 Women in the silk-weaving workshops continue the 'eating out' event despite the onset of rain (photo by Millie Creighton)

decided which color threads she would use for the crosswise threads for her pieces. The resulting cloth showed both collective engagement because the lengthwise threads were set, and individuality in the threads each woman used as crosswise threads. This reflects Japanese cultural emphasis on collectivism over individualism while not negating individuality. Despite the lengthwise threads being the same for all newcomers, the resulting pieces showed great visual variety. For each newcomer to be able to take the pieces of cloth she wove home, the long cloths had to be cut at the woven spaces between the women's segments. (See Figure 9.5 showing the women holding the collective silk woven cloths before they were cut into individual segments at the workshop's end.)

Cutting the cloth seemed like a metaphor for cutting ties with each other. The women had been socialized into multiple foci of group membership, being a member of the smaller A-*han* or B-*han* groups, of all the newcomers or repeaters, and of the entire workshop group. This socialization in collective involvement reiterated Japanese cultural emphasis on the interdependent, rather than individualistic, nature of human beings. As Kondo writes:

> In the factory, in the neighborhood, in language, in the use of space, in attitudes toward nature and toward material objects, the most insistent refrain, repeated over and over again and transposed into countless different keys of experience, was the fundamental connectedness of human beings to each other. It was a conception that exploded my Western ideas about the

9.5 The women show their silk creations at the end of the residential workshop. (The author is shown second from right; photo by the author.)

relationship between self and the social world, and it was an inescapable motif in the lives of people I knew.[14]

Some women had to leave before the farewell dinner. Female-*sensei* would make everyone stop what they were working on and go outside to send off each woman. Everyone remained in place waving until her taxi could no longer be seen. As each participant left the following day, *onna-sensei* again had everyone remaining go out to send her off. This reflected a strong Japanese cultural emphasis on nurturing relationships. A few years after my involvement in these silk-weaving workshops, I participated in a three-week residential workshop on research methods in the US. Participants also became close during the three weeks. When it came time to leave, participants each left individually, usually without farewells or even without others knowing. In the last two days, it was unclear who was there and who had gone. Given my experience with the Japanese workshops, I was highly aware of this, and longed for a stronger recognition of our departures from each other.

Japanese women weavers, similarity, diversity, and constraints

For the subtitle of her edited book on modern Japanese women, Takie Sugiyama Lebra[15] uses constraint and fulfillment – not freedom and fulfillment, not choice and fulfillment, not careers and fulfillment. Japanese women seek fulfilling, meaningful lives but find themselves enmeshed in constraints, which may guide ways they seek fulfillment. Constraints include family obligations such as being the primary caretakers of children and the elderly. In Japan, the context is understood as something that may limit and restrict individuals. Likely this is not unique to Japan and applies to modern Western cultures, but the emphasis on individualism in the West may deter one from clearly seeing the various obligations and constraints that impede one.

Japanese women share a culture, a language and often a way of perceiving things, resulting in an ethos they have been culturally socialized into, that includes a strong value on human interconnectedness. This does not mean they have the same opinions, as even debates about whether silkworms are 'cute' or 'gross' reflect. The differences among the women I met in repeated workshop pursuits often reflected age and life stage differences. The majority were middle-aged women whose children had grown. Their life stage made it easier for them to go off for a week or more to pursue silk weaving. They had reached a level of authority in their households not held by new brides and younger married women with children. These women's pursuits reflect a sub-stratum of Japanese women similar to those described by Kato, who wrote about women returning to or commencing Tea Ceremony (*chanoyu*) study after their children were grown.[16]

The second most common grouping was women seen as being before marriage, and sometimes a married woman who had not yet had children. There seemed an expectation that the single women would marry, and married women without children would have a child or children. However, as Japanese family structure has been transitioning, and universal marriage is no longer expected, this might not have happened for all. The single women were at a phase considered free in Japan, allowed to pursue activities they enjoyed, with their incomes, though small, considered their own discretionary funds, in contrast to expectations prior to the Second World War and into the 1960s that an unmarried daughter brought her income home to her parents to help with family expenses (often with daughters' incomes supporting sons' educations). Even without children, married women needed an understanding husband to attend, or a so-called salaryman husband for whom her absence might allow him to concentrate more on company duties, staying even later at night.

The third type, married women with a young child or children, was rare but occurred. For such women the educational role of the workshops and their value in retaining Japanese traditions was important to gaining, if not permission for their absence, an acceptance of their absence. These women were often reliant on their mothers-in-law for childcare. A Japanese saying claims the mother-in-law hates the daughter-in-law while she loves the grandchildren the daughter-in-law bears. Another Japanese saying claims the mother-in-law scolds the daughter-in-law as a bad mother if she leaves a child in her care while she secretly loves having the child for a while. When I first met a young mother with a child left in her mother-in-law's care to attend the workshops, she said it was not a problem; her mother-in-law loved caring for the child and was happy she was attending. When the younger woman left the room, a middle-aged woman said to me, 'You realize that was *tatemae* don't you; of course, her mother-in-law gave her a hard time.' In Japanese, *honne* refers to the real thing, or true voice, in contrast to *tatemae*, the polite front people put on something. *Tatemae* is not considered 'false' because Japanese are supposed to know what is really happening; it is part of everyone saving face and maintaining harmonious interactions. A woman in this young mother's situation must negotiate with family to attend, and those who cannot do so successfully cannot attend because of such constraints.

Among the single women I met were low-paid OLs (office ladies) without chance of advancement, women with higher or professional education pursuing careers, and one divorcee. One professional single woman was a pharmacist who had aimed at a career. She had no objections to marrying but wanted to make sure she could make her own living, in a field that interested her. She grew up in an extended household in which silk weaving was part of life. She longed to buy a full floor loom, the kind she remembered from childhood, but these were extremely expensive and she could not afford one. She reminisced about hearing the sounds of the large loom, *ton, ton, ton, ton*, throughout the household, as her grandmother wove. When my grandmother died, she said, my mother burned the loom. Her mother may have been eager to embrace modernity and modern conveniences just as Japanese were striving for the 'bright life' (*akurui seikatsu*) in the 1960s and so-called labor-saving devices. Her mother may also have seen burning the loom as symbolically ending the yoke of her own mother-in-law on her.[17]

Weaving, like many forms of handmade textiles, can involve seemingly tedious labor to those who do not understand how fulfilling it can be. Sashiko embroidery, typically involving white accent stitching on blue (often indigo) cloth, is another textile tradition considered a Japanese identity icon, and one noted for the particular region of Tohoku, the northeastern area of Honshu (Japan's 'main island'). As in the case of silk weaving in Nagano prefecture, women have been pivotal in revitalizing Tohoku sashiko embroidery. In addressing the idea mentioned above, that such work can seem tedious to others, Hayes emphasizes that it only seems tedious to those who do not grasp the creative fulfillment women achieve from such forms of work. Additionally, in a boost to these women's textile pursuits and attempts to revitalize sashiko embroidery there have been shifting perspectives outside Japan, from seeing such pursuits as tedious, to a modern, internationalized view of the slow stitch-by-stitch engagement now being seen as a pathway to mindfulness.[18]

Women's involvement in other Japanese textile traditions

There are many revitalizations of textile traditions often more geared towards women. These are symbols of Japanese identity, while associated with regional identities, again showing that the culturally construed concept of Japanese identity has a certain flexibility and can amalgamate diverse traditional forms. As area traditions they connect places with varying past and sometimes present lifestyles, into a Japanese *uchi* (inside) identity. As mentioned, Hayes presents women revitalizing sashiko embroidery associated with Tohoku. Like Nagano, Tohoku is on Honshu, but in a different region. Tohoku once had a relationship to the central Tokyo area resembling a colonized area. Scholars have analyzed Tohoku's triple disasters of 11 March 2011 (largest recorded earthquake in Japan, huge tsunami, and nuclear power plant breakdown) in relation to the historic and ongoing treatment of Tohoku.[19]

There are multiple regional traditions on each of Japan's four main islands, stemming from specific environmental adaptations and historic processes in each, again showing Japan as having diverse areas and backgrounds. At least one example of each is given here. Hokkaido, north of Honshu, is often characterized as having a different background from the other main islands and smaller islands of Japan and being more like the West. Although indigenous Ainu inhabit Hokkaido and have their own characteristic textile traditions, until this century Japanese history of Hokkaido has emphasized Japanese settlement. Hokkaido developed along Japanese attempts to Westernize. Its more northern climate was amenable to crops associated with Western countries. With advisors from the West, its space and farmlands were developed like those in the American Midwest or prairie provinces of Canada. Thus Japanese have seen Hokkaido as a more Western placescape within the Japanese identity umbrella.

In the 1980s, 1990s, and into the twenty-first century, while the Nagano silk-weaving workshops offered Japanese women nostalgic journeys to a sense of their earlier Japanese selves, residential knitting workshops in Hokkaido offered Japanese women nostalgic engagement in rural Hokkaido. Although knitting and crocheting using sheep's wool have associations of Western traditions brought into Japan, they are also seen as long-existing Japanese pursuits in Hokkaido, and hence part of Japanese tradition. The patterning of the knitting workshops showed similarities to the silk-weaving workshops. Women did learn to knit, but were also required to learn many other things, again reflecting an emphasis on knowing all elements of one's pursuit. Women learned to care for sheep, shear sheep, card wool, clean and transform it to wool batting, spin wool yarns, and dye them. These were things the Japanese knitters would likely never do again. However, in the experiential learning of them, they would understand the underlying processes in the background of wool and knitting or crocheting endeavors.

Shikoku, in the southwestern part of Japan, is the smallest of Japan's four main islands. Japan is an archipelago with thousands of islands, so although being the smallest of the four main islands gives Shikoku a quaint image for many on the other main islands, it is still the fourth largest of the islands that comprise Japan. One of Shikoku's famous textile traditions involves large, colorful banners traditionally and still flown by fishing families with sons in the Kochi region, as Boys' Day, 5 May (sometimes on calendars called Children's Day) nears.[20] Boys' Day is celebrated throughout Japan, but the massive colorful flag-like banners (different from *koinobori* or 'flying fish' flown in Japan around Boys' Day) are unique to the Kochi area. Another prefecture, Tokushima, is famous for indigo-dyed textiles. Indigo cloth products (jackets, shirts, blouses, cell phone holders) are sold at Tokushima City's Awa-Odorikan, or the Awa-Odori exhibit building. Tokushima is also famous in Japan for Awa-Odori, the Awa-Dance, with Awa being the older pre-industrial, pre-Western name for the region. Awa-Odorikan is most active in the August dance festival period, but is open all year, presenting icons of Tokushima identity, including Awa-Odori, indigo-dyed textiles, sudachi (citrus fruit smaller than but similar to limes), and wisteria.

Tokushima indigo-dyeing and weaving workshops are popular among textile enthusiasts, both Japanese domestic tourists and international tourists. The Tokushima indigo-dyeing workshops I participated in were day-long ones, shorter than the silk-weaving workshops of Nagano or knitting workshops of Hokkaido. Participants are more often women. Men participate, but are often husbands going because of their wives' interest. In a day-long workshop participants learn to find and harvest indigo plants, wrap or tie cotton cloth, make resist patterns on the cloth, and dye it. The resulting textile has a pattern of dark blue with white designs. The workshops offer something participants can make and take home, such as handkerchiefs, place mats, cloths to sew into small bags, and cell phone holders. The day-long indigo-dyeing workshops allow those interested, passing through for other purposes, or visiting Tokushima for the Awa-Odori to participate in a textile tradition, while not requiring the same commitment as the residential silk or knitting workshops.

Kyushu is famous for kasuri textiles, similar to Indonesian ikat in which cotton threads are first tied and dyed, then woven into desired patterns. It is thought the area of Kurume has been producing kasuri for eight hundred years. There are overlaps with other traditions. Kasuri also involves indigo dyeing, showing a traditional icon does not have to be totally different to function as a regional and national identity symbol, because distinctiveness is found in its full configuration. Women seem to have the most interest in learning about this textile tradition, and often do so as part of tourism. For women its role as an identity icon of a particular region can again cloak travel with the aura of legitimate engagement in an educational pursuit. Kurume kasuri is prominent in Japan travel and tour guides. It is integrated into group tours involving Kyushu. Tourists can take all-day indigo-dyeing workshops, and shorter workshops teaching kasuri weaving. Kurume kasuri attracts Japanese and international followers of traditional textiles. It has also resulted in Japanese women entrepreneurs, knowledgeable about Kurume kasuri, operating their own tours or being tour guides for international tourists.

This look at some traditional regional textile pursuits, shows diversity in such Japanese traditions, while at the same time reflecting similarities with each other and with the Nagano silk-weaving workshops. They are gendered pursuits, directed at women, or attracting more women. The regional textile traditions contribute to the fabric of a national Japanese tradition. They represent traditions once requiring a community, village, family, or some collective to carry out, and were not fully individualistic pursuits. Fascination with them reflects nostalgia for a Japanese pre-Westernized past that romanticizes more remote areas, where a sense of Japanese identity and values were thought to thrive. Interest in them merges with desire to travel, cloaking participation in the culturally valued work of one's life-long self-education.

Conclusions

This chapter explored residential silk-weaving workshops for women in Japan's Nagano Alps, with brief portraits of traditional textiles in an additional area of Honshu and on Japan's other three main islands. Contemporary interest in textile traditions and their revivals burgeoned when Japan reached the long-sought goal of becoming modernized, Westernized, and, in the process, intensely urbanized. These journeys into traditional textile making are gendered. Men are involved and sometimes orchestrate processes. However, women largely account for participants, returning to processes that were once expected as women's domestic labor. In the modern revivals, however, women claim control over these processes and products of their work, whereas once the male head of household could decide what to do with the handmade products (keep, sell, trade) of their grandmothers' or great-grandmothers' generations. Such pursuits are cloaked in Japanese values surrounding education and life-long self-development through *shumi*. Traphagan shows the legitimacy of personal interest pursuits increases from middle age to older adulthood, because they are thought to help avoid *boke* (mental functions becoming less strong as people age) which causes inconvenience for others.[21] Women's textile pursuits gain legitimacy as consistent with cultural expectations that women be the curators of tradition, passing such knowledge to further generations while raising children or teaching the young.

Involvement in traditional textile revivals reflects agency and fulfillment for Japanese women, who nonetheless make participation decisions under cultural constraints. There is a strong women's movement in Japan. However, careers have not necessarily been accepted by most Japanese women as the answer to gendered constraints. Japanese women often feel trapped in a system of hegemonic control whether they pursue careers, work part time, or become homemakers. They are aware of continuing difficulties in Japan for women who want both children and a career, and the double burden of both for most women who are not among elite social groupings. Many also feel that if they have children they want to spend time with them. This problematic resulted in Keiko Higuchi, a leading Japanese feminist, suggesting women should resist exploitation by male-based Japanese capitalist institutions, instead devoting themselves to raising their children; a pronouncement ironically echoing many Japanese male conservatives.[22]

Economist Tachibanaki claims the recession beginning in Japan in the 1990s, and persisting through the first two decades of the twenty-first century, has brought greater gender inequality and disparities among women, who are now polarized into elite and non-elite tracks. He captures this problematic in his book title, *The New Paradox for Japanese Women: Greater Choice, Greater Inequality.*[23] His work comes at a time when Japan is transitioning away from a full-time working husband and full-time domestic housewife model, that even when it was more common did not accurately reflect most Japanese families. Japanese feminist scholar, Ueno Chizuko[24] has suggested women find fulfillment through non-career activities, specifying the consumer realm. This does not simply mean shopping. Recall that women enrolled in self-development pursuits such as the workshops and other textile traditions through department stores, or urban culture centers, part of Japan's consumer realm, just like travel and tourism.

The silk-weaving workshops presented here, along with other diverse textile pursuits considered to represent Japanese traditions, allow Japanese women to pursue fulfilling personal pursuits stemming from their own individual interests, while at the same time engaging in Japanese tourism suggesting reunion with Japan's past and identity. Women perceive and discuss their pursuits as learning about Japanese textile traditions and contributing to their retention. The workshops reflect underlying Japanese values that reiterate meaning for Japanese women participants. These include the importance of collectivity, working in groups, and the importance of cultivating human relationships. It is worthwhile in closing to reiterate Dorinne Kondo's recognition that, in contrast to her socialization in the United States, in Japan 'the most insistent refrain, repeated over and over again and transposed into countless keys of experience, was the fundamental connectedness of human beings to each other' and her additional comment that 'it was an inescapable motif in the lives of people I knew.'[25] Likewise, in my participant observation of the silk-weaving workshops I found that these pursuits invoked for the Japanese women participants this Japanese conception of what it means to be human, which can be expressed as: to be human is to be connected. The silk cloths and other textiles woven, knit, dyed, made, are a metaphor for this. Individual threads or yarns signify things that cannot in themselves be useful as clothing, garments, or other textiles, but when woven together or in other ways connected together, they can.

Notes

1. *Ton, Ton* is pronounced more like 'tone' or 'toe-n' in English. It is onomatopoeia for a soft, repetitive striking sound, such as that made when working the looms.
2. Nelson H. H. Graburn, ed., *Ethnic and Tourist Arts: Cultural Expressions from the Fourth World* (Berkeley: University of California Press, 1976).
3. Soba is a common type of noodles eaten in Japan.
4. Carol Hayes, 'Sashiko Needlework Reborn: From Functional Technology to Decorative Art,' *Japanese Studies*, 39, no. 2 (2019): 263–280.
5. Isamu Kurita, 'Revival of the Japanese Tradition,' *Journal of Popular Culture*, 17, no. 1 (1983): 131–132.
6. In earlier writing, I used Mr *Sensei* and Mrs *Sensei* to reflect them as a married couple. However, I felt contradictions in doing so. I agree with the inherent status differential of using 'Mrs' as part of titles that define women, but not men, by

marital status. In Japan such unequal title usage is not invoked and the title for both would be *sensei*, or teacher. Japanese participants in the workshops tended to call them 'male teacher' (*otoko sensei*) and 'female teacher' (*onna sensei*).

7 See Millie Creighton, 'Dancing Lessons from God: To Be the Good or the Good Bad Ethnographer,' in John-Guy Goulet and Bruce G. Miller, eds, *Extraordinary Anthropology: Transformations in the Field* (Lincoln: University of Nebraska Press, 2007), pp. 380–417.

8 Eyal Ben-Ari, 'Disputing About Day-Care,' *International Journal of Sociology of the Family*, 12, no. 2 (1987): 197–215; Joy Hendry, *Becoming Japanese* (Manchester: Manchester University Press, 1986); Lois Peak, 'Learning to Become Part of the Group,' *Journal of Japanese Studies*, 15, no. 1 (1989): 93–123; Joseph Tobin, David Wu, and Dana Davidson, *Preschools in Three Cultures* (New Haven: Yale University Press, 1989); Thomas Rohlen, *Japan's High Schools* (Berkeley: University of California Press, 1983).

9 Dorinne Kondo, *Crafting Selves: Power, Gender, and Discourses of Identity in a Japanese Workplace* (Chicago: University of Chicago Press, 1990).

10 Emiko Ohnuki-Tierney, 'The Ambivalent Self of the Contemporary Japanese,' *Cultural Anthropology*, 5, no. 2 (1990): 197–216.

11 Esther Goody, 'Learning, Apprenticeship and the Division of Labor,' in Michael W. Coy, ed., *Apprenticeship from Theory to Method and Back Again* New York: State University of New York Press, 1989).

12 Millie Creighton, 'Marriage, Motherhood, and Career Management in a Japanese "Counter Culture,"' in Anne Imamura, ed., *Re-imaging Japanese Women* (Berkeley: University of California Press, 1996).

13 For example, Alex Kerr, *Utsukushiki Nihon no Zanzo* [Beautiful Japan Traces] (Tokyo: Shinchosha, 1993); Ales Kerr, *Lost Japan* (Melbourne: Lonely Planet Journeys, 1996).

14 Dorrine Kondo, *Crafting Selves: Power, Gender, and Discourses of Identity in a Japanese Workplace* (Chicago: University of Chicago Press, 1990), p. 9.

15 Takie Sugiyama Lebra, ed., *Japanese Women: Constraint and Fulfillment* (Hawaii: University of Hawaii Press, 1985).

16 Etsuko Kato, *Tea Ceremony and Women's Empowerment in Modern Japan: Bodies Re-presenting the Past* (New York: Routledge, 2004).

17 Millie Creighton, 'Japanese Craft Tourism: Liberating the Crane Wife,' *Annals of Tourism Research*, 22, no. 2 (1995): 463–478.

18 Carol Hayes, 'Sashiko Needlework Reborn: From Functional Technology to Decorative Art,' *Japanese Studies*, 39, no. 2 (2019): 263–280, at 277.

19 For example, Theodore Bestor, 'Disasters, Natural and Unnatural: Reflections on March 11, 2011, and Its Aftermath,' *Journal of Asian Studies*, 72, no. 4 (2013): 763–782; Millie Creighton, 'Wasuren! We Won't Forget! The Work of Remembering and Commemorating Japan's and Tohoku's (3.11) Triple Disasters in Local Cities and Communities,' *Journal of Global Initiatives: Policy, Pedagogy, Perspective*, 9, no. 1 (2014): 97–119; Yuko Nishimura, 'A Tohoku Utopia: Alternative Paths After March 11, 2011,' *Global Ethnographic* (2014), https://globalethnographic.com/index.php/a-tohoku-utopia-alternative-paths-after-march-11-2011-2/ (accessed 18 August 2023).

20 Japanese celebrate two days recognizing children and the obligations of adults to raise children well. These are Girls' Day (also called *momo no sekkyu* or the Peach Festival) on 3 March, and Boys' Day on 5 May. At some point the 5 May date was legislated as a national holiday by the Japanese government to stand for both days. Later, it also became part of the series of holidays known as 'Golden Week' during which many Japanese take their vacations. Thus calendars list 5 May as Children's Day (*kodomo no hi*) even though Japanese typically still celebrate the two occasions differentially as Girls' Day on 3 March and Boys' Day on 5 May.

21 John Traphagan, *The Practice of Concern: Ritual, Well-Being and Aging in Rural Japan* (Durham: Carolina Academic Press, 2004).
22 Keiko Higuchi, '*Shufu' to iu na no Zaken*' [The Rights of Those Called Housewives]. *Sekai*, 478 (1985): 24–35.
23 Toshiaki Tachibanaki, *The New Paradox for Japanese Women: Greater Choice, Greater Inequality* (Tokyo: International House of Japan, 2010).
24 Ueno Chizuko, 'The Japanese Women's Movement: The Counter Values to Industrialism,' in Gavin McCormack and Yoshio Sugimoto, eds, *The Japanese Trajectory: Modernization and Beyond* (Cambridge: Cambridge University Press, 1988).
25 Dorrine Kondo, *Crafting Selves: Power, Gender, and Discourses of Identity in a Japanese Workplace* (Chicago: University of Chicago Press, 1990), p. 9.

Bibliography

Ben-Ari, Eyal. 'Disputing About Day-Care.' *International Journal of Sociology of the Family* 12, no. 2 (1987): 197–215.

Bestor, Theodore. 'Disasters, Natural and Unnatural: Reflections on March 11, 2011, and Its Aftermath.' *Journal of Asian Studies* 72 no. 4 (2013): 763–782; Yuko Nishimura, 'A Tohoku Utopia: Alternative Paths After March 11, 2011.' *Global Ethnographic*. 2014. https://globalethnographic.com/index.php/a-tohoku-utopia-alternative-paths-after-march-11-2011-2/ (accessed 18 August 2023).

Chizuko, Ueno. 'The Japanese Women's Movement: The Counter Values to Industrialism.' In *The Japanese Trajectory: Modernization and Beyond*. Edited by Gavin McCormack and Yoshio Sugimoto. Cambridge: Cambridge University Press, 1988.

Creighton, Millie. 'Dancing Lessons from God: To Be the Good or the Good Bad Ethnographer.' In *Extraordinary Anthropology: Transformations in the Field*. Edited by John-Guy Goulet and Bruce G. Miller. Lincoln: University of Nebraska Press, 2007.

Creighton, Millie. 'Japanese Craft Tourism: Liberating the Crane Wife.' *Annals of Tourism Research* 22, no. 2 (1995): 463–478.

Creighton, Millie. 'Spinning Silk, Weaving Selves: Gender, Nostalgia and Identity in Japanese Craft Vacations.' *Japanese Studies* 21, no. 1 (2001): 5–29.

Creighton, Millie. 'Wasuren! – We Won't Forget! The Work of Remembering and Commemorating Japan's and Tohoku's (3.11) Triple Disasters in Local Cities and Communities.' *Journal of Global Initiatives: Policy, Pedagogy, Perspective*, 9, no. 1 (2014): 97–119.

Creighton, Millie. 'Weaving the Future from the Heart of Tradition: Learning in Leisure Activities.' In *Learning in Likely Places*. Edited by John Singleton. Cambridge: Cambridge University Press, 1998).

Graburn, Nelson H. H., ed. *Ethnic and Tourist Arts: Cultural Expressions from the Fourth World*. Berkeley: University of California Press, 1976.

Hayes, Carol. 'Sashiko Needlework Reborn: From Functional Technology to Decorative Art.' *Japanese Studies* 39, no. 2 (2019): 263–280.

Hendry, Joy. *Becoming Japanese*. Manchester: Manchester University Press, 1986.

Kato, Etsuko. *Tea Ceremony and Women's Empowerment in Modern Japan: Bodies Re-presenting the Past*. New York: Routledge, 2004.

Keiko, Higuchi. '*Shufu' to iu na no Zaken*.' [The Rights of Those Called Housewives.] *Sekai* 478 (1985): 24–35.

Kondo, Dorinne. *Crafting Selves: Power, Gender, and Discourses of Identity in a Japanese Workplace*. Chicago: University of Chicago Press, 1990.

Kurita, Isamu. 'Revival of the Japanese Tradition.' *Journal of Popular Culture* 17, no. 1 (1983): 131–132.

Peak, Lois. 'Learning to Become Part of the Group.' *Journal of Japanese Studies* 15, no. 1 (1989): 93–123.

Rohlen, Thomas. *Japan's High Schools*. Berkeley: University of California Press, 1983.

Sugiyama Lebra, Takie, ed. *Japanese Women: Constraint and Fulfillment*. Hawaii: University of Hawaii Press, 1985.

Tachibanaki, Toshiaki. *The New Paradox for Japanese Women: Greater Choice, Greater Inequality*. Tokyo: International House of Japan, 2010.

Tobin, Joseph, David Wu, and Dana Davidson. *Preschools in Three Cultures*. New Haven: Yale University Press, 1989.

Traphagan, John. *The Practice of Concern: Ritual, Well-Being and Aging in Rural Japan*. Durham: Carolina Academic Press, 2004.

PART III
Creative voices for change: textiles, gender, and artivism

10

Entangled histories of craft and conflict: the story of *phulkari* textiles in The Singh Twins's *Slaves of Fashion*

Cristin McKnight Sethi

In 2017, Amit and Rabindra Kaur Singh, who produce and exhibit work singularly as The Singh Twins, launched a new series, *Slaves of Fashion* (Figure 10.1), with the goal of exploring 'hidden narratives of Empire, Colonialism, conflict and slavery through the lens of India's textile trade and their relevance to modern day legacies and debates around ethical consumerism, racism, and the politics of trade.'[1] Initially, the series consisted

10.1 The Singh Twins with her *Slaves of Fashion* lightbox artworks series exhibition hosted by Norwich Castle Museum and Art Gallery in 2022/23

of eleven digital lightbox portrait-panels, which when installed in the darkened gallery space seem to float, like large technicolored miniature paintings. The Singh Twins's series embodies ideas of artistic activism, that is, to use creative work to challenge power relations and bring about social change.[2] Indeed, the artist has long been engaged with depicting politically charged subject matter that critiques colonial histories and power dynamics, constructions of gender, and issues of migration and 'national belonging from the point of view of the minority subject.'[3]

Drawing upon these themes, each portrait-panel offers richly symbolic visual content with evocative titles to match. In one panel, the central figure is Arjumand Banu Begum, more popularly known as Mumtaz Mahal: the beloved wife of the seventeenth-century Mughal emperor Shah Jahan and the woman whose tomb, the Taj Mahal, is one of the most iconic architectural sites in the world (Figure 10.2).[4] In the portrait-panel, Mumtaz stands holding a small globe and sporting a pair of bright blue trousers, a reference to the origin of the 'dungarees,' a coarse indigo-dyed twill weave cotton trouser historically worn by laborers in the city of Dongri, just outside of Mumbai. This panel, titled *Indigo: The Colour of India*, directly references the global trade of the dyestuff *indigofera tinctoria*, which is indigenous to India and was enormously valuable as a cash crop and trade commodity in the sixteenth and seventeenth centuries.[5] Indigo was used as a currency and was at the heart of the African slave trade; one length of indigo-dyed cloth could be exchanged for one human body.[6] During the period of British colonial rule in India, peasant farmers were forced to grow indigo under atrocious conditions – a social cause which would later be picked up by Mohandas 'Mahatma' Gandhi as part of his anticolonial nationalist campaign.

The Singh Twins references this checkered history of the famous blue dye. We see Mumtaz Mahal (a personification of indigo, perhaps?) using her high-heeled sandal to step on the back of a dark-skinned figure who appears crouching and enchained. An emaciated man (perhaps an indigo farmer who succumbed to one of the devastating famines in Bengal) sits nearby and clings to an early version of the Indian flag known as the *swaraj* flag, which was adopted in 1931 by the Indian National Congress, the political party of which Gandhi was a leader. *Swaraj* means 'self-rule' and was a key tenet of Gandhi's approach for securing India's independence from Britain, an achievement realized in 1947, just before Gandhi's death.

The connection between politics and trade, slavery, and textiles continues in another portrait-panel titled *Coromandel: Sugar and Spice, Not so Nice* (Figure 10.3). Here the artist depicts the Dutch East India Company's dominance in the seventeenth-century spice trade, in which Indian cotton fabrics were exchanged for nutmeg, black pepper, and cloves grown throughout Indonesia and particularly in the Molucca Islands. At the center of the composition a white Dutch woman appears wearing an overcoat

10.2 *Indigo: The Colour of India (Slaves of Fashion* series), 2017

10.3 *Coromandel: Sugar and Spice, Not so Nice (Slaves of Fashion series)*, 2017

fashioned from mordant-printed and -painted cotton fabric (known by a variety of names, including chintz) which was produced along the Coromandel Coast of India and was a major trade commodity and fashion trend in seventeenth- and eighteenth-century Europe.[7] A small flowering bush that recalls the stylized 'tree of life' motifs that were popular on bed covers or *palampores* made along the Coromandel Coast for the European market, appears just behind the central figure. An interesting comparison is a circa 1760 fragment of a *palampore* that depicts a woman in Japanese attire sitting at a dressing table and floating among the birds and flowers that seem to emanate from the tree's serpentine branches (Figure 10.4). This is a reminder of the hybrid nature of these *palampores* in which Indian textile artisans interpreted Persian and East Asian decorative motifs as they were translated by European merchants and buyers, the latter of whom often collapsed regional stylistic differences into a generic 'Orientalist' aesthetic.[8] A diminutive Japanese woman (an Orientalist metonym for the entire region of East Asia, perhaps) also appears in The Singh Twins's portrait-panel. We see the woman fanning herself and seated next to a tray holding blue and white porcelain vessels, reminding the viewer that both tea and 'china' were major trade commodities of East Asia and circulated around the world on ships of the Dutch East India Company.[9] In fact, we see a depiction of one such ship sailing in a tumultuous sea, the water of which is reminiscent of Katsushika Hokusai's famous woodblock print *The Great Wave off Kanagawa*.[10] Hanging from the tree's branches the artist has depicted the body of a black man, dangling like some tortured, exotic fruit, and referencing the Dutch practice of using profits from their trade of Indian textiles to purchase enslaved people from Africa for use on sugar plantations in South America.[11]

Another portrait-panel, *Cotton: Threads of Change*, focuses on The Singh Twins's home county of Lancashire, England and the rise of Liverpool and Manchester as cotton-manufacturing centers in the eighteenth and nineteenth centuries, which competed against Indian-made cloth in the global textile market (Figure 10.5). At the center of the composition the artist depicts Sophia Duleep Singh, the daughter of the last Sikh maharaja to rule Punjab, who was deposed by the British East India Company in 1849, converted to Christianity, and lived in exile in England. Maharaja Duleep Singh appears in a medallion in the upper left corner of the panel. Punjab has long been an important agricultural region on the Subcontinent and was central to the cultivation and production of cotton, since at least the period of Mughal rule, and later exploited under the British Raj.[12]

In the frame behind Sophia Duleep Singh, Gandhi appears wearing his iconic loin cloth (*dhoti*) and shawl while walking on a sea of blood that surrounds a cartographic rendering of the Indian Subcontinent. The words *swaraj* (self-rule) and *swadeshi* (self-sufficiency) float in the red water and

236 Creative voices for change

10.4 *Palampore*, c. 1760, India (made). Painted cotton chintz

recall key tenets of Gandhi's campaign for India's independence from British rule: to support locally made products, especially textiles, and to boycott British-, specifically Lancashire-made, goods. Central to this campaign, Gandhi promoted the spinning and weaving of *khadi* (handspun cotton fabric) as an alternative to the British cloth that was flooding Indian markets and devastating indigenous textile producers (represented in the

10.5 Cotton: Threads of Change (Slaves of Fashion series), 2017

portrait-panel by a young girl dressed in rags and grasping the *swaraj* flag). A tumultuous sky above Gandhi's head ends in a scalloped halo that references the 'Khadi Movement' on one side and 'Jallianwala Bagh' on the other – a massacre that occurred in the city of Amritsar, Punjab in which British officers fired their rifles into a crowd of unarmed Indian civilians, who had gathered to celebrate the Hindu and Sikh holiday of Baisakhi (solar new year) and to peacefully protest the arrest of two nationalist leaders. The officers responsible for the massacre at Jallianwala Bagh killed at least 379 people and injured over a thousand more. The violence of this event and the loss of human life is countered by a depiction of environmental catastrophe and pollution in the form of the red-hot kilns of the foundries of the Black Country, a region in the West Midlands (UK) that was the heart of the industrial revolution and produced enormous quantities of coal, steel, iron, and bricks.

The choice to feature Sophia Duleep Singh as the center of this portrait-panel underscores the intersecting histories and political dynamics between Punjab and England at this time: Sophia was born and raised in England and was an active promoter of women's rights, particularly the rights of female cloth workers in Lancashire. As The Singh Twins explains, 'Sophia was a product of Empire. Her heritage, homeland and life were shaped by British commercial exploitation and conquests in India in ways that exemplify some of the many legacies of Empire: most notably, material and cultural loss, geographic displacement, migration and multiculturalism.'

The numerous intricate depictions on these portrait-panels remind viewers of the violent and exploitative history of European colonialism throughout the Indian Ocean region and render in hyper-realistic detail the practices of cultural appropriation by white colonizers and the subjugation of colonized black and brown bodies in the name of capitalism and exploration. The Singh Twins is quite literally showing us the slaves of fashion: the human costs of commodity culture and the deep roots of exploitation at the heart of the global textile industry.

Following the success of the digital lightbox portrait-panels, The Singh Twins created a series of tapestry-woven textile portrait-panels that feature the same rich iconography as the digital lightboxes (Figure 10.6). For the remainder of this chapter, I would like to focus on another one of the portrait-panels in the *Slaves of Fashion* series, titled *Phulkari: Craft and Conflict*, which directly references a vernacular form of embroidery with historical roots in pre-Partition Punjab and continues to be an iconic art form in both the Punjab province in Pakistan and the state of Punjab in India (Figure 10.7). I first encountered this portrait-panel in its tapestry form, as a soft, woven textile, in the home of a private collector – it was not a digital lightbox nor was it displayed alongside other portrait-panels in a gallery. This initial encounter affected my experience and interpretation of

10.6 The Singh Twins with two of her *Slaves of Fashion* tapestry artworks (inspired by the *Slaves of Fashion* lightbox artworks series)

the object: not only did I see the portrait-panel as referencing an important form of textile art originally from South Asia (that of *phulkari*), but the object itself was very much a textile, a category of thing that embodies a range of associations (e.g. three-dimensional, connected to the body, haptic by nature and layered with histories of touch) and one which is distinct from the two-dimensionality and glowing flatness of the digital lightbox portrait-panels.

In the pages that follow, I argue that the *Phulkari* portrait-panel – indeed the entire *Slaves of Fashion* series – is more than simply an example of artistic activism, a role the portrait-panels easily assume when

10.7 *Phulkari: Craft and Conflict (Slaves of Fashion series)*, 2017

considered as part of the narrative of colonial exploitation inscribed in the series. Instead, these portrait-panels are about histories of power; about The Singh Twins asserting her agency and reclaiming power from colonial institutions; and about using strategies of non-linear narratives to decolonize archives and collections.[13] Additionally, the composite images woven together in The Singh Twins's portrait-panels operate like a dynamic visual collection or archive that pulls together multiple histories and experiences into a single pictorial frame. In doing so, the portrait-panels suggest that the by-products of colonial intervention on the Indian Subcontinent – particularly intervention in the form of collecting, cataloging, and writing about handcrafted textiles, like *phulkaris*, which we see flourishing during the height of British colonial rule in the last twenty years of the nineteenth century – have created textile traditions with shared, entangled histories and hybrid cultural identities.

When looking historiographically at the history of scholarship on Indian textiles – particularly studies that discuss *phulkaris* – the first major publications emerge at the end of the nineteenth century and continue through the turn of the twentieth century. These initial studies are then followed by an explosion of texts after 1947, when India gained independence from British colonial rule and the nation state of Pakistan was formed.[14] Not surprisingly, in the wake of these political revolutions, published histories of textiles are steeped in nationalist rhetoric. From 1947 onwards, scholarship on textiles seem intent on celebrating the cultural specificity of textiles and humanizing regional styles – a move that is distinctly different from colonial catalogs and late nineteenth-century essays that treat Indian textiles as both ethnographic specimen and object of good design, waiting patiently for European appropriation and consumption.[15] Textile scholars of the post-1947 period, such as renowned craft advocate Kamaladevi Chattopadhyaya, positioned Indian textiles as significant art forms with deep, ancient roots and wide global reach, which suffered a 'calculated destruction' during the period of British colonial intervention largely due to the 'introduction of machines' (read: industrial modernism imagined as centered in 'the West') and competition from British mechanized looms.[16] For Chattopadhyaya, and other nationalist writers of India's textile history, the goal of the post-independence period was to return textiles to the people and specifically to the idealized 'village community' that was imagined as somehow untouched by colonial rule:[17]

> In the peace and quiet seclusion of the countryside the village community evolved a culture of its own out of the steady flow of its own life and of the nature around it. The community acted as a single personality because of the common integrated pattern of life, in responding to the common joys and burdens of life, to the common occasions and landmarks that stood out in the flux of time and the change of seasons. Out of a million coloured strands of tradition filled with song and verse, legends, myths, native romances and episodes,

from the substance of the everyday life of the community, and out of nature's own rich storehouse, was woven a rich, creative and forceful art.[18]

While Chattopadhyaya's work was a necessary, critical step in localizing Indian textile production, what this nationalist view fails to recognize is that the documentation and collection of Indian textiles that occurred during – and in many ways because of – colonial intervention, forms the basis for almost all subsequent studies of Indian textiles. In other words, without colonial taxonomies and catalogs produced by the British, the work of Chattopadhyaya and others would not be possible. Instead of the history of Indian textiles being written as a long continuous thread that was interrupted by colonial intervention, it is helpful to acknowledge the ways in which colonial intervention facilitated the writing of India's textile history itself.[19] From the acquisition of actual textiles and their incorporation into museum collections; to catalogs that sought to differentiate textile genres; to the concept of 'History' itself as defined through post-Enlightenment thought,[20] British engagement with Indian textiles created the frame through which later scholars see and understand these materials, whether consciously or not. In this way, histories of Indian textiles are also histories of British textiles: the messy entanglements of colonialism resulted in art forms that are hybrid in nature.

The Singh Twins's *Phulkari* portrait-panel offers one lens through which to see this entangled history. At the center of this portrait-panel is artist Amrita Sher-Gil, whose short career (she died at the age of twenty-eight), bi-racial heritage (her father was Punjabi, her mother was Hungarian), and position as one of the few female *avant garde* painters working in India in the 1930s has made her an alluring and enigmatic icon of modernism.[21] In the portrait-panel Sher-Gil faces the viewer, but doesn't meet their gaze. Instead she appears to look just beyond the margins of the picture to a distant place or perhaps a moment in time referenced in the elaborate composition that surrounds her. Sher-Gil holds in her right hand a copy of *Tales of the Punjab* by Flora Annie Steel, a British Orientalist writer who lived in India during the last two decades of the nineteenth century and authored several titles, including this one of well-known folktales from the region of Punjab which she published in 1894. Steel also held a position within the British colonial government in India as the Director of Education for Punjab. In this capacity she traveled throughout the region managing colonial government-run schools and also interacted with many local women from whom she learned about and collected examples of the indigenous embroidery of the region, which was known as *phulkari*.[22]

The name *phulkari* translates as 'flower work' or 'floral embroidery' and references the stylized flowers that appear in many of these textiles.[23] Typically taking the form of large cloths known as *chaddars* and most often worn as shawls or *odhnis*, *phulkaris* were traditionally made by women to be included as part of their trousseaux upon marriage.²⁴ Brides wore very elaborate *phulkari*s during the many ceremonies associated with Punjabi weddings. However, *phulkari*s are more than simply examples of embroidery from Punjab, but instead have taken on iconic status within Punjab (both in India and Pakistan) as well as in the global Punjabi diaspora. Many of the tropes about *phulkari*s that emerge in scholarship on these textiles over the last hundred and fifty years continue to dominate popular conceptions of this art form. *Phulkari*s have long been associated with romanticized rural settings and the domestic labor of women. Writing in 1888, Flora Annie Steel describes the making of *phulkari*s with rhetoric typical of Victorian Orientalists. She explains that women, who 'after doing yeoman's service with father or husband in the fields, sit down in the cool of the evening to watch their threshing floors, and leaning… against the heaps of golden grain, darn away with patient clumsy fingers at the roll of ruddy cloth upon their lap.'²⁵ Steel continues by emphasizing the slowness of this embroidery practice and the time it takes to complete a *phulkari odhni*: 'It is a beauty to be manifested later on … when the worker will, perhaps for the first time, unfold the veil, to see and wear the fruits of her labours.'²⁶ This emphasis on duration (and, indeed, it often took months, sometimes years, to create a single *phulkari odhni*) and the idealized picture of rural Punjab and its productive women (they are farmers *and* embroiderers in addition to being mothers/daughters/daughter-in-laws/sisters/wives, etc.), endures in later scholarship on *phulkari*s.²⁷ Relatedly, the making of a *phulkari* has been for centuries deeply tied to constructions of femininity. An often-quoted reference to embroidery (*kashida*) in Punjab attributed to the fifteenth-century founder of Sikhism, Guru Nanak, asserts that when a woman is able to embroider her own blouse, only then will she be considered 'an accomplished lady.'²⁸

More recent scholarship on *phulkari*s has enumerated a robust taxonomy that classifies different types of embroidered textiles from Punjab all within the umbrella term of *phulkari*s. There are *sainchi*s, *darshan dwar*s, *bagh*s, *chope*s, and *phulkari*s with specific names that identify dominant motifs in a composition or additional materials used.²⁹ Indeed, the diversity of embroidered textiles that fall under the category of *phulkari*s is as diverse as pre-Partition Punjab itself. The Singh Twins has similarly included diverse visual references in the portrait-panel. For example, the small flowers that appear on the *kurta* (tunic) and *dupatta* (scarf) worn by Sher-Gil in the portrait-panel recall the wheel-like floral forms that appear at the center and in the four corners of many *sainchi phulkari*s (Figure 10.8). Other characteristic motifs and compositions associated with *phulkari*s which The Singh Twins depict in the portrait-panel include grids of floral and vegetal forms, like those found in extant nineteenth-century *phulkari*s and mirrored in Steel's essay illustrations from the same period.³⁰ Similar *phulkari* patterns appear in the border that frames Sher-Gil's body in the

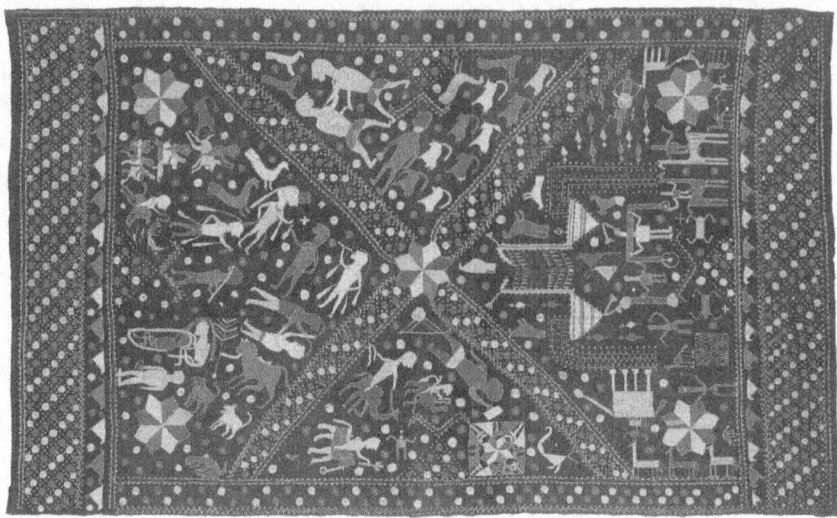

10.8 *Sainchi phulkari,* twentieth century

portrait-panel. Another quintessential *phulkari* style is known as *baghs* ('gardens') in which the embroidery is so densely applied to the surface of the cloth that the base fabric beneath is obscured, as in one example of an *odhni* from the twentieth century now in the George Washington University Museum and the Textile Museum collection (Figure 10.9). The subtle lozenge pattern created from golden-yellow silk threads in this *bagh* is similar to the shawl in the portrait-panel that drapes across Sher-Gil's right arm and around her back. Steel also includes *baghs* among the illustrations in her 1888 essay, which suggests the longevity of this particular form of embroidery and the diverse geographical origins of these textiles, which, from at least the last quarter of the nineteenth century, were made throughout the vast region of Punjab.[31]

Indeed, *phulkaris* appear throughout the portrait-panel, both as visual depictions and indirect referents. Above Sher-Gil's head we see two *phulkaris* draped like a canopy across the upper right portion of the composition. While traditionally these textiles circulated in domestic settings and were most typically worn by women closely connected to the embroiderer, if not by the embroiderer herself, by the late nineteenth century there was a strong commercial demand for *phulkaris*, not just in India but also abroad. European and American merchants (like Walsh & Co. referenced in the portrait-panel) sold *phulkaris* to be used as curtains in the homes of wealthy clients.[32] Commercialization of *phulkaris* also occurred with elite Indians commissioning the embroidery of multiple *odhnis* in preparation for a bride's wedding, and *phulkaris* were available for purchase in the markets of Amritsar, Delhi, and Lahore.[33] Accompanying the depiction of

10.9 *Phulkari bagh*, twentieth century

the curtain-like *phulkaris* above Sher-Gil's body in the portrait-panel are the words 'Manchester Bagh' and 'Jubilee Bagh,' references to two styles of *phulkaris* which Steel disparages in her 1888 essay on this embroidery genre (Figure 10.10). In a caption accompanying two chromolithographic prints used to illustrate her essay, Steel explains that the Manchester Bagh is a 'specimen of the cause of phulkari deterioration' and the 'result of native bad taste.'[34] By contrast, Steel describes the Jubilee Bagh as a 'result of English bad taste' – a reference to foreign demand for these textiles and British intervention into the design and production of *phulkaris*. The patterns and composition of the *phulkari* canopy in The Singh Twins's portrait-panel are identical to the fragmented *phulkaris* in Steel's illustration. Their inclusion in the portrait-panel underscores this other life of *phulkaris* – as objects that circulated outside of domestic settings and romanticized rural Punjabi landscapes, and whose patterns reflected market trends and influences from outside Punjab.

The base for most *phulkaris* is hand spun, plain weave cotton fabric known as *khadder*, upon which an embroiderer typically adds untwisted silk threads using a technique of counted darning stitches to achieve long floats of shiny thread over the surface of the comparatively rough *khadder* base ('the ruddy cloth' of Steel's description).[35] While the silk threads for *phulkaris* came from many different sources and often originated outside of Punjab (in Kashmir, Bengal, or even China), the *khadder* base cloth was, by contrast, locally produced using cotton that was spun at home (by women) and then woven by neighborhood weavers (typically men).

10.10 'Manchester Bagh' and 'Jubilee Bagh' as depicted in Figures 27 and 28 in Flora Annie Steel's essay on *phulkaris* in the *Journal of Indian Art*, vol. 2, 1888

In fact, spinning cotton thread was a commonly practiced pastime of Punjabi women and is one of the few documented forms of female textile labor that appear in paintings and photographs from the nineteenth century.[36] In the bottom left corner of The Singh Twins's *phulkari* portrait-panel, the artist depicts a small, light-skinned female figure sitting at a traditional Indian *charkha* or spinning wheel while wearing elaborate clothing and jewelry associated with a bride's festive wedding attire. This diminutive figure stands in for ideals of female beauty, labor, and domesticity that were popular in Punjab in the late nineteenth and early twentieth centuries: her light-colored skin, ornate but modest clothing, and position at the wheel all suggest she is a model of femininity and decorum. A pamphlet leaning against the base of the *charkha* advertises 'Fast Magenta Dye' and references the industrialization of textile dyes beginning in 1856 with the creation of the first aniline dyes by William Henry Perkin – an invention that forever changed the course of textile production in India and around the world.[37]

Beyond these specific references to *phulkari*, the portrait-panel also includes depictions that refer more generally to objects and artistic practices identified as 'craft' – a discursive term that gained traction in India in the second half of the nineteenth century as a way to articulate difference between handmade things and objects of industrial manufacture as well as distinctions between art created by indigenous Indian makers and 'fine art' objects made by Europeans.[38] In the lower left side of the panel, The Singh Twins includes a portrait of the architect Bhai Ram Singh, in a nearly identical pose, turban, and tunic as he appears in the 1892 painting by Austrian artist Rudolf Swoboda.[39] Bhai Ram Singh holds an architect's ruler and a scroll that reads: 'Kipling, Mayo School' – a reference to John Lockwood Kipling, the British-born artist who served as Principal of the Mayo School of Art and curator of the adjacent Lahore Museum from 1875 until his return to England in 1893. Under Kipling's leadership, Mayo School developed an arts curriculum that centered on traditional 'crafts,' particularly those unique to Punjab.[40] Among his many architectural projects, Ram Bhai Singh worked closely with Kipling to create the Durbar Room at Osborne House, a royal residence for Queen Victoria on the Isle of Wight. This connection is made by The Singh Twins in the portrait that appears directly opposite that of Ram Bhai Singh on the panel: Queen Victoria holds a scroll that reads 'Osborne House.' These two figures, and their mirroring scrolls, draw the viewer's eye towards the bottom of the portrait-panel and to a colourful *pida* chair, a few handmade bowls, and a newspaper advertising the Punjab Industrial Exhibition, a colonial-style exhibition held in Lahore in 1864 that featured traditional arts and mechanized goods from Punjab. In many ways the portrait-panel celebrates the central role that Punjab played in discourses on craft and the handmade during the period of colonial rule. It reminds the viewer of the British writers (Steel), artists (Kipling), and patrons (Queen) who championed traditional art forms from Punjab and worked to bring those art forms to the attention of a European, and ultimately, a global audience.

The viewer is also reminded of the less savoury history of British colonialism in India and its impact, specifically, on Punjab. References to the violence and subjugation at the hands of the British Raj is embodied most directly in the person of the Queen, but also in the allusions to warfare that appear in the portrait-panel. In the background behind Amrita Sher-Gil, The Singh Twins depicts a meandering line of blood that flows along the Sutlej River, dividing India from Pakistan and reminding the viewer of the millions of lives lost and people displaced during Partition. The blood spilled from Partition extends to the bottom of this small scene in which three British officers hold captive a white-clad follower of the Kuka or Namdhari sect of Sikhism, a reform movement that aimed to return Sikh rule to Punjab and whose members fought in the freedom movement against the British in the early 1870s. The pivotal role that Punjabi Sikh men played as soldiers in the British Raj military is underscored in an image on the panel's side border.

The overall composition of the portrait-panel recalls the format of many *phulkari odhnis*, with their central decorative field framed by side and end borders in complementary patterns. This is also the overall format of flatwoven rugs or *dhurries* made throughout Punjab. Additionally, this framing strategy recalls the interplay of central image and border in numerous Indo-Persian 'miniature' paintings – a style and format in which The Singh Twins has worked extensively. Aside from the depictions of *phulkari* embroidery, other patterns in The Singh Twins's portrait-panel are atypical of Indian textiles, which were prized by Victorian-era designers for their flatness and bold use of color.[41] Instead, many of the patterns in the portrait-panel, such as the small carpet that lies beneath Amrita Sher-Gil's feet, recall British designs from the nineteenth century, such as carpets created by John Henry Dearle and William Morris, which were often inspired by Persian and Turkish carpet-weaving traditions.[42]

The idea of collision conjured by the subtitle of the portrait-panel (*Craft and Conflict*) is not only a reference to military violence or competing cultural forms, but also alludes to the idea of religious difference. Implied by the depiction of the river of blood that stands as a metonym for Partition is the political division of Punjab along religious lines (most prominently, Hindu and Muslim). The reference to the Kuka Revolt underscores further religious divisiveness in colonial Punjab and the desire felt by some within the Sikh community for a Punjab ruled exclusively by Sikhs. To underscore this, the artist depicts a church above the word 'Missionaries' in the side border of the portrait-panel, which references the 'civilizing mission' of British colonial intervention in India and specifically goals of evangelical Christian missionaries to create, in the words of critical theorist Homi

Bhabha, a 'reformed, recognized Other' or 'mimic man' using 'Christianity as a form of social control.'[43] The church in the portrait-panel is strikingly similar in style to the Sacred Heart Cathedral in Lahore, which stands in stark architectural contrast to the Sikh gurdwaras depicted at the very top of the composition.

The idea of mimicry, framed through Bhabha's writing, is useful for understanding The Singh Twins's *Phulkari* portrait-panel and the kinds of cultural and historical references it visualizes. Bhabha describes mimicry as an ambivalence of colonial discourse; it is 'a subject of a difference that is almost the same, but not quite.'[44] In many ways, the *Phulkari* portrait-panel is itself an object of mimicry. In its hyper-realistic renderings and exquisitely detailed imagery it mimics a miniature painting, but it is not a miniature painting. Its overall compositional format and juxtaposition of pattern mimic flat woven/pile woven/knotted carpets, but it is not a carpet. We see motifs that mimic actual *phulkaris* (i.e. hand-embroidered *phulkari odhnis*), but it is not a *phulkari*. In fact, the *phulkaris* depicted on the portrait-panel are more akin to the chromolithographic prints of *phulkaris* included in Steel's essay rather than actual *phulkaris* from real life: they appear more like depictions of textiles that have been flattened and repeated through mechanical reproduction, disembodied from their wearers and void of the hand.[45] In all cases, the portrait-panel renders forms that are *almost the same, but not quite*.

An important difference for the way Bhabha speaks about mimicry and the way I am proposing to use it for interpreting the portrait-panel, is a consideration of the artist's positionality and agency. For Bhabha, the discourse of mimicry is constructed by colonial power and affects both the colonizer and the colonized: it is the way that the colonizer imagines the colonized subject as 'almost the same, but not quite' and 'continually produce[s] its slippage, its excess, its difference' despite the discomfort the colonizer may feel in constructing the colonized subject as a 'mimic man.'[46] In the case of the portrait-panel (which I propose is the ambivalent subject of mimicry), the producer is an artist who is an English citizen and member of the Punjabi diaspora in the UK. The Singh Twins acknowledges that part of her creative process in making the *Slaves of Fashion* series was to engage in deep research in archives and holdings of the National Museums Liverpool, a collection that boasts over forty thousand objects from the nineteenth century that were collected from cultures around the world by British merchants, missionaries, naval officers, colonial administrators, and explorers.[47] Accordingly, the histories and experiences depicted in the portrait-panel do not simply belong to Punjab or to India, but also very much reflects the patrimony of Liverpool. There is a kind of double mirroring that occurs in The Singh Twins's portrait-panel in the way that it depicts the history of *phulkaris* as recorded in archives held by an institution at the heart of the British Empire and then projected back by a diasporic artist who herself constantly plays with the idea of the copy and syncretic identity.[48]

There is also a feeling of visual discomfort that emerges when looking closely at the iconography of the portrait-panel: an odd juxtaposition of meticulous three-dimensional renderings *and* emphatically flat and graphic patterns of textiles and ornamental flourishes creates an uneasy play between the foreground and the background of the composition and collapses any semblance of planar logic (e.g. the three-dimensionality of Sher-Gil's face and *churidar* trousers, the expansive linear perspective of the cityscape behind her right shoulder, the faces and bodies that populate the cartouches in the borders vs the two-dimensionality of the textiles depicted throughout the composition). Similarly, the dramatic shift in scale between various figures in the portrait-panel destabilizes any sense that the viewer is encountering a space grounded in reality: this is not a window into another world, but a non-linear dreamscape fashioned from historical characters and moments, snippets, and fragments, woven together on a mechanical loom, or, in the case of the digital lightboxes, pressed against Plexiglas.

The broader implications for art history are the ways this portrait-panel invites us to consider how histories of textiles from South Asia, and sometimes the actual textiles themselves, are hybrid forms that emerge through colonial discourse. *Phulkari*s are not cultural practices or material things that are somehow 'untouched' by colonial intervention (e.g. the labor of idealized, anonymous female figures working in Punjabi villages), but rather became objects of study and 'works of art' through global collecting practices that began in the second half of the nineteenth century, even if the historical roots of the art of embroidery may have been centuries earlier. Through publications such as Steel's writings, and in colonial exhibitions (like the Punjab Industrial Exhibition referenced on the portrait-panel), *phulkari*s were reframed, and remade, through colonial encounter. The creation of a *phulkari* was not solely the purview of rural housewives and brides-to-be ('darning away with patient clumsy fingers,' as Steel would have us believe) or working solely in idyllic rural settings; but instead, making *phulkari*s also occurred as part of colonial commodification of Indian craft, as objects bought and sold by British merchants and consumed internationally. *Phulkari*s were not just the richly embroidered shawls worn by Punjabi brides, but also the 'Jubilee' and the 'Manchester' *bagh*s which mark in their forms and names a hybrid identity: both Punjabi *and* British, even if uncomfortably so. Similarly, the historiography of *phulkari*s includes Guru Nanak's early reference to embroidery as part and parcel of the construction of ideal femininity, as well as the writings of Flora Annie Steel. Hundreds of extant historical *phulkari*s are housed not only in museums and private collections in India and Pakistan, but also in London, Paris, Philadelphia, Toronto, and Washington D. C. – to name just a few.[49] Indeed, so much of the story of *phulkari*s is one that is deeply inculcated in the history of the British colonial presence in Punjab, and accordingly these objects are hybrid in nature and active participants in narratives of migration and displacement. They are, as Arjun Appadurai has suggested of many museum objects, migrants or 'accidental refugees,'[50] displaced and redefined through colonial intervention. As Bhabha describes, 'cultural hybridities ... emerge in moments of historical transformation,'[51] an assertion that seems particularly apt for thinking about *phulkari*s, and the ways in which they came to the fore during the dominance of the British East India Company and subsequent British Raj rule in Punjab, amid rising anticolonial nationalism, and the cultural and political upheaval of Partition (an experience which is, in many ways, continually unfolding).

The Singh Twins's decision to feature Amrita Sher-Gil as the central figure in the portrait-panel further emphasizes the idea of cultural hybridity inherent in the art of *phulkari*s. Sher-Gil herself embodied hybridity and often assumed a role of an artistic go-between or translator: through her body and her parentage, as a bi-racial Indo-European woman; through her bi-sexuality; through her artistic training, living and studying in both Europe and India; and the style of her painting, embracing both European forms of artistic modernism and indigenous subjects and painting traditions of India.[52]

The Singh Twins's choice, too, of creating this portrait-panel as both a digital lightbox *and* a tapestry-woven cloth hanging further plays with ideas of hybridity, ambivalence, and mimicry. On the one hand the tapestry, which is made with hundreds of colorful cotton threads, references the pliability, softness, tactility, and comfort of textiles as well as the acoustic buffering that such woven objects might provide when hung in a room. On the other hand, its doppelganger, the digital lightbox, distances the viewer in ways that are completely at odds with the haptic, sensorial experience of engaging with textiles. In the gallery, the digital lightbox portrait-panels are things that pulsate with light and blur the lines between human-made/machine-made, fine art/popular culture, colonizer/colonized, England/Punjab, and remind us of the entangled histories of objects that emerge through colonial encounter. The lightbox mounts of the portrait-panels also invite parallels to glowing LED screens and digital hardware like smartphones that transmit diverse sources of information and visual imagery to viewers across time zones and cultural spaces. Furthermore, mounting the portrait-panels as digital lightboxes allows the artist to control the viewing experience: we are only encouraged to look and consider, but not to touch these objects.

The Singh Twins's gift for culling numerous visual and historical references and compiling them into dynamic compositions is reminiscent of the practice of collecting and archiving itself. As numerous scholars have discussed, the practice of collecting often entails bringing together dispersed objects and narratives, shaping them through the identity of the collector, and redefining them as part of a collection.[53] I would like to end by returning to the depiction of the 'Manchester Bagh' and the 'Jubilee Bagh' curtains in the *Phulkari* portrait-panel as a way to illustrate the strategy of collecting-archiving that the artist employs. The actual textiles that Steel references in her 1888 essay, which are meticulously reproduced as chromolithographic prints by William Griggs, no longer exist; I have been searching for these textiles – from London to Lahore – for the last decade or so to no avail. Steel mentions in another publication about her intent to donate her collection of *phulkari*s (some of which, presumably, include those that she references in the 1888 essay) to the Lahore Museum, which she may have done before she left India.[54] However, these textiles are not currently in Lahore, and if they were at one time, they may have been transferred to a regional museum in Punjab in the decades following Partition.[55] All this to say that the 'Manchester Bagh' and the 'Jubilee Bagh' that The Singh Twins reference in the *Phulkari* portrait-panel are not depictions of actual textiles. Rather, these are depictions of depictions of *phulkari*s – simulacra of a sort – recreated as colorful threads into the composition of the portrait-panel. As such, the primary source for these curtains in the portrait-panel is constructed through British colonial perspectives (both Steel's and Griggs's) of what good *phulkari*s look like and how they should be valued (remember, Steel's assertion that both of these *bagh*s illustrated 'bad taste' in one form or another). Steel never elaborates as to why these *bagh*s specifically represent the 'deterioration' of the art of *phulkari*s, except to say that they depart from her preference for tight darning stitches (what she calls 'diapering') rendered in even, rhythmic patterns without the use of running stitch guides, as in the 'Anar Bagh' illustrated elsewhere in her essay that serves as the hallmark of *bagh*s attributed to the Hazara region of present-day Khyber Pakhtunkhwa province in Pakistan. In fact, Steel disparages several other *phulkari*s in her essay in order to instruct the reader how to distinguish 'good specimens' from bad. By including these very specific textile images, that of the 'Manchester Bagh' and the 'Jubilee Bagh' as rendered in Steel's essay, The Singh Twins is participating in an act of reclaiming these lost textiles and removing them from the sole ownership of the colonial archive (Steel's essay and the pages of the *Journal of Indian Art*). Depicting the 'Manchester Bagh' and the 'Jubilee Bagh' in the *Phulkari* portrait-panel is an act of reappropriating and reinventing these textiles as a narrative of the history of *phulkari*s on The Singh Twins's terms (into her own visual collection, of sorts); it is a kind of conceptual repatriation that decolonizes colonial archives, like the National Museums Liverpool. As such, their presence in the portrait-panel becomes a reference not of 'bad taste' but rather of the diversity of *phulkari* motifs and the entangled histories of Britain and Punjab in making these textiles the iconic forms that they are today.

Notes

1. My use of the singular pronoun to refer to The Singh Twins throughout the chapter is intentional and reflects the desire on the part of the artist to produce and exhibit as one. See Saloni Mathur, 'Diasporic Body Double: The Art of the Singh Twins,' *Art Journal*, 65, no. 2 (Summer 2006): 34–56.
2. For a succinct definition, see the essay authored by Stephen Duncombe and Steve Lambert, co-founders of the Center for Artistic Activism, in their self-published booklet, 'Why Artistic Activism: Nine Reasons': https://c4aa.org/2018/04/why-artistic-activism (accessed 28 August 2023).
3. Mathur, 'Diasporic Body Double,' 47.
4. A circa 1860 double portrait on ivory depicting Mumtaz Mahal and Shah Jahan shows the princess wearing similar headgear and jewelry. See Victoria and Albert Museum, London. IM.150–1926.
5. Jenny Balfour-Paul, *Indigo* (London: British Museum Press, 1998).
6. Catherine McKinley, *Indigo: In Search of the Color that Seduced the World* (New York: Bloomsbury USA, 2011).
7. For an example of a similar overcoat, see Gown, c. 1780, Coromandel Coast (made), Netherlands (tailored). Cotton, resist- and mordant-dyed, block-printed, painted and lined. 62 inches (back of neck to base of hem length). Victoria and Albert Museum, London. T.217-1992. For more on chintz, see Sarah Fee, ed., *Cloth that Changed the World: The Art and Fashion of Indian Chintz* (Toronto: Royal Ontario Museum, 2020).
8. John Irwin, 'The Tree of Life in Indian Textiles,' in Lokesh Chandra and Jyotindra Jain, eds, *Dimensions of Indian Art: Pupul Jayakar Seventy* (New Delhi: Agam Kala Prakashan, 1986).
9. Ellen Huang, 'China's China: Jingdezhen Porcelain and the Production of Art in the Nineteenth Century,' PhD dissertation (University of California, San Diego, 2008); and Vimalin Rujivacharakul, *Collecting China: The World, China, and a History of Collecting* (Newark: University of Delaware Press, 2011).
10. See Katsushika Hokusai, *Under the Wave off Kanagawa* (*Kanagawa oki nami ura*), also known as *The Great Wave*, from the series *Thirty-six Views of Mount Fuji* (*Fugaku sanjurokkei*), c. 1830–1832, Japan. Woodblock print; ink and color on paper. 10 ⅛ × 14 15/16 inches. Metropolitan Museum of Art, JP1847.
11. From The Singh Twins's description provided in the exhibition: https://estherschreuder.wordpress.com/2018/04/11/liverpool-slaves-of-fashion/.
12. John F. Richards, *The Mughal Empire* (Cambridge: Cambridge University Press, 1995).
13. This is akin to what Saloni Mathur describes as 'micronarrative modalities of the miniature form' (multiple stories within a story) when discussing other work by The Singh Twins. Mathur, 'Diasporic Body Double,' 42.
14. For a comprehensive bibliography on South Asian textiles, see Donald Clay Johnson, *Agile Hands and Creative Minds: A Bibliography of Textile Traditions in Afghanistan, Bangladesh, Bhutan, India, Nepal, Pakistan, and Sri Lanka* (Bangkok: Orchid Press, 2000).
15. For examples of colonial-era catalogs and studies of Indian textiles, see J. Forbes Watson, *The Textile Manufactures and the Costumes of the People of India* (London: Allen, 1867); and Owen Jones, *The Grammar of Ornament: A Visual Reference of Form and Colour in Architecture and Decorative Arts* (London: Day & Son, 1856).
16. Kamaladevi Chattopadhyaya, *Indian Handicrafts* (New Delhi: Indian Council for Cultural Relations, 1963), pp. 2, 31–33.
17. Chattopadhyaya's position on the rural roots of many indigenous art forms, including textiles, draws heavily upon Mohandas 'Mahatma' Gandhi's valorization of village spaces and his dream of Sarvodaya, a self-sustaining rural community.

See, for example, M. K. Gandhi, *Ruskin Unto This Last: A Paraphrase*, translated from Gujarati by Valji Govindji Desai (Ahmedabad: Navajivan Trust, 1956).
18. Chattopadhyaya, *Indian Handicrafts*, p. 3.
19. This argument parallels Partha Chatterjee's assertion that nationalist political leaders, in their anticolonial rhetoric, inadvertently borrowed the language of colonial discourse. See Partha Chatterjee, *Nationalist Thought and the Colonial World: A Derivative Discourse?* (London: Zed Books for the United Nations University, 1986).
20. For more on the influence of Enlightenment thinking on the study of Indian art, see Partha Mitter, *Much Maligned Monsters: Histories of European Reactions to Indian Art* (Oxford: Clarendon Press, 1977); and Tapati Guha-Thakurta, *Monuments, Objects, Histories: Institutions of Art in Colonial and Post-Colonial India* (New York: Columbia University Press, 2004).
21. See Sonal Khullar, 'An Art of the Soil: Amrita Sher-Gil (1913–1941),' in *Worldly Affiliations: Artistic Practice, National Identity, and Modernism in India, 1930–1990* (Berkeley: University of California Press, 2015).
22. Cristin McKnight Sethi, 'Women's Work: *Phulkari*, Flora Annie Steel, and Collecting Textiles in British India,' in Melia Belli Bose, ed., *Women, Gender* and *Art in Asia, c. 1500–1900* (London: Routledge, 2016).
23. For an expanded discussion on the name *phulkari*, see Cristin McKnight Sethi, 'The Many Meanings of Punjabi Phulkaris,' in *Phulkari: The Embroidered Textiles of Punjab from the Jill and Sheldon Bonovitz Collection* (Philadelphia: Philadelphia Museum of Art, 2017).
24. Ibid., p. 19.
25. Flora Annie Steel, 'Phulkari Work in the Punjab,' *Journal of Indian Art and Industry*, 2, no. 24 (October 1888): 71–72 with several pages of color plates.
26. Ibid., 71.
27. See, for example, S. S. Hitkari, *Phulkari: The Folk Art of Punjab* (New Delhi: Phulkari Publications, 1980). For a comprehensive review of the historiography of *phulkaris* see Cristin McKnight Sethi, 'Mapping Phulkaris: The Production, Circulation, and Display of Embroidered Textiles from Punjab,' PhD dissertation (University of California, Berkeley, 2015).
28. For further discussion of this quote, see McKnight Sethi, 'Many Meanings,' p. 19.
29. For an expanded discussion on these 'types' of *phulkaris*, see ibid., pp. 14–18.
30. For example, see Phulkari, Punjab, Victoria and Albert Museum, London 05615, and 'Bagh Punjab' as depicted in Figure 20 in Steel's 'Phulkari Work in the Punjab.'
31. For example, see 'Bagh Anar' as depicted in Figure 16 in ibid.
32. George Watt, *Indian Art at Delhi, 1903: Being the Official Catalogue of the Delhi Exhibition, 1902–1903* (Calcutta: Superintendent of Government Printing, India, 1903).
33. Michelle Maskiell, 'Embroidering the Past: Phulkari Textiles and Gendered Work as "Tradition" and "Heritage" in Colonial and Contemporary Punjab,' *Journal of Asian Studies*, 58, no. 2 (May 1999): 361–388. The *phulkaris* which Caspar Purdon Clarke purchased for the South Kensington Museum (now V&A Museum) similarly attest to this.
34. Steel, 'Phulkari Work in the Punjab,' 72.
35. *Khadder* is another word for *khadi*, which was popularized by Gandhi during his *swadeshi* campaign. For more on *khadi* see Rebecca Brown, *Gandhi's Spinning Wheel and the Making of India* (London: Routledge, 2010); and Emma Tarlo, *Clothing Matters: Dress and Identity in India* (Chicago: University of Chicago Press, 1996).
36. See chapter 4, 'Gender and the Modern Charkha,' in Brown, *Gandhi's Spinning Wheel*.
37. Jan Hicks, 'William Henry Perkin and the First Synthetic Dye,' blog of the Science and Industry Museum (25 August 2017): https://blog.scienceandindustrymuseum.org.uk/.

38 Abigail McGowan, *Crafting the Nation in Colonial India* (New York: Palgrave Macmillan, 2009), pp. 11–16. For an elaboration on the historiography of the term 'craft' with reference to *phulkari*s, see McKnight Sethi, 'Mapping Phulkaris,' ch. 4.
39 See Rudolf Swoboda (1859–1914), *Bhai Ram Singh*, signed and dated 1892. Oil on panel. 30.1 × 18.2 cm. Royal Collection Trust. RCIN 403750.
40 Julius Bryant and Susan Weber, eds, *John Lockwood Kipling: Arts and Crafts in the Punjab and London* (New Haven: Yale University Press, 2017).
41 T. J. Barringer, *Men at Work: Art and Labour in Victorian Britain* (New Haven: Paul Mellon Centre for Studies in British Art, 2005).
42 See, for example, John Henry Dearle and William Morris (designers), Morris & Co. (maker), 1889 (made), London. 764.8 × 398.8 cm. Victoria and Albert Museum, London. T.31–1923.
43 Homi Bhabha, *The Location of Culture* (London: Routledge, 1994), pp. 122–125.
44 Ibid., p. 122.
45 McKnight Sethi, 'Women's Work,' pp. 181–185.
46 Bhabha, *Location of Culture*, p. 122.
47 https://www.liverpoolmuseums.org.uk/collections/world-cultures.
48 For more on copying, syncretism, and the concept of 'twinning' in The Singh Twins's work, see Mathur, 'Diasporic Body Double.'
49 See McKnight Sethi, 'Mapping Phulkaris.'
50 Arjun Appadurai, 'Museum Objects as Accidental Refugees,' *Historische Anthropologie*, 25, no. 3 (2017): 401–408.
51 Bhabha, *Location of Culture*, p. 3.
52 Sonal Khullar, 'Painting as Translation: The Art of Amrita Sher-Gil,' in Susanne Gaensheimer, Maria Muller-Schareck, and Nora Luckacs, eds, *Museum Global: Micro-histories of an Ex-centric Exhibition* (Dusseldorf and Cologne: Kunstsammlung Nordrhein-Westfalen and Wienand Verlag, 2018). [Published in German as 'Malerei als Ubersetzung. Die Kunst von Amrita Sher-Gil.']
53 See, for example, Jean Baudrillard, 'Marginal System: Collecting,' in *The System of Objects*. Translated by James Benedict (London: Verso, 1996). [First published as *Le système des objets*, 1968.].
54 See McKnight Sethi, 'Women's Work,' pp. 180–181.
55 This assertion is based on my analysis of the *phulkari* collection and related conversations with the collections management team at the Lahore Museum in January 2018.

Bibliography

Appadurai, Arjun. 'Museum Objects as Accidental Refugees.' *Historische Anthropologie* 25, no. 3 (2017): 401–408.

Balfour-Paul, Jenny. *Indigo*. London: British Museum Press, 1998.

Barringer, T. J. *Men at Work: Art and Labour in Victorian Britain*. New Haven: Paul Mellon Centre for Studies in British Art, 2005.

Baudrillard, Jean. 'Marginal System: Collecting.' In *The System of Objects*. Translated by James Benedict. London: Verso, 1996. First published as *Le système des objets*, 1968.

Bhabha, Homi. *The Location of Culture*. London: Routledge, 1994.

Brown, Rebecca. *Gandhi's Spinning Wheel and the Making of India*. London: Routledge, 2010.

Bryant, Julius and Susan Weber, eds. *John Lockwood Kipling: Arts and Crafts in the Punjab and London*. New Haven: Yale University Press, 2017.

Chatterjee, Partha. *Nationalist Thought and the Colonial World: A Derivative Discourse?* London: Zed Books for the United Nations University, 1986.

Chattopadhyaya, Kamaladevi. *Indian Handicrafts*. New Delhi: Indian Council for Cultural Relations, 1963.

Duncombe, Stephen and Steve Lambert. 'Why Artistic Activism: Nine Reasons.' https://c4aa.org/2018/04/why-artistic-activism (accessed 28 August 2023).

Fee, Sarah ed. *Cloth that Changed the World: The Art and Fashion of Indian Chintz.* Toronto: Royal Ontario Museum, 2020.

Gandhi, M. K. *Ruskin Unto This Last: A Paraphrase.* Translated from Gujarati by Valji Govindji Desai. Ahmedabad: Navajivan Trust, 1956.

Guha-Thakurta, Tapati. *Monuments, Objects, Histories: Institutions of Art in Colonial and Post-Colonial India.* New York: Columbia University Press, 2004.

Hicks, Jan. 'William Henry Perkin and the First Synthetic Dye.' Blog of the Science and Industry Museum, 25 August 2017. https://blog.scienceandindustrymuseum.org.uk/.

Hitkari, S. S. *Phulkari: The Folk Art of Punjab.* New Delhi: Phulkari Publications, 1980.

Huang, Ellen. 'China's China: Jingdezhen Porcelain and the Production of Art in the Nineteenth Century.' PhD dissertation, University of California, San Diego, 2008.

Irwin, John. 'The Tree of Life in Indian Textiles.' In *Dimensions of Indian Art: Pupul Jayakar Seventy.* Edited by Lokesh Chandra and Jyotindra Jain. New Delhi: Agam Kala Prakashan, 1986.

Johnson, Donald Clay. *Agile Hands and Creative Minds: A Bibliography of Textile Traditions in Afghanistan, Bangladesh, Bhutan, India, Nepal, Pakistan, and Sri Lanka.* Bangkok: Orchid Press, 2000.

Jones, Owen. *The Grammar of Ornament: A Visual Reference of Form and Colour in Architecture and Decorative Arts.* London: Day & Son, 1856.

Khullar, Sonal. 'An Art of the Soil: Amrita Sher-Gil (1913–1941).' In *Worldly Affiliations: Artistic Practice, National Identity, and Modernism in India, 1930–1990.* Berkeley: University of California Press, 2015.

Khullar, Sonal. 'Painting as Translation: The Art of Amrita Sher-Gil.' In *Museum Global: Micro-histories of an Ex-centric Exhibition.* Edited by Susanne Gaensheimer, Maria Muller-Schareck, and Nora Luckacs. Dusseldorf and Cologne: Kunstsammlung Nordrhein-Westfalen and Wienand Verlag, 2018. Published in German as 'Malerei als Ubersetzung. Die Kunst von Amrita Sher-Gil.'

Maskiell, Michelle. 'Embroidering the Past: Phulkari Textiles and Gendered Work as "Tradition" and "Heritage" in Colonial and Contemporary Punjab. *Journal of Asian Studies* 58, no. 2 (May 1999): 361–388.

Mathur, Saloni. 'Diasporic Body Double: The Art of the Singh Twins.' *Art Journal* 65, no. 2 (Summer 2006): 34–56.

McGowan, Abigail. *Crafting the Nation in Colonial India.* New York: Palgrave Macmillan, 2009.

McKinley, Catherine. *Indigo: In Search of the Color that Seduced the World.* New York: Bloomsbury USA, 2011.

McKnight Sethi, Cristin. 'Mapping Phulkaris: The Production, Circulation, and Display of Embroidered Textiles from Punjab.' PhD dissertation, University of California, Berkeley, 2015.

McKnight Sethi, Cristin. 'The Many Meanings of Punjabi Phulkaris.' In *Phulkari: The Embroidered Textiles of Punjab from the Jill and Sheldon Bonovitz Collection*. Philadelphia: Philadelphia Museum of Art, 2017.

McKnight Sethi, Cristin. 'Women's Work: *Phulkari*, Flora Annie Steel, and Collecting Textiles in British India.' In *Women, Gender and Art in Asia, c. 1500–1900*. Edited by Melia Belli Bose. London: Routledge, 2016.

Mitter, Partha. *Much Maligned Monsters: Histories of European Reactions to Indian Art*. Oxford: Clarendon Press, 1977.

Richards, John F. *The Mughal Empire*. Cambridge: Cambridge University Press, 1995.

Rujivacharakul, Vimalin. *Collecting China: The World, China, and a History of Collecting*. Newark: University of Delaware Press, 2011.

Steel, Flora Annie. 'Phulkari Work in the Punjab.' *Journal of Indian Art and Industry* 2, no. 24 (October 1888): 71–72.

Tarlo, Emma. *Clothing Matters: Dress and Identity in India*. Chicago: University of Chicago Press, 1996.

Watson, J. Forbes. *The Textile Manufactures and the Costumes of the People of India*. London: Allen, 1867.

Watt, George. *Indian Art at Delhi, 1903: Being the Official Catalogue of the Delhi Exhibition, 1902–1903*. Calcutta: Superintendent of Government Printing, India, 1903.

11

The politics of wastefulness and 'the poetics of waste':[1] Ruby Chishti's sartorial interventions

Saleema Waraich

Human choices are devastating the planet at every stage of production, distribution, consumption, and disposal. Of all the types of waste buried in the upper sedimentary layers of our landfills, especially confounding are the tons of cheap, disposable clothing worn less than a handful of times (if at all), purchased mainly by Western consumers but made by laborers in countries like China, Bangladesh, and Turkey in unsafe, toxic factories for unlivable wages. Our consumption of fast fashion – and its disregard for the planet and the lives of the less fortunate – hastens the demise of our ecosystems and ourselves.

How fast fashion emerged in the late twentieth century can be traced to the desire for accessible and affordable textiles from a century and a half earlier that drove the colonization of the South Asian Subcontinent and ignited the industrial revolution. As textiles became more easily and rapidly manufactured, the desire for cotton further propelled the enslavement of millions of people from the African continent, which further fueled the Western projects of colonization, industrialization, and consumption. Analogous to the role cotton once played, fast fashion today perpetuates the depletion of the earth's resources, ecological destruction, and modern enslavement. Yet these vital problems largely go overlooked or ignored.

It is within this socio-economic context that I turn to Ruby Chishti,[2] an artist trained in sculpture at the National College of Arts in Lahore and now residing in New York City, for whom fabrics are at the heart of her work. Tracing Chishti's engagement with clothing proposes a path for recovering its possibilities and potential, while still stressing the costs – environmental, human, personal – of clothes we mindlessly throw away. Chishti's early engagements with textiles sought to maintain connections to absent family members, then attempts to construct 'home' untethered from a physical location, after relocating to a new country and losing her family home in Pakistan. Her later monumental installations connect to the forced migrations of refugees and larger geopolitical and environmental crises. Her choice of practice and material engages with a series of issues plaguing society, including those related to fast fashion. In particular, Chishti's more recent works with discarded clothing transform cheap, ephemeral waste into sculptural and architectural monuments, thereby resisting the abbreviated life span (by design) of fast fashion and reflecting upon its ramifications.

'The Cloth that Changed the World' for better, then for far worse

As suggested by the title of a recent exhibition, *The Cloth that Changed the World: India's Painted and Printed Cottons*,[3] India's exquisitely painted and/or printed cottons (now popularly referred to as chintz in the West), exquisite muslins, and finely woven woollens (pashmina) had become enormously popular with global consumers, from Japan to Africa to Europe, by the seventeenth century. As European trading companies realized that the regions where they were seeking spices were more interested in South Asian textiles than what Europeans offered, their desire to control and appropriate textile production and distribution fueled not only the colonization of the Subcontinent but also the devastation of local economies. Over time, South Asian textile industries were transformed from global producers of coveted cotton products to suppliers of raw cotton to support British manufacturing and finally to a captive market for Britain's lower-quality cotton goods.[4]

In her superb study, *The Intimacies of Four Continents*, Lisa Lowe notes how the British fetishism of colonial commodities led to a national 'economic story of success through innovation and mechanization.'[5] Cotton and textile factories were central to the development of the industrial revolution, the rise of capitalism, and our globalized capitalist system.[6] Rather than something to be celebrated, 'the textile industry has always been one of the darkest realms of global economies,'[7] revealing the structural inequalities and injustices rooted in the practices of colonization and enslavement. The West's continuing desire for 'cotton, cloth, and clothing'[8] is similarly marked by the destruction of local industries and ecosystems, enslaved labor to supply factories, and the exploitation of immigrants, women, and child labor. Today's abuses are built on a long history of producing *more*: more goods, more quickly, more cheaply, more profitably. The same impulse leads to outsourcing as well as deplorable labor conditions faced by garment workers in China, Bangladesh, and Vietnam. Although clothing production today has largely left the US and UK, immigrant workers from Los Angeles to London and beyond remain victims of wage theft and exploitation. The fashion industry continues to depend on 'the toil of the powerless and the voiceless.'[9] Today's corporations mirror

Western colonizers in their exploitation of natural resources and human labor, just as the supply chains for major fashion companies rely on the same trade routes from centuries past.[10]

Fast fashion's rise and our fall

The rise of British colonialism in South Asia was intimately tied to cotton, which eventually led to manufacturing cotton products quickly and cheaply 'at home' and devastating the cotton industry in South Asia. In recent decades, the increased drive to manufacture 'fast fashion' – or 'throwaway fashion' – has further damaged the relationship between people and the clothes they wear and wreaked havoc on the environment by creating mountains of waste, oceans of pollution, and significantly contributing to climate change.

From bespoke clothing (custom-made clothing for an individual) to ready-to-wear clothing (pre-made clothing in standardized sizes) – it was once common practice for individuals to build a wardrobe over time, with savings and patience. When selecting fabric or clothing, one may appreciate the color, texture, fall and drape, and movement. Those with means would purchase well-made pieces; those with opportunity would alter their clothes to be more flattering or more comfortable. Mending and patching likewise would extend the life of a given piece of clothing. For many, clothing meant an investment, and consumers needed to be thoughtful, careful, and selective about purchases. When clothing requires time, money, and choice, the clothes we wear communicate aspects of our identity – how we understand and communicate our values and how we wish to be seen. In this sense clothing said something, meant something, and signaled our commitments and priorities.

The fashion industry of course has long sought to stimulate more active consumer demand. For example, in *haute couture*, *prêt-à-porter*, and mid-price ready-made garments, a fashion year came to operate in two basic cycles: a spring/summer collection and an autumn/winter collection. But today's fast fashion works relentlessly, in a constant loop. In the pre-fast-fashion model, trends and styles were determined by designers and manufacturers, then showcased on runways and in department stores, and class imitation was viewed as responsible for the dissemination of fashion trends through society, with quality being compromised as a given style 'trickled down' to less privileged consumers.[11] Fast fashion, however, has been touted as reversing this trend, with fads instead being set by consumers. The pioneers of fast fashion were headquartered in Europe (H&M, 1947 in Sweden and Zara, 1975 in Spain) and initially targeted Western European consumers. The term 'fast fashion' was coined by the *New York Times* in the late 1980s when Zara opened in New York, based on the speed of production model.[12] By the time the first H&M store opened in the US in

April 2000, according to New York retail analyst Howard L. Davidowitz, it had become 'chic to pay less.'[13] This alleged 'democratization of fashion,' enabled by mass production, was extolled for allowing consumers more access to clothing regardless of their social and economic backgrounds. As Teri Agins wrote in 2000, 'the power belongs to us, the consumers, who decide what we want to wear, when we buy it, and how much we pay for it.'[14] But such democratization was an exclusive privilege for Western consumers made possible by the exploitation of people in 'non-Western' countries. What, then, are consumers of fast fashion actually communicating? Their democratization or their privilege? Their eye for a bargain or their disregard for its consequences? Along these lines, scholars of fast fashion and hedonism argue that creativity and uniqueness appear to be important facets for the pleasure-seeking fast-fashion customer. Consumers comment on how the limited supply and availability of fast-fashion trends means other consumers are unable to copy 'their' look.[15] Ironically, but perhaps not surprisingly, these developments mirror the exclusivity of *haute couture*; a single design, worn once.

With fast fashion, the customary bi-annual fashion cycle has metamorphized into as many as fifty-two weekly micro-seasons, resembling 'a feed of constant product drops.'[16] This strategy aims to attract continuous media attention, and round-the-clock social media advertising seeks to lure primarily young consumers into retail stores or even and ever more often to online websites every week, or every day. As described by correspondent Kate Abnett, '[t]oday, trends are born and die within an infinitely faster and more turbulent environment, in which brands, celebrities, magazines, bloggers and end consumers on social media all jostle for influence over what's "in" and "out" of fashion.'[17] Targeted young consumers have disposable income and a need for instant gratification, exemplified by the social media applications they use.[18] Fast-fashion brands reach out to young consumers and encourage them to take fashion selfies that perpetrate the dizzying cycle. The result is an industry now predicated on barely perceptible micro-trends.[19]

It is important to underscore that since most fast fashion is now purchased online, consumers don't see consistent shades of colors (i.e. colors do not display consistently across platforms, screens, manufacturers), cannot get an accurate sense of texture or construction, and are unable to gauge the feel, fall, and movement of fabric. Even the fit of clothing can't be properly assessed until it arrives and often a cheap garment is not worth the time, effort, and cost of return. Nevertheless, rates of return are high enough to have led more companies to introduce charges for returns, leading to further environmentally detrimental consequences.[20] As a result, fast fashion often veers away from buying an item to last towards sampling an item of which to dispose. This is magnified by consumerism's strategy to sustain itself, to create and then feed off consumers' insecurities, which marketing assures will be resolved by purchasing this or that object.[21] This results in 'a lot of people conflat[ing] the search for self with the search for stuff,' writes psychologist April Lane Benson. Shopping therefore becomes a 'quick fix,' as she puts it, for other underlying issues.[22]

Although fast fashion began in the 1990s, the early 2000s saw much wider consumer uptake, and it has grown exponentially over the last two decades, relying on a business model that makes up for low profit margins through enormous volume. 'A store like H&M produces hundreds of millions of garments per year,' Elizabeth Cline says. 'They put a small markup on the clothes and earn their profit out of selling an ocean of clothing.' To keep manufacturing costs low, these companies outsource to countries such as China and Bangladesh, hiring workers at low wages and using cheap, synthetic materials and rudimentary manufacturing processes.[23] This further ensures the continued sale of oceans of clothing since these items are not designed, structurally or conceptually, to be worn more than a few times; these products are designed to be used and discarded. 'Once fashion trends move on, the aesthetic value of a garment declines. It becomes waste.'[24] This philosophy influences 'wasteful' consumer behavior, where clothes are discarded not necessarily because they are worn out but rather because they are outdated and no longer desirable. Clothing has become so disposable that the average US consumer throws away approximately 81 pounds of clothing each year.[25] Collectively, according to the Environmental Protection Agency, Americans generated 16 million tons of textile waste in 2019, as compared to 11.15 million tons in 2017, and a dramatic contrast to 1.7 million tons in 1960. Of the 16 million tons of waste, over 3 million tons were incinerated and 10 million tons were sent to landfill.[26] According to the United Nations Environment Programme, this translates to one trash truck's worth of textiles either burned or sent to a landfill *every second*.[27]

'Fast fashion isn't free. Someone, somewhere, is paying.' – Lucy Siegle[28]

The low prices of fast fashion obscure its ultimate costs. We may be spending substantially less of our income on clothing today, but we are buying more clothes than ever – the average US or European consumer now purchases 60% more clothing than they did fifteen years ago. Fashion's environmental problems plague all levels of the industry, from manufacturing to overproduction to disposal. The textile and apparel industries are among the world's largest polluters, trailing only the oil industry: the Intergovernmental Panel on Climate Change and the United Nations Environment Programme have calculated that the fashion industry produces 10% of global carbon dioxide emissions every year, contributing 'more [to climate change] than international air travel and shipping combined.'[29] This is because an inordinate amount of fossil fuel is used in production (petroleum-based fabrics), manufacturing (coal-powered processing), and distribution (gasoline used to transport the majority of clothes halfway around the world). In other words, we are depleting non-renewable resources, including petroleum, to produce clothes that are often used only for a short period of time, which soon end up incinerated or decaying in landfills.

From pesticides to chemical waste to microplastics, pollution from fabric production has reached crisis levels. More than 60% of today's fabric fibers are now synthetic, derived from fossil fuels.[30] Nearly 70 million barrels of oil are used each year to make the world's polyester, the most commonly used fiber in clothing.[31] Synthetic materials derived from petrochemicals do not decompose, but rather break down into smaller and smaller fragments called microfibers. This means that when our clothing ends up in a landfill it will not biodegrade but rather release a toxic brew of pollutants.[32] Fast fashion also relies on chemical-intensive processes such as intensive farming, textile washing and bleaching, and fabric dyeing and treatment. The fashion industry uses around 1.5 trillion liters of water annually and is responsible for producing 20% of global wastewater, including run-off pollution that contaminates soil, rivers and oceans, and affects animal, marine and human life.[33] Hazardous chemicals endanger farmers' and workers' health; toxic chemicals in the synthetic textiles pollute the air, land, and water.

The fashion apparel industry is especially labor intensive. One-sixth of people around the globe work within some element of the global fashion industry. Although North America and Europe generate most of the demand for fast fashion, most production takes place outside of North America and Europe.[34] Likewise, although the US ranks as the leading market, with 88% of US consumers purchasing fast fashion, only 2.5% of the clothing purchased in 2012 was manufactured stateside. The fashion industry is also notorious for its inhumane treatment of workers, from the era when European colonizers and US settlers controlled cotton markets, to today's factories in China, Bangladesh, Vietnam, and Indonesia – countries with low-wage economies and scant environmental and labor regulations.[35] The treatment of workers is unconscionable: meager wages; excessive overtime; hazardous conditions; child labor violations; harassment of the largely female workforce; physical abuse; even forced labor and virtual slavery. Oxfam reported in 2019 that 0% of Bangladeshi garment workers and 1% of Vietnamese garment workers earned a living wage.[36] The fact that the fashion supply chain funnels more money towards modern enslavement than any other industry after the technology industry means that the record of Western countries – the forces that drive this industry – must be reassessed for their complicity in human rights violations.[37] As fast fashion makes overwhelmingly clear, the desires of the most privileged countries on earth still dictate which lives matter and which don't.

Ruby Chishti's sartorial investments

Grappling with the crises surrounding fast fashion – environmental, ethical, global, political, individual – will require far more activism and intervention from all corners. One particularly inspired response to these acute challenges can be found in the inventive and powerful work of artist Ruby Chishti. The arc of her career offers a moving tribute to the lasting power and intimacy of cloth and clothing, in direct conversation with and opposition to the current fashion market that fetishizes the new and enforces wastefulness.[38] Ruby Chishti (born 1963 in Jhang, Pakistan, now living in Brooklyn, New York) trained as a sculptor in a Western classical manner at the National College of Arts (NCA) in Lahore. Later she abandoned her initial training in clay, stone, wood, and metal in favor of materials commonly associated with domestic, feminine spaces – namely, cloth and clothing – as well as the detritus of daily life: remnants of clothing, pantyhose, twigs, feminine sanitary napkins. I will focus on her choice of material as her medium and explore how the meanings of her sculptures and her engagement with materials have shifted over time, from personal narratives to social reflections and societal indictments. Broadly speaking, her work interrogates persistent, interrelated themes of absence, love, and loss; as she says, it is 'about being human.'[39] Her relationship to clothing in particular has emerged as a vital intervention in the age of fast fashion.

To understand her distinctive relationship to cloth and clothing, it is necessary to understand Chishti's personal history. She suffered a series of major losses beginning at an early age: her father when she was twelve, her elder brother nearly five years later, her mother after a decade-long illness that left her immobile and uncommunicative, and several years later, her family home. Over the years, and before she began integrating them into her artistic work, Chishti collected pieces of cloth, remnants of materials used for her and her family's clothing. Part of this stemmed from being raised in an environment where resources were limited and where the majority of people repurpose, preserve, and pass down items; as a child, she learned to sew in order to make her own dolls and eventually stitch her own clothes:

> Early on I learned how to sew, make and mend. ... This activity shaped my general approach towards life; it taught me not to discard or waste things quickly and instead to strive to mend and keep and the lesson extended to life, to relationships, associations and so on.[40]

After losing her father and then her brother, she couldn't bear throwing out their clothes. As she poignantly notes, 'people leave, their clothes remain.' She describes the act of throwing away clothing and other meaningful textiles such as personal quilts as 'ruthless.'[41] For this reason, she held onto their clothing, 'just like we tend to adhere passionately to our joys as well as sorrows.'[42] When she moved to the United States in 2002, Chishti brought suitcases filled with scraps of fabric on her journey, much to the surprise of customs agents anticipating 'exotic' memorabilia.[43]

Chishti's experiences as a long-term caregiver for her mother also contributed to these perspectives. In 1991, a few years after graduating from NCA, she put her artistic pursuits on hold to care for her mother, who had been paralyzed by a stroke. It was not until 1999 that Chishti fully 'discovered cloth as a medium of sculpture.' She recalls a particularly alarming incident, while trying to help her mother dress, when her mother fell 'just like a rag doll.'[44] Chishti had not thought of a body as doll like before that moment and she 'felt a connection between the exhausted castoffs [of clothing that she'd been collecting over the years] and a frail body of an inert being ... my mother. All those heaps of scraps of fabric started transforming into figurative forms that I had collected over the years and never wanted to throw away.'[45] In response to this distressing incident, she began using remnants from her collection of family clothing 'to make dolls that were like my mother's body.' Her earliest works of this type transformed the clothing of her absent family members into 'something else that isn't as painful.' The surviving scraps of cloth became for Chishti the 'most beautiful way of remembering someone.'[46]

Chishti's sensibilities and pursuits explore the possibilities, meanings, and affective impact of fabric in ways that fast fashion denies. For Chishti, personal clothing and textiles are the most precious of our possessions, since memories of one's upbringing and relationship become interwoven with their threads. The potential and preciousness of fabric possesses the ability to signify one's sense of self as well as connections to others, perhaps especially in their absence; as noted by Emma Tarlo, 'clothes are frequently perceived as expressions and even extensions of the people who wear them.'[47] As Chishti continued working with this material as her primary medium, she connected with its tactile qualities, its pliability, and its fragility and vulnerability.[48] Textiles have traditionally not been considered suitable material for a sculptor or artist, but rather associated with women's domestic work. That little value and prestige has been associated with fabric was another reason she chose to work with textiles. By using scraps of cloth to make *sculpture*, or fine art, her work upends distinctions between female domestic activity, folk craft, and fine arts. As Chishti comments: '[fabric is] not so snobby, or, it's not that there's so much respect attached to it like high art materials [such as] bronze, wood.' She continues, 'I feel so comfortable with this material that I don't feel [with] other sculpture's materials,' it's material that's like 'talk[ing] to your friend.'[49]

Cloth is a very communicative medium. Everyone has a relationship to cloth and clothing: it is accessible, familiar, personal, and inviting. We can all connect to and relate to it, which for Chishti facilitates a close connection between her work and her audience. In fact, Chishti has noticed how people read her work the same way around the world: 'there's nothing exotic that I use, my materials they are throw away materials.'[50] This is a significant point, especially for artists who originate in the global south, since contemporary art markets tend to reinforce colonial desires for 'authenticity,' which frequently translate to Western desires for the exotic.[51]

The familiarity of fabric is thus an asset, yet it is precisely for this reason that cloth has been undervalued, if not dismissed, for being commonplace. In addition, when viewed through the lens of Sufi philosophy, which values modesty, humility, and submissiveness, Chishti's embrace of a 'lowly' medium enables her to uphold Sufi ideals. Not only does her choice of used clothing itself resonate with Sufi sartorial practices – such as wearing simple garments that are repeatedly mended and repaired over the years – but her choice of a material associated with women's work connects with the female voices historically used by Sufi poets in Punjabi literature.[52] The same applies to her choice 'deliberately to extend the craft and skill of sewing, considered to be a low art form, into my art practice.'[53]

Chishti's earliest cloth works were made by stitching together remnants of clothes she made with fabrics from her family members' belongings. These figures of humans (Figure 11.1), crows (Figure 11.2), and buffaloes (Figure 11.3) – all stuffed with straw, an act akin to 'feeding

11.1 *My Birth Will Take Place a Thousand Times No Matter How You Celebrate It* (2001). Recycled cloth, thread, straw, yarn. Height 45.7 cm each

Ruby Chishti's sartorial interventions 267

11.2 *Crows* (2001). Recycled cloth, thread, polyester, steel, wood. Approximately (crow-) life size

11.3 *Giving End* (2001). Fabric, straw, thread. H: approx. 96.5 cm

them'⁵⁴ – embody 'narratives of dignified pathos and gentle sadness.'⁵⁵ In addition to honoring family members, Chishti's work encourages viewers to collapse their perceived distinctions between dolls and sculpture, craft and art, female and male practices, and domestic settings and elite exhibition spaces. The female figures in *My Birth Will Take Place a Thousand Times No Matter How You Celebrate It* (Figure 11.1) were created out of remnants of her father's forty-year-old *rizai* (quilt) 'and other pieces of fabric that had similar associations.'⁵⁶ While embodying her personal loss and grief, these cloth women also mourn the 'individual tragedies of [the] unwanted, discriminated existence [that] millions of female[s] experience in this part of the world.'⁵⁷ These doll-like figures, made of cloth and connecting intimately with Chishti's personal history, powerfully combine materials and practices that speak on behalf of the larger themes of women's work and the extensive historical experiences of women.

Another recurring element of Chishti's installations are crows fabricated from scraps of old and worn fabric remnants (Figure 11.2). Like the remnants of cloth that carry memories of her family, these birds bear witness to her history: she associates them with traumatic moments in her life but as sources of personal comfort and companionship. Crows are also symbols of resilience and survival, known for their ability to survive in a variety of climates and habitats worldwide: they lived in the trees surrounding her home in Lahore and she encounters them today in New York. Citing the *Compendium of Materia Medica*, Chishti also speaks of the kindness of crows, upheld as symbols of filial piety in the Chinese text for feeding their parents when they are old and weak.⁵⁸ Indeed, crows are one of the few species of birds that are known to remain with their parents for a number of years.⁵⁹ Chishti's early US exhibitions often featured crows – made out of fabric scraps from her mother's clothing that Chishti shipped from Lahore – which memorialize the loss of family members as well as bear witness to her physical and personal journey. In this way her work again infused the personal and domestic into 'pristine gallery spaces.'⁶⁰

When Chishti moved from Lahore to the Bay Area in northern California in 2002, she left her belongings, including her clothing, in her family home, expecting to return soon after. But it was not until 2006 that Chishti was able to return to Lahore for the first time. She found that her home was gone, and along with it, all of her and her family's belongings had been disposed of in her absence. Thirty years of accumulated belongings and memories of the people she'd loved and lost disappeared: 'When I came back it was like the house had never been there, there was wilderness.'⁶¹ The dramatic loss of her family home profoundly affected her, haunting her days, nights, and dreams. Her longing for home, a home that now existed only in the mind, compelled her to begin exploring architectural structures, made of discarded clothing. This shift would also change her practice. Whereas she previously stitched, stuffed, and made doll-like sculptural forms, she began using fabric in a different way: she would cut used clothing into long strips, fold and compress the strip, and hand-stitch the folded layers together. She would sew through five or six of these stitched layers and then sew them into a wire mesh armature (please see Figure 11.6b, below, for a detail of one of her sculptures, showing the folded, layered slips). The layers upon layers of folded fabric that form the building blocks of her monuments invoke earth's sedimentary layers, the geological record of the passage of time; here the material layers signify time, memory, and identity. Her process of stitching layers of material together enables us to view the works produced at this time within Kirsty Robertson's 'expanded field of quilting,' which Robertson defines as the extension of quilting practice in the work of artists 'who do not create traditional quilts but who use the processes of quilting (and patching, suturing and appliqué) to draw together knowledge, facts, images and artifacts into quilted wholes.'[62]

Coming to terms with the loss of her home would eventually result in a new body of work, animated by a new approach. The loss of her physical 'home' made her acutely aware of 'home' as an idea. Reflecting upon the similarities between the structure of a house and the structure of a body, she began thinking about the body as a house, as home. As she describes this shift: 'in architecture people live; in bodies memories live, and my home also.'[63] Her reconceptualization also brought the desire to associate home with a tangible location, wanting to keep a home 'like a toy,' one that never leaves you, or one you never part from. Before 2008, she had always stitched, stuffed, or cast her figures with remnants from her and her family's collection of scraps of fabrics. Moving forward, she began building single-structure sculptures, not only adopting a new technique but turning to discarded clothing found in neighborhood thrift shops that she would systematically dissemble into strips and reassemble into numerous layers.

These major shifts in form, technique, and source material were further informed by another physical move, this time from the Bay Area to New York City. She was immediately entranced by the city, one of the world's capitals of fashion and of architecture. And she found neighborhood thrift shops in Brooklyn equally inspiring, full of unexpected and fascinating items that sparked her curiosity. She imagined the many people that wore these clothes, the places where they came from, the diverse immigrant communities they represented, and the multitudes of stories woven into the fabric. She treats 'each scrap of fabric [from the clothing of unknown people] with the same meticulous care and sensitivity I would have offered the humans who once wore them.'[64] In this way, Chishti's dis- and reassemblage of used clothing from her neighborhood resonates with one reading of quilts, which Robertson describes as providing 'comfort and succor, income, and community, [quilts] are seen as important historical documents, as text/iles recording lives, kinships and relationships.'[65]

Simultaneously, Chishti learned of a fast-fashion trend where 'stylish young men and women' purchase the latest fashion trends, wear it once, and then discard it. She described feeling overwhelmed by how quickly such shoppers discarded clothes.[66] Due to her early experiences of loss of family, of home, and the ways in which clothing and textiles helped her navigate loss, she immediately recognized the loss of meaning and value in her neighbors' sartorial practices. As a result, Chishti's works, like those of Jarod Charzewski, Derick Melander, and Guerra de la Paz (a collaboration between artists Alain Guerra and Neraldo de la Paz) also comment on rampant over-consumption by involving 'mass amounts of [material] debris … created by late capitalism.'[67] As such, as Robertson persuasively argues, activist quilting makes 'issues intimate, understandable, but never solely comforting';[68] a description that aptly pertains to Chishti's installations.

Chishti's experiences of loss, relocation, and rediscovery culminated in her first sculptural/architectural piece, *Live, Laugh, Love* (2009) (Figure 11.4), which was later reworked and retitled *Sublime Architecture* (2013) (Figure 11.5). When she began making this sculpture/structure in California, it was intended to be 'a home kind of place'; however, as she continued working on it after her move to Brooklyn, she started exploring her desire to assimilate in her new environment, reinforced by 'a connection I felt when I took other people's clothing; a practice that made me feel a part of a new environment.'[69] The process of working with, of touching other people's clothes, fabric that had touched other people's bodies, is an intimate one, and created a deep connection with people who she didn't know. This sentiment is shared by another artist, Derick Melander, who eloquently wrote, 'As clothing wears, fades, stains and stretches, it becomes an intimate record of our physical presence.'[70] This work was both a 'human collection,' but also created a human connection that she was searching for,[71] as symbolized by the open doll house windows – 'where inside and outside meet and cross'[72] – that are part of the quilted fabric of the sculpture/structure.

At a later residency at Bose Pacia Gallery in Brooklyn, Chishti started to explore the possibility of wearing this sculptural-architectural piece:

> I had built it earlier as a sculptural form with a complex armature inside full of wires and wire mesh sewn with fabric strips. When I decided to wear it, I had to cut the inside armature to make it wearable, but the moment I cut the complex armature inside, the whole form collapsed just as a building without having a structure. I had to stitch it vertically with vertical supports in it.[73]

She subsequently wore this sculpture-dress as a performance piece in an art festival in 2011, making manifest her past, her experiences, and her memories as an untethered 'home,' while simultaneously fostering connections with the people she now lived among by transforming their discarded clothes into an embodied communal fabric. As eloquently described by

11.4 *Live, Laugh, Love* (2009). Recycled clothing, thread, wood, paper, wire mesh. 83.8 cm × 55.9 cm × 30.5 cm. Private collection

11.5 *Sublime Architecture* (2013). Recycled clothing, thread, wood (performance still). 193 cm × 10.1 cm × 76.2 cm

Nafisa Rizvi, Chishti's dresses 'remind one of the nests that crows make using debris and detritus, specially finding and utilizing scraps of cloth so [ingeniously] so as to make solid, unyielding homes that weather violent winds and rain.'[74] From recycled clothing to sculpture-structure to a dress-as-home, Chishti collapses distinctions between the body, dress, and architecture, continuing to push past the divisions and boundaries that confine us.

Chishti's work was stalled because of health issues during 2012–2014. But she continued collecting discarded clothing during this period, cutting these garments into thousands upon thousands of strips, then stitching together layer after layer. As her health improved, she was able to pursue an artistic residency in Colombo (Sri Lanka). During a trip to the city of Jaffna, ravaged by thirty-five years of civil war, the layers of fabric began to take a distinct and monumental turn. There she encountered abandoned houses containing dust-covered belongings of people who had been forced to leave. The ravaged homes evoked her own loss, but she was struck more by the difference between her having decided to leave her home and the Jaffna residents being forced to leave not only their homes but also their physical surroundings, their entire communities. She recalled: 'I left by choice under good circumstances and yet I miss my home *that* much; what about people who are forced to leave with nothing?'[75]

Chishti's subsequent artistic move from single buildings to sprawling environments marks an important transition, from reflecting upon personal experiences to broader experiences of forced migration, experiences that continue to increase around the globe every year. Similar to the ways in which she perceived the traces of people in the clothes they once wore, her work began to address the presence of absent residents. Do migrants carry their memories with them or do memories remain within the walls they left behind? How do homes reflect or remember their former occupants? The abundant supply of stitched layers that Chishti had in reserve enabled her to construct two large, sprawling environments: *The Present is a Ruin Without the People* (2016, with sound) (Figure 11.6a and 6b) and *We Leave, We Never Leave, We Return Endlessly* (2017) (Figure 11.7), both made from recycled textiles, thread, wood, and wire mesh. Chishti describes *The Present is a Ruin Without the People* as an audio-visual installation addressing the issues she grappled with over the years of its construction:

> The overall form is a juxtaposition of architectural and human body structures ... a framework I use to explore the codependent relationship between personal experience and the socio-political narratives amplifying the voices of those who have survived emotional and physical trauma resulting from conflict, war and the universal subject of mortality. ... It is my way of engaging with the persistence and tenuous fragility of human existence, while exploring materials and reinventing sculptural forms that can forge a sense of collective human connection.[76]

These large installations build on earlier themes in her work: the interweaving of personal and family histories, the relationship between clothing and bodies, the entangling of loss and memory, and imagining collective connections. Her work suggests that when bodies are absent, when people depart, their haunting presence remains in the homes they abandoned, in the cloth and clothing they have discarded. Chishti's approach draws not only on the people who wore this clothing but also invokes the people who originally made the clothing. Whereas today's consumers often do not know or consciously disregard who stitched their clothing, Chishti actively imagines and invokes garment workers – their time-intensive process, their physical labor, their sewing posture – as she hand-stitches the strips of fabric that compose her work. By honoring them through her own time-consuming and labor-intensive practice, Chishti connects the local and the global.

In a recent interview, Chishti expressed a shift in meaning and direction. While her focus remains on personal and societal narratives, she now seeks to emphasize 'the challenge of survival in hostile socio-ecological climates.'[77] Inspired by the ravages of war, her built environments – decaying, collapsing structures of discarded clothing – signify a moment

11.6 (a) *The Present is a Ruin Without the People* (2016). Recycled textiles, thread, children's clothing, embellishments (lace, metal scraps), wire mesh, wood, paint, archival glue; with soundscape. 207.5 cm × 324.8 cm × 29.7 cm. Qatar Museums; and (b) *The Present is a Ruin Without the People* (2016), detail

when all has been lost. As she has continued to work on these sculptures, she also has come to understand them in environmental terms, invoking regions devastated by natural disasters as a result of climate change. The installations bear witness to our twenty-first-century world, to living in a

11.7 *We Leave, We Never Leave, We Return Endlessly* (2017). Recycled textile, wire mesh, thread, wood, archival glue. 209.5 cm × 327.6 cm × 34.3 cm. Kiran Nadar Museum of Art

time of unprecedented and accelerating environmental collapse. In particular, an aesthetic of 'patching,' or 'combining mismatched fabrics or reworking "salvaged" jackets,' as discussed by Alison Gill, prompts visions of what 'it is to live with an "ensuing" environmental crisis that may well bring dramatic reductions in resources.'[78] As much as the decaying, dilapidated buildings of Sri Lanka propelled this stage of her growth, Chishti was also struck by the vibrancy of the lush greenery that covered everything, the overgrown ruins signaling the force of nature. As a reminder of our inevitable return to earth, her installations now incorporate green materials that represent the moss that will eventually envelop these structures, and perhaps our world should we continue on a path of self-destruction.

Chishti's unruly installations, made up of layer upon layer of discarded clothing, invoke environmental disaster and push back against a throwaway society. Her relationship to cloth, including fast fashion, shows us a different path, one in which we value, preserve, and elevate earth's resources as well as foster connections with those near, far, and absent. Carla Binotto and Alice Payne's inspiring discussion of a 'poetics of waste'; one that offers a jarring metaphor of a 'life in thrall to the fury of extinction' perfectly applies to Chishti's works.[79] In Chishti's installations, waste thus carries the capacity to provoke thought and reflection on the vulnerability of our planet and our lives.[80] An 'aesthetic of the worn and wasted' elevates rather than disguises trash, the latter approach perpetuating obliviousness, disavowal, and apathy, and Chishti's artistic practice draws attention to its affective possibilities of repair and repurposing. This poetics of waste channels the 'potency and poignancy of rubbish … to reflect on universal ideas of grief, loss and renewal.'[81] Chishti's embrace of discarded fast fashion resists the very industry that depends upon us not placing any value on what we (briefly) wear. Unlike consumers who purchase such clothes online without touching them, much less trying them on, Chishti contemplates the textures, colors, patterns, and embellishments of the clothing she thoughtfully selects as fabric sources. And from cheap, disposable garments, she creates enduring, evocative structures that underscore the fragility and preciousness of our lives and environments.

Conclusion

Chishti's work weaves together a number of subversive strategies. She reimagines – through reconfigured 'female' materials – sculptural and architectural practices historically associated with men and offers rivals to 'the heroics of colossal masculinity.'[82] She replaces an elite, male-dominated medium with a feminine practice, recasting, for example, dolls as sculpture and using discarded clothing to build sprawling sculptures of architecture. Her approach is anti-hierarchical in method and material, necessarily invoking and questioning traditional practices as well as global systems of inequity and injustice. From the waste emerging out of self-indulgent consumerism, she constructs communal, collective monuments. Her work destabilizes boundaries between craft and art, mass culture and high culture, domestic space and elite museum culture. In the face of global disaster and environmental catastrophe, Chishti's work exhibits mindful, meditative, and inspirational qualities, yet without making false promises by retaining an aesthetic of decay, deterioration, and loss.

Speaking back to the hubris and hedonism of mindless, rampant consumerism, best exemplified by fast fashion, Chishti transforms disposed materials into monumental structures. Through this ultra-resourceful approach – nothing discarded, everything up for transformation and reuse – Chishti simultaneously challenges and critiques elitist artistic precedents as well as modern consumers. Her sculptural architecture, or architectural sculpture, invokes a 'history of thriftiness' that recalls time-honored traditions of creating quilts by recycling patchwork material.[83] At the same time, her approach relies on and responds to a contemporary culture of waste, reanimating 'the detritus of a consumerist society where the overconsumption of clothing is the norm.'[84] In our era of gluttony and neglect, Chishti's installations function at once as memorials of loss and monuments to obscenity, offering grim and inspired visions of our future.

Notes

1. Carla Binotto and Alice Payne, 'The Poetics of Waste: Contemporary Fashion Practice in the Context of Wastefulness,' *Fashion Practice*, 9, no. 1 (2017): 5–29.
2. My discussion of Ruby Chishti's work is born from a series of interviews from August 2015 and May 2022. I sincerely appreciate her generosity and kindness over the years. All quotes, unless otherwise noted in the text, are drawn from these conversations. I'd also like to thank Melia Belli Bose for her enduring support, encouragement, and patience.
3. Royal Ontario Museum in Toronto, 12 September 2020 to 2 January 2022, www.rom.on.ca/en/exhibitions-galleries/exhibitions/the-cloth-that-changed-the-world-indias-painted-and-printed (accessed 2 August 2023).
4. Lisa Lowe, *The Intimacies of Four Continents* (Durham: Duke University Press, 2015), p. 90.
5. Ibid., p. 91.
6. Andrew Brooks, *Clothing Poverty: The Hidden World of Fast Fashion and Second-Hand Clothes* (London: Zed Books, 2015), p. 5.
7. Tatiana Schlossberg, 'How Fast Fashion Is Destroying the Planet,' *New York Times*, 3 September 2019, www.nytimes.com/2019/09/03/books/review/how-fast-fashion-is-destroying-the-planet.html (accessed 2 August 2023); Dana Thomas, 'Introduction,' *Fashionopolis: The Price of Fast Fashion – and the Future of Clothes* (New York: Penguin Books, 2019).
8. Brooks, *Clothing Poverty*, p. 5.
9. Schlossberg, 'Fast Fashion'; Tansy Hoskins, 'Made in Britain: UK Textile Workers Earning £3 Per Hour,' *The Guardian*, 27 February 2015, www.theguardian.com/sustainable-business/sustainable-fashion-blog/2015/feb/27/made-in-britain-uk-textile-workers-earning-3-per-hour (accessed 2 August 2023).
10. Aditi Meyer and Ayesha Barenblat, 'Why Fashion Brands are Today's Masters,' *Eco Age*, 6 November 2020, https://eco-age.com/resources/why-fashion-brands-are-todays-colonial-masters/ (accessed 2 August 2023).
11. Andrew Reilly and Jana Hawley, 'Attention Deficit Fashion,' *Fashion, Style & Popular Culture*, 6, no. 1 (2019): 85–98, at 86.
12. Anne-Marie Schiro, 'Fashion; Two New Stores That Cruise Fashion's Fast Lane,' *New York Times*, 31 December 1989, www.nytimes.com/1989/12/31/style/fashion-two-new-stores-that-cruise-fashion-s-fast-lane.html (accessed 2 August 2023); Suzy Hansen, 'How Zara Grew into the World's Largest Retailer,' *New York Times Magazine*, 9 November 2012, www.nytimes.com/2012/11/11/magazine/how-zara-grew-into-the-worlds-largest-fashion-retailer.html (accessed 2 August 2023).
13. Ruth La Ferla, '"Cheap Chic" Draws Crowds on 5th Ave,' *New York Times*, 11 April 2000, www.nytimes.com/2000/04/11/style/cheap-chic-draws-crowds-on-5th-ave.html (accessed 2 August 2023).
14. Teri Agins, *The End of Fashion: How Marketing Changed the Clothing Business Forever* (New York: William Morrow Paperbacks, 2010), cited in Reilly and Hawley, 'Attention Deficit Fashion,' 87. It is worth noting that the idea of 'democratizing fashion' was promoted by Amancio Ortega, founder of Zara, one of the most highly successful fast-fashion chains, who became the third richest person in the world by 2012, worth $58.3 billion. Hansen, 'How Zara Grew.'
15. Karen Miller, 'Hedonic Customer Responses to Fast Fashion and Replicas,' *Journal of Fashion Marketing and Management*, 17, no. 2 (2013): 160–174, at 167–168.
16. Kate Abnett, 'Do Fashion Trends Still Exist?' *Business of Fashion*, 9 January 2012, www.businessoffashion.com/articles/retail/fashion-trends-still-exist (accessed 2 August 2023).

17 Ibid.
18 For example, SnapChat images last for no more than 10 seconds and Twitter limits texts to 280 characters. Reilly and Hawley, 'Attention Deficit Fashion,' 89, 90.
19 Ibid.,90.
20 As reported by Sophie Benson, returned clothing is more likely to end up in landfills than resold and those items that are processed, and there are other considerable time and environmental costs involved. Sophie Benson, 'Past the Parcel: How the End of Free Returns Will Change the Way We Shop,' *The Guardian*, 20 July 2022, www.theguardian.com/commentisfree/2022/jul/20/end-free-returns-fast-fashion-online-shoppers (accessed 2 August 2023).
21 J. Francis Davis, 'The Power of Images: Creating the Myths of Our Time,' *Media & Values*, Issue 57 (1992), www.medialit.org/reading_room/article80.html (accessed 3 August 2023).
22 April Lane Benson, *To Buy or Not To Buy: Why We Overshop and How to Stop* (Boston and London: Trumpeter, 2008), cited in Marc Bain and Quartz, 'The Neurological Pleasures of Fast Fashion,' *The Atlantic*, 25 March 2015, www.theatlantic.com/entertainment/archive/2015/03/the-neurological-pleasures-of-modern-shopping/388577/ (accessed 2 August 2023).
23 Elizabeth Cline, *Overdressed: The Shockingly High Cost of Cheap Fashion* (New York: Portfolio/Penguin, 2012), cited in Jim Zarroli, 'In Trendy World of Fast Fashion, Styles Aren't Made To Last,' *NPR*, 11 March 2013, www.npr.org/2013/03/11/174013774/in-trendy-world-of-fast-fashion-styles-arent-made-to-last (accessed 2 August 2023).
24 Alice Payne, 'Nourishing or Polluting: Redefining the Role of Waste in the Fashion System,' in Emma Felton, Oksana Zelenko, and Suzi Vaughan, eds, *Design and Ethics: Reflections on Practice* (New York: Routledge, 2012), p. 205.
25 Nicholas Gilmore, 'Ready-to-Waste: America's Clothing Crisis,' *Saturday Evening Post*, 16 January 2018, www.saturdayeveningpost.com/2018/01/ready-waste-americas-clothing-crisis/ (accessed 2 August 2023).
26 Beth Porter, 'What Really Happens to Unwanted Clothes?' *Green America*, Winter 2019, www.greenamerica.org/unraveling-fashion-industry/what-really-happens-unwanted-clothes (accessed 2 August 2023).
27 Samantha Masunaga, 'Does Fast Fashion Have to Die for the Environment to Live?' *The Los Angeles Times*, 3 November 2019.
28 Lucy Siegle in *The True Cost* (documentary), directed and written by Andrew Morgan, Life is My Movie Entertainment; an Untold Production, 2015.
29 Textile production alone is estimated to release 1.2 billion tons of carbon dioxide into the atmosphere every year. House of Commons Environmental Audit Committee, 'Fixing Fashion: Clothing Consumption and Sustainability,' Sixteenth Report of Session 2017–19, House of Commons, February 2019.
30 Gustav Sandin and Greg M. Peters, 'Environmental Impact of Textile Reuse and Recycling – A Review,' *Journal of Cleaner Production*, 184 (2018): 353–365.
31 James Conca, 'Making Climate Change Fashionable – The Garment Industry Takes On Global Warming,' *Forbes*, 3 December 2015, www.forbes.com/sites/jamesconca/2015/12/03/making-climate-change-fashionable-the-garment-industry-takes-on-global-warming/?sh=5d38114e79e4 (accessed 2 August 2023).
32 Schlossberg, 'Fast Fashion.'
33 Nicola Davis, 'Fast Fashion Speeding Toward Environmental Disaster, Report Warns,' *The Guardian*, 7 April 2020, www.theguardian.com/fashion/2020/apr/07/fast-fashion-speeding-toward-environmental-disaster-report-warns (accessed 2 August 2023).
34 Adler Bowman and Alaina Baumohi, 'What's Hot This Season,' *Washington University Political Review*, 26 October 2019, www.wupr.org/2019/10/26/whats-hot-this-season (accessed 2 August 2023); Brooks, *Clothing Poverty*, p. 6.
35 Brooks, *Clothing Poverty*, p. 5.

36 S. Nayeem Emran, Joy Kyriacou, and Sarah Rogan, *Made in Poverty: The True Price of Fashion* (Oxfam Research Report), Oxfam Australia, February 2019, p. 9, www.oxfam.org.au/wp-content/uploads/2021/11/Made-in-Poverty-the-True-Price-of-Fashion-Oxfam-Australia.pdf (accessed 2 August 2023).
37 'Modern Slavery, A Hidden, Everyday Problem,' *The Global Slavery Index*, Walk Free Foundation, 2018, www.globalslaveryindex.org/ (accessed 2 August 2023).
38 Aisha Khan, brochure accompanying exhibit *We Leave, We Never Leave, We Return Endlessly* (Twelve Gates, Philadelphia, 4–26 September 2015); Binotto and Payne, 'The Poetics of Waste,' p. 8.
39 Personal communication.
40 Conversation with Ruby Chishti, 'Ruby Chishti,' *Art Now*, 1 May 2012, www.artnowpakistan.com/ruby-chishti/ (accessed 2 August 2023).
41 Personal communication.
42 Ruby Chishti, Artist Statement, Indo-American Arts Council 7th Annual Erasing Borders Exhibition of Contemporary Indian Art of the Diaspora (New York, 2010), www.iaac.us/erasing_borders2010/RubyChishti/bio.htm (accessed 2 August 2023).
43 Personal communication.
44 Ibid.
45 Chishti, Artist Statement, Indo-American Arts Council.
46 Personal communication.
47 Emma Tarlo, 'Introduction: The Problem of What to Wear,' in *Clothing Matters: Dress and Identity in India* (Chicago: University of Chicago Press, 1996), p. 16.
48 Personal communication; Salima Hashmi, *Unveiling the Visible: Lives and Works of Women Artists of Pakistan* (Islamabad: Salima Hashmi and ActionAid, 2002), p. 151.
49 Personal communication.
50 Ibid.
51 As recent debates involving the neo-miniature practice of painting, which has emerged as the international face of contemporary art in Pakistan, demonstrate.
52 Personal communication.
53 Conversation with Ruby Chishti, 'Ruby Chishti.'
54 Chishti had to stop working in straw because it's live material and couldn't travel; it also presents a problem for galleries and museums.
55 Staff, 'Creating Art with Detritus of Daily Life,' *Pakistan Today*, 19 April 2011, https://archive.pakistantoday.com.pk/2011/04/19/creating-art-with-detritus-of-daily-life/ (accessed 2 August 2023).
56 Anita Sharma, 'Transparent Studio: Interview with Ruby Chishti – Part 1,' *+91 Archives Blog*, 5 April 2012, https://plus91archivesblog.wordpress.com/2012/04/05/transparent-studio-interview-with-ruby-chishti/ (accessed 2 August 2023).
57 Chishti, Artist Statement, Indo-American Arts Council.
58 Personal communication.
59 Kevin McGowan, 'Family Lives of the Uncommon American Crow,' *Cornell Plantations Magazine*, 51, no. 1 (Spring/Summer 1996): 1–4; also available here: www.birds.cornell.edu/crows/planta.htm (accessed 2 August 2023).
60 Conversation with Ruby Chishti, 'Ruby Chishti.'
61 Personal communication.
62 Kirsty Robertson, 'Quilts for the Twenty-first Century: Activism in the Expanded Field of Quilting,' in Janis Jefferies, Hazel Clark, and Diana Wood Conroy, eds, *Handbook of Textiles* (London: Bloomsbury Press, 2014), p. 197.
63 Personal communication.
64 'Local Stories: Meet Ruby Chishti,' *Shout Out Miami*, 12 May 2021, https://shoutoutmiami.com/meet-ruby-chishti-visual-artist/?__FB_PRIVATE_TRACKING__=%7B%22loggedout_browser_id%22%3A%22e2df03b1d96a638c3234eee29b4a21708096f796%22%7D&fbclid=IwAR0av9Ig9zEB24i7vTWGKae1qxCWD0WHmVxxmx74c1h8ACb3hqO-zNSSfCc (accessed 2 August 2023).

65 Robertson, 'Quilts for the Twenty-first Century,' p. 199.
66 Personal communication. Also, I refer to Derick Melander's structure, *Into the Fold* (2009) made from 3,615 pounds of recycled clothing, the amount of second-hand clothing in reference to the amount of textile waste created by New Yorkers every five minutes. https://derickmelander.com/clothing-sculpture-all-works/into-the-fold-brooklyn-borough-hall-2009/ (accessed 2 August 2023).
67 Robertson, 'Quilts for the Twenty-first Century,' p. 205.
68 Ibid., p. 205.
69 Personal communication.
70 Robertson, 'Quilts for the Twenty-first Century,' p. 203.
71 Personal communication.
72 A Performance Art series curated by SAWCC, The South Asian Womxn's Creative Collective, Brooklyn, 28 and 29 September 2013, www.sawcc.org/sublime/ (accessed 2 August 2023).
73 Anita Sharma, 'Transparent Studio: Interview with Ruby Chishti – Part 2,' *+91 Archives Blog*, 15 May 2012, https://plus91archivesblog.wordpress.com/2012/05/15/transparent-studio-interview-with-ruby-chishti-part-2/ (accessed 2 August 2023).
74 Nafisa Rizvi, brochure accompanying exhibit *We Leave, We Never Leave, We Return Endlessly* (Twelve Gates, Philadelphia, 4–26 September 2015).
75 Personal communication.
76 'Ruby Chishti,' Karachi Biennale, 2017, www.kbcuratorial.com/artists/ruby-chishti (accessed 2 August 2023).
77 'Meet Ruby Chishti,' *Shout Out Miami*, 12 May 2021.
78 Alison Gill, 'Deconstruction Fashion: The Making of Unfinished, Decomposing and Re-assembled Clothes,' *Fashion Theory*, 2, no. 1 (1998): 25–49, at 33–34.
79 Binotto and Payne, 'The Poetics of Waste,' 8.
80 Ibid., 7.
81 Ibid., 6, 12.
82 Yashodhara Dalmia and Salima Hashmi, *Memory, Metaphor, Mutations: Contemporary Art of India and Pakistan* (New Delhi: Oxford University Press, 2007), p. 64.
83 Robertson, 'Quilts for the Twenty-first Century,' p. 9.
84 Ibid., p. 10.

Bibliography

Abnett, Kate. 'Do Fashion Trends Still Exist?' *Business of Fashion*, 9 January 2012. www.businessoffashion.com/articles/retail/fashion-trends-still-exist (accessed 2 August 2023).

Agins, Teri. *The End of Fashion: How Marketing Changed the Clothing Business Forever*. New York: William Morrow Paperbacks, 2010.

Bain, Marc and Quartz. 'The Neurological Pleasures of Fast Fashion.' *The Atlantic*, 25 March 2015. www.theatlantic.com/entertainment/archive/2015/03/the-neurological-pleasures-of-modern-shopping/388577/ (accessed 2 August 2023).

Benson, April Lane. *To Buy or Not To Buy: Why We Overshop and How to Stop*. Boston and London: Trumpeter, 2008.

Benson, Sophie. 'Past the Parcel: How the End of Free Returns Will Change the Way We Shop.' *The Guardian*, 20 July 2022. www.theguardian.com/commentisfree/2022/jul/20/end-free-returns-fast-fashion-online-shoppers (accessed 2 August 2023).

Binotto, Carla and Alice Payne. 'The Poetics of Waste: Contemporary Fashion Practice in the Context of Wastefulness.' *Fashion Practice* 9, no. 1 (2017): 5–29.

Bowman, Adler and Alaina Baumohi. 'What's Hot This Season.' *Washington University Political Review*, 26 October 2019. www.wupr.org/2019/10/26/whats-hot-this-season (accessed 2 August 2023).

Brooks, Andrew. *Clothing Poverty: The Hidden World of Fast Fashion and Second-Hand Clothes*. London: Zed Books, 2015.

Chishti, Ruby. Artist Statement, Indo-American Arts Council 7th Annual Erasing Borders Exhibition of Contemporary Indian Art of the Diaspora. New York, 2010. www.iaac.us/erasing_borders2010/RubyChishti/bio.htm (accessed 2 August 2023).

Cline, Elizabeth. *Overdressed: The Shockingly High Cost of Cheap Fashion*. New York: Portfolio/Penguin, 2012.

Conca, James. 'Making Climate Change Fashionable – The Garment Industry Takes On Global Warming.' *Forbes*, 3 December 2015. www.forbes.com/sites/jamesconca/2015/12/03/making-climate-change-fashionable-the-garment-industry-takes-on-global-warming/?sh=5d38114e79e4 (accessed 2 August 2023).

Dalmia, Yashodhara and Salima Hashmi. *Memory, Metaphor, Mutations: Contemporary Art of India and Pakistan*. New Delhi: Oxford University Press, 2007.

Davis, J. Francis. 'The Power of Images: Creating the Myths of Our Time.' *Media & Values* Issue 57 (1992). www.medialit.org/reading_room/article80.html (accessed 3 August 2023).

Davis, Nicola. 'Fast Fashion Speeding Toward Environmental Disaster, Report Warns.' *The Guardian*, 7 April 2020, www.theguardian.com/fashion/2020/apr/07/fast-fashion-speeding-toward-environmental-disaster-report-warns (accessed 2 August 2023).

Emran, S. Nayeem, Joy Kyriacou, and Sarah Rogan. *Made in Poverty: The True Price of Fashion*. Oxfam Research Report. Oxfam Australia, February 2019, p. 9. www.oxfam.org.au/wp-content/uploads/2021/11/Made-in-Poverty-the-True-Price-of-Fashion-Oxfam-Australia.pdf (accessed 2 August 2023).

Gill, Alison. 'Deconstruction Fashion: The Making of Unfinished, Decomposing and Re-assembled Clothes.' *Fashion Theory* 2, no. 1 (1998): 25–49.

Gilmore, Nicholas. 'Ready-to-Waste: America's Clothing Crisis.' *Saturday Evening Post*, 16 January 2018. www.saturdayeveningpost.com/2018/01/ready-waste-americas-clothing-crisis/ (accessed 2 August 2023).

Hansen, Suzy. 'How Zara Grew into the World's Largest Retailer.' *New York Times Magazine*, 9 November 2012. www.nytimes.com/2012/11/11/magazine/how-zara-grew-into-the-worlds-largest-fashion-retailer.html (accessed 2 August 2023).

Hashmi, Salima. *Unveiling the Visible: Lives and Works of Women Artists of Pakistan*. Islamabad: Salima Hashmi and ActionAid, 2002.

Hoskins, Tansy. 'Made in Britain: UK Textile Workers Earning £3 Per Hour.' *The Guardian*, 27 February 2015. www.theguardian.com/sustainable-business/sustainable-fashion-blog/2015/feb/27/made-in-britain-uk-textile-workers-earning-3-per-hour (accessed 2 August 2023).

House of Commons Environmental Audit Committee. 'Fixing Fashion: Clothing Consumption and Sustainability.' Sixteenth Report of Session 2017–19, House of Commons. February 2019.

La Ferla, Ruth. '"Cheap Chic" Draws Crowds on 5th Ave.' *New York Times*, 11 April 2000. www.nytimes.com/2000/04/11/style/cheap-chic-draws-crowds-on-5th-ave.html (accessed 2 August 2023).

'Local Stories. Meet Ruby Chishti.' *Shout Out Miami*, 12 May 2021. https://shoutoutmiami.com/meet-ruby-chishti-visual-artist/?__FB_PRIVATE_TRACKING__=%7B%22loggedout_browser_id%22%3A%22e2df03b1d96a638c3234eee29b4a21708096f796%22%7D&fbclid=IwAR0av9Ig9zEB24i7vTWGKae1qxCWD0WHmVxxmx74c1h8ACb3hqO-zNSSfCc (accessed 2 August 2023).

Lowe, Lisa. *The Intimacies of Four Continents*. Durham: Duke University Press, 2015.

Masunaga, Samantha. 'Does Fast Fashion Have to Die for the Environment to Live?' *The Los Angeles Times*, 3 November 2019.

McGowan, Kevin. 'Family Lives of the Uncommon American Crow.' *Cornell Plantations Magazine* 51, no. 1 (Spring/Summer 1996): 1–4. www.birds.cornell.edu/crows/planta.htm (accessed 2 August 2023).

Meyer, Aditi and Ayesha Barenblat. 'Why Fashion Brands are Today's Masters.' *Eco Age*, 6 November 2020. https://eco-age.com/resources/why-fashion-brands-are-todays-colonial-masters/ (accessed 2 August 2023).

Miller, Karen. 'Hedonic Customer Responses to Fast Fashion and Replicas.' *Journal of Fashion Marketing and Management*, 17, no. 2 (2013): 160–174.

'Modern Slavery, A Hidden, Everyday Problem.' *The Global Slavery Index*. Walk Free Foundation. 2018. www.globalslaveryindex.org/ (accessed 2 August 2023).

Payne, Alice. 'Nourishing or Polluting: Redefining the Role of Waste in the Fashion System.' In *Design and Ethics: Reflections on Practice*. Edited by Emma Felton, Oksana Zelenko, and Suzi Vaughan. New York: Routledge, 2012.

Porter, Beth. 'What Really Happens to Unwanted Clothes?' *Green America*, Winter 2019. www.greenamerica.org/unraveling-fashion-industry/what-really-happens-unwanted-clothes (accessed 2 August 2023).

Reilly, Andrew and Jana Hawley. 'Attention Deficit Fashion.' *Fashion, Style & Popular Culture* 6, no. 1 (2019): 85–98.

Rizvi, Nafisa. Brochure accompanying exhibit *We Leave, We Never Leave, We Return Endlessly*. Twelve Gates, Philadelphia, 4–26 September 2015.

Robertson, Kirsty. 'Quilts for the Twenty-first Century: Activism in the Expanded Field of Quilting.' In *Handbook of Textiles*. Edited by Janis Jefferies, Hazel Clark, and Diana Wood Conroy. London: Bloomsbury Press, 2014.

Royal Ontario Museum in Toronto. 12 September 2020 to 2 January 2022. www.rom.on.ca/en/exhibitions-galleries/exhibitions/the-cloth-that-changed-the-world-indias-painted-and-printed (accessed 2 August 2023).

'Ruby Chishti.' *Art Now*, 1 May 2012. www.artnowpakistan.com/ruby-chishti/ (accessed 2 August 2023).

Sandin, Gustav and Greg M. Peters. 'Environmental Impact of Textile Reuse and Recycling – A Review.' *Journal of Cleaner Production* 184 (2018): 353–365.

Schiro, Anne-Marie. 'Fashion; Two New Stores That Cruise Fashion's Fast Lane.' *New York Times*, 31 December 1989. www.nytimes.com/1989/12/31/style/fashion-two-new-stores-that-cruise-fashion-s-fast-lane.html (accessed 2 August 2023).

Schlossberg, Tatiana. 'How Fast Fashion Is Destroying the Planet.' *New York Times*, 3 September 2019. www.nytimes.com/2019/09/03/books/review/how-fast-fashion-is-destroying-the-planet.html (accessed 2 August 2023).

Sharma, Anita. 'Transparent Studio: Interview with Ruby Chishti – Part 1.' *+91 Archives Blog*, 5 April 2012. https://plus91archivesblog.wordpress.com/2012/04/05/transparent-studio-interview-with-ruby-chishti/ (accessed 2 August 2023).

Sharma, Anita. 'Transparent Studio: Interview with Ruby Chishti – Part 2.' *+91 Archives Blog*, 15 May 2012. https://plus91archivesblog.wordpress.com/2012/05/15/transparent-studio-interview-with-ruby-chishti-part-2/ (accessed 2 August 2023).

Staff. 'Creating Art with Detritus of Daily Life.' *Pakistan Today*, 19 April 2011. https://archive.pakistantoday.com.pk/2011/04/19/creating-art-with-detritus-of-daily-life/ (accessed 2 August 2023).

Tarlo, Emma. 'Introduction: The Problem of What to Wear.' In *Clothing Matters: Dress and Identity in India*. Chicago: University of Chicago Press, 1996.

Thomas, Dana. 'Introduction.' *Fashionopolis: The Price of Fast Fashion – and the Future of Clothes*. New York: Penguin Books, 2019.

Zarroli, Jim. 'In Trendy World of Fast Fashion, Styles Aren't Made To Last.' *NPR*, 11 March 2013. www.npr.org/2013/03/11/174013774/in-trendy-world-of-fast-fashion-styles-arent-made-to-last (accessed 2 August 2023).

12

Made in Rana Plaza: Dilara Begum Jolly's garment factory-themed art

Melia Belli Bose

On the morning of 24 April 2013 in Savar, an industrial suburb of Dhaka, Bangladesh, an eight-story commercial building collapsed, killing a confirmed 1,135 people and injuring approximately 2,500, many of whom are permanently maimed (Figure 12.1). The building, named Rana Plaza, housed a bank, shops, and garment factories that manufactured low-cost ready-made clothing for several popular European and North American

12.1 Rana Plaza collapsed on 24 April 2013, killing over one thousand garment workers and injuring thousands more

brands. One of the deadliest industrial accidents in history, Rana Plaza's collapse is attributed to a number of factors: the eight-story concrete structure, which was located on reclaimed swampland, was built largely of substandard materials. Zoned for commercial use, it was not structurally equipped for the factories' heavy, vibrating machinery. Rana Plaza's upper four floors, on which the factories were housed, were in violation of building codes and were added illegally without permits. Two days before the collapse, inspection teams identified prominent cracks in the building's walls. While the bank and shops on the lower floors immediately closed, the factory owners ordered their workers to return the following day, upon threat of employment termination.[1]

Images of the behemoth pile of shattered concrete slabs and twisted metal, littered with glass and scraps of fabric, circulated across the globe. They quickly became a symbol of global inequality, exploitation, corporate greed, the true cost of so-called 'fast fashion,' and what can happen when neoliberalism and globalization go horribly wrong. Throughout Europe and North America, people furtively checked the labels of their clothes to see if they were made in Bangladesh.

The collapse of Rana Plaza was not the first industrial catastrophe associated with Bangladesh's booming garment industry, which is the world's second largest after China's.[2] Approximately eighty% of the nation's estimated 4 million workers are young, non-literate women from low-income families in rural areas,[3] whose circumstances make them particularly vulnerable to systems of structural violence.[4] In the past decade alone, at least 2,200 Bangladeshi garment workers have died in factory accidents and hundreds more have been injured.[5] In a single week in 2006, two garment factory complexes collapsed and another was destroyed by fire, collectively killing and injuring hundreds of workers.[6] The industry's largest-scale disaster prior to Rana Plaza was the 2012 fire that gutted the nine-story Tazreen Fashions factory, which was a major supplier to numerous Western chains. At least 112 people burned to death or were crushed in the stampede to the building's few unlocked exits (managers frequently bolt fire exits from the outside to prevent workers from stealing merchandise or leaving during their up to nineteen-hour shifts).[7]

Activists and organizers have mobilized in force since the Tazreen Fashions fire to organize strikes, protests, and union activity. They are also establishing non-governmental organizations (NGOs), worker complaint hotlines, and legal aid agencies to combat structural violence by empowering workers and helping to establish a safer, more equitable workplace.

Among the Bangladeshis working for these changes are artists based in Dhaka and Chittagong, the nation's second-largest city and another center of ready-made garment production. Chittagong-based multi-media artist Dilara Begum Jolly (b. 1960) created a series of videos, installations, and works on paper in response to the Tazreen Fashions factory fire and the Rana Plaza collapse. These artworks point directly to the greed, negligence, and structural violence which are the root causes of the disasters. They frankly confront the various guilty parties, demanding their accountability and acknowledgment of their victims as individuals by emphasizing the pain (both physical and psychological) and personhood of their subaltern subjects, often through the inclusion of their names, faces, and personal effects recovered from the disaster sites. Jolly's affective garment factory-themed art elicits an aesthetic response of empathy within its viewers, which, beyond its capacity to educate, may ultimately serve as a catalyst for change.[8]

This body of work is in conversation with a well-established tradition of art that takes the Bengali poor as a subject to various ends. In 1943, Zainul Abedin, a towering figure of Bangladeshi modern art, created the *Famine Sketches*, a series of monochrome drawings of people dying of starvation on the streets of Calcutta during the Bengal Famine of that year. Although Abedin sketched his famine victims from life, he describes their faces with sketchy features and they are not individuals. Rather, they are a trope in service to a wider critique on colonialism and Britain's mismanagement of food distribution that caused the disaster.[9] The work of other celebrated East Bengali/Bangladeshi artists, such as Safiuddin Ahmed and the contemporary painters, Shakoor, Mintu Dey, and Kanak Chakma, also features peasants, both Bengali and tribal villagers, as its subjects. However, as in Abedin's sketches, in their work, the peasants are anonymous. Moreover, Ahmed, Shakoor, Dey, Chakma, and many other artists render a utopian agrarian idyll, devoid of poverty and populated by well-fed, satisfied peasants.

A career of cultural activism

Jolly began her artistic career in the early 1980s, during the military dictatorship of Husain Muhammad Ershad. This era in the young nation's history was marked by artistic and media censorship, as well as the erosion of secularism after Islam was officially designated the state religion in 1988.[10] The Ershad years afforded little scope for creative commentary on politics, religion, or gender. Nevertheless, since this tumultuous period in her nation's history, Jolly has been an engaged cultural activist, drawing from media, politics, and her commitment to social justice to create art that confronts abuses of women in Bangladesh and the world.[11] Over the past three decades, she has emerged as one of her nation's most celebrated artists, both within Bangladesh and abroad; she has had numerous solo exhibitions in Bangladesh's best-known galleries; participated in group exhibitions, including some of the largest art fairs in Asia, the Middle East, Europe, and North America; and her work is owned by collectors and institutions throughout the world.

Jolly's encounter as a college student in Dhaka with a group of older men on the street who chastised her for not covering her head was a creative turning point in her career. The impasse inspired her first major painting series, *Lal Shallu*, in 1985. The paintings criticize what the artist perceives as the religious patriarchy's oppression of women. Based on Syed Waliullah's 1948 Bangla novel of the same name, the paintings examine the relationship between a headstrong young woman and an older *mullah* (priest) whom she is forced to marry. A central theme is religious hypocrisy; the respected *mullah* is a charlatan. He unsuccessfully attempts to temper his wife's willfulness through religious instruction and prayer. A painting from the series depicts the husband and wife at a *dargah* (Sufi grave) (Figure 12.2). The *mullah* looms over his wife, his arms extended like a puppet master. His prayer beads touch her extended arm, reminiscent of a puppet's strings, and suspend her above a candle's leaping flame. The wife's head is uncovered, exposing her long, unbound hair – inappropriate at a *dargah*. In the foreground three women with appropriately covered heads gather reverently around the *dargah*, representing the *mullah*'s ideal wife and the ideal Bangladeshi woman in the eyes of the marauding religious conservatives who harassed the artist. As a secular feminist in Ershad's Bangladesh, Jolly surely identified with and applauded the wife's rebelliousness in the novel.

Nearly three decades later, the wars in Iraq and Afghanistan prompted Jolly to set her sights beyond Bangladesh. In particular, the artist was anguished by the Iraqi and Afghan women whose children were killed. In her 2001–2006 mixed media on paper series *Excavating Time*, Jolly introduced themes that remain central in her oeuvre today: women's pain, loss, and production (both biological and material). Typical of Jolly's art of the early 2000s, *Sculpting Time 2* is executed in an exuberant, jewel-hued palette, which belies the painting's darker subject and meaning (Figure 12.3). The torso and splayed legs of a primordial mother goddess occupy the center of the composition. A succession of eggs emerges from her dark womb, in which a butterfly spreads its wings. She is flanked by therianthropic soldiers who brandish rifles and trample her eggs. The painting and others in the series articulate a paradoxical futility, which is a reoccurring leitmotif in Jolly's art: although the world is unfit for new life, women are compelled to perform their reproductive roles. In this tragically senseless cycle, in war women give birth to children destined to die.

The goals of the *Shomoy* ('Time') artistic group of the 1980s also shaped Jolly's art. *Shomoy*, of which Jolly and her artist husband, Dhali Al Mamoon, were among the founding members, was dedicated to creating art rooted in contemporary times (hence the name). The *Shomoy* artists also sought to ground their work in their own place, and to this end looked to aesthetics and media from vernacular Bengali visual cultures,

12.2 Dilara Begum Jolly, untitled painting from the *Lal Shallu* series, 1985, oil paint on cardboard, approx. 63 × 45 cm

particularly tribal and domestic crafts. Local visual cultures also provided Jolly with a history, media, and visual language rooted in the feminine local.

Jolly's most conspicuous and enduring appropriations of Bengali visual culture are references to textiles, both heritage and contemporary, as signifiers of feminine labor and women's quotidian lives. The artist

12.3 Dilara Begum Jolly, *Sculpting Time 2*, mixed media on paper, 2005, 60 × 76 cm

began her textile appropriations in 2006 with the acrylic on canvas painting series *Tahader Kotha* ('Their Words'), in which she recreates the distinctive stitches and symbols of Bengali *nakshi kantha* quilts embroidered by women.

Dominated by graduations of red, yellow, and orange, *Tahader Kotha 4* articulates a cross-section of an ovary as if stitched in a *nakshi kantha* (Figure 12.4). Regularly placed punctiliously rendered dots, lines, and dashes covering the painting's surface mimic running stitches. Mapping a trajectory of matrilineal descent, the central lotus blossom-like organ is ringed by women's heads, recalling maturing follicles in an ovary. A lotus bulb with eyes for seeds emerges from the ovary, evoking a placenta. The lotus references are apt; in *nakshi kantha* iconography, these plants signify fertility and endurance, as they emerge from the depths of village ponds and survive prolonged periods without water. As with other paintings in the series and later works by the artist, *Tahader Kotha 4* visually unites women's physiology and the prescribed heteronormative domestic duties of textile production.

Jolly's textile appropriations are at once local, personal, and participate in global gendered conversations. During her childhood, the artist sat with her female relatives while they gossiped, shared their travails, and provided emotional support as they embroidered – hence, the title of the painting series. For Jolly the stitches are paradoxes of familial joy, pain, and domesticity, a synecdoche for her past, and a link to her

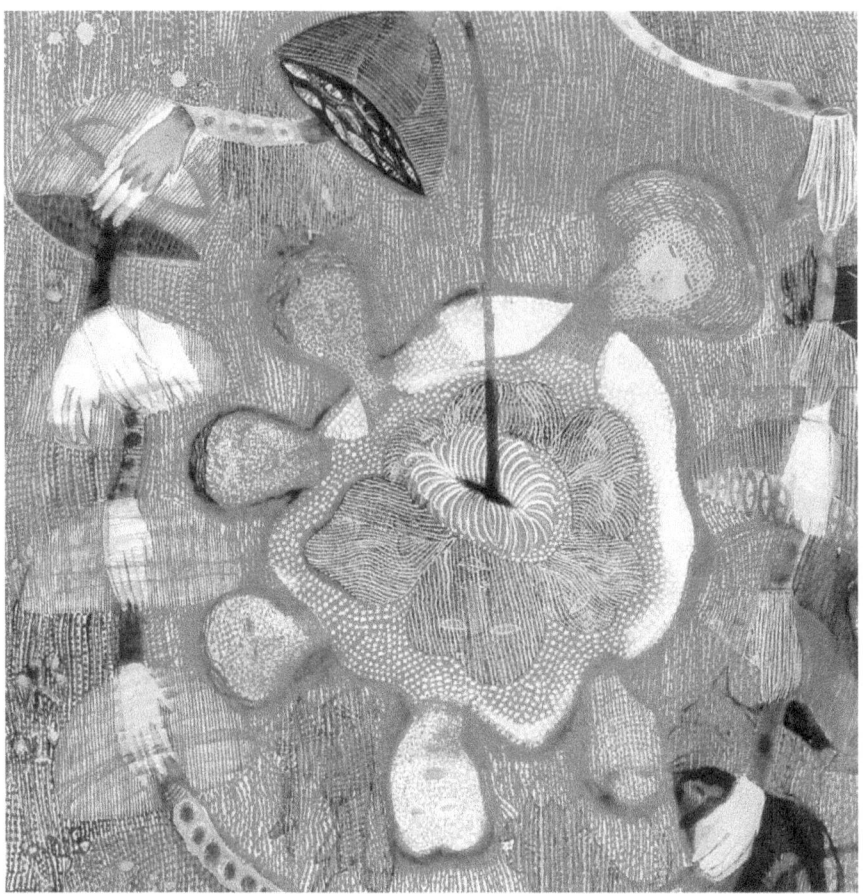

12.4 Dilara Begum Jolly, *Tader Bola 4*, acrylic on canvas, 2008, 90 × 90 cm

ancestors and other Bengali women. Textile references in Jolly's art also resonate with the work of North American feminist artists such as Judy Chicago and Miriam Schapiro, founder of the Pattern and Decoration Movement in the mid-1970s. Among others, these two artists are known for championing what is often dismissively regarded as 'women's art' and diffusing entrenched distinctions between 'high art' and craft – including textiles – which, throughout the world, have historically been produced by women.[12]

Jolly's *nakshi kantha*-inspired art perhaps holds closest parallels with the work of Korean artist Kimsooja, who incorporates *bottari* (lit. 'bundle'; appliqué bedcovers that double as makeshift travel bags handsewn by women) in her installations. Both Jolly and Kimsooja engage with the practice of 'femmage,' and performativity in their lengthy production processes. Miriam Schapiro and Melissa Meyer coined the portmanteau 'femmage' (feminist collage) to refer to and reclaim creative activities historically practiced by women, such as sewing, knitting, and scrapbooking.[13] Both also appropriate from their respective domestic textile traditions to explore imbrications of gender, memory, domesticity, and women's homosocial relationships. They consider the performative act of sewing a metaphor for physical and mental pain, as evoked through the action of piercing the surface of the textile with a sharp object. Jolly and Kimsooja also examine the textiles' role as a site of memory. Women sew *nakshi kantha*s and *bottari*s from scraps of older textiles, each with its own history and impresses of its former users. These two categories of textiles are traditionally passed from mother to daughter, and form part of the latter's trousseau. In a daughter-in-law's new home, childhood *nakshi kantha*s and *bottari*s cover their marital beds in which they lie with their husbands, give birth, rest, and often die.[14]

Jolly continues to engage with these tropes – textiles, memory, and the objectification of women as (re)producers – in the art she creates in response to the two garment factory disasters. What changes from her earlier work is an increased emphasis on stress, anguish, loss, and sorrow. Jolly's latest works also offer an expanded media; the artist moves from the two-dimensional surface of the paper or canvas to installations of textiles, resins, and found objects, as well as video to critique aspects of her country's ready-made garment industry. She also engages with her materials in a directly embodied manner, thereby facilitating her viewers' affective responses.

An embodied empathy

Bangladesh's booming garment industry is a mixed blessing for the factory workers, who are among its greatest beneficiaries and most vulnerable. On one hand, the industry accounts for nearly 70% of female employment in the country. With little, if any, formal education, garment factory work offers many a much-needed opportunity to financially contribute to their families, who typically remain in the workers' home villages. Such an opportunity is empowering, and workers often report feeling valued by their relatives for the first time in their lives.[15] On the other hand, in addition to the potentially life-threatening working conditions, long, physically demanding hours, and low wages, garment factory work is dangerous for numerous reasons. Workers face health risks from prolonged exposure to chemicals, repetitive strain, and the continual roar of the machines, which is associated with noise-induced hearing loss. Gender-based violence and harassment are endemic in garment factories and employed by male managers to supervise and reaffirm workplace hierarchies.[16] Few workers receive an employment contract, placing them in a precarious situation that renders them subject to the whims of the factory managers – they may thus be easily bullied into returning to a visibly structurally compromised building, such as Rana Plaza. Additionally, in a city such as Dhaka, where real estate is at such a premium, accommodation is difficult to secure. Factories rarely provide housing or transport for their employees and female workers report being regularly sexually harassed on their journey home at night.[17]

In the late 1970s the young nation focused on manufactured goods for the global export market, namely ready-made garments. The industry has been a phenomenal economic boon for Bangladesh: the output of nearly 4,500 factories accounts for 75% of the country's export earnings, and grosses over 9 billion dollars annually. The industry provides employment for approximately three and a half million workers, the overwhelming majority of whom are women from poor families.[18] One of the secrets to Bangladesh's success in the international ready-made garment industry is that it produces the cheapest products for its foreign buyers. One of the reasons the country is able to do this is because it offers some of the cheapest human labor on the planet. As of 2016, the national minimum monthly wage for garment workers was sixty-eight American dollars, significantly less than that of their counterparts in other garment-producing countries. Under constant pressure to outbid factories within Bangladesh and in other developing nations, factory owners and managers also consistently cut costs in areas such as building safety.[19]

Jolly addressed these darker aspects of the garment industry in two series and solo exhibitions of the same name that were held in Dhaka. The first, *Threads of Testimony* was a multi-media exhibition held in 2014 at the Bengal Art Lounge, then the capital's trendiest upscale commercial gallery. The second, *Wound*, was an exhibition of works on paper at the Kala Kendra, a small, non-profit artists' collective, in 2016. In contrast to the vibrant palette characteristic of the artist's earlier work, artworks from both later series are dominated by stark, and deeply significant, black and white. These pieces also mark a turning point in Jolly's oeuvre, in terms of her embodied engagement in the production of the art, and in some cases, its display. While her earlier artworks certainly have great capacity to elicit an emotional response to global institutions of structural violence (particularly gender inequality), Jolly's more direct physical engagement with the creation of the works in *Threads of Testimony* and *Wound* maps a trajectory of suffering, affect, and empathy from her subaltern subjects to her viewers.

To a contemporary Dhakaite, Jolly's choice of colors would immediately recall the thousands of missing persons posters families of lost workers made, photocopied, and plastered throughout Dhaka in the wake of Rana Plaza. For several months in 2012 and 2013, these indexical signs were ubiquitous in the capital city's urban fabric and remain ingrained in its residents' collective memory. Jolly incorporated the posters throughout the exhibition, as synecdoches of the human cost of gendered vulnerability, exploitation, and greed that is so entrenched in the global ready-made garment industry.

Jolly silk-screened a series of white *saris* with actual missing persons posters (Figure 12.5). (Like several other Bangladeshi artists, Jolly personally assisted with the rescue efforts at Rana Plaza and interviewed several survivors and victims' families. She incorporated the posters with permission from the victims' families.). Interspersed with reproduced posters bearing the missing victims' faces and biodata are reproductions of the many posters of young women whose families were too poor to afford a camera or a session at a photographer's studio, and are thus conspicuously devoid of an image. In their stead is the frank statement: 'there is no photograph of our daughter.' Roland Barthes argued that 'Every photograph is a certificate of presence,' confirming that what it depicts occurred, and who it depicts existed.[20] As a corollary, the imageless posters and their text suggest that these young women did not truly exist as individuals; but simply as producers of textiles (for the neoliberal global market) and money (for their families). At the opening of the *Threads of Testimony* exhibition, Jolly, Saydia Gulrukh, a prominent labor activist and anthropologist, and Firdausi Priyabhashini, the celebrated artist and first woman to publicly come forward as a *Birangona* (lit: 'Brave Woman'; woman raped by Pakistani soldiers and/or their Bengali collaborators during the Bangladesh Liberation War), each wore one of the poster *saris*.[21] In so doing, the three women performed their nation's history of exploiting, objectifying, and abusing the female body. Particularly as the sexual violence endured by the *Birangonas* is such a controversial – and for many Bangladeshis, shameful – national memory, equating the opposition's abuse of the *Birangonas* to the structural violence visited upon the garment workers' bodies would certainly have been arresting, and unsettling for many viewers.

The nearly one dozen pen and ink drawings on paper in the *Threads of Testimony* exhibition continued the trope of the exploited female body. In the 2012 drawing *Amara* ('Placenta'), a dense web of regularly spaced dashes – again, reminiscent of stitches – articulates the profile of a woman in a *burqa* with a featureless face silhouetted against a white background (Figure 12.6). A distortedly large powder-pink knitted yarn placenta hovers across the figure. The placenta's hieratic scale and its media, coupled with the absence of facial features, emphasizes women's reduction to their (re)productive roles and, once again, stresses woman's value for her ability to create and nourish new life and perform domestic and money-generating labor – such as textile production – but not as an individual. In *Amara* the disparate tropes of women's biological and social roles, and their anonymity, are literally framed by the *burqa*, thus hearkening back to the artist's earliest works, which similarly examine imbrications of rising religious conservatism and gendered identity in Bangladesh.

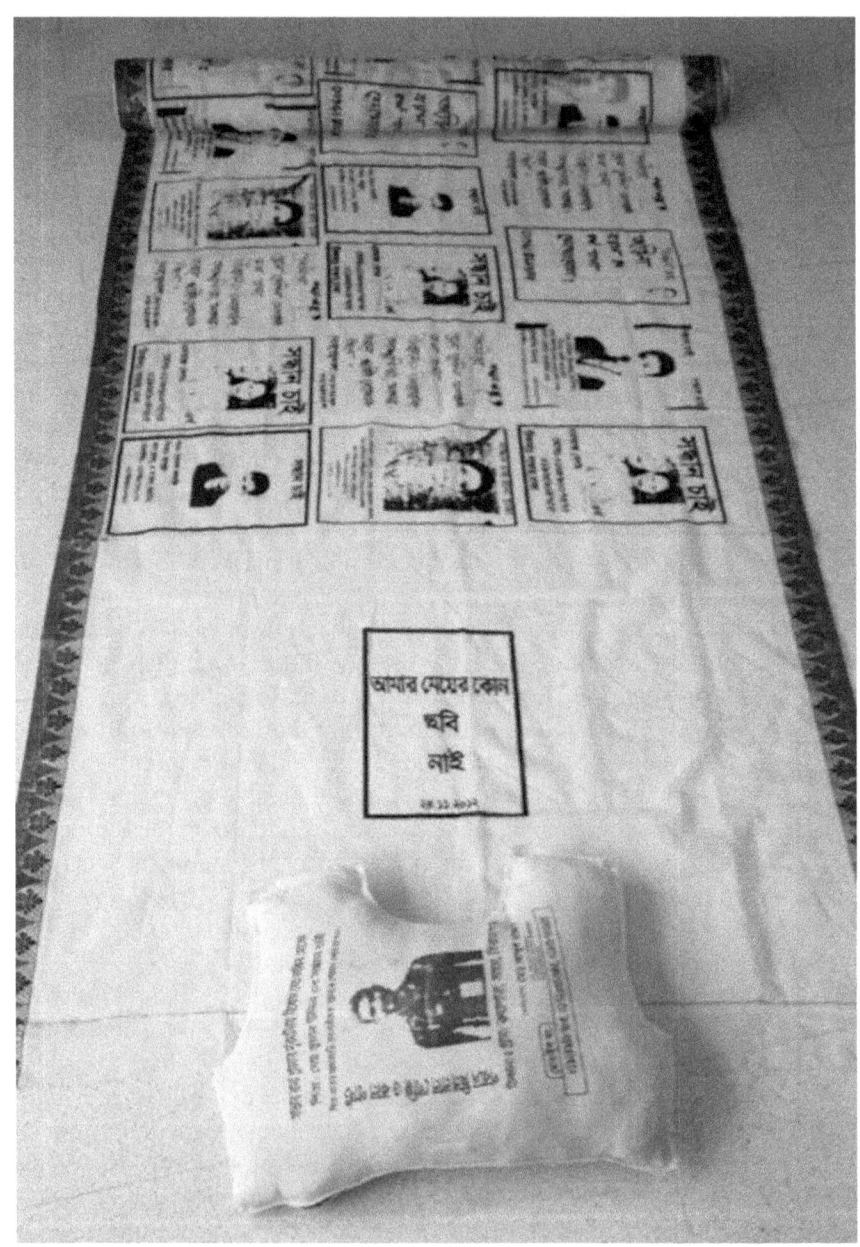

12.5 Dilara Begum Jolly, sari with missing persons posters (and detail), 2013, from the *Threads of Testimony* series

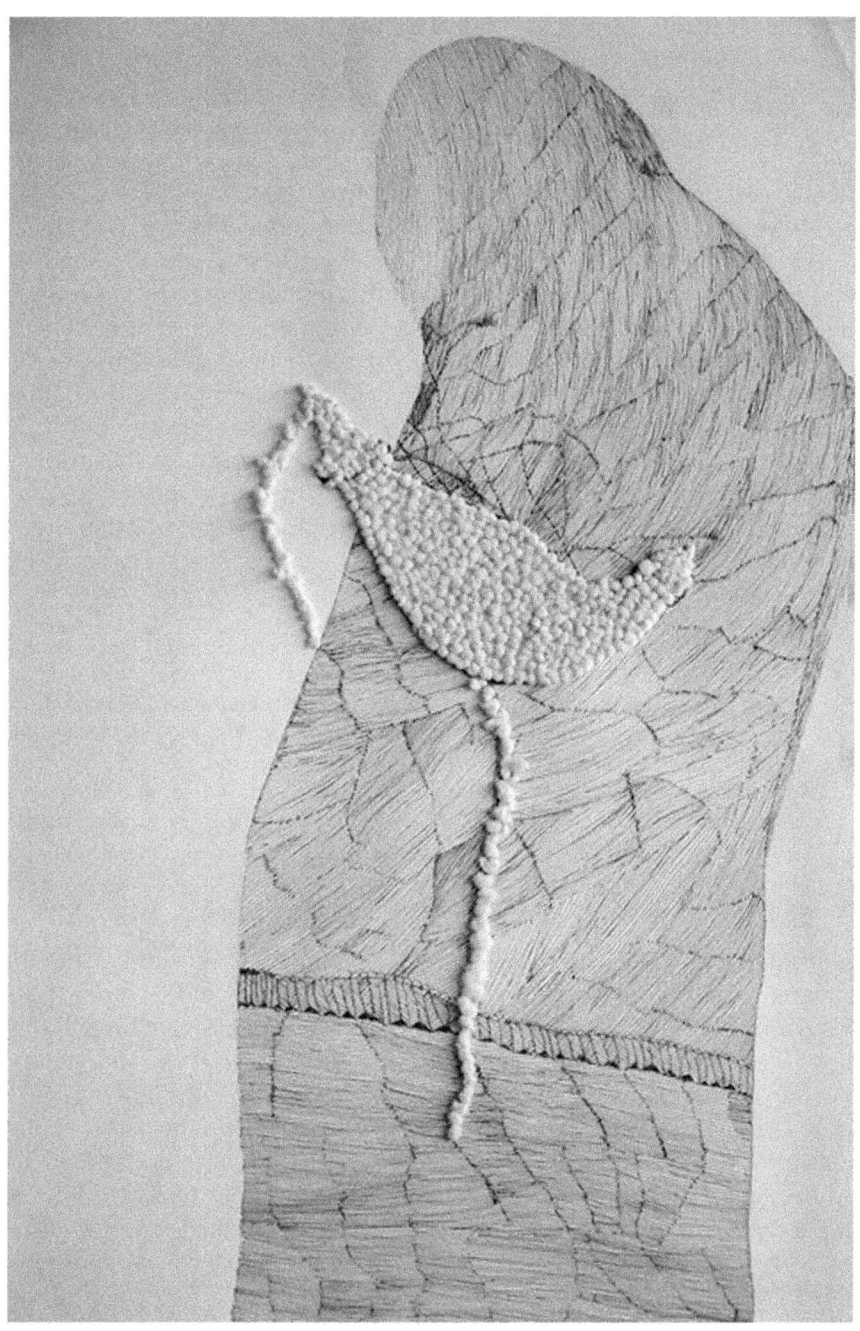

12.6 Dilara Begum Jolly, *Amara*, 2012, pen, ink, and yarn on paper, approx. 43 × 30 cm

The fine ink lines in *Amara* and other drawings in *Threads of Testimony* mark the beginnings of Jolly's embodied, purposely laborious, and even painful methods of execution. It took the artist dozens of hours to execute the hundreds of delicate lines. The work was exacting, and as a repetitive action, wore on the joints in her hand and wrist.[22] Such repetitive, punctilious, and uncomfortable actions appositely recall the process of sewing.

In contrast to the 'everywoman' in *Amara*, other drawings in *Threads of Testimony* foreground the pain and individual personhood of the victims and those who mourn them. Several drawings titled *Bayana* ('Weaving') incorporate missing persons posters through the artist's process of wetting the poster and pressing it to the surface of the paper. The transfer blurs the faces, rendering them appropriately specter like in their liminal spaces of uncertainty. Jolly's process also reverses the faces and text, as if unsettlingly viewed in a mirror. By extension, viewers of these works experience themselves as the missing workers, whose liminal status consigns them to a ghostly heterotopia of neither this world, nor that of the confirmed dead. Foucault describes such a dislocating scenario in his identification of mirrors as heterotopias:

> The mirror really exists and has a kind of comeback effect on the place that I occupy. ... I find myself absent from the place where I am, in that I see myself in there. Starting from that gaze which to some extent is brought to bear on me, from the depths of that virtual space which is on the other side of the mirror, I turn back on myself, beginning to turn my eyes on myself and reconstitute myself where I am in reality. Hence the mirror functions as a heterotopia, since it makes the place that I occupy, whenever I look at myself in the glass, both absolutely real – it is in fact linked to all the surrounding space – and absolutely unreal, for in order to be perceived it has of necessity to pass that virtual point that is situated down there.[23]

In these pieces, Jolly 'reverses the gaze,' enabling us to empathize with the victims by briefly viewing ourselves as them.

Threads of Testimony 4 renders the face of a woman – a mother, sister, or wife – whose tear is linked to a poster superimposed on a shirt, signifying the industry for which the young man featured lost his life (Figure 2.7). Other drawings in the series superimpose posters on objects – bobbins and pieces of furniture – signifying each woman's worth as a producer, whose labor enables her family to purchase consumer items. In *Bayana 6* the mirror of a vanity table reflects a poster of a seated young woman, under which is written backwards '1,135' – the confirmed number of deaths at Rana Plaza (Figure 12.8). Viewed together, the *Bayana* drawings complicate the issue of culpability; greed is not the sole prerogative of neoliberal Western consumers who demand ever-cheaper clothing. The drawings apportion equal blame to families who compel their young members to engage in dangerous, exploitative work so that they too can acquire consumer goods.

Dilara Begum Jolly's garment factory-themed art

12.7 Dilara Begum Jolly, *Bayana 2*, pen and ink on paper, 2014, 76 × 56 cm

For the *Threads of Testimony* exhibition, the central room in the Bengal Art Lounge was dominated by an installation; the artist laid a table with ten place settings, each comprising a dish of molded resin encasing victims' personal effects – hair clips, identification cards, safety pins, grains of boiled rice from smashed lunchboxes – she collected at Rana Plaza, as well as their hair (Figure 12.9a, b, c). Some also offered DNA laboratory reports used to identify the corpses. (These reports, which victims' relatives granted Jolly permission to use, are also printed in black and white,

12.8 Dilara Begum Jolly, *Bayana 6*, sketch from the *Bayana* series, 2013, pen and ink on paper, approx. 43 × 30 cm

infusing the exhibition's dominant colors with greater signification).[24] Missing persons posters were repurposed as placemats and each piece of cutlery was wound with strips of white t-shirt material like corpses in winding shrouds. The guests of (dis)honor for this imaginary dinner party were the owners and managers of Tazreen Fashions and Rana Plaza, whom Jolly personally invited to the exhibition's opening. Her intention was to confront key figures who, in her view, are the most immediately liable for the two disasters – for egregiously defying building safety codes, and, in the case of Rana Plaza, for blatantly ignoring structural faults and bullying their employees into returning to a clearly dangerous work environment. As a witness to the destruction of the two disasters and the permanent physical, psychological, and financial damage it inflicted, through the installation, Jolly demanded the owners' and managers' accountability and acknowledgment of their victims as individuals. Clearly uninformed of the exhibition's theme, one manager did accept Jolly's invitation, and, as reported in major newspapers, insulted, promptly left.[25]

Jolly began to experiment with performance and video after the Tazreen Fashions fire. Two performances relate directly to the two garment factory disasters: *Tazreen Nama* and *Rana Plaza*.[26] In the former, over the course of seven minutes, enveloped in a cloak of flame-like red, orange, and yellow textile strips, the artist moves in slow motion against a dark background to the sound of crackling flames, performing

12.9 (a) Dilara Begum Jolly, *Threads of Testimony*, multi-media exhibition, 2014. View of the installation, consisting of a table and plates (molded resin encasing found objects)

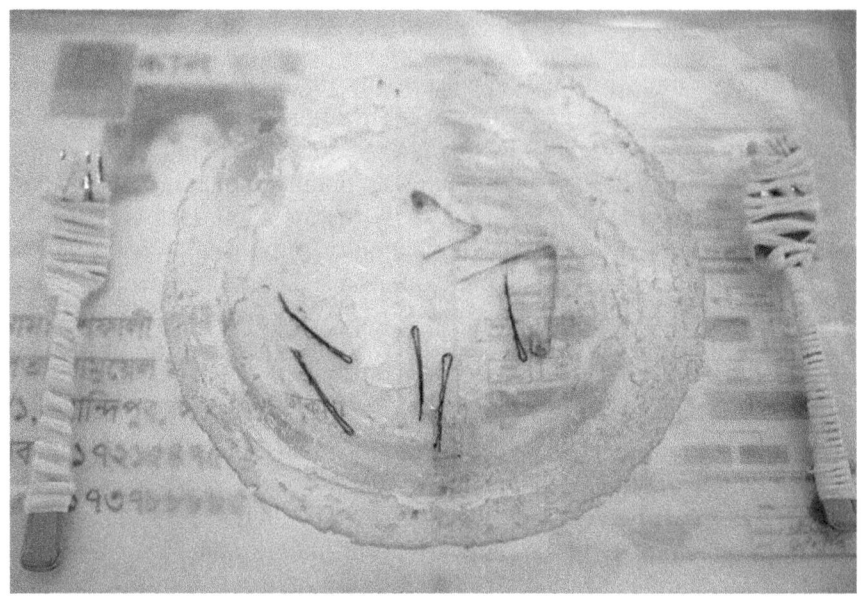
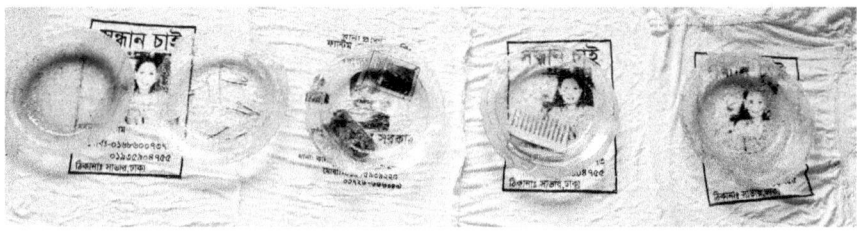

12.9 (b, c) Dilara Begum Jolly, 'Object,' resin and found objects, 2014

the role of a burning factory worker. The performance concludes with her collapsed and still on the floor as white powder (recalling the lime used to prevent the spread of disease and decomposition, presumably until the corpse can be identified) is poured over her against the sound of a distraught woman reciting a *bilāp* (a dirge). As with her garment factory-themed works on paper, central to *Tazreen Nama* performance is Jolly's foregrounding of pain. Here, through her reenactment of the workers' immolation (surely one of the most painful ways to die), Jolly embodies and internalizes, and then conveys to the audience, the victims' pain. Jolly made a two-channel video of *Tazreen Nama* for the *Threads of Testimony* exhibition.

Another two-channel video that aired during the exhibition was the nearly three-minute *Rana Plaza*. The video cuts between crowds of young women – garment factory workers – in *burqa*s or *hijab*s filing through a busy street on their way to work, and the disaster site.

At the Bengal Art Lounge, both videos were projected above dozens of plastic bags Jolly filled with her own breath, another deliberately laborious and physically exhausting act, which signified the victims' desperate gasps in the fire and as they were pinned between slabs of concrete at Rana Plaza. Similarly, for her contribution to the 2016 Dhaka Art Summit, one of the largest art festivals in Asia,[27] Jolly projected her video *Dbitīya Ābaraṇa* on a vessel filled with water surrounded by bags filled with her breath, upon each of which was printed a missing persons poster. In the approximately three-minute video, Jolly, dressed in a flame cloak, writhes on the floor as she winds her head tightly with strips of white t-shirt material against the droning clangor of sewing machines. The installation's title translates to *Second Skin*, and, by extension, clothing. The message is clear: factory workers give their lives – if not literally, as in the Tazreen Fashions fire, then metaphorically through their arduous labor – for the global market of ready-made garments.

Caroline Turner, who has written extensively about the social roles of art, particularly in relation to human rights, describes an artist's ability to convey a sense of tragedy about an injustice through their work as 'witnessing,'[28] an appropriate designation for Jolly's garment factory-themed art. Jolly's main research methodology for the *Threads of Testimony* project was ethnographic: she conducted interviews with survivors and family members of deceased and missing victims, and visited Rana Plaza numerous times. The experiences deeply affected her, filling her with sorrow and anger. Through her embodied, uncomfortable production of the drawings, the artist became a conduit, experiencing (to a degree) what her subjects endured for a majority of each day. In underscoring the personhood of her subjects – incorporating their names, biodata, faces, and possessions – and adopting the allusive color scheme, Jolly charted a trajectory of pain that enables viewers to 'feel into' these artworks and experience a profound empathetic response. Such a trajectory, from subject, to artist, to viewer, approximates the late nineteenth-century German philosopher of aesthetics Robert Vischer's concept of *einfühlung* (literally: 'feeling into'; being moved). Significantly, Vischer devised his theory of *einfühlung* in relation to visual art, applying it to the process whereby works of art enable the viewer to 'feel into' the artist's emotions.[29]

Turner asserts that when artists serve as witnesses, they may testify to traumatic and unjust circumstances and events, but rarely call for retribution or offer correctives.[30] Similarly, with her artworks in *Threads of Testimony* Jolly does not explicitly urge us to arms, or to rally or boycott. These artworks are testimonies of pathos and hopelessness. While they may be interpreted as exposing complicit parties, ultimately, of course, the guilty is not a single individual, or even a group. At the root are entrenched local and international systems of power entwined with gender, privilege, greed, globalization, capitalist market systems, and violence.

Foucault describes power as an omnipresent and amorphous network of relationships that weave a dense web from innumerable institutions and apparatuses without being localized in any single one.[31] If power is so pervasive and hydra like, how can these deep-seated systems of inequality and structural violence be altered? How can tragedies such as Rana Plaza be averted in future? How can the conditions of Bangladeshi garment workers, or anyone who performs exacting manual labor in dangerous conditions for less than a living wage, be made more equitable? Foucault offers hope through the possibility of resistance: 'As soon as there is a power relation, there is the possibility of resistance. We are never trapped by power: we can always modify its grip in determinate conditions and according to a precise strategy.'[32]

Resistance, Foucault opines, dons myriad guises. It manifests more frequently in the form of smaller everyday actions, which he refers to as a 'point' or – apposite in a textile context – a 'knot' of resistance to unequal power structures, than in radical ruptures, such as revolutions.[33] Art may be such a 'knot' of resistance. If, as Vischer claims, *einfühlung* can guide the viewer towards empathy and the ability to appreciate the condition of another human being,[34] surely works of art with this quality possess power beyond the didactic? They may also be an incentive to positive action, by first eliciting empathy and then a resolve to work towards change.

The cultural activist artists who run the Kala Kendra artists' collective and gallery (many of whom are *Shomoy* members) would certainly subscribe to the power of *einfühlung* as a vehicle for social transformation. Jolly's exhibition *Wound* was part of the Kala Kendra series *Celebrated Violence!*. Wakilur Rahman and Kehkasha Sabah, the series curators, sought to draw attention to the pervasiveness of violence; its ubiquity in media, social media, advertising, entertainment, and our daily lives. The omnipresence of violence makes us not only inured to it, but also paranoid, and, consequently, isolated and unfeeling.[35]

Jolly addressed our habituation to structural and physical gendered violence through eighteen 'drawings' on thick, untextured white paper (Figure 12.10 a, b). Rather than articulating images through pen or pencil strokes, she repeatedly pricked the paper's surface with a needle, rendering the images as networks of keloid scars. The surface of the paper evokes human skin and the repetitive action of puncturing it, the violent act of stabbing, again drawing a parallel with the Kimsooja's textile work. Despite the hundreds of pinpricks on each, these 'wounds' yield no blood, signifying our inability to recognize our own or another's pain. Jolly's choice of instrument, her precise and laborious method of production, and her choice of color (white is the color of death and mourning throughout Asia) again recall the gendered act of sewing, pain, and the structural (as well as physical) violence to which women are routinely subjected. The subjects in the *Wound* series are physiological – women's reproductive organs, such

Dilara Begum Jolly's garment factory-themed art 303

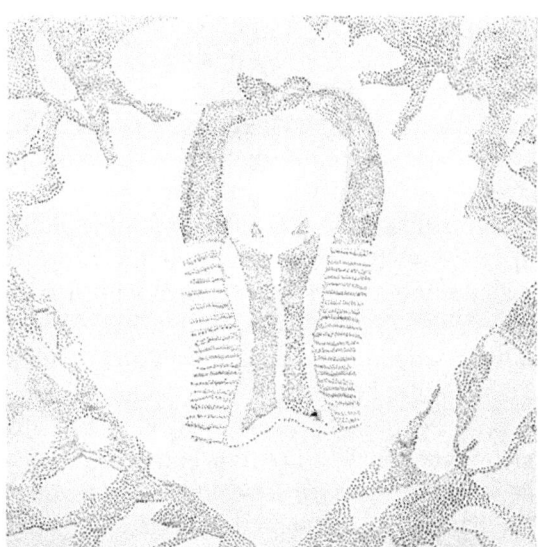

12.10 (a, b) Dilara Begum Jolly, hands (approx. 38 × 36 cm), cross-section of uterus (approx. 43 × 30 cm), pierced paper, 2015. *Wound* series, exhibited at Kala Kendra's *Celebrated Violence!*, 2016

as a (here monochromatic white) bleeding uterus, and domestic utensils – again stressing women's primary (re)productive value.

Gendered hierarchies are exposed and reaffirmed in daily language, as Jolly demonstrates in a number of artworks that interrogate the Bangla word *chelemye*. Literally 'boy-girl,' the word refers to children in general, thus laying the foundations of structural violence and inculcating in females from an early age that their worth is less than that of males. In one of the unnamed *Wound* 'drawings,' Jolly 'flips the script' by reversing both the sequence of the word's components, and each letter, again as if viewed in a mirror. *Meyechele* ('girl-boy') is etched through profuse pinpricks in a void between two fallopian tubes. Looming above is a comparatively small, disembodied torso. The word *meyechele* is in fact derogatory, indicating a tomboy or woman who does not behave in a normatively appropriate feminine manner. With its laboriously executed delicate pinpricks, reminiscent of the (often) uncomfortable labor of needlework, which is 'women's work,' perhaps we should also understand Jolly's piece as reinterpreting and taking pride in the insult. The reversal of the components of the word and its letters suggests a heterotopia devoid of gendered hierarchies, created by the removal of one of a child's first introductions to gender-based structural violence.

Conclusion: a possibility to effectuate change?

Making affective art that foregrounds the inequalities pervading Bangladesh's ready-made garment industry is an act of cultural activism, which harbors potential to effect positive change. Critics of socially engaged art (especially featuring victims) point out that it changes nothing and does not improve the lot of its subjects.[36] Regarding Jolly and other Bangladeshi artists' garment factory-themed work, some of my own friends and colleagues criticize the artists' privileged socio-economic distance from their subaltern subjects, and accuse them of capitalizing on others' pain and being emotionally manipulative for their own gain. Certainly, the majority of contemporary artists who deal with trauma in their work experienced such criticism themselves.[37] American artist Martha Rosler, whose work addresses gender inequality, war, and homelessness, is similarly removed from her subjects and faces criticism on similar grounds. She notes that socially engaged artworks may in fact positively impact the lives of their victim-subjects – albeit not immediately. In her exhibition on homelessness, *The Bowery in Two Inadequate Descriptive Systems*, Rosler concedes that photographs on their own cannot present reality or effect change. However, showing the environment the homeless inhabit is a start.[38] Similarly, although Jolly's art does not change the lives of the garment workers directly, by exhibiting her affective artworks in diverse venues, Jolly ensures that a wide cross-section of society becomes aware of their situation. When *Threads of Testimony* was at the Bengal Lounge and *Dbitīya Ābaraṇa* was displayed at the Dhaka Art Summit, it was viewed by diverse groups of people, including wealthy and politically influential Bangladeshis and foreigners, such as those in NGOs and the foreign service. Beyond reaching and educating a wide audience, as Caroline Turner and Jen Webb examine in relation to contemporary cultural and political activist artists in Southeast Asia, art has the potential to be a catalyst for real change when it instills a sense of agency and responsibility in the audience. Building on Jacques Rancière's writing on spectatorship, Turner and Webb posit that art has the capacity to encourage thought and mobilize others into action, thereby generating personal, social, and political change within society.[39] The Kala Kendra, where Jolly exhibited *Wound*, is visited largely by local artists. Rather than effecting 'top down' policy changes, perhaps these works on paper encouraged other artists to take on similarly difficult subjects in their work.

In works such as *Bayana*, Jolly (literally) holds a mirror to her audience and draws them into a heterotopia in which they see themselves as her victim-subjects, and are thus compelled to empathize with them. Implicit in these works is a demand that the audience acknowledge their role in the global garment industry. Drawing from Walter Benjamin's writings on photography, scholar of information and media studies Sharon Sliwinski notes how photographs of human suffering and trauma engender a sense of pathos and responsibility, as they force the viewer to examine their own identity:

> in looking at another's pain one might rightly wonder whether knowledge of their suffering is a restorative act or complaisant with the violence witnessed. Can the tiny faces see us doing nothing to help them? Of course not, but this interminable, painful labor of attending to and – failing to attend – to the other's suffering might be the very basis of responsibility itself.[40]

What Sliwinski describes is *einfühlung*, to which she adds an additional layer of affect-responsibility for not assisting those who suffer. Similarly, Jolly's affective images of factory workers and their bereaved loved ones elicit a sense of responsibility in her audience. By cutting corners on workers' safety and paying them the lowest possible wages, Bangladeshi factory owners and managers are responding to global demand for ever-cheaper clothing. The millions of clothing consumers in developed nations are equally responsible. Viewers of Jolly's garment industry-themed exhibitions take away an understanding of their own role in these two disasters.

The situation is, of course, far more nuanced. It is impractical not to buy garments made in Bangladesh, or China, Indonesia, or any other country where workers are not treated equitably, for that matter. Furthermore, such a boycott would be counterproductive and do a disservice to the millions of women who have no other means to support themselves and their families than through their manual labor. Equally complex is that not all consumers in the global north have the luxury of being able to buy ethically, as such garments are inevitably more expensive. While finding the works uncomfortable, and the changes required inconvenient, the majority of viewers of Jolly's garment factory-themed art are moved to want a more equitable life for garment workers. If strong enough, that desire may just inspire audiences to demand grassroots changes, and vote to change policies, thus transforming Jolly's art into a small but powerful 'knot' of resistance to one system of structural violence.

Acknowledgments

Research for this project was supported by the American Institute of Bangladesh Studies, the Asian Cultural Council, and the Edith O'Donnell Institute of Art History at the University of Texas at Dallas. I am also indebted to Mustaque Ahmad for his support and hospitality in Dhaka, and to Hadrien Diez for his insightful comments on this and other essays. Most of all, I wish to thank Dilara Begum Jolly and Dhali Al Mamoon for sharing their art with me, discussing it over many hours, and for being gracious hosts in Chittagong.

Notes

1 Julifikar Ali Manik and Jim Yardley, 'Building Collapse in Bangladesh Leaves Scores Dead,' *New York Times*, 24 April 2013, www.nytimes.com/2013/04/25/world/asia/bangladesh-building-collapse.html (accessed 16 May 2018).
2 In 2016 the industry was valued at US$ 25 billion (Rina Chandran, 'Three Years after Rana Plaza Disaster, Has Anything Changed?' *Reuters*, 21 April 2016, www.reuters.com/article/us-bangladesh-garments-lessons-analysis-idUSKCN0XJ02G (accessed 17 May 2018).
3 Simon Parry, 'The True Cost of Your Cheap Clothes: Slave Wages for Bangladesh Factory Workers,' *South China Morning Post*, 11 June 2016, www.scmp.com/magazines/post-magazine/article/1970431/true-cost-your-cheap-clothes-slave-wages-bangladesh-factory (accessed 1 June 2018).
4 Psychologist and scholar of violence and public health, Bandy X. Lee distinguishes behavioral from structural violence, defining the latter as: 'the avoidable limitations society places on groups of people that constrain them from achieving the quality of life that would have otherwise been possible. ... The harm is *structural* because it is a product of the way we have organized our social world; it is *violent* because it causes injury and death' ('Causes and Cures VII: Structural Violence,' *Aggression and Violent Behavior*, 28 (2016): 109–114, at 110). These limitations may be economic, political, cultural, religious, or legal, and have their origins in institutions or systems with authority over certain subjects. Salient to an analysis of Bangladesh's garment industry, Lee notes that structural violence frequently manifests in gender disparities, such as imbalances in education, healthcare, and wages. Moreover, the excessive rates of injury, disability, and death among certain groups – such as poor, uneducated Bangladeshi women employed in garment factories – are the direct result of structural violence. Structural violence often goes unnoticed, as it is so entrenched

in social structures; people are habituated to it and accept manifestations of it as unavoidable trials to be endured over the course of a lifetime (ibid., 109–112).
5 Shahidur Rahman, *Broken Promises of Globalization: The Case of the Bangladesh Garment Industry* (Plymouth: Lexington Books, 2013), p. ix.
6 Geertjan, 'Three Tragedies Hit Bangladesh Factories in One Week, Leaving Scores Dead, Wounded,' *Clean Clothes Campaign*, https://cleanclothes.org/news/2006/02/27/three-tragedies-hit-bangladesh-factories-in-one-week-leaving-scores-dead-wounded (accessed 1 June 2018).
7 Vikas Bajaj, 'Fatal Fire in Bangladesh Highlights the Dangers Facing Garment Workers,' *New York Times*, 25 November 2012, www.nytimes.com/2012/11/26/world/asia/bangladesh-fire-kills-more-than-100-and-injures-many.html (accessed 5 June 2018); Richard Bilton, 'Bangladeshi Factory Workers Locked in on 19-Hour Shifts,' BBC News, 23 September 2013, www.bbc.com/news/business-24195441 (accessed 1 September 2020). The Tazreen Fashion fire recalls the Triangle Shirtwaist Factory fire of 1911 in Manhattan, in which 146 young, emigrant, women garment workers died. Although the fire catalyzed labor reforms across the US, it ultimately led to the outsourcing of garment production in the global south, where labor is less regulated. As I have explored elsewhere, American and Bangladeshi artivists are creating textile-based work that highlights the similarities between these two disasters ('Uncomfortable Quilts: Textile-Based Artivism in Response to Bangladeshi Garment Factory Disasters,' *South Asian History and Culture*, forthcoming).
8 'Empathy' is an imprecise word in English and there is widespread disagreement regarding its exact definition. Here, I refer to the term's affective capacity: the visceral sharing of another's psychological and emotional state, as developed by the German philosopher Robert Vischer in relation to the experience of viewing art (*einfühlung*) in the late nineteenth century. British psychologist Edward Tichener translated the term as 'empathy,' which is the path by which it came into English (Harry Francis Mallgrave and Eleftherios Ikonomu, *Empathy, Form, and Space: Problems in German Aesthetics 1873–1893* (Los Angeles: Getty Center for the History of Art, 1993), pp. 17–29, 89–125). Significant to an analysis of Jolly's garment factory-themed art is that recent reinterpretations of empathy include a compassionate action component, which inspires the audience not only to feel, but also to desire to rectify a negative situation (Karla McLaren, *The Art of Empathy* (Boulder: Sounds True, 2013), p. 18).
9 For more on Abedin's famine sketches, see Abul Hasnat, 'Images of Famine,' in Rosa Maria Falvo, ed., *Great Masters of Bangladesh: Zainul Abedin* (Milan: Skira, 2012), pp. 57–61.
10 At its creation in 1971 Bangladesh was officially a secular nation, as outlined in its constitution. Although a Muslim-majority nation, there are also sizeable Hindu, Buddhist, and Christian communities.
11 Melia Belli Bose, 'Entangled Tensions: Bangladeshi Women Artists,' *ArtAsiaPacific*, 96 (November/ December 2016): 90–98. I refer to Caroline Turner and Jen Webb's use of 'cultural activism,' which they distinguish from political activism, identifying the former as 'the production of creative artefacts and events designed to mobilize affect.' Conversely, Turner and Webb identify political activism as 'the process by which citizens organize and participate in actions designed to achieve political change.' Political activism frequently entails working more directly through political channels, such as organizing rallies, campaigning, circulating petitions, and other means to initiate policy or legislative changes. These two categories of activism intersect, and artists often work across both. Moreover, cultural activism may pave the way for political activism through affectual engagement, which in turn may mobilize viewers. Caroline Turner and Jen Webb, *Art and Human Rights: Contemporary Asian Contexts* (Manchester: Manchester University Press, 2016), pp. 36–37.

12 Norma Broude, 'The Pattern and Decoration Movement,' in Norma Broude and Mary D. Garrard, eds, *The American Movement of the 1970's, History and Impact* (New York: Harry N. Abrams, 1996), pp. 208–226.
13 Miriam Schapiro and Melissa Meyer, 'Waste Not Want Not: An Inquiry into What Women Saved and Assembled – FEMMAGE,' *Heresies*, I, no. 4 (Winter 1977–1978): 66–69.
14 For more on the significance of *bottari* in Kimsooja's art, see, among others, Sun Jung Kim, 'Kim Sooja's Bottari and Her Journey,' in *Reinventing Textiles, Volume Two 'Gender and Identity'* (Winchester: Telos Art Publishing, 2001), pp. 131–142; and Joo-eun Lee, 'Sooja Kim's Wrapping Cloth: The Aesthetics of Paradox,' *Woman's Art Journal*, 36, no. 1 (Spring/Summer 2015): 19–26.
15 Conversation with Bangladeshi anthropologist, documentary photographer, and garment worker activist, Taslima Akhter, June 2015.
16 Dev Nathan, Silliman Bhattacharjee, Rahul S. Shikha, Purushottam Kumar, Immanuel Dahagani, Sukhpal Singh, and Padmini Swaminathan, *Reverse Subsidies in Global Monopsony Capitalism: Gender, Labour, and Environmental Injustice in Garment Value Chains* (Cambridge: Cambridge University Press, 2022), pp. 112–131.
17 Syeda Sharmin Absar, 'Women Garment Workers in Bangladesh,' *Economic and Political Weekly*, 37, no. 29 (20–26 July 2002): 3012–3013 + 3015.
18 Khondoker Abdul Mottaleb and Tetsushi Sonobe, 'An Inquiry into the Rapid Growth of the Garment Industry in Bangladesh,' *Economic Development and Cultural Change*, 60, no. 1 (October 2011): 67–89; Anu Muhammad, 'Wealth and Deprivation: Ready-Made Garments Industry in Bangladesh,' *Economic and Political Weekly*, 46, no. 34 (20–26 August 2011): 23–27.
19 Rina Chandran, 'Three Years after Rana Plaza Disaster, Has Anything Changed?' *Reuters*, 21 April 2016), www.reuters.com/article/us-bangladesh-garments-lessons-analysis-idUSKCN0XJ02G (accessed 3 July 2019).
20 Roland Barthes, *Camera Lucida: Reflections on Photography*, trans. Richard Howard (New York: Farrar, Straus and Giroux, 1981), pp. 82–85.
21 The honorific term *Birangona* has been problematic since Bangladesh's first President, Sheikh Mujibur Rahman, coined it to refer to the estimated 200,000–400,000 war rape victims. Many women's rights activists prefer *Mukti Bahini* ('Freedom Fighter'). These women inhabit a liminal and controversial space in Bangladeshi history. On one hand, there have been numerous efforts to valorize them and reintegrate them into society. On the other, for many, they remain a source of national shame and embarrassment. Many such women were ostracized and disowned by their families. With such social stigma attached to the experience, for Ferdousi Priyabhashini to publicly acknowledge her multiple rapes was a demonstration of great courage. For more on sexual violence during the Bangladesh Liberation War and public regard of its victims, see Nayanika Mookherjee, *The Spectral Wound: Sexual Violence, Public Memories, and the Bangladesh War of 1971* (Durham: Duke University Press, 2015).
22 Conversation with Dilara Begum Jolly, Chittagong, August 2019.
23 Michel Foucault, 'Of Other Spaces: Utopias and Heterotopias,' in Neil Leach, ed., *Rethinking Architecture: A Reader in Cultural Theory* (New York: Routledge, 1997), p. 332.
24 Only with an official DNA report confirming the victim's identity could family members collect compensation from the major brands with factories inside the building. American NGOs donated hundreds of kits to test samples from the corpses against that of relatives. However, Bangladesh lacks sufficient numbers of facilities to process the samples in a timely fashion. Months after the catastrophe, dozens of corpses remained unidentified, and relatives were unsure of their loved ones' fate and unable to claim compensation, while suffering major financial (in addition

to emotional) hardship in the face of their reduced income (Jane Deith, 'Dhaka Factory Collapse: No Compensation Without DNA Identification,' *The Guardian*, 17 October 2013and www.bbc.com/news/magazine-24080579) (accessed 10 July 2019).
25 Conversation Dilara Begum Jolly, Chittagong, August 2019.
26 *Nama* means 'the story of': thus, 'the story of Tazreen.' Tazreen is not only the name of the burned garment factory, but a popular Muslim woman's name, reiterating the objectification of women as producers.
27 That year the biennale attracted a total of nearly a hundred and forty thousand Bangladeshi and foreign visitors.
28 Caroline Turner, 'Art and Images,' in David Forsythe, ed., *Encyclopedia of Human Rights* (Oxford: Oxford University Press, 2009), p. 105. See also Caroline Turner and Nancy Sever, eds, *Witnessing to Silence: Art and Human Rights* (Canberra: Australian National University Press, 2003).
29 For more on *einfühlung* and the optic, psychological, physiological, and even haptic impacts on viewers, see Mallgrave and Ikonomu, *Empathy, Form, and Space*; and Juliet Koss, 'On the Limits of Empathy,' *Art Bulletin*, 88, no. 1 (March 2006): 139–157.
30 Turner, 'Art and Images,' p. 105.
31 Michel Foucault, *The History of Sexuality Volume I: An Introduction*, Robert Hurley, trans. (New York: Pantheon Books, 1978), p. 96.
32 Ibid., pp. 95–96.
33 Ibid., pp. 95–96.
34 Mallgrave and Ikonomu, *Empathy, Form, and Space*, p. 107.
35 Personal communication.
36 See, for example, Cara Ober, 'Martha Rosler: Art as Activism, Democratic Socialism, and the Changing Role of Women Artists as They Age,' *BmoreArt*, 4 July 2019.
37 See for examples Margo Machida, 'Trauma, Social Memory, and Art,' in *Unsettled Visions: Contemporary Asian American Artists and the Social Imaginary* (Durham: Duke University Press, 2008), pp. 120–193; Boreth Ly, *Traces of Trauma: Cambodian Visual Culture and National Identity in the Aftermath of Genocide* (Honolulu: University of Hawaii Press, 2020).
38 Martha Rosler, 'In, Around, and Afterthoughts (on Documentary Photography),' in *Martha Rosler, 3 Works* (Halifax: The Press of the Nova Scotia College of Art and Design, 1981).
39 Turner and Webb, *Art and Human Rights*, p. 65.
40 Sharon Sliwinski, 'A Painful Labor: Photography and Responsibility,' in Maria Pia Di Bella and James Elkins, eds, *Representations of Pain in Art and Visual Culture* (New York: Routledge, 2013), pp. 72–73.

Bibliography

Absar, Syeda Sharmin. 'Women Garment Workers in Bangladesh.' *Economic and Political Weekly* 37, no. 29 (20–26 July 2002): 3012–3013 + 3015.

Bajaj, Vikas. 'Fatal Fire in Bangladesh Highlights the Dangers Facing Garment Workers.' *New York Times*, 25 November 2012. www.nytimes.com/2012/11/26/world/asia/bangladesh-fire-kills-more-than-100-and-injures-many.html (accessed 5 June 2018).

Barthes, Roland. *Camera Lucida: Reflections on Photography*. Translated by Richard Howard. New York: Farrar, Straus and Giroux, 1981.

Belli Bose, Melia. 'Entangled Tensions: Bangladeshi Women Artists.' *ArtAsiaPacific* 96 (November/ December 2016): 90–98.

Bilton, Richard. 'Bangladeshi Factory Workers Locked in on 19-Hour Shifts.' BBC News, 23 September 2013. www.bbc.com/news/business-24195441 (accessed 1 September 2020).

Broude, Norma. 'The Pattern and Decoration Movement.' In *The American Movement of the 1970's, History and Impact*. Edited by Norma Broude and Mary D. Garrard. New York: Harry N. Abrams, 1996.

Chandran, Rina. 'Three Years after Rana Plaza Disaster, Has Anything Changed?' *Reuters*, 21 April 2016), www.reuters.com/article/us-bangladesh-garments-lessons-analysis-idUSKCN0XJ02G (accessed 3 July 2019).

Deith, Jane. 'Dhaka Factory Collapse: No Compensation Without DNA Identification.' *The Guardian*, 17 October 2013.

Foucault, Michel. 'Of Other Spaces: Utopias and Heterotopias.' In *Rethinking Architecture: A Reader in Cultural Theory*. Edited by Neil Leach. New York: Routledge, 1997.

Foucault, Michel. *The History of Sexuality Volume I: An Introduction*. Translated by Robert Hurley. New York: Pantheon Books, 1978.

Geertjan. 'Three Tragedies Hit Bangladesh Factories in One Week, Leaving Scores Dead, Wounded.' *Clean Clothes Campaign*. https://cleanclothes.org/news/2006/02/27/three-tragedies-hit-bangladesh-factories-in-one-week-leaving-scores-dead-wounded (accessed 1 June 2018).

Hasnat, Abul. 'Images of Famine.' In *Great Masters of Bangladesh: Zainul Abedin*. Edited by Rosa Maria Falvo. Milan: Skira, 2012.

Kim, Sun Jung. 'Kim Sooja's Bottari and Her Journey.' In *Reinventing Textiles, Volume Two 'Gender and Identity.'* Winchester: Telos Art Publishing, 2001.

Koss, Juliet. 'On the Limits of Empathy.' *Art Bulletin* 88, no. 1 (March 2006): 139–157.

Lee, Bandy X. 'Causes and Cures VII: Structural Violence.' *Aggression and Violent Behavior* 28 (2016): 109–114.

Lee, Joo-eun. 'Sooja Kim's Wrapping Cloth: The Aesthetics of Paradox.' *Woman's Art Journal* 36, no. 1 (Spring/Summer 2015): 19–26.

Ly, Boreth. *Traces of Trauma: Cambodian Visual Culture and National Identity in the Aftermath of Genocide*. Honolulu: University of Hawaii Press, 2020.

Machida, Margo. 'Trauma, Social Memory, and Art.' In *Unsettled Visions: Contemporary Asian American Artists and the Social Imaginary*. Durham: Duke University Press, 2008.

Mallgrave, Harry Francis and Eleftherios Ikonomu. *Empathy, Form, and Space: Problems in German Aesthetics 1873–1893*. Los Angeles: Getty Center for the History of Art, 1993.

Manik, Julifikar Ali and Jim Yardley. 'Building Collapse in Bangladesh Leaves Scores Dead.' *New York Times*, 24 April 2013. www.nytimes.com/2013/04/25/world/asia/bangladesh-building-collapse.html (accessed 16 May 2018).

McLaren, Karla. *The Art of Empathy*. Boulder: Sounds True, 2013.

Mookherjee, Nayanika. *The Spectral Wound: Sexual Violence, Public Memories, and the Bangladesh War of 1971*. Durham: Duke University Press, 2015.

Mottaleb, Khondoker Abdul and Tetsushi Sonobe. 'An Inquiry into the Rapid Growth of the Garment Industry in Bangladesh.' *Economic Development and Cultural Change* 60, no. 1 (October 2011): 67–89.

Muhammad, Anu. 'Wealth and Deprivation: Ready-Made Garments Industry in Bangladesh.' *Economic and Political Weekly* 46, no. 34 (20–26 August 2011): 23–27.

Nathan, Dev, Silliman Bhattacharjee, Rahul S. Shikha, Purushottam Kumar, Immanuel Dahagani, Sukhpal Singh, and Padmini Swaminathan. *Reverse Subsidies in Global Monopsony Capitalism: Gender, Labour, and Environmental Injustice in Garment Value Chains*. Cambridge: Cambridge University Press, 2022.

Ober, Cara. 'Martha Rosler: Art as Activism, Democratic Socialism, and the Changing Role of Women Artists as They Age.' *BmoreArt*, 4 July 2019.

Parry, Simon. 'The True Cost of Your Cheap Clothes: Slave Wages for Bangladesh Factory Workers.' *South China Morning Post*, 11 June 2016. www.scmp.com/magazines/post-magazine/article/1970431/true-cost-your-cheap-clothes-slave-wages-bangladesh-factory (accessed 1 June 2018).

Rahman, Shahidur. *Broken Promises of Globalization: The Case of the Bangladesh Garment Industry*. Plymouth: Lexington Books, 2013.

Rosler, Martha. 'In, Around, and Afterthoughts (on Documentary Photography).' In *Martha Rosler, 3 Works*. Halifax: The Press of the Nova Scotia College of Art and Design, 1981.

Schapiro, Miriam and Melissa Meyer. 'Waste Not Want Not: An Inquiry into What Women Saved and Assembled – FEMMAGE.' *Heresies* I, no. 4 (Winter 1977–1978): 66–69.

Sliwinski, Sharon. 'A Painful Labor: Photography and Responsibility.' In *Representations of Pain in Art and Visual Culture*. Edited by Maria Pia Di Bella and James Elkins. New York: Routledge, 2013.

Turner, Caroline. 'Art and Images.' In *Encyclopedia of Human Rights*. Edited by David Forsythe. Oxford: Oxford University Press, 2009.

Turner, Caroline and Jen Webb. *Art and Human Rights: Contemporary Asian Contexts*. Manchester: Manchester University Press, 2016.

Turner, Caroline and Nancy Sever, eds. *Witnessing to Silence: Art and Human Rights*. Canberra: Australian National University Press, 2003.

Index

advocacy 12, 162, 180, 190, 201
alternative economies 181, 183, 202, 205
Antoinette, Marie 151, 152
artivism xii, 13, 14, 19, 21, 307

Bangladesh 284, 285, 286, 287, 291, 292, 293, 302, 304, 305, 306, 307, 308, 309, 310, 311
Bengal Art Lounge 305
Bhutan xvi, 8, 11, 18, 19, 21, 92–112
Bhutan (Royal Government of) 93, 101, 106, 111

Cambodia xv, 2, 12, 16, 21, 158–179, 309, 310
Cixi (Empress Dowager) xvii, xviii, 10, 12, 18, 20, 21, 31, 37, 38, 39, 40, 41, 42, 44, 45, 137, 138, 139, 140, 141, 142, 143, 144, 146, 148, 152, 153, 154, 156, 157
climate change 260, 262, 274, 278, 281
colonialism 7, 51, 62, 67, 70, 94, 231, 238, 242, 248, 260, 286
Color Silk 158, 163, 168, 169, 170, 171, 172, 173, 174, 176, 177, 178
consumerism xvi, 9, 14, 53, 65, 66, 70, 73, 149, 231, 276
cotton 5, 7, 11, 12, 14, 17, 18, 19, 21, 25, 34, 47–71, 115, 141, 142, 191, 196, 223, 232, 235, 236, 237, 245, 247, 251, 253, 258, 259, 260, 263

Dell'Orefice, Carmen 12, 137, 149, 152
diaspora 13, 114, 243, 249, 279, 281
dye 80, 82, 98, 113, 118, 120, 121, 123, 125, 126, 127, 128, 129, 130, 131, 165, 166, 167, 171, 192, 193, 195, 196, 198, 207, 214, 215, 222, 223, 225, 232, 247, 253, 254, 256, 263

embroidery x, 13, 17, 19, 20, 21, 28, 64, 80, 81, 82, 101, 116, 117, 126, 127, 120, 130, 131, 140, 142, 143, 146, 153, 221, 238, 242, 243, 244, 245, 248, 250
empathy/*einfühlung* 286, 291, 292, 301, 302, 305, 307, 309

factory workers 61, 291, 300, 301, 305, 306, 307, 310, 311
fast fashion 2, 3, 10, 14, 15, 16, 17, 18, 19, 20, 21, 22, 258–265, 270, 275, 276, 277, 278, 280, 281, 282, 283, 285
Fashion 'n Fashions 79, 83, 84, 89
femme fatale 137, 149, 152, 153, 156

gendered agency 173
gendered labor 4, 62, 63, 68
globalization xvii, 8, 11, 14, 63, 71, 74, 93, 96, 99, 108, 111, 203, 206, 285, 301, 307, 311

Guo Pei 9, 12, 18, 22, 135, 136, 137, 138, 144–156

heritage textiles 8, 9
haute couture 3, 9, 12, 135, 136, 137, 138, 144, 148, 151, 152, 153, 260, 261

imperial China xvi, 17, 18, 20, 21, 26, 38, 114, 135, 138, 142, 146
indigo 13, 30, 34, 44, 80, 82, 118, 120, 121, 122, 125, 126, 127, 128, 221, 222, 223, 232, 233, 253, 255, 256
information and communication technology (ICT) 181, 182, 183, 196, 198, 200, 201, 202, 204, 205, 206

Japan xv, xvi, 5, 8, 12, 13, 15, 16, 19, 22, 31, 42, 43, 45, 46, 47, 48, 51, 53, 55, 56, 58, 62, 64, 82, 159, 169, 207–228, 253, 259
jeans xviii, 11, 72–91

Kala Kendra 292, 302, 303, 305
kesi woven silk 33, 34, 40, 43
Khemara 158, 161, 162, 163, 174, 175, 178

leisure xvi, 2, 8, 13, 106, 110, 213, 227
Levi Strauss 72, 73, 74, 80, 87, 88, 90
Lin, Brigitte 80, 82, 83

matriarchy 12, 135, 152, 153
Miao (people) xvi, 88, 80, 113–131
memory xv, 7, 17, 20, 114, 269, 273, 280, 281, 291, 292, 293, 309, 310
migration 172, 232, 238, 251, 259, 273

nakshi kantha 6, 14, 18, 22, 289, 290
nationalism 17, 19, 43, 45, 67, 70, 88, 91, 204, 251
nostalgia xvi, 100, 173, 209, 216, 223, 227

Orientalism 111, 135, 155, 156

Paris Peace Accords 161
patriotic capitalism 58, 66
patronage 10, 97

personhood 113, 117, 118, 123, 128, 129, 286, 296, 301
Philippines xvii, xviii, 2, 5, 12, 17, 180–206
photograph 35, 36, 38, 39, 40, 41, 43, 44, 45, 48 55, 56, 63, 66, 70, 76, 77, 85, 87, 98, 102, 138, 141, 142, 143, 148, 153, 154, 156, 208, 247, 293, 304, 305, 308, 309, 311
phulkari 1, 13, 14, 17, 18, 21, 22, 23, 238–257
Punjab 1, 6, 13, 17, 18, 20, 21, 235, 238, 242–257, 266

Qing (Empire) 12, 17, 18, 21, 28, 30, 31, 32, 33, 34, 35, 37, 38, 41, 42, 43, 45, 55, 74, 88, 89, 91, 92, 114, 135, 137, 138, 140, 144, 146, 148, 149, 150, 152, 153, 154, 155, 156, 157
quilt/quilting 6, 264, 268, 269, 270, 276, 279, 280, 282, 289, 307

Rags2Riches 181, 184, 185, 186, 187, 188, 189, 197, 199, 200, 201, 203, 204, 205, 206
Rana Plaza 3, 14, 15, 16, 20, 21, 172, 284, 285, 286, 292, 293, 296, 297, 299, 300 301, 306, 308, 310
reproduction xvii, 11, 113, 116, 117, 118, 129, 131, 204, 205, 249, 293

self-education 208, 223
sericulture 5, 6, 12, 13, 16, 17, 22, 160, 161, 162, 171, 207, 209
Shidong xvi, 11, 113–132
Sikh/Sikhism 235, 238, 243, 248, 249
silk xv, xvi, 1, 5, 9, 10, 12, 13, 16, 19, 21, 25–30, 33, 34, 37, 38, 40, 42, 43, 46, 48, 49, 50, 51, 54, 55, 57, 59, 60, 61, 62, 63, 64, 68, 70, 98, 101, 115, 135–157, 158–179, 207–228, 244, 245, 293
Singh Twins (The) 8, 13, 14, 231–257
Silk Associations of Cambodia 163, 165, 167, 168, 173, 174
Slaves of Fashion 13, 231, 233, 234, 237, 238, 239, 240, 249, 253
social activists 2, 183

social enterprise 12, 158, 176, 180, 183, 186, 187, 189, 190, 191, 198, 201
social entrepreneurship xviii, 168, 173, 181, 183, 184, 194, 202, 203, 205, 206
social welfare 180, 181, 187 194, 197
soft power 12, 137, 138, 142, 143, 144, 148, 149, 152, 153, 156

Taiwan Women's Monthly 78, 83
Tazreen Fashions factory 15, 20, 285, 299, 300, 301, 307, 309
Tazreen Nama 299, 300
textile art 6, 9, 11, 17, 19, 21, 42, 45, 109, 111, 200, 235, 239
'Thirteen Gals' 76
tourism xvi, 94, 96, 99, 110, 190, 208, 223, 225, 226, 227
tradition xvi, 5, 8, 15, 16, 18, 19, 20, 21, 22, 26 27, 32, 34, 44, 45, 62, 98, 101, 102, 105, 106, 109, 110, 111, 112, 137, 152, 153, 154, 156, 196, 203, 205, 207, 208, 209, 221, 222, 223, 224, 225, 227, 228, 243, 254, 256, 286
transorientalism 136, 150, 153 156

velvet 25, 33, 36, 37, 38, 146
violence 14, 114, 238, 248, 285, 286, 291, 292, 293, 301, 302, 303, 304, 305, 306 308, 310

Wangchuck (Her Majesty The Gyaltsuen Jetsun Pema) 11, 93, 97, 101, 105, 106
wastefulness 14, 264, 277, 280
weaving 5, 8, 11, 12, 16, 17, 33, 51, 58, 62, 67, 97, 98, 113–132, 158–179, 180, 184, 185, 188, 190, 194, 198, 207–228, 236, 248, 273, 296
women's empowerment 163, 171, 174, 181, 182, 226, 227
wool 8, 11, 13, 47, 48, 55–66, 70, 71, 98, 222, 259
work xv, xvi, xvii, 2, 3, 4, 5, 6, 7, 8, 9, 11, 12, 14, 16, 17, 18, 19, 21, 60, 61, 63, 80, 82, 84, 92, 102, 105, 106, 108, 110, 136, 151, 152, 159, 162, 165, 169, 174, 178, 181, 183, 184, 185, 186, 187, 188, 189, 190, 194, 200, 201, 202, 205, 206, 207, 208, 212, 214, 221, 223, 224, 226, 227, 231, 232, 242, 253, 254, 255, 256, 257, 258, 263, 264, 265, 266, 268, 269, 270, 272, 273, 274, 276, 277, 286, 287, 290, 291, 292, 296, 299, 300, 301, 302, 304, 305, 307

yang (yin-yang) 29, 115
yishu mei (single tree) 25

EU authorised representative for GPSR:
Easy Access System Europe, Mustamäe tee 50,
10621 Tallinn, Estonia
gpsr.requests@easproject.com